MANAGEMENT AND MOTIVATION

MANAGEMENT
An Introduction

HARPER & ROW, PUBLISHERS
New York, Hagerstown, San Francisco, London

AND MOTIVATION

to Supervision

Jay L. Todes
John McKinney
Wendell Ferguson, Jr.
RICHLAND COLLEGE

Sponsoring Editor: John Greenman
Special Projects Editor: Mary Lou Mosher
Project Editor: David Nickol
Designer: Gayle Jaeger
Production Supervisor: Stefania J. Taflinska
Photo Researcher: Myra Schachne
Compositor: American Book–Stratford Press, Inc.
Printer: The Murray Printing Company
Binder: Halliday Lithograph Corporation
Art Studio: Eric G. Hieber, E.H. Technical Services

Articles in Appendix 2 and Appendix 3 reprinted by permission of *Nation's Business*.

MANAGEMENT AND MOTIVATION:An Introduction to Supervision
Copyright © 1977 by Jay L. Todes, John McKinney, and Wendell Ferguson, Jr.

Library of Congress Cataloging in Publication Data

Todes, Jay L
    Management and motivation.

    Includes index.
    1.   Industrial management.   I.   McKinney, John,
Date-   joint author.   II.   Ferguson, Wendell,
joint author.   III.   Title.
HD31.T633   658.4   76–54696
ISBN 0–06–046636–7

CONTENTS

APPENDICES

CUSTOM FURNITURE CASES

PREFACE

Since the development of the factory system, management has searched for a plan that would motivate workers to become more production oriented. Adam Smith and other classical economists theorized that in capitalism, money or the threat of its loss would be sufficient to raise the worker and the employer to ever higher levels of production, thereby helping themselves and society. However, in our present economy of abundance, the worker is less motivated by money than in earlier times. Psychological needs such as self-fulfillment and self-actualization have become more important to workers today.

The modern manager must understand worker behavior. If money does not motivate as it was once thought to do, then what inspires people? If just giving orders does not always get results, then how does one communicate with workers? If a decent income, job security, and good working conditions are not enough to satisfy workers, then what does satisfy them? These are some of the questions that this book asks. We do not pretend to have all the answers, but we have tried to report the findings of some of the most authoritative administrators, writers, and behavioral scientists in a way that will be easily understood by students, workers, and managers.

This book is intended for use in three ways. First, it is written primarily as a textbook for management courses in four-year state schools and in community and junior colleges. The four parts of the book are divided into thirteen chapters. Instructional objectives are included at the beginning of each chapter and a case problem is found at the end, as well as discussion questions and notes. There are also a series of related cases on the Custom Furniture Company that start and end each chapter.

Second, we believe this book will be helpful to all those who want to advance from their present positions to become members of management. Our aim is to provide them with a guide that will aid in understanding the management concepts needed to make progress.

Third, for those already in management, we hope that this book will be useful as a reminder and also as an opening to new insights into the behavior of people at work so that you may be more effective in your daily, face-to-face relationships with the work group.

We hope that we have been successful in presenting the problems that confront supervisors and managers daily. We hope even more that we have presented some practical advice on ways to meet these problems.

J. L. T.
J. M.
W. F.

MANAGEMENT AND MOTIVATION

THE MANAGER'S JOB

CONFERENCE ROOM

ONE

JOHN
TAYLOR
GENERAL
MANAGER

BILL
JONES
OFFICE
MANAGER

HISTORICAL STUDIES

1

CECIL
MOONEY
HEAD
DESIGNER

SAM BROWN
FACTORY
SUPERINTENDENT

Go to the end of this chapter, to page 14, for an explanation of the case method and further information about the Custom Furniture cases, in which these four men are the featured cast of characters.

GENERAL PURPOSES
OF CHAPTER 1

1. To gain an insight into the history of management
2. To learn the advantages and disadvantages of scientific management
3. To look at the results of the Hawthorne experiments
4. To examine the Prudential studies concerning styles and attitudes of supervisors

LEARNING OBJECTIVES

1. To list at least two assumptions of Frederick W. Taylor's principles of scientific management
2. To list at least two advantages of the applied principles of scientific management. List at least two disadvantages
3. To give the initial reason for the beginning of the Hawthorne experiments at Western Electric
4. To list three concepts of the experiments that could have influenced the results
5. To name the principal revelation that emerged from these studies
6. To describe four conclusions that were derived from the observance of the bank-wiring group
7. To define a production-centered supervisor
8. To define an employee-centered supervisor

Before about 1800, most Americans lived and worked on farms. Those who were engaged in other forms of production were either part of the "putting-out" system or were involved in a master-apprentice program. In the "putting-out" system the worker remained at home. Using his or her own tools, the worker processed the raw materials that were delivered by an early entrepreneur. In town, a young man might serve as an apprentice or journeyman to learn a trade. If he worked hard and saved his money, he could go into business for himself after a few years. There was very little management involved in either of these systems, just the relations between a man and his boss. These were often more like family than business relationships. A person learned a skill and, when the job was finished, could be proud of the result.

On the farm the family was the basic economic unit. Father and son worked the fields while mother and daughter provided the meals, spun the yarn, and made the clothes. A man did not have a boss, but he knew that if he did not work the fields, his family would not be provided for.

With the invention of the steam engine and the start of the industrial revolution, drastic changes came. People were brought together in factories to produce items formerly made at home. Many came from farms. In trying to make factory workers out of farmers, supervisors resorted to many harsh and degrading practices. Human problems were of little or no concern to the manager, the government, or the general public. Workers were paid meager wages for long hours and were supposed to know their place and stay in it.

In this situation, the authority of the supervisor was considerable. It was limited only by the company owners, who were mostly interested in keeping workers dependent on their jobs for their very existence. The owners could use the threat of discharge to force workers to accept even the worst treatment. The theory was that the lower classes were born to work hard and be poor. Mill owners were mostly men who had worked their way up the ranks and started their own business. They were principally interested in machines and production. These new machines had made it possible to hire people, including women and children, who had little skill, since the machines performed all the skilled operations. Social problems were not felt to be the company's concern. The facts that there were no strong unions and that Americans looked upon hard work almost as a religious duty allowed these harsh conditions to flourish, but also set the stage for the great industrial growth of the United States.

Scientific Management

As factories became larger, more workers were employed and production problems became more complex. Manager-owners began to look for better ways to improve production efficiency.

At the Midvale Steel Company plant in the 1880s, a young foreman named Frederick W. Taylor became interested in the relationship between the worker and the machine. He noticed that workers were all producing at their own pace and doing the job in any way they saw fit. Taylor considered the individual as important to production as the machine. He undertook studies at Midvale to record the motions and the time required for each job in the plant. As a result of these and other studies he is frequently called the father of scientific management. Taylor believed that there was one best way to do a job and that better ways could be found to do almost any job if the job was studied carefully.

Some have said that Taylor neglected to consider the feelings and needs of people when he developed his methods of improving production. This may seem true when one looks at his zealous efforts to get the most out of the workers. However, when one studies his ideas about the division of the profits in a company, it seems that he did have certain interests of the worker at heart. It was his contention that most disputes between labor and management centered on the issue of how this surplus, which came from their joint efforts, was to be divided. He believed that if both parties would disagree less about the division of the surplus and work more to increase its size, there would be enough money to provide for a large increase in wages and for an equally large increase in profits.

Taylor was the first to introduce piecework into the factory. There was much opposition at first, but when the workers found that by using Taylor's scientific methods and the new pay plan they could make $1.85 per day instead of the $1.15 they had been making, much of the opposition disappeared. He even used this scientific method to analyze such a simple task as shoveling by asking the question "At what shovel load will a man do his biggest day's work?" He began by finding the maximum load on a shovel; it turned out to be about 38 pounds. He then reduced the load until it was determined that at 21 pounds a man did his greatest day's work. The conclusion was that, no matter what material the man is shoveling, he should have a shovel that holds 21 pounds. A shovel room was built and equipped with a number of different-sized shovels, so that each worker would always have just a 21-pound load. It was then necessary to plan the work for 500 men so that they would each have the right shovel and be in the right work station in the yard.

Each day the men were told how well they had done the day before and exactly what they were supposed to do that day. They were given slips of paper in pigeonholes, which they were required to check each morning. If a worker found a yellow slip, he knew that he had not done a first-class job the day before. A white slip told him which implement to use that day. He would take this slip to the tool room, where he was issued the proper shovel and told where in the yard he would be working.

If any worker did not meet the assigned quota of work for three or four days, a teacher was sent to find out what the trouble was. The teacher probably would find out that the worker had simply forgotten something about how he had been taught to shovel. Taylor and his people had prescribed a certain way: put the right arm down on the right hip, hold the shovel on the left leg and put the weight of the body into the shovel when digging into the pile. Do not take the shovel and just shove it into the pile. This is an example of the way Taylor applied his method to the simplest jobs. As a result of his work, management became conscious of people as well as machines, in the work situation.

Pros and Cons of Scientific Management

At Midvale, production increased as much as 100 percent. There is the story of a certain Schmidt, who weighed only 130 pounds. By using Taylor's scientific methods, he consistently loaded 47 tons of pig iron a day when the prevailing standard was 12.5 tons. Naturally the increased productivity and lower costs resulting from the work simplification were very appealing to industrialists. (Among its strongest devotees was Henry Ford.) However, Taylor's conception of employees as purely "economic men" to whom money and material gain meant everything became the very reason that the movement did not solve all management's problems, as he had hoped it would. His concept neglected human needs and wants that quite often override the desire for high pay. These needs include, for example, desire for affiliation, security, recognition, self-esteem, and self-fulfillment. Furthermore, although Taylor intended to increase the total amount of profit that management and labor would have to split, labor was to have no choice as to how much of the surplus it would receive. The amount was to be decided by the company. Individual workers were also to have no voice in how to do the job. It was assumed that they had neither the ability nor the intelligence to offer valuable suggestions about even their own actions or job.

The system was eventually attacked by the public and the government. Federal laws were passed against time studies. Unions attacked this method of "exploiting" the workers; companies who retained the system denied that they were doing so. Fortunately, many of the firms that continued Taylor's practices began to temper them with more consideration for human behavior and for people's needs and wants.

Human Relations Research

During the 1920s, social researchers were coming to the conclusion that workers did not like work and that, therefore, money would not motivate them. There were many attempts to find other benefits for workers that would make them more productive. The most significant research during this period was that involved in the Hawthorne studies, which were the start of the modern human relations movement in business.

The Harvard Studies at Hawthorne

The Hawthorne studies, the most famous in the field, were directed by Elton Mayo and a group from Harvard at the Hawthorne works of the Western Electric Company (Chicago) between 1927 and 1932. Mayo and his research team were called in to study the effect of lighting on worker fatigue and efficiency. Two groups of workers were selected for the experiment. One worked under the same lighting at all times and the other worked under varying lighting conditions. These illumination experiments yielded no clear-cut results since production increased in both groups, regardless of the lighting. In fact, two volunteers continued working until the light was reduced to that of a moonlit night; they were still able to maintain efficiency. They even reported being less tired and experiencing no eye strain. This part of the experiment was discontinued since it apparently was not yielding any important conclusions. However, the researchers realized that they were into something that went much deeper than lighting, so a new experiment was set up. Five volunteer women—experienced telephone relay assemblers and one layout operator—were set up in an experimental shop. They were told that they were to be studied for effects of rest periods and differing workweek hours on production. The women were to continue their normal telephone relay assembly work.

These experiments went on for 238 weeks. Working days ranged from 4 to 5.5 days per week; hours per day from 7.75 to 8.75; rest periods from six five-minute rests per day to two rest periods that totaled twenty-five minutes per day. Relative output per week climbed steadily from 100 to 140, and when the women returned to the original conditions existing at the start of the experiment, output dropped to only 138. This was still a new high level for every operator. The researchers began to search for other explanations for the upward trend in production, since rest periods and work hours did not appear to be the cause. In going back over the experiments they found a number of factors that could have influenced the results. The women had been interviewed about their problems at work and also about their home lives, recreational pursuits, and other off-the-job activities. They were asked to make suggestions about their jobs and any changes that would affect them.

There was no hard-boiled supervisor to put pressure on them. They were allowed to set their own pace, which gave them a more relaxed attitude, especially as the production figures steadily increased. The women felt special because they had been singled out for a research project. They realized that management felt they were important. The social contact and good relations among the women made the work more pleasant. This feeling of participating in something special and working hard because of it has since become known as the *Hawthorne effect.*

Out of this preliminary research came the revelation that social relations among workers and between the workers and their boss have a profound effect on the motivation to work, on productivity, and on the quality of work performed. To investigate this premise further, a group of fourteen men was selected. These men wired banks of equipment, soldered them, and then inspected them. They were put into a special room, where they could be watched by a trained observer who simply sat in the corner of the room. After the men realized that the observer was not a menace, they relaxed and went on with their normal work routines. The observer came to several conclusions about the work group in the bank-wiring room.

First, he saw that there were two cliques within the work group: those in the front of the room and those at the back. However, some workers did not belong to either clique. The men in front felt they were superior and claimed that their jobs were more difficult than those of the back group. There was a good deal of competition between the groups. Each seemed to have its own set of norms and values.

Second, some of these norms concerned the production rate of the group. The rate had been set at 6000, well below what could be produced, but a rate that seemed to satisfy management. Two other norms were that (1) no one would be a rate buster (that is, produce more than others in the group) and (2) no one would be a chiseler (that is, produce too little relative to the others). If a worker violated these norms, he faced social ostracism until he got back into line. Since all workers were producing at a level below their abilities, they were practicing what is now known as *restriction of output.*

Third, the men consistently violated company policy against trading jobs. They tried to escape the boredom of their work by changing from wiring to soldering and back again. This also let them make contact with different people in the room.

Fourth, there was a great variance in individual production that could not be traced to dexterity or intelligence. The high-status group was constantly nagging the low-status group about low production. Since they all were being paid on a base rate plus a percentage of a group bonus for high production, the low-status group was attempting to retaliate by restricting its efforts.

These studies told much about informal social organizations, restriction of output under an incentive plan, and workers' distrust of management. It was discovered that work is a group activity and that acceptance into the work group is more important to many workers than financial incentives when the two conflict. As a result of this information, management began to give more attention to nonfinancial rewards.

The Institute for Social Research

Since 1947 the Institute for Social Research, under the direction of Rensis Likert, at the University of Michigan has conducted research on work groups. These studies concentrate mainly on the effects on production of supervisors' attitudes and styles. A supervisor was rated as production centered if he used close supervision and was autocratic in putting on pressure for production. If the supervisor had good personal relationships with subordinates and attempted to create positive motivation in order to get production, he was considered employee centered.

It was found that most high-producing supervisors did not do the same work as their subordinates, but actually supervised; did not practice close supervision and were not afraid to delegate; were employee centered rather than production centered; and were part of a work group that got along well together.

The Prudential Studies

Probably the best known of the Michigan studies was carried on in several large clerical departments at the headquarters of the Prudential Insurance Company of American in Newark shortly after the end of World War II. The institute was trying to determine what effect certain supervisory styles had on the productivity of each department.

On the basis of interviews, supervisors were placed in three groups: those who were predominantly *production centered,* those who were *employee centered,* and those who were using a *mixed pattern.* A production-centered supervisor was one who felt fully responsible for production and who considered it the duty of subordinates to do only what they were told. A supervisor was defined as employee centered if he felt that subordinates could assume responsibility for deciding how the work should be done after they knew what they were expected to accomplish.

The statistics gained from these studies showed that the highly productive groups usually had an employee-centered supervisor, whereas the less productive groups had production-centered supervisors. Even when autocratically controlled groups showed higher production, the high production did not last. Morale suffered and good employees quit. There was animosity toward high producers in these groups.

Certain assumptions were made as a result of these studies, which at

12

the time were highly controversial. For example, many workers, if given a certain amount of autonomy on their jobs, would *like* to work and would want to be productive.

Not many supervisors can be considered either completely production centered or completely employee centered. Most use a mixed pattern. In addition to the supervisor's own ability, the important thing is how well the supervisor is able to adapt to the needs of the job and of the people being supervised. It is a matter of the correct balance between direction and control based on a proper estimate of subordinates. Certain groups may become lazy and unproductive without strong guidance. Others may grow uncooperative if a supervisor does not grant them certain freedoms they feel they deserve.

Summary

Frederick W. Taylor believed that there is one best way to do a job and that better ways could be found to do almost any job if the job were studied carefully. He believed that managers and workers should strive to increase the funds of the enterprise and should share the benefits. Taylor's ideas made workers efficient economically but failed to deal with human needs of security, recognition, and self-esteem.

The Hawthorne studies told us much about informal social organizations, restriction of output under an incentive plan, and workers' distrust of management. It was discovered that work is a group activity and that acceptance into that group is more important to many workers than financial incentives when the two conflict. Studies at the University of Michigan found that most high-producing supervisors did not do the same work as their subordinates, but actually supervised; did not practice close supervision and were not afraid to delegate; were employee centered rather than production centered; and were part of a work group that got along well together. The Prudential studies stressed the need for a supervisor to adapt to job needs, people needs, and individual abilities in all supervisor-subordinate relationships.

Discussion Questions

1. *In what ways were working conditions changed by the advent of the industrial revolution?*
2. *What is the main premise of Taylor's "scientific management"?*
3. *Discuss the principal advantages and disadvantages of scientific management as conceived by Taylor.*

4. *What was the principal aim of the Hawthorne experiments at the beginning?*
5. *What were the principal outcomes of the Hawthorne experiments when they were completed?*
6. *Discuss the main differences between a production-centered and an employee-centered supervisor.*
7. *Can many supervisors be characterized as completely production centered or completely employee centered?*

Chapter Case 1

Joe Horn is the supervisor of a records department for an insurance company. He is very conscientious and wants to get maximum production from his employees, most of whom are female. The files are automated, and he has instructed the women not to waste time looking for files. If they are not exactly where they should be, the clerk is to notify him and go on to something else. The beginning and end of breaks are announced by ringing a bell. Joe purposely has his desk located so that he can check on all the clerks at any time. He spends a lot of time patrolling his area, and if he sees any mistakes occurring, he steps in and corrects them himself.

Another department engaged in similar work is managed by Bill Jackson. Bill is also very conscientious. Actually his production is greater than that of Joe Horn. Bill is relaxed with his employees. He lets the women get their own supplies from the supply room, and they are allowed to schedule their own breaks as long as they do not abuse the privilege. There is a lot of laughter and conversation among the women. Bill seems to enjoy the sociability as long as it does not interfere with the work.

1. *What type of supervisor is Bill Jackson?*
2. *Why is Bill's production greater than that of Joe?*
3. *Which group is likely to be more fatigued at the end of the day?*
4. *Is turnover and absenteeism likely to be greater in Joe's group? Why?*

Case Method of Instruction

The case method of instruction began at Harvard Business School, and from there the idea has spread throughout the world. Today in many colleges, especially in upper division courses, the case method is the basic tool of instruction. There are several aspects of this type of instruction that are different from the traditional methods of teaching. In mathematics and many other subjects, the student is given the problem and told to arrive at the correct solution. In a business case, the problem is not so evident. It may be buried within the facts or it may be so disguised that it is difficult to identify. The first step in solving a case is identifying the problem(s).

One of the most frequently heard complaints of students beginning this method is that they do not have enough information. This fact does not take away from the value of case studies when we realize that in real-life situations we frequently do not have all the information we would like to have at our disposal for solving problems. It is often not possible to get all the facts because of limits on time or money. It is therefore necessary for the student to make realistic assumptions based on the available information.

It is not enough in analyzing a case to say that a problem exists. The student must decide what is to be done about the problem. It is not enough, for instance, to report that the concept of unity of command is being violated in the case; it may be necessary to recommend a change in the way the firm is organized or at least in the organization of a particular department.

Why has the case study method of instruction become so popular as a teaching tool? One reason is that it is a way of exposing the student to actual business experiences and problems. It is one way, though admittedly imperfect, to bring the real world into the classroom. It gives the student an arena for trying out some of the theories that he or she has been studying in situations where the resources of the firm are not actually being risked. Further, the student learns that no two situations in business are exactly the same, that there is probably no single "right" solution to the problem at hand, and that errors in decisions bring consequences. The learner can become personally involved in the problems and can employ some self-direction in the learning process. Finally, in the group meetings involved in solving the cases, students are encouraged to be open-minded and allow the contributions of others in the meeting to blend with their own thinking. They may even change their positions when they are convinced that the ideas of others are superior to their own.

This method of instruction places burdens on both the instructor and the students. The teacher must create a democratic climate in which people feel free to join the discussion and do not fear embarrassment or censure from the teacher or from fellow students. Students who do not prepare the cases hold back the whole class. Some may be too sensitive to enter the discussion for fear of being ridiculed, and others may be so closed-minded that they attempt to dominate the class and discourage suggestions from others.

Problem Solving

In conjunction with the case method of instruction the following model for problem solving was presented at Harvard Business School:

1. Statement of the problem(s)
2. Statement of the pertinent facts
3. Statement of alternative courses of action
4. Advantages and disadvantages of alternatives
5. Evaluation of advantages and disadvantages
6. Selection of best alternative

The authors propose the following extension of this model for the purpose of problem solving:

1. Statement of the problem(s)
2. Statement of facts
3. Statement of alternatives
4. Examination of limiting factors
5. Evaluation of alternatives
6. Reexamination of objectives
7. Selection of best alternative
8. Implementation of selected alternative
9. Follow-up for actual results

Statement of the Problem

It is obviously impossible to arrive at an effective solution to a problem unless the problem selected is the proper one. One obvious but effective method of isolating *the* problem is to make a list of all possible problems and then select one the analyst believes to be critical. Never attempt to solve more than one problem at a time, because many complex problems become so complicated that one can easily get lost in their tangles.

After the problems have been listed, examine the list and arrange the problems according to the urgency of their solution. It is entirely possible that some of the factors that seem most urgent are actually of little importance. However, the most urgent problems are *usually* those that need first attention. Avoid the tendency to solve those problems that in the first reading of the case seem to stand out. They may be only indications of much deeper problems. Remember to look for the problem that is at the root of the trouble.

Try to state the problem as broadly as possible. Do not state possible solutions as part of the problem. For example, do not ask the question "Should we . . . ?"; rather, ask the question "What should we do about . . . ?"

Statement of Facts

We have already mentioned that most cases do not have all the information that might be desired. It is sometimes possible to get some of the desired information through research. However, eventually the analyst is forced to make some assumptions. This is permissible as long as the assumptions are stated as such and as long as there is reasonable evidence that these assumptions are logical ones.

Statement of Alternatives
At this point it is often helpful to write down all possible alternatives, no matter how extreme. Then go back and arrange these bits and pieces in their order of likelihood, discarding those that are obviously not feasible. For example, here are some possible alternatives to the handling of an employee who has been found drunk on the job (for the first time):

Discharge him
Reprimand him
Lay him off
Advise him to join A.A.
Send him home and ignore the offense
Determine the cause for this behavior; then do one of above

Limiting Factors
You naturally discard some of the alternatives as you write them down, but it is still wise to put them down for examination. As you go over the list of possible solutions, it will be necessary to discard some because of factors that may be beyond your control. Often these factors include time (usually it is necessary to act quickly) and money. For instance, it may be too costly to gather all the information you would like to have before you make a decision, or the decision you favor may be too costly to implement, so that you must choose an alternative. Other constraints that may hamper a decision could be customs of the firm or community, legal restraints, moral considerations, or economic conditions.

Evaluation of Alternatives
It is now time to consider the advantages and disadvantages of the remaining alternatives. If the problem is complex, it is helpful to list them like this.

ALTERNATIVE _____

Advantages	Disadvantages

Do not make the mistake of considering this as too rudimentary or too simple. It is very useful to see these merits and shortcomings side by side and makes the decision much easier. As you are listing these, think about the eventual outcomes of each. Also, list them as you think of them. Do not spent time wondering if they should be added to the lists, just get them down. Later, when you go back over them, you can correct any mistakes. Quality is not important when you first get the list together; you must concentrate on ideas at this time.

When you have listed all the advantages and disadvantages that you can think of, evaluate them. First organize both sides of your list to be sure that the ideas are all clear and that there are no duplications. Then cross out all that are insignificant. After the list has been cleaned up and certain items have been discarded, prepare a new list from which to select the best alternative.

Reexamination of Objectives
It is sometimes easy to get so involved in finding the problem and selecting various alternatives that one forgets to consider the objectives of the firm or the department that will be affected by the alternative chosen. So it is advisable at this stage to get those goals firmly in mind so that they play a large part in selecting the alternative.

Selecting the Best Alternative
With some problems it is easy to compute the actual costs and gains associated with each alternative and then it is simple to select the alternative that either costs the least or gains the most. However, in the majority of problems, the decision is not easy or mechanical, especially when it involves people and their needs and wants. The problem still needs the judgment of the decision maker, which must be based on training, experience, and common sense. The decision maker must look at the advantages and disadvantages of each alternative and decide on the one that is best under the existing circumstances.

Implementation of Selected Alternative
In the case study method it is not possible actually to implement the decision. The most that we can do is to state in what way we would implement the chosen alternative if we could. In doing this it is necessary to consider again the objectives to which the unit is committed and to attempt to implement the action in such a way as to gain the advantages inherent in this alternative but not bring about any of the disadvantages. Any decision improperly implemented will turn into a bad decision.

Follow-up for Actual Results
It is not possible to do follow-up in a class situation, but the analyst should report on the ways that the decision will be checked on during and after its implementation. A procedure must be worked out to discover whether a proper decision has been made and if it is being carried out. It may even turn out that the decision is a bad one and needs to be changed. Without a follow-up procedure there is no way of comparing actual results with expected results.

Custom Furniture Company and Its Problems

In order to use the case study method, the authors have set up a fictitious company, Custom Furniture Company. A brief description of the
firm and some of its employees follows. At the end of most chapters
there is a short case dealing with typical problems that arise in the day-
to-day activities of the Custom Furniture company. There are questions
at the end of each case to help you through the nine steps involved in
problem solving. These cases can also be role-played. Remember, there
is no single right answer. It is in the process of studying the cases and
going through the problem-solving steps that learning takes place.

THE CUSTOM FURNITURE COMPANY: AN INTRODUCTION

The Custom Furniture Company is a relatively small firm that manufactures and sells custom-built furniture to motels and hotels. The company is organized along line-and-staff methods. The departments are production, sales, office, warehouse, and design.

Personnel in the various departments are as follows:

General Manager
John Taylor, age fifty-five, formerly head of the design department, recently appointed to general manager. John is trying to pull the company out of a slump that has been continuing for the past two years. He is a very creative person, easy to talk to, and very considerate of the feelings of his people. This is the first time in his career that he has had to worry about budgets, costs, and production; he is working very hard to make a success of the company. He has been with the firm for fifteen years and intends to stay until he retires at age sixty-five.

Office Manager
Bill Jones, age thirty, declared surplus by the company that owns Custom Furniture and transferred here two years ago. Bill is very stubborn and is mostly interested in figures and reports. He thinks that the sales force is a necessary evil that just makes more work for him and that every job in the warehouse over which he has control must be done exactly as he says. He spends most of his time working on reports and telling people in the warehouse what to do and how to do it. He would like to learn another field and go into business for himself.

Head Designer
Cecil Mooney, age thirty-four, supervisor of three other designers; also works as decorator, designing furniture and interiors for motel and hotel customers. A great deal of the furniture is built in the Custom factory and the balance is brought from other manufacturers all over the country. Cecil is a very insecure person and is often more concerned with his reputation in his field than with the profits of the company. He works very hard at his job but he is resented by the three designers who work for him, each of whom thinks that he or she should have had the promotion.

Factory Superintendent
Sam Brown, age forty-five, hired from a large furniture factory in North Carolina, where he worked his way up through the plant, a union shop, to superintendent. Sam is very capable, but his whole theory of management is "a fair day's work for a fair day's pay." He believes that people must be told what to do and that they should do it without any questions. There has been one attempt to unionize the shop but it

was successfully fought off, mostly through the efforts of John Taylor, the general manager.

There are twenty workers in the factory, most of them skilled machine operators who run lathes, planing machines, and jointers. The warehouse has eight employees, including two truckdrivers. These warehouse employees are under the direction of Bill Jones, whereas the people in the factory report to Sam Brown. Jones also is responsible for all office personnel, most of whom are typists and clerical workers. Credit problems are handled by the parent company.

There are eight salespeople who are responsible for contacting customers in their territory involved in new construction and those who are upgrading and refurnishing their motels and hotels. Four of these salespeople work out of the local office; the others are based in Miami, Los Angeles, Chicago, and Denver. These four come into the main office at least twice a year for conferences.

STYLES OF LEADERSHIP

2

Mr. Taylor, I just don't believe there is a way in the world that I can continue to work here.

Why is that?

It's that Sam Brown. I just can't take any more of his pushing.

For the full story, turn to the case on page 38.

GENERAL PURPOSES
OF CHAPTER 2

1. To learn the assumptions in Douglas McGregor's Theory X and Theory Y
2. To examine the concepts of the managerial grid
3. To gain an insight into the characteristics of management by objectives and its goal-setting philosophy
4. To contrast autocratic and democratic leadership
5. To take a look at the relative merits of participative management

LEARNING OBJECTIVES

1. To describe briefly the three assumptions in Theory X
2. To describe briefly the six assumptions of Theory Y
3. To give four reasons for the difficulty of implementing Theory Y
4. To list the five major leadership styles described in the managerial grid and give a brief description of each
5. To name the five major steps in a management-by-objective program
6. To list the eight major steps in goal setting according to Charles L. Hughes
7. To describe an autocratic manager by giving at least three characteristics of his or her style
8. To name two disadvantages of the autocratic style of leadership
9. To give at least three characteristics of the democratic leader
10. To list at least six conditions necessary for participation to work effectively

Certain people are referred to as "born leaders." Earlier in the history of management, many believed that a person's having certain traits would determine capability for leadership. However, later studies showed there were so many variations in the traits possessed by leaders that the theory had to be abandoned.

The appropriate style of leadership depends on the situation and the people involved. Managers are faced with the problem of how to be democratic in relations with employees and at the same time exercise the authority needed to make a profitable operation. In this chapter we consider some different patterns of leadership available to managers as they relate to their subordinates.

McGregor: Theory X and Theory Y

Douglas McGregor believed that management's assumptions about people were unrealistic and that the way in which managers were implementing these assumptions frequently contributed to the uncooperativeness that meant the failure of many well-laid plans. He called management's customary view of direction and control Theory X and described it like this:[1]

1. The average human being has an inherent dislike to work and will avoid it when he can.
2. Because of this human characteristic of dislike of work, most people must be coerced, controlled, directed, threatened with punishment to get them to put forth adequate effort toward the achievement of organization objectives.
3. The average human being prefers to be directed, wishes to avoid responsibility, has relatively little ambition, wants security above all.

The work by social scientists in the field of human relations prompted him to come up with a new set of assumptions about people at work. He called it Theory Y and described it as follows:

1. The expenditure of physical and mental effort in work is as natural as play or rest. The average human being does not dislike work. Depending upon controllable conditions, work may be a source of satisfaction (and will be voluntarily performed) or a source of punishment (and will be avoided if possible).
2. External control and the threat of punishment are not the only means for bringing about effort toward organizational objectives. Man will exercise self-direction and self-control in the service of directives to which he is committed.
3. Commitment to objectives is a function of the rewards associated with their achievement. The most significant of such rewards, e.g.,

the satisfaction of ego and self-actualization needs, can be direct products of effort directed toward organization objectives.
4. The average human being learns, under proper conditions, not only to accept but to seek responsibility. Avoidance of responsibility, lack of ambition, and emphasis on security are generally consequences of experience, not inherent human characteristics.
5. The capacity to exercise a relatively high degree of imagination, ingenuity, and creativity in the solution of organizational problems is widely, not narrowly distributed in the population.
6. Under the conditions of modern industrial life the intellectual potentialities of the average human being are only partially utilized.

There are few people in management who consistently resort to either Theory X or Theory Y. Most fall somewhere between the two. Which theory to use depends on many things—the situation, the people involved, the organization itself, the labor market, and other complex factors. McGregor realized that there are some controls that must be kept. Further, he recognized that there were certain individuals or work groups that would try to take advantage of a Theory Y supervisor. A good supervisor, however, would use authoritarian methods of control described in Theory X only when necessary and not as a day-by-day method of supervising.

Theory Y is not easily implemented. First, it means that management must give up some traditional authority. Management must accept some of the blame for people's attitudes toward work because they have learned these attitudes in work experiences. Further, it must treat workers as mature and responsible people. Managers should realize that when most people are treated this way, they develop mature and responsible attitudes.

Second, when it is necessary to use certain controls, workers should be given reasons for the direction. They should have an opportunity to discuss these reasons and possibly even come up with a better alternative. This participation, which is discussed in later chapters, is often profitable to management, especially when it concerns matters relating to the individual's own job. However, many managers are reluctant to allow this freedom.

Third, Theory Y does not let a manager be aloof. It calls for inquiry into the capabilities and, more important, the wants and needs of the individual employee. This does not mean catering to whims, as some critics of Theory Y contend, but it does mean finding out what the individual can do, what his or her aims in life are, and how that person likes to be treated.

Fourth, use of Theory Y means that workers must be informed of the company's goals in easily understood terms, that their personal goals must be determined, and that, in consultation with them, ways must be found in which they can meet their personal goals while working toward organization objectives. If people are committed to company objectives because such commitment helps meet their own goals, they exercise self-direction and self-control in their work.

In spite of the difficulties associated with Theory Y, many believe it is worth the effort in the long run, even though Theory X may show more immediate benefits. The authoritarian approach may motivate people briefly, but it can bring out distrust and ill feelings toward management that eventually may result in slowdowns, sabotage, and strikes. The more democratic approach seeks to create a work climate where there is mutual trust and respect, where there is upward as well as downward communication, and where management and employees pull together for the mutual accomplishment of their objectives.

The Managerial Grid

A different way of showing the extremes of managerial styles is found in the book *The Managerial Grid,* by Robert R. Blake and Jane S. Mouton. In the preface, the "either/or" style of leadership is discussed. These styles have been called by various names, such as autocratic versus democratic, authoritarian versus participative, production-centered versus employee-centered, and Theory X versus Theory Y. According to these authors, such labels are confusing and inadequate. They believe that the grid theory shows how a manager can use both production-centered and employee-centered methods at the same time.

The basis of understanding this theory is a grid (see Figure 2-1.) The horizontal axis shows concern for production, whereas the vertical axis shows concern for people. Each axis is divided into a nine-point scale, with 1 representing lowest concern and 9 standing for highest concern. In the upper-left corner is found 1,9 style, which represents a minimum concern for production but a maximum concern for people. In the lower-right corner is shown the 9,1 style. This is the exact opposite, a high concern for production with a low concern for people. In the upper-right corner is the 9,9 style, the "ideal" or "team" manager. At this point the maximum concern for both people and production is reached. In the center is the 5,5 style, where there is a medium amount of both kinds of concerns.

When the grid is applied to groups, participants are placed in certain theoretical management situations. Their behavior in these situations is ranked and then scored in the grid area that best describes the style selected by the participant. A brief description of the five major leadership styles may help to clarify the theory.

The *Exacting task master* style (9,1) appears in the lower-right-hand

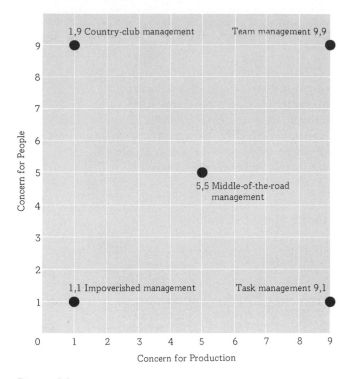

Figure 2-1
Blake and Mouton's Managerial Grid. They identify five possible styles to typify areas on the grid. The styles differ as follows:
1,1—*Impoverished*. Bare minimum effort. Little concern for persons and little concern for production.
9,1—*Task*. High concentration of production. Little concern for persons.
1,9—*Country Club*. High concern for persons. Little concern for production.
5,5—*Middle of the Road*. Enough concern for persons and production to be somewhat effective as a leader.
9,9—*Team*. High concern for both persons and production. The truly effective manager who concentrates on task efficiency while developing group relationships. Source: From *Management: The Individual, the Organization, the Process* by Gerald H. Graham. Copyright © 1975 by Wadsworth Publishing Company, Inc., Belmont, California 94002. Reprinted by permission of the publisher.

corner of the grid. This manager is interested in only one thing—production. People are expected to do what they are told, with no say as to how they are to do it. This closely approaches McGregor's Theory X. As far as goals are concerned, this manager's concern for organizational goals is apt to be very great, but the goals of subordinates are completely

28

ignored. Quotas may be set by management to be met by those lower in the hierarchy using any means necessary.

Country club style (1,9) is in the upper-left-hand corner of the grid. This style of manager has a low concern for production but a high concern for people. To him or her the wants and needs of people are important. Work is arranged so that it is easy and comfortable for the workers; they gain a sense of security. Such a manager may be found doing the work of subordinates rather than supervising. Under this type of management, there will probably be no quotas imposed high in the hierarchy nor will goal setting be done for the employee. The aim is to see that the people adopt general goals that everyone can support.

Impoverished management (1,1) is located in the lower-left-hand corner of the grid. It couples low concern for people with low concern for production. People expect little from this manager, and that is what they get. The manager is frustrated and discouraged. The attitude is one of "don't kick sleeping dogs." People are put on jobs and are supposed to work out the best way to do the job while left strictly to themselves. Goals are almost nonexistent, except they do survive within the system in an inconspicuous manner. Workers get paid and eventually retire.

Middle of the road (5,5) is in the center of the grid. The philosophy of such a manager is to find a position about half-way between concern for people and for production. Some emphasis is placed on production and some consideration is given to people. There is conscious use of the "ask-and-sell" method to get people to work. Rules and procedures are relied on heavily to get things done; pressures are applied through the informal group. When action is not clear, the manager asks other supervisors or managers what they would do under the given set of circumstances. When questioned about an order, this person is apt to say, "We have to do it because *they* want it done." Goals under this system are likely to become "targets," which are not the firm quotas found under 9,1 but rather are easily met production goals. Individual goals tend to be very conservative. Conformity is the rule, sometimes even to the point of mediocrity.

The *ideal style* (9,9) is located in the upper-right-hand corner of the grid. Characterized by a high concern for people and a high concern for production, this style says there need be no conflict between organizational objectives and personal goals of employees. Workers should be involved in setting the conditions and methods under which they are to do their job. The assumption is that when people are aware of organizational objectives and of their part in them, they will not need direction and control; rather, they will exercise self-control and self-direction. In this context, company goals and individual goals can be met at the same time if the goals are understood and agreed upon. Under this system, employees can see themselves as working for themselves, not just the corporation. Goal setting becomes an important force in all the planning, organizing, controlling, and leading that takes place in the organization. This style embraces the assumptions of McGregor's Theory Y.

Goal Setting

An ancient philosopher said: "If a man does not know to what port he is steering, no wind is favorable to him." Goal setting is a process for deciding where you want to go. It is an integral part of "management by objectives," first introduced by Peter Drucker, elaborated on by Douglas McGregor, and adapted to all phases of management since 1965 by George S. Odiorne. Goals have played an important part in all the philosophies mentioned here, including those of McGregor, Likert, Blake and Mouton, and Mayo, as well as many who are mentioned later. All have been looking for ways to make the organization and its members work together for the common cause and for the accomplishment of personal objectives.

The major characteristics of a management-by-objectives program can be stated as follows:

1. Identify the goals of the organization
2. Clarify the working organization chart
3. Set objectives for the period agreed upon with each individual
4. Check periodically on progress toward goals
5. Measure results against goals at the end of the period

In identifying the goals of the organization, top management must understand and agree on the use of such a program as management by objectives. Individual lower-level managers must know what the measures of organization performance are before they can realistically propose their own goals. Many managers, when asked about the goals of their organization, answer with one word—*profit*. Certainly this is one of the ultimate aims of any business, but there are other goals that, if neglected, can defeat the accomplishment of the profit goal. Some of these other goals are productivity, competitive position, technology, employee development, and responsibility to the public.

The organization chart should be clarified so that a manager works on goals only with those under the manager's direct supervision. In accomplishing this task, the chart may have to be clarified and updated.

As a manager, in setting objectives with individuals under your supervision, the first step should be to ask them to list some objectives that they have in mind for the coming period. Mention that they should keep in mind the overall objectives of the company when setting their own goals. List some objectives that you might have in mind. In a second meeting, talk over these objectives and make your suggestions.

Tell them that you wish to do whatever you can to help them meet their goals.

During the goals period there should be intermediate checks to see if milestones along the way are being reached. Also, it should be determined if targets should be changed or amended. Events may have taken place that make it impossible for workers to reach these goals in the time decided upon. Tell employees at this time if they are doing a good job. If they have made some mistakes, take this opportunity to counsel them and see if they are receiving all the help they need.

In measuring results against goals, ask the employees to submit written statements of how well they have progressed in accomplishing the set objectives. They should give reasons for any failures and also list any accomplishments that were not considered when the goals were set. This is a good time to talk about job-related problems. Do not get involved in personality discussions and do not use this time to discuss promotions or raises.

The Goal-Setting Process
In his book *Goal Setting,* Charles L. Hughes gives the following steps for goal setting.[2]

1. Establishing specific goals to support stated purpose
2. Determining the importance of these goals
3. Making plans for action
4. Arriving at performance standards and measurement criteria
5. Stating anticipated problems
6. Weighing the resources required to carry out the planned action
7. Providing for the interaction of organizational and individual goals
8. Following up with actual performance measurement and evaluation

Specific goals must be both short- and long-range. They must be stated in easily understood terms. This helps everyone avoid the pitfall of deciding on actions before really thinking about what they are for. For a company it is very important that long-range objectives be considered in every planned strategy. Each individual must want to reach stated goals and make a commitment to self and to others. There is no substitute for a written statement of these commitments.

In helping people plan for action, top management must allow planning to extend as far down the levels of management as possible, especially in the area of short-range planning. People are much more motivated to achieving both company goals and personal goals if they are given independence in determining the exact action they will take in the achievement process.

Performance standards and target dates must be set so that both the company and the individual have a way of knowing how well they are doing. In many circumstances it is possible to allow the employee to set standards. A manager must be careful on this point with a highly motivated worker to be sure that the standards set are not unreasonably high.

In setting goals, certain areas must be watched carefully so that, if it becomes necessary, tactics or possibly the goal itself can be changed. The individual must realize that there may be certain problems, either personal or organizational, that slow down or even make impossible the achievement of personal goals. In the company it may mean lack of chance for advancement. Many times, however, this barrier is an example of rationalization by the worker. The true block may be a lack of knowledge about the company's plans or an unwillingness to gain further training that would qualify the individual to move up in the organization. Often a willingness to understand the goals and objectives of others in the company who can help is a giant step in the right direction.

Management by objectives is especially effective in measuring actual performance against goals set. Performance review is the time to look back over the period and discover what success the individual and the organization have had; what actions contributed to that success; what factors blocked the attainment of some objectives; and what steps can be taken to improve the accomplishment of goals during the next cycle. The supervisor is in a large degree responsible for the success of the evaluation interview. The supervisor can best help the task-oriented employee become goal oriented, working for the accomplishment of both personal goals and those of the company. During the interview a manager should act as a counselor giving advice on how to accomplish objectives, not as a judge of the employee's performance. The interview and other phases of this type of appraisal are discussed in more detail in Chapter 12.

Leadership Styles

We have seen that there are many styles of leadership. There are thousands of variations of the ways in which managers use their power to get the job accomplished. However, there are three styles usually recognized: autocratic, democratic, and laissez faire. Laissez faire actually means the abandonment of all leadership and is seldom found in a work situation.

Autocratic Leadership
Autocratic leadership is characterized in Theory X and in grid style 9,1. It is production centered. All decisions regarding tasks are made for employees. They do what they are told, no more and no less. The leader assumes full authority and full responsibility. It is autocratic style to

rule more with negative leadership than with positive; that is, offer more penalties than rewards. These penalties take the form of reprimands, layoffs, and firings. It is rule by fear. This type of manager is more a boss than a leader.

Autocratic leadership can be effective in some situations if it has rewards as well as penalties. Certain people respond well to this strong-hand approach because they have been conditioned to it by parents in their childhood or by bosses in past work situations. It works in certain emergency situations because decisions take less time when made by only one person. However, for the long term, it can have harmful side effects, such as poor quality of output, slowdowns, strikes, and low morale. These side effects may more than offset any immediate gains.

The main disadvantages of this style of leadership are that (1) it develops frustration, which may lead to aggression and conflict, and (2) it stifles creativity. People work only because they have to, not because they want to.

There are many forces that limit the power of the autocratic leader. The growth of unions, the increasing numbers of better-educated workers, the intervention of government, and the enlightened policies of many companies have restricted the autocrat's authority to coerce and control workers. Autocrats can still make the major decisions, but they must conform to a union contract, to the laws for protecting employees, and to the pressures exerted by groups, both formal and informal. Even top management must operate under obligations to stockholders, employees, customers, and the community where the business is located.

Democratic Leadership

The democratic leader functions under the assumptions of Theory Y and grid style 9,9. Employee-centered in thinking, the democrat still realizes that the main task is to get the job done. This manager believes that the best way to keep up production is to create a climate where the employees want to do their best to meet company objectives. Decisions are arrived at after consultation with subordinates and participation on their part. In order for them to participate, employees are informed about conditions and changes that affect their job. The individual is respected and efforts are directed at trying to synthesize goals for the workers rather than attempting to force them to meet goals that are not their own.

Participation

When a manager uses the democratic approach, the work group acts as a social unit in getting the tasks done. The manager still has responsibility for operations, but is willing to share this responsibility with the group. In this environment, employees can become goal oriented rather than task oriented. They are eager to contribute to group and company objectives because they know that in this way personal goals can also be met. Democratic leadership is usually prevalent in these organizations where you may hear the employees referring to the company as *we* rather than *they*.

Further, in line with Theory Y, people are encouraged to use self-direction and self-control. They are willing to accept responsibility because they are working at something they *want* to work at. They have dignity because their work has not been oversimplified. They exercise self-control because the company has recognized their value as human beings who really want to work actively at their jobs with support from the company but not with stifling controls. Their supervisor has realized that he or she cannot do an effective job without the help of subordinates and so is willing to sacrifice enough power to make this possible. This does not mean that the superviser just holds meetings, asks opinions, and attempts to convince the employees that they are participating, when they know that the boss has already decided what action will be taken. Employees soon see through this kind of manipulation. Participation is more than getting approval of something already decided upon. When workers find themselves in this situation, they quit making any effort to contribute, because they know that only their mechanical skill is involved, not their mental and emotional involvement.

Successful participation depends on many things. The following are some prerequisite conditions for effective participation: [3]

1. There must be time to participate before action is required. Participation is hardly appropriate in emergency situations.
2. The financial cost of participation should not exceed the values, economic and otherwise, that come from it. Employees cannot spend all their time participating, to the exclusion of other work!
3. The subject of participation must be relevant to the participant's organization or something in which he is interested, else he will look on it merely as busy work.
4. The participant should have the ability, such as intelligence and knowledge, to participate. It is hardly advisable, for example, to ask the janitor in a pharmaceutical laboratory to participate in deciding which of five chemical formulas deserves research priority, but he might participate in other problems related to his work.
5. The participants must be able mutually to communicate—to talk each other's language—in order to be able to exchange ideas.
6. Neither party should feel that his position is threatened by participation. If a worker thinks his status will be adversely affected, he will not participate. If a manager feels that his authority is threatened, he will refuse participation or be defensive.
7. Participation for deciding a course of action in an organization can take place only within the group's areas of job freedom. Some degree of restriction on subunits is necessary in any organization in order to maintain internal unity.

Participation does have some shortcomings. Employees may want to participate in all decisions. A certain amount of education is needed in using the principle so that employees can be made to understand that when some policy or change affects their job, their participation is welcome, even solicited. However, when general policies or top-management decisions are based on information that only management has, the employee cannot contribute much to the decision-making process.

For participation to work effectively, there must be considerable trust within the group. If interpersonal relations are strained, this trust probably will not exist; in fact, members may even prefer an authoritarian approach by the supervisor. Communications are also vital. In a group without trust, it is doubtful that communication can be open. A barrier certainly exists in this kind of climate.

In spite of its limitations, participation has been quite successful in many instances in bringing about improved morale, acceptance of change, more job satisfaction, and commitment to goals. It must be worked at constantly and cannot be developed overnight, but it is well worth the effort.

A recent report prepared by a panel of experts for the Department of Health, Education and Welfare states:[4]

Dull, repetitive, seemingly meaningless tasks, offering little challenge or autonomy, are causing discontent among workers at all occupational levels. This is not so much because work itself has greatly changed; indeed, one of the main problems is that work has not changed fast enough to keep up with the rapid and widespread changes in worker attitudes, aspirations and values.

The panel suggests that a "great part of the staggering national bill in the areas of crime and delinquency, mental and physical health, manpower and welfare are generated in our national policies and attitudes toward work." It adds, "Most important, there are the high costs of lost opportunities to encourage citizen participation: The discontent of women, minorities, blue-collar workers, youth and older adults would be considerably less were these Americans to have had an active voice in the decisions in the workplace that most directly affect their lives."

Summary

The styles of leadership presented in this chapter are not absolute managerial theories, but a series of guides to influence the thinking of supervisors in all organizations. For example, in presenting his Theory X and Theory Y, McGregor identified two approaches to management. Each style has specific implications for managers using Theory X or Theory Y. The goal of Theory Y is a democratic approach that creates a climate of mutual trust and respect, where there is open communication and management and employees pull together to accomplish mutual objectives.

Blake and Mouton structured a managerial grid that placed participants in certain theoretical management situations. Their behavior in these situations is ranked and then scored in the grid area that best describes the style selected by the participant. All five leadership styles exhibit a high degree of concern for the task or for people in a given work situation.

Goal setting plays an important part in the management views of McGregor, Blake and Mouton, and others to be mentioned later. In identifying the goals of the organization, top management must understand and agree on the use of such a program as management by objectives. Each individual must want to reach stated goals and make a commitment to self and to others. People are much more motivated to achieving both company goals and personal goals if they are given independence in determining the exact action to take in the achievement process. Management by objectives is especially effective in the measurement of actual performance against goals set.

Autocratic, democratic, and laissez-faire leadership styles provide three choices to any manager seeking to direct the work of people in an organized setting. Autocratic leadership is characterized in Theory X and in grid style (9,1). Changing internal and external forces have severely limited the autocratic leadership style in modern organizations. The democratic leader functions under the assumption of Theory Y and grid style (9,9). Participation is a key ingredient to a democratic leadership style. For participation to work effectively, there must be considerable trust within the group. If interpersonal relations are strained, this trust probably will not exist, in fact, members may even prefer an authoritarian approach by the supervisor. In spite of its limitations, participation has been quite successful in many instances in bringing about improved morale, acceptance of change, more job satisfaction, and commitment to goals.

Discussion Questions

1. *Name and explain the assumptions contained in McGregor's Theory X.*
2. *In what ways does Theory Y differ from Theory X?*
3. *Discuss four reasons why it is difficult to implement Theory Y.*
4. *Compare the concepts in the managerial grid to those of Theory X and Y and apply the grid to the Prudential studies mentioned in Chapter 1.*
5. *Why is the (9,9) position on the grid considered ideal?*
6. *Why is it important in a management-by-objectives program that*

employees be allowed to set their own goals (subject to review by their supervisor).

7. Discuss the importance of the realization that goals should always be considered as subject to change.
8. Discuss the differences in autocratic and democratic leadership.
9. Relate the concept of participation to Theory Y and to goal setting.
10. What sort of climate is necessary in the organization if employee participation is to be effective?

Chapter Case 2

Tim Gabe is an assistant supervisor. His boss, Fred Gurney, has been with the company for many years and has been a supervisor for ten years. Fred is an advocate of the idea that subordinates should be given orders in a way that tells them exactly what they should do and how they should do it. On the other hand, Tim likes to give his staff all the freedom that he can and still see that the jobs get done. He especially likes to let them choose their own methods of doing their jobs as long as production is kept at a high level. The morale of the employees is very high in Tim's section.

Fred Gurney has discovered that one of the members of Tim's crew is performing his duties in a manner that is not consistent with the way that the methods department has specified in his job description. He says that management sets the standards and specifies how the job is to be performed and that the worker is not to think or plan, just perform the duties as specified.

1. Discuss the advantages and disadvantages of Fred Gurney's method of supervising.
2. Discuss the strengths and weaknesses of Tim's methods.
3. How can Tim practice democratic supervision in this situation?
4. Should employees be allowed to have a say in how their work is performed?
5. What will happen to morale if Tim starts supervising like Fred Gurney does?

Notes

1. D. N. McGregor. *The Human Side of Enterprise.* New York: McGraw-Hill, 1960.
2. Charles L. Hughes. *Goal Setting: Key to Individual and Organizational Effectiveness. American Management Association,* New York, 1965.
3. Robert Tannenbaum, Irving R. Weschler, and Fred Masserick. *Leadership and Organization: A Behavioral Science Approach.* New York: McGraw-Hill, 1961, pp. 88–100.
4. *U.S. News and World Report,* December 25, 1972, p. 52.

CUSTOM FURNITURE CASE: "I QUIT"

John Taylor sat sipping a cup of coffee and looking out of his office window; he was perplexed. Within the past week three plant workers had given John three weeks notice that they would be leaving the company. John had talked to Sam Brown, the plant superintendent about this matter, and when he asked why these workers were resigning, Brown replied, "John, you know how things are nowadays. Nobody wants to work; they just want to draw their paychecks and put out as little as possible. When you jump them about laying down on the job, the first thing they want to do is quit. Give them a day or two and they'll change their minds." This did not satisfy John, so he decided to call the men in and attempt to find out the problem. All the men were young, wore their hair long, and participated in a certain amount of horseplay and banter back and forth while they did their jobs in the finishing department of the plant. However, even Sam Brown admitted that they turned out their fair amount of production and were not slowing up the line.

John had his secretary ask Randy Hill to come to his office where they could talk privately. When Randy came in, he had a look of apprehension on his face.

"Sit down, Randy," John said. "I'd like to talk to you for a few minutes. Want a cup of coffee?"

"Please," Randy answered. This gesture seemed to put him a little more at ease.

"Randy," said John, "I really hate to see you leave the company and I was hoping that if we talked things over, perhaps I could convince you to stay."

There was a long pause and Randy finally said, "Mr. Taylor, I just don't believe there is a way in the world that I can continue to work here."

"Why is that?"

"Well," continued Randy, "I wasn't going to say anything, but now that you have asked me, I'll tell you. It's Sam Brown. There is just no way to please him. No matter how hard you work and how much you turn out, he is never satisfied. He wants you to do more and more. I think he even resents it when we take time to go to the rest room. I just can't take any more of his pushing."

"Now, Randy," John said, "I know that Sam is concerned about production, but is it really as bad as you say it is?"

"Yes, sir, it is. And if you don't believe me, just ask any man in the plant who has any self-respect and I'll bet he will tell you the same thing."

John Taylor saw that Randy was getting excited, so he thanked him for coming in and told him he was free to return to work.

When Don Alexander was called in and queried in the same manner, he answered, "Mr. Taylor, I really need this job. When I first came here, I had determined to stay until I retired, working my way up through the organization until I had Sam Brown's job. But if it takes his way of doing things to keep his job, well, I don't want any part of it."

John asked, "What do you mean by 'his way of doing things,' Don?"

"Well, after I had been here awhile, I saw where some of the operations could be handled more efficiently and I began to use some of my own ways of doing things. You know some of the jobs out in the plant get sort of boring at times and some of us started trading around on some of the operations—just the ones that we can all do, you understand. It made the day pass a little faster and didn't hurt anything, but when Sam noticed what we were doing, he put a stop to it fast and told us to stick to what we were told to do. Now we are back in the same old rut again and frankly, I have just lost interest in the job. This is exactly why I am quitting."

John Taylor dismissed him with a promise to look into the matter and see what could be done about it. He decided to go back into the plant to talk to Darrell Tyler.

As he approached Tyler's work station, he saw that Sam Brown and Darrell were having an animated converstion. Sam's finger was pointed at the face of Tyler and Tyler was standing with hands on hips, his face crimson. Sam was saying in a loud voice, "If I have told you once, I have told you a thousand times not to stand there all day rubbing those drawer fronts. You're not refinishing an expensive antique, you are supposed to be building commercial furniture and turning it out fast so the company can make a profit and you can earn your paycheck!"

Neither of them had seen John Taylor approaching and at this point Tyler threw down his materials and stormed into the washroom.

1. What is the main problem here?
2. What kind of leader is Sam Brown?
3. You are John Taylor. How will you solve the problem?

THE ORGANIZATION

3

I have so many people asking me to do things and all of them want their work done first.

What kind of things are they asking you to do?

The sales people want to get their own orders billed out right away so they will have more commission coming.

For the full story, turn to the case on page 55.

GENERAL PURPOSES
OF CHAPTER 3

1. To define the organization
2. To look at various methods of organizing
3. To define line and staff positions in the organization
4. To examine the concepts of span of control and unity of command
5. To see some possible effects of organization on people

LEARNING OBJECTIVES

1. To give the definition of an organization
2. To list three assumptions that organizations make about supervision
3. To name at least three disadvantages of the tall organization
4. To give three advantages of the flat form of organization
5. To define *decentralization*
6. To list six methods for accomplishing departmentation and define each
7. To describe briefly the main advantage of the project form of organization
8. To discriminate between line and staff in an organization
9. To define *unity of command*
10. To define *span of control*
11. To list at least six behaviors to which employees may resort in order to combat frustration

Almost from the day we are born we all belong to some organization. Most of us are born in a hospital, an institution that is highly structured. When we are taken home, we become members of a not so highly structured group, the family. Later we proceed through school, may join a church, and eventually go to work for some organization to earn a living. Yet how often do we think about what an organization is? We speak of business organizations, fraternal organizations, social organizations, religious organizations, and many others. What do they all have in common that makes us call them organizations? The first thing that comes to mind is people. Organizations must be composed of people. Next, we may think of objectives. There must be some reason, some goal, for these people to come together and organize. Third, we consider structure. If a number of people have joined together to accomplish some objective, there must be a structure, a plan that aids in getting the tasks done. Finally, a relationship exists between these people as they work to accomplish their objectives. So we can define organizations as follows: *Organizations are people joined together by a structure that attempts to define the relationships needed to accomplish their objectives.*

There are many ways in which people can be organized. However, there are certain assumptions that are made by all companies organized along traditional lines. One is that formal authority is the most effective means of exercising control. Most organizations have an organization chart similar to that in Figure 3-1. These charts are drawn so that every person has a position on the chart, and that person's responsibilities are recognized by everyone else on the chart. Another assumption is that task specialization is the most effective way of assuring that various jobs are accomplished. Finally, there are several assumptions about supervision:

1. Each employee should report to only one supervisor.
2. One supervisor should have control over a relatively small number of subordinates.
3. Along with responsibility given to supervisors must also go authority.

The Tall Organization

The preceding assumptions provide for what is known as a "tall" organization, with many layers of authority between the hourly employee and top management. (See Figure 3-1.) When organizations are too tall, people at the top tend to lose contact with those at the bottom. Elaborate systems of reports and other means for keeping informed develop. All decisions are made at the top levels; systems of controls are tight. Con-

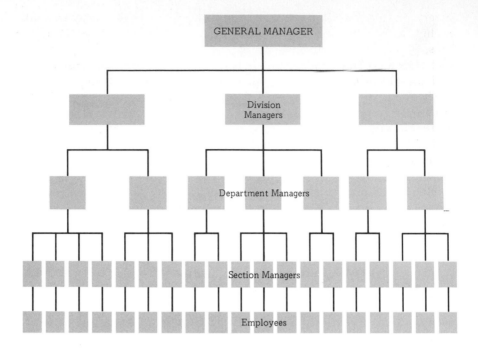

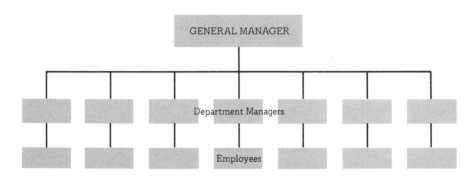

Figure 3-1
"Tall" and "flat" organization structures. Source: Herbert J. Chruden and Arthur W. Sherman, Jr., "Personnel Management," South-Western Publishing Company, Cincinnati, Ohio, 1972, p. 82.

formity is encouraged, so people do only what they are told to do, problems are simply passed up to the next level, and initiative is discouraged. An employee is expected to exhibit the same kind of behavior that his or her supervisor displays. The supervisor is expected to make a good showing under the particular system that has been set up. The supervisor thus has little regard for other departments that may depend on him or her, but that may have an entirely different set of controls. This, in turn, throws an extra burden on higher levels of management, that of settling differences and trying to secure cooperation among the various work groups.

The tall organization may also destroy any pride or real meaning that the workers might find in the job. Jobs are often functionalized to such a degree that workers have no chance to see the whole process of which their duties are only a small part. They can only see the dull, monotonous, repetitive tasks to which they are assigned. Therefore, they tend to have little feeling of responsibility for their tasks or for production as a whole. Management must maintain production, so it exerts increasing pressure on employees. They meet this pressure with resistance, and management exerts more pressure. The cycle is maintained and employees band together, either in formal or informal groups, to fight this increasing pressure from management.

The Flat Organization

A "flat" organization is usually composed of only three or four levels of management. (See Figure 3-1.) There is more personal leadership; lines of communication are shorter and decisions can be made more quickly. In a flat organization the individual manager is decidedly more independent. The manager has greater responsibility and is much more visible; that is, any mistakes are quickly seen and there is no one to whom the buck can be passed. The qualities of self-confidence and initiative are highly valued in this type of organization. If a manager is able to function in such a climate, he or she probably passes on these qualities to subordinates. An individual with tease qualities might not stay long with a "tall" organization, where a premium is placed on conformity and self-direction is stifled.

An example of the use of a "flat" organization is the Sears, Roebuck retail stores division. In this organization, a vice-president may have 100 stores under his or her direction, and a store manager may be responsible for as many as thirty-five or forty department managers. James C. Worthy tells of research conducted by Sears in the field of employee attitudes and morale.[1]

Intelligent planning on the part of management in setting up the formal structure of organizations can do much to improve the quality of human relations in industry. Flatter, less complex structures with a maximum of administrative decentralization tend to create a potential for improved attitudes, more effective supervision, and greater individual responsibility and initiative among employees. Moreover, arrangements of this type encourage the development of individual self-expression and creativity which are so necessary to the personal satisfaction of employees and which are an essential ingredient of the democratic way of life.

Decentralization

Organizations in which top management retains most of the authority and the decision-making power may be considered centralized. Those in which there is a high degree of delegation of power and authority to lower levels in the organization may be called decentralized. Decentralization distributes authority to the smallest practical unit while at the same time keeping tight enough controls to assure that all units are working toward the same company objectives. The term has nothing to do with the geographical location of the company or its branches.

There is a certain amount of risk involved in delegating power to the lower levels. More ability and experience are required of the managers of lower-level units. Higher managers must be willing to allow these decision-making processes to function, even though they are still responsible for the outcome of their subordinates' decisions. This risk is more than offset by the fact that under this system people are allowed to make decisions about things that affect them and their jobs. They do not feel that they are simply numbers in the organization to be manipulated for the sake of productivity and profit. It is much easier for employees to see the relation between company goals and their own personal objectives. They then become better managers and are more qualified to take over the responsibilities of higher management positions.

Unfortunately there has been a trend in recent years for a return to centralization. One reason for this is the increased use of computers, which can furnish information to top management with incredible speed. This same information was formerly supplied by middle-level managers, who were on the spot and may have been the only ones with enough current information to make certain decisions. Another reason is the intervention of big government and big labor unions, which necessitates uniform policies administered by top management.

Actually, there is no clear-cut choice between centralization and decentralization. Some degree of each is always necessary. The proper degree of decentralization results in better performance and more effective organization. People are more motivated when they have the authority necessary to carry out their duties. It is frustrating for employees to feel that they do not have authority commensurate with their ability. It is just as frustrating, however, when people have too much authority with not enough boundaries and guidelines for its use. The ideal solution is to grant authority to managers that is in line with their ability to use it and also with the degree of difficulty associated with their positions.

Communication is also greatly affected by the degree of centralization in an organization. If it is highly centralized, communication is mostly downward, through the many levels of authority. Decentralization provides more upward and lateral communication and lessens the demand for a highly organized communication system. Improved communication and higher motivation are two of the main reasons that decentralization is considered as an important step in developing managerial ability among the members of an organization.

Line and Staff

A major source of friction in many organizations is the concept of line and staff. A basic reason for the friction is the lack of understanding by many of a proper definition of these two terms. Classically, line personnel are described as those who have direct responsibility for accomplishing the goals of the enterprise and staff personnel are those who help the line officials in some way. This seems to say that staff people do not contribute to the objectives of the organization. If this were true, it would indicate that they are not necessary. Staff persons, because of these erroneous definitions, have been delegated an inferior status in many organizations. In reality, however, staff is not inferior to line. There is no inferiority or superiority relationship that should be assumed between line and staff. True, line authority provides the right to direct others to conform to policies and procedures, whereas a staff person does not normally issue orders (except to direct subordinates). It is the staff official's function to give advice and counsel to all members of the organization who may need special services. Most organizations have become so complicated that there are very few managers who can effectively direct the operations of their companies or institutions without the assistance of such staff people as personnel, legal counsel, administrative assistants, and others. Although these very important officials may not give orders, their objective is the same as that of line personnel, namely, the achievement of organization goals. Their authority lies principally in the expertise and knowledge that they possess in a particular field.

Although supervisors may have staff positions as far as the overall company is concerned, in their own departments they assume a line relationship with their subordinates and have direct control over them, with the authority to issue orders and see that they are executed in line with company policy.

A typical staff operation is the personnel department. Its function is to recruit applicants, screen applicants for interviews by managers or supervisors, keep personnel records, assist in wage and salary determination, participate in labor negotiations, and in other ways provide assistance to line managers. However, in most instances, the line manager is free to accept the advice and assistance of the personnel manager or to ignore it. In some cases, the personnel manager may serve a line function. It is not possible to determine a line or staff capacity by a title. A position is what top management says it is, and the entire organization must be examined to determine the intent as to staff or line authority of a given position.

Unity of Command

The concept of unity of command was laid down as a principle for administrators by Henri Fayol in 1916. It states that for any action whatsoever, an employee should receive orders from one superior only. If A is accountable to B and B is accountable to C, C will never give orders to A, nor should A ever go to C for help. A must go through B. There are several reasons for this principle. First, conflicting orders from two bosses may mean the subordinate is frustrated trying to decide which order to follow. In the extreme case of an employee always reporting to two supervisors, the worker never knows exactly which one to follow. Second, the employee may be left with unwanted decision responsibilities when two supervisors disagree or when each gives orders for different assignments that must be carried out at the same time. Finally, morale suffers in a department where subordinates are criticized for not obeying orders from one or the other of the supervisors.

It is very difficult for a manager to be responsible for an employee's performance if that employee is being directed by someone else, such as the first-line supervisor. In order to prevent such a situation, each employee should be clearly informed both about what his or her exact duties are and about to whom he or she should report. Most organizations have a job description that should give this information to a new employee, as well as an organization chart showing the flow of authority. Employees should be made to understand that they report only to one supervisor, and that if anyone else attempts to give them orders or directions, they should refer that person to the supervisor.

Span of Control

Along with unity of command goes the traditional view that a manager can supervise only a certain number of subordinates. During World War I, a British general, Sir Ian Hamilton, asserted that a superior should have no more than six immediate subordinates and that their work should be interrelated. Supposedly the fewer the subordinates, the better the management. This point of view has been partly responsible for the tall organizations that permeate industry today, with as many as ten or twelve levels between the production employees and top management.

Certainly there is a limit to the number of people that a supervisor can effectively direct, but it varies under different situations, depending on the ability of the supervisor and subordinates, the nature of the tasks being performed, and the amount of staff assistance available to the supervisor.

A supervisor who is willing to delegate some responsibilities and who spends time supervising rather than attempting to accomplish the tasks assigned to subordinates can naturally supervise more employees than can another supervisor who must try to do everything personally. Being willing to give self-direction to subordinates frees the supervisor to spend more time on managerial responsibilities and also enlarges the span of control. The span of control may also be broader in a department where the duties are routine and repetitive, such as on an assembly line. If the activities are varied, such as in a research and development department, the span tends to be less broad.

If the supervisor has to recruit, hire, and train all employees, then much valuable time that should be spent on managerial tasks will be sacrificed. However, most organizations today large enough for this to be a problem have a personnel department to furnish staff assistance in these matters and free the supervisor so that the span of control can be broader.

Broader spans of control make for "flatter" organizations where subordinates carry out their duties with less direct control from supervisors and where there are more lateral than hierarchical relationships. When circumstances permit a flat organization, it is the most desirable form, according to the research findings of the behavioral scientists.

Departmentation

Grouping people and jobs occurs in all organizations and at all levels. The process is commonly referred to as departmentation. It is usually accomplished by (1) function, (2) product, (3) territory, (4) customer, (5) time, or (6) process. Effective division of work may call for mixing two or more of these methods.

Function

Function simply means "the jobs to be done." This is usually the first type of departmentation that occurs as a small business begins to grow. The simplest way to divide work is by grouping together those who have certain skills, such as all salespeople in the sales department or the warehouse and delivery personnel in a shipping and receiving department. In large organizations functions can be identified as marketing, production, finance, and research and development. If marketing is not involved, as in some nonprofit organizations, public relations may replace sales as a department.

Product

It may be more feasible to departmentalize by product, where each product or a closely related group of products is placed in a certain department, than by function. A good example of this is General Motors, with its various divisions for marketing Chevrolets, Pontiacs, Oldsmobiles, and its other automobiles. Each division is a fairly independent unit within the overall framework of General Motors, responsible for its own profit picture.

Territory

As the name suggests, the territory method is governed by geographical boundaries. It is usually reserved for larger companies, which may be divided by territories, states, cities, counties, or even nations for those that are large enough to have international divisions.

Customer

In the customer type of departmentation, particular attention is paid to individual needs of customers. For example, there are several large chains of department stores that operate discount stores under other names in an effort to satisfy both the type of customer who desires and is willing to pay for services such as deliveries, credit, and personal attention and the type who would rather have lower prices than some of the frills. Other companies may sell both wholesale and retail and have a separate department or even a separate business for each operation.

Time

Many manufacturing firms that operate two or three shifts group activities according to time. However, this is not complete departmentation, as the activities of one shift overlap in most instances with those of another. So a company may be divided by function or product and also have the division of shifts because of the need to operate around the clock.

Process

Sometimes tasks are grouped according to the process involved. This method of departmentation is very similar to grouping by function. For example, in a data-processing department, it is true that only certain functions are performed, but the division occurs because of the type of equipment involved and the training required to operate this equipment.

A supervisor may have mixed departmentation, such as a production supervisor (by function) in the Southwest branch (by territory) in the wholesale division (by customer). It is important that the supervisor realize that these options are open in the process of grouping people and jobs.

Project Organization

Another method of organizing that has become increasingly popular in recent years, especially among those companies engaged in government projects such as the space missions, is project organization. These organizations are set up on a temporary basis to accomplish a particular task and are disbanded when the task is completed. This type of organization is used when there is a mission that requires complex skills, all of which cannot be found in one department. Personnel with these skills are drawn from permanent departments and placed under the authority of the project manager for the duration of the project. They remain, however, under the direct authority of their permanent department manager.

This pooling of talent can contribute to solutions of very difficult problems by having highly skilled personnel focus all their attention to one project and by reducing the long lines of communication usually associated with the formal organization. It is also an excellent way of motivating people by letting them work on a project where they can see the end result. They tend to become very personally involved and in so doing are able to satisfy to some extent their social, egoistic, and self-fulfillment needs. This effect is covered later in the discussion on motivation.

One disadvantage of project organization is that department heads are forced to give up some of their best personnel for the length of the project. Another is that some do not find it comfortable to work for the project manager and still be under the authority of the head of the department to which they will probably return at the end of the project. The success of this transition depends a lot upon the ability of the product manager to recognize that it may be a problem.

Despite its problems, project organization has an excellent record of success. However, this does not mean that it is a panacea for all organizational problems. The important thing to know is whether it is appropriate for the particular tasks at hand. When innovation and flexibility are essential to the successful accomplishment of a mission, project management is deemed to be a desirable form of organization. However, the role ambiguity necessary for the persons involved can be very frustrating. It is necessary that participants be given a thorough understanding of the role of the project manager. The manager functions as a coordinator and mediator between the diverse groups working on the project. Less emphasis is placed on permanent rank within the organization, and authority is granted by the group on the basis of knowledge and talents. The problem to be solved becomes the main concern and the organization for the project becomes a very flat one.

Effects of Organization on People

There have been many critics of the struggle of employees with their organizations. In 1956, William H. Whyte, Jr., published *The Organization Man* and in 1957 Chris Argyris followed with *Personality and Organization*. Whyte sees the individual as a victim of a custodial approach to managing people in which they are "looked after" by the employer and expected in turn to be grateful. Whyte is especially adamant against personality testing, bureaucracy, and conformity. Chris Argyris contends that the employers want dependence from the workers whereas the workers are looking for independence. The result of this conflict, Argyris says, is frustration and loss of self-esteem. Both writers urge workers to fight the organization, stopping only short of self-destruction.

Regardless of these opinions, it is agreed by most that organizations must have people and that people must have organizations. The answer lies in using the principles of good organization to form a plan that fits the needs of the people of the organization in such a way that the individual members use their abilities to accomplish the objectives of the organization while at the same time reaching their own personal goals.

When workers are unable to reach their goals, frustration occurs. People are apt to resort to one of the following behaviors in an attempt to resolve this conflict:

1. Rationalization
2. Projection
3. Withdrawal
4. Repression
5. Aggression
6. Regression

Rationalization is the creation of various false reasons to justify the failure to achieve goals. A student does not want to work on an assigned term paper. The student may convince himself that by going to a concert, the work on the paper will go better. After the concert, he may decide to visit with a friend because it is too late to start the paper now anyhow.

Projection is used when a person is trying to hide failures by putting the blame on others. A student who has failed an exam may blame the professor, saying that the test covered material that had not been stressed in class. An employee who is not doing his job may say it is because others will not cooperate or someone is "out to get him."

Withdrawal is the removal of oneself from a frustrating situation. It is quite often related to an illness, real or imaginary, such as when a young student gets a bad stomachache just before time to leave for school on the day that a test is to be given.

Repression is the putting out of one's mind of anything that is distasteful. A student, for example, may "forget" a term paper that is due if it interferes with something that the student would rather do.

Aggression is almost always the result of frustration. The person who is overly aggressive lashes out at everyone, resents authority, and usually has a very negative frame of mind. The stronger the desire to reach a personal objective, the greater will be the aggressive tendencies if the goal is not reached. Also, the aggression will be directed at those who are near at the time, regardless of whether they created any of the frustration.

Regression is evidenced when a person returns to childish acts. An employee may storm out of a meeting because others are not agreeing with his or her suggestions. People may feel that they cannot face situations as they are, consequently, they retreat to another time in which they were more comfortable.

All these behaviors may be destructive to an organization and its members. The organization should not create frustration; it should do away with it, or at least attempt to keep it to a minimum. It is much easier to provide outlets for release of pressures and tensions that build up to frustration in a relatively flat organization than in a tall organization, which has many levels of authority. There must be a sincere effort within the organization to achieve a balance between control, on the one hand, and self-direction, on the other, if the goals of both the organization and the individual are to be parallel rather than divergent.

Summary

Organizations consist of people who are joined together by a structure and attempt to accomplish their objectives within it. One way to exercise control over an organization is to use formal authority to accomplish a given task. For example, tall organizations create layers of authority relationships between hourly employees and top management. Flat organizations stress personal leadership, shorter lines of communication, and a shorter time span for making decisions.

Decentralization distributes authority to the smallest practical unit while at the same time keeping tight enough controls to assure that all units work toward the same company objectives. Decentralization provides more upward and lateral communication and lessens the demand for a highly organized communication system.

A major source of friction in many organizations is the lack of understanding of the terms *line* and *staff*. Although supervisors may have a staff position as far as the overall company is concerned, in their own departments they have a line relationship with their subordinates and have direct control over them, with the authority to issue orders and see that they are executed in accordance with company policy.

The principle of unity of command was formulated for administrators by Henri Payol in 1916. It states that employees should always receive orders from one superior only. Employees should be made to understand that they report only to one supervisor, and that if anyone else attempts to give them orders or directions, they should refer that person to the supervisor.

Along with unity of command goes the traditional view that a manager can supervise only a certain number of subordinates. Certainly there is a limit to the number of people that a supervisor can effectively direct, but that number varies, depending on the ability of the supervisor and subordinates, the nature of the tasks being performed, and the amount of staff assistance available to the supervisor.

People and jobs are grouped in all organizations and at all levels. This process is commonly referred to as departmentation. It is usually accomplished by (1) function, (2) product, (3) territory, (4) customer, (5) time, or (6) process. Effective division of work may call for mixing two or more of these methods.

Another method of organizing that has become increasingly popular in recent years, especially among those companies engaged in government projects such as the space missions, is project organization. These organizations are set up on a temporary basis to accomplish a particular task and are disbanded when the tasks are completed. The problem to be solved becomes the main concern and the organization for the project becomes a very flat one.

When workers are unable to reach their goals, frustration occurs. People relieve their frustrations through rationalization, projection, withdrawal, repression, aggression, and regression. All these behaviors may be destructive to an organization and its members. There must be a sincere effort within the organization to achieve a balance between control, on the one hand, and self-direction, on the other, if the goals of both the organization and the individual are to be parallel rather than divergent.

Discussion Questions

1. *Define* organization.
2. *What are some assumptions made by firms that are organized along classical lines?*
3. *What is meant by a tall organization and what are some of its disadvantages?*
4. *Describe some advantages of a flat organization.*
5. *Define* decentralization.
6. *What is your opinion of a current trend to return to centralization?*
7. *Describe the differences between* line *and* staff.
8. *Give your opinion of the concept of unity of command.*
9. *What factors govern the span of control of a manager?*
10. *Discuss the various methods of departmentation.*
11. *Name some problems that may be encountered in a project form of organization.*
12. *What are some causes of frustration among workers and what methods are employed to combat this frustration?*

Chapter Case 3

The XYZ Corporation is divided into regions and branches. Because of the size of the Metroplex area of Dallas–Fort Worth, the region and the branch in this location occupy the same headquarters in Dallas. The regional sales manager for this region is supposedly responsible to the regional vice-president.

Recently one of the largest accounts serviced by the Dallas branch has been giving most of its orders to a local competitor and the branch manager has been instructing the regional sales manager about tactics that should be used to get this account back. Naturally, the sales manager resists this criticism. When he tries to discuss this with his superior, he is told that he will have to work out the problem on his own. Some of his commissions and expenses are paid by the branch manager.

1. *What action should the regional sales manager take?*
2. *What principles of classical organizational theory are being overlooked?*
3. *What would you do if you were the regional vice-president?*
4. *What would you do if you were the branch manager?*

Note

1. James C. Worthy. "Organizational Structure and Employee Morale," *American Sociological Review*, Vol. 15, April, 1950, pp. 169–179.

CUSTOM FURNITURE CASE: WHAT TO DO FIRST?

Rita Sanchez is a clerk-typist for the company. Among other duties, she is responsible for mailing invoices to customers when shipments are made. She also makes out the travel vouchers from which the salespeople are reimbursed for travel expenses, and she types the bills of lading from which the shipping department schedules shipments. Her boss is Bill Jones, who has set up rather elaborate systems and scheduled dates when Rita is to perform certain duties.

Rita is a very friendly, outgoing person who tries to fulfill every request that is made of her. The salespeople have come to regard her as their partner in getting their paper work done, a task which most of them regard as something from which they should be relieved.

John Taylor prides himself on being well tuned in to the feelings of all his subordinates and he has noticed that lately Rita seems agitated and very unsettled. Her desk, usually neat and uncluttered, is suddenly covered with papers. Taylor senses that she is spending an inordinate amount of time trying to decide which piece of paper to process next. He starts to speak to her about it, but he remembers how sensitive Bill Jones is about his authority and determines to discuss the matter with Bill instead at their next weekly meeting.

"Bill," Taylor asked next Monday morning, "what is the matter with Rita?"

"What do you mean? I haven't noticed that anything is wrong. Has she been in here complaining? I told her to take up any problems with me."

"No, she hasn't been complaining. I just passed her desk the other day and she seemed very disorganized. Now you know that this is very unusual for Rita," said John.

"Oh, hell! I guess those salespeople are at it again. They think Rita is their personal aide. They are always trying to get her to do their work. I don't know how many times I've told them to go through me when they want something done."

John asked, "Who seems to be the worst offender?"

"It's got to be Bryan Mitchell. He thinks that because he is our top salesman, he should get special treatment, and he's always after Rita to do something for him. If we didn't have to pamper these salespeople, everything would sure be a lot easier for everyone."

"Oh, come on, Bill. I know some of them are a little temperamental, but you must remember they are the ones who keep the doors open. I'll talk to Bryan."

However, after thinking it over, John decided to go ahead and discuss the matter with Rita first. He called her into his office and the following conversation ensued:

John: "Well, Rita, how is everything going on your job?"
Rita: "Just fine, Mr. Taylor."
John: "Are you keeping on top of everything?"
Rita: "Pretty well, Mr. Taylor, although I do have a little trouble sometimes deciding about priorities."
John: "What do you mean? Don't you understand what your job is?"
Rita: "Yes, sir, I think I understand that. It's just that I have so many people asking me to do things and all of them want their work done first."
John: "What kinds of things are they asking you to do?"
Rita: "Well, you know that the salespeople work on commission and they want to get their own orders billed out right away, especially toward the end of the month, so they will have more commission coming."
John: "I thought Bill Jones was supposed to give you the orders that are ready for billing?"
Rita: "That's right, but sometimes the sales people get impatient and bring it to me, especially Bryan. I realize he is our best sales person and I don't want to upset him. He gets mad enough if I don't get his commission figured right away. I'm not really complaining but it is sometimes hard to figure out whom I'm working for."

John: "Yes, Rita, that is a difficult situation to be in. Let me see what I can do about it."

Since Bryan Mitchell has been mentioned by both Rita and Bill Jones as the principal offender in this matter, John decides to have lunch with him the next day and discuss the problem.

Lunch is finished and the restaurant is not crowded as John turns the conversation to this topic.

John: "Bryan, I have something that I want to talk to you about."

Bryan: "What is it, John? I can tell you that I have exceeded my quota."

John: "Yes, Bryan, I know you have and I want you to know how much the company and I appreciate your efforts. Keep up the good work. However, I didn't want to talk to you about sales. It's about Rita Sanchez."

Bryan: "I hope she's not in trouble. She's one of the best girls we have and certainly one of the few people in the organization that appreciates and tries to help the sales force."

John: "No, she is not in trouble. But I am afraid we might lose her if we don't get some things straightened out about her job."

Bryan: "Just tell me what I can do. We sure don't want her to leave."

John: "Well, it looks as if we have the recurring problem of you salespeople telling her what to do without going through Bill Jones. Why do you continue to do this?"

Bryan: "Oh, so Bill has been griping again about usurpation of his authority. He'd be tickled to death if we didn't have to have a sales force and he could sit back there and make out his reports. He just won't realize that without us, he wouldn't have any reports to complete. Well, let me tell you if the procedures that he has worked out didn't take so long, there wouldn't be any reason for us to bother Rita. Sometimes a customer doesn't get billed until two weeks after the order has been shipped and then commissions don't get figured until the next month. I never know how much money to count on. But he gets his salary every two weeks no matter what."

John: "Bryan, I appreciate your frankness, but please quit confusing Rita until I can get this worked out."

John returned to his office determined to work out a solution to this problem that would be equitable to all concerned.

1. What principle is being violated in this situation?
2. Who is right, Bill Jones or Bryan Mtichell?
3. How would you handle this matter if you were John Taylor?
4. Discuss Rita's behavior in this circumstance. What should she have done?

HUMAN RESOURCES

TWO

WORK GROUPS

4

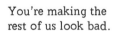

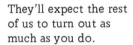

For the full story, turn to the case on page 86.

GENERAL PURPOSES
OF CHAPTER 4

1. To gain a better understanding of the reasons why informal groups are formed in the work situation
2. To define group norms and learn how they may affect production
3. To learn some of the benefits of the informal organization
4. To acquire knowledge of the role of the supervisor in working with the informal group

LEARNING OBJECTIVES

1. To name and explain briefly six main reasons why people join together in groups in the work situation
2. To list six factors that contribute to the unity of an informal group
3. To define group norms and explain how they can affect production
4. To explain why an informal leader arises from within a group
5. To give four benefits of informal groups
6. To explain the role of the informal group in affecting changes by giving three reasons why it is easier to make changes through the group
7. To explain the role of the supervisor in working with the informal group

Work groups are a permanent part of organizational realities. They represent all people in the firm. Work groups exist in the executive, managerial, and employee levels in every organized work environment. As a major element in an enterprise, work groups can exert a positive influence on the activities of the enterprise, or they can destroy its effectiveness. All levels of management must read, understand, and interpret work groups in order to supervise them effectively and achieve the company's objectives. Recognizing that work groups do exist is the first step in creating a cooperative environment among all organizational levels.

The Formation of Work Groups

People tend to associate with other people who work at a similar position, who work in the same physical location of the plant or office, and who feel a concern for common issues. Another reason for the formation of work groups is the presence of goals, interests, and aspirations that create a cohesive work group striving to reinforce the personal views of each individual member as well as to meet the objectives of the formal organization. Work groups set a hierarchy of relationships based on communication channels, influence, positions held, and leadership traits of one or more members of the group. With any group activity, there will develop a hierarchy with three distinct relationships. The director shapes the direction and accomplishments of the group. The primary members directly influence the actions taken by the director of the group, and the secondary members exercise little or no influence over group activities.[1]

Work groups tend to reflect a common set of desires that may or may not be evident on the surface. Research has suggested several common threads that tend to exist in all group structures. These common threads consist of (1) the desire to fill the need for positive social interaction among group members, (2) the need to control the actions of group members by setting standards of expected behavioral outcomes, (3) the need to protect individual members through a collective representation of individual views, (4) the desire to exercise greater influence over the work environment through group interaction, and (5) the desire to enhance group effectiveness by pooling individual assets to achieve a given objective.[2]

Work groups represent a broad spectrum of views and have a common purpose. A supervisor should construct work groups carefully, but he should recognize their limitations in achieving organizational goals. In contrast to informal groups, work groups are created by functional relationships within the organization. Work groups usually have some direction or control by institutional authority. They tend to change in size and makeup, depending upon changing needs of the formal structure. For example, the growth of computer technology has influenced the activities of some work groups by upgrading entrance requirements into a group, demanding more specialization to meet a given goal, and increasing the level of achievement required by all work groups in an enterprise. Another example is the creation of new work groups in the fields of ecology, environmental hazards, and equal employment opportunities. Again, the creation or demise of work groups is a function of economic, organizational and societal needs, interests, and desires in the life of an institution. In the final analysis, the effectiveness of any work group depends upon the ability of the formal leadership to maintain, change, or redirect the activities of all group endeavors within the sphere of functional interrelationships.[3]

Moreover, an effective group possesses the following traits:

1. A clear sense of direction
2. A flexible schedule to work toward a goal
3. A clear communication process
4. The ability to make decisions without destroying group cohesiveness
5. The authority to achieve human and economic objectives
6. The ability to utilize group leadership by sharing group responsibilities
7. A cohesive spirit that does not destroy individual freedom
8. The ability to utilize each member
9. The ability to avoid domination by one person
10. The ability to adjust to changing external or internal environmental conditions
11. The ability to function on a rational basis without negative emotional influences[4]

Informal Groups

Informal groups are based on informal power in a network of personal and social relationships. Power to influence the group is based on the cooperation of group members, not on formal position or authority. In order to anticipate the actions of informal groups, a supervisor must pay less attention to functional work groups and try instead to identify the attitudes, values, and aspirations of the informal structure. Understanding informal groups is essential to motivate them toward the collective achievement of organizational goals. Similarly, informal groups are not static but change to reflect new ideas, new interpersonal relationships, and new communication channels. Supervisors and management should take a positive attitude toward informal groups by influencing the beliefs, aspirations, and attitudes of individual group members.

The major concern of an informal group is to have an impact on the work environment. The cohesiveness of an informal group can be increased by creating:

1. a team identity by altering job assignments
2. an environment that encourages cooperation
3. an informal group that reduces personal friction among antagonistic personnel
4. a desire to compete as a team instead of against individual members, and
5. a work environment that strives to meet the personal and organizational needs of people.[5]

Finally, informal groups can be a managerial tool that a supervisor can employ to increase the social, economic, and psychological growth of people, organizations, and managers in any organized endeavor.

A few examples of the effectiveness of informal groups may help to reinforce their importance. (1) A major function of the informal group is to establish, maintain, and perpetuate the attitudes, values, and goals of the group within the formal organization. For example, the attitude people take toward quality of workmanship reflects group views instead of formal guidelines. Another example is the degree of employee theft in a given firm; this reflects the views of the informal group rather than the desires of formal influences. (2) Another major function of an informal group is to achieve social identification within a large general universe. Many people in our complex society tend to feel alienated from personal relationships because of the size, the indifference, and the inability of formal structures to meet personal needs to belong, to have identity, and to achieve social success. (3) Another function of informal groups is communication among group participants. Informal groups are a vital link in the communication process because they reflect a clearer view of what the group expects to accomplish than the formal policies in a static organization structure. An understanding of what the informal group is saying is essential to channel the activities of informal groups effectively. (4) A final function of informal groups is to establish norms governing the activities of members in internal or external relationships. These norms set dress codes, productivity goals, and social standards to govern the actions of individual group members.[6]

The benefits of informal groups are closely related to the functions performed by informal group structures. One benefit is the flexibility provided by informal activities in the accomplishment of formal policies, procedures, and directives. For example, an emergency or a dynamic environment provides an opportunity for the informal group to react to changes in a positive manner faster than is the case with most formal structures. A similar benefit is the ability of individual members to obtain social satisfaction by achieving a sense of belonging. Although this process is not automatic, it does protect individual members from harassment from external forces. As stated earlier, groups usually have a director, primary members, and secondary members. Thus, an individual's role is determined by his or her influence with and acceptance by other group members.

A personal benefit to the supervisor is a cooperative attitude that, if nourished, can build mutual respect as well as enhance the productivity of the group. In Chapter 2, we discussed leadership styles and concluded that a democratic style tends to increase the self-direction of individual workers. Also, such a leadership style gives a supervisor more time to plan, to create, and to improve working relationships with informal elements.

A spin-off of group self-direction and cooperation is the reinforcement of management goals by the informal group's willingness to pick up the slack in crisis or peak-load periods. Also, a supervisor can overcome personal managerial deficiencies by using the expertise of informal groups to achieve formal organization objectives. This is not manipulation but is an avenue to allow the group to grow. The group receives credit for its initiative and willingness to cooperate with a supervisor.

Another benefit of the informal group is that it forces a supervisor to make judicious decisions, for a bad decision reduces the leader's formal authority. An adverse effect related to that produced by a bad decision is the decline of a supervisor's informal influence on the attitudes of the informal group.[7]

Group Loyalty

In every organization there are pressures to increase the loyalty of employees to the firm. Informal pressures strive to enhance the loyalty of the individual to the peer group. As a result, divided loyalties cause frustration if management fails to unite formal and informal loyalties around a common goal. Likewise, a threat to the group's loyalty has an immediate adverse impact on organizational relationships. Building mutual loyalties in formal and informal groups is a constant process of education, training, and employee self-development.

The strength of group loyalties is related to the group's ability to satisfy needs, to control members' behavior, and to produce a cohesive course of action. Also affecting group loyalties are the personality traits of each member. For example, someone with a negative self-image may work harder to sustain group loyalty because this enhances association with group members. An opposite view is taken by a person with such traits as dominance, ego, strength, and self-reliance. This individual may adhere to group loyalty if it seems to be in his or her best interest but may disregard group loyalties if they conflict with personal aspirations. Consequently, the continuity of group loyalties is, at the least, elusive because of the divergent personalities existing in formal or informal groups.

A related issue in discussing group loyalty is the situation at any specific time. Some factors that influence group loyalties are the following:

1. How cohesive is the group? (Is there pressure for divergent views?)
2. How will change affect group loyalties? (Weaken or strengthen?)
3. How important is the issue? (Group-individual members)
4. How important is it for the group or the individual to be right?
5. How important is the view of one or more group members?[8]

Another factor in group loyalty is the group's ability to punish the deviate member. An experiment conducted several years ago was designed to test the group's ability to alter or punish deviate behavior of individual members. (See Figure 4-1.) One person assumed the role of

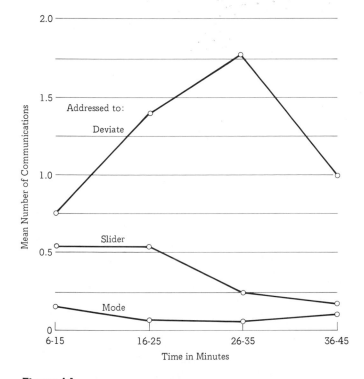

Figure 4-1
Communications to deviate, slider, mode. Source: "Creativity and Conformity: A Problem for Organizations," Foundation for Research on Human Behavior, Ann Arbor: Braun & Brumfield, March 1965, p. 27.

"mode," who was always to agree with the majority. The group virtually ignored this person. Another person assumed the role of "slider," who changed from opposition to agreement with the group's position. At first the group listened to this person but ignored the person entirely after "slider" agreed with the majority. A third person assumed the role of "deviate," who took an opposite view and refused to change. As expected, this person received the most attention but lost attention when other members saw the "deviate" was not going to change position. Communication received by the "deviate," the "slider," and the "mode" is illustrated in Figure I.

Later, the group was asked to nominate an executive committee to make policy for the group and a correspondence committee to handle housekeeping details. The "deviate" received no nominations to the executive committee but received the most votes for the correspondence committee. Also, the "deviate" was rated as the least desirable member of the group. Such an experiment reinforces the belief that the behavior of individual members can be shaped, altered, or conformed to meet the desired outcomes of the majority. Similarly, the person who does not change will be penalized or will fail to receive an anticipated reward. Loyalty to a group is a function of group personalities, group ideals, group situations, and group pressure to punish or alter behavior of "deviate" members.[9]

Behavior Patterns

In viewing work groups, our discussion has dealt with the formation of groups, the structure of informal groups, and the loyalty of group members. All these ideas reflect the behavior patterns of groups in various stages of development. However, to analyze the behavior of any group is to examine the (1) background, (2) rate of group participation, (3) communication techniques, (4) group's attractiveness, (5) group's atmosphere, (6) various subgroups, (7) standards of the group, (8) group's operating procedures, (9) group's goals, and (10) leadership pattern. A brief definition of each behavior pattern follows.

Group background—consisting of both its previous experiences and the personal notions and attitudes which the members bring to the group. This history will affect the work of the group as well as the relationships of its members.

Group participation—consisting of individual task, group task, and the readiness of the group to function collectively. This participation uses the abilities of each member and eliminates the negative influence of internal or external pressures.

Group communication—consisting of oral, written, and non-verbal forms of expression. Such communication reflects a willingness to share experiences, a clear expression of ideas, an understanding of what is being said, and the development of a group art of listening to the views of all participants.

Group cohesion—the attractiveness of the group in terms of likes and dislikes as well as commitment to a common group goal.

Group atmosphere—consisting of cooperation or conflict in internal or external relationships. Such an atmosphere is based on the freedom each member has to express his ideas, how well the group supports an individual member, and how well the group adjusts to the needs of various tasks.

Sub groups—consisting of special interests that tend to divide the cohesiveness of the group. The effectiveness of the group depends on their ability to overcome divisiveness of special interest groups.

Group standards—consisting of a code of operation adopted by a group. Such standards pertain to their own operations, may or may not be open to reexamination, and will change standards that are no longer useful.

Group procedures—consisting of a methodology to obtain the productivity to maintain the operating effectiveness of the group. Such a procedure tends to reflect group size, group purpose, group task, and group understanding of existing operating procedures.

Group goals—consisting of personal or group achievements the group wishes to make an objective to be obtained within a prescribed time period. Objectives should relate to group resources, be realistic, be attainable, and be in line with the long-range objectives of the group.

Group leadership—consisting of complete leader dominance or mutual responsibility for leadership of the group. Leadership seeks to complete a given task, to maintain interpersonal relationships, and to fulfill the individual needs in performing a task or in maintaining interpersonal relationships.[10]*

Production Restrictions

A direct consequence of negative group behavior in organized entities is reduced physical output and distortion of quality standards. Severe cases result in physical damage to company property, products, or services. An excellent example is found in the film "The Blue Collar Trap," which shows one employee on an auto plant assembly line who dropped cars, miscounted cars, and carried out other activities to disrupt the work of the formal organization. The major areas of restrictive behavior result from changes that alter production schedules, working relation-

* This text is from the monograph "The Leader Looks at Group Effectiveness," by Gordon L. Lippitt and Edith W. Seashore, published and copyrighted by Leadership Resources, Inc., One First Virginia Plaza, 6400 Arlington Blvd., Suite 344, Falls Church, Va. 22042. It is reproduced here by special written permission of the publisher.

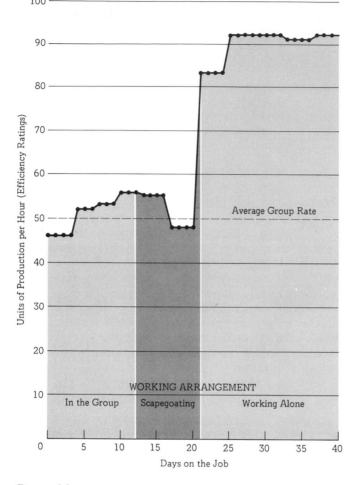

Production Record for One Presser in a Sewing Factory
for the Forty Days after Hiring

Figure 4-2
Group pressures and production. Source: "Creativity and Conformity: A
Problem for Organization," Foundation for Research on Human Behavior, Ann
Arbor: Braun & Brumfield, March 1965, p. 23.

ships, or alter the job content of an individual position. The impact of
such changes tends to lower morale, increase employee turnover, and
increase grievances. A study of one group in a garment factory illustrates the impact of group pressures on productivity. As shown in Figure
4-2 a new employee exceeded the normal rate of fifty units an hour,
which brought direct group actions that forced her again below fifty
units an hour. However, this employee's rate went to ninety units an

hour after the group was restructured and she was allowed to work alone.[11]

A similar experiment was conducted to overcome group hostility toward style changes by increasing group participation in decision making. Group A received a directive on the need for change and a statement on the new rates. Group B was given representative participation in setting new standards. Group C was given total group participation in setting new pay rates and job standards. The results are shown in Figure 4-3. Group A dropped from sixty to fifty units. Group B declined in

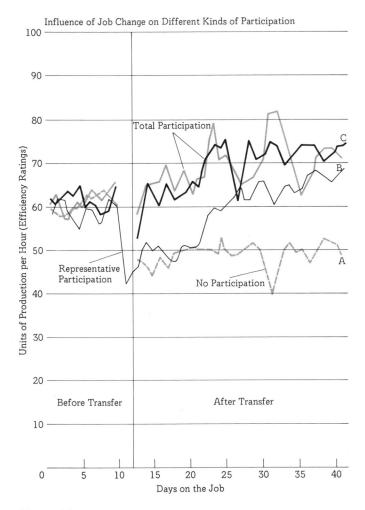

Figure 4-3
Productivity in groups. Source: "Creativity and Conformity: A Problem for Organizations," Foundation for Research on Human Behavior, Ann Arbor: Braun & Brumfield, March 1965, p. 24.

production but returned to the standard of sixty units within two weeks. Group C recorded an increase in productivity to seventy units after forty days on the job. A side benefit was reduced turnover, fewer grievances, and less hostility toward management.[12]

Group pressures worked in all three groups to increase as well as decrease productivity. The positive impact of group participation redirected group pressures away from conflict to cooperation. Group pressures can serve management when a favorable climate of mutual trust, respect, and concern is fostered. Figure 4-4 shows the standard deviations from the group production rate before and after a major style change for groups A, B, and C. These results picture clearly the impact of managerial actions on group productivity. Likewise, the impact of negative group actions on productivity is illustrated in Figures 4-2, 4-3, and 4-4.[13]

The negative impact of group pressures may cause wasteful organizational practices. Compromise decisions tend to satisfy a majority of needs without giving adequate consideration to the needs of the formal structure. Another practice with a negative impact is that of utilizing people below their capacities because of rigid job descriptions, promotion policies, or inadequate personnel training. A related managerial belief is that growth in group size and complexity is proof of managerial success. This belief does not take into account organizational, human, or efficiency needs. We are all creatures of habit, which means we tend

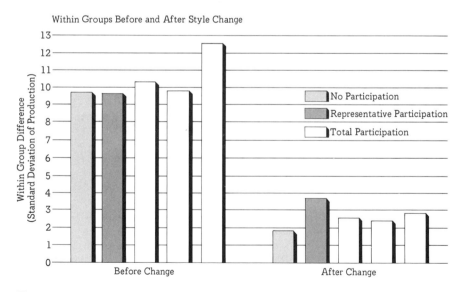

Figure 4-4
Differences in production in clothing factory. Source: "Creativity and Conformity: A Problem for Organizations," Foundation for Research on Human Behavior, Ann Arbor: Braun & Brumfield, March 1965, p. 26.

to reinforce previously stated policies, procedures, and rules. Conflict of personal goals with those of the firm causes clashes in loyalties as well as reducing the impact of formal controls over group activities. The desire of managers to protect their areas from budget cuts results in inflating personnel needs and inflating performance figures in annual reports. As we look at formal or informal groups, group pressure is evident in reduced employee productivity and in wasteful organizational practices.[14]

Similar dysfunctional practices are found in all formal and informal groups. Several are (1) avoiding responsibility for group actions, (2) placing the blame for failure on other organizational aspects, (3) ignoring a problem and leaving it for someone else to solve, (4) multiplying the responsibility for a decision to distort the concept of individual accountability, and (5) adhering to conforming influences without considering the need to obtain positive results.[15]

As noted earlier, restricting output often reflects the frustrations felt by employees in their inability to influence their environment. Morale has a direct impact on products, profits, and priorities. Moreover, morale measures the individual's ability to satisfy personal needs as well as receive satisfaction from the total job situation. An effort to enhance morale through job enrichment is shown in the following example: A group of educated and intelligent women were assigned the task of handling correspondence with stockholders. Working under close supervision as well as in a highly structured environment, the quality of work of the women was low and employee turnover was high. To overcome this problem a job enrichment program was established that required each woman to sign each business letter, to be personally responsible for letter quality, and to develop skills in areas that appealed to them. Experts were provided for consultation regarding problem subjects. Six months later this test group showed a dramatic improvement in terms of productivity, reduced absences, increased promotions, and reduced labor cost.[16] We have to assume that the morale of people has a direct impact on productivity, product quality, and employee attitudes toward the formal organization. The end result was that as jobs became more meaningful to people in terms of content, sense of accomplishment, and recognition, there was a dramatic improvement in morale and productivity.

Another factor in restricting employee's output is the worker's physical and psychological orientation to the firm. For example, vast amounts of money have been spent to modernize America's productive facilities but the rate of growth in employee productivity has remained at 3 percent each year since the early 1960s. The physical resources exist but the desire to use them is missing, as is the desire to design, implement, and create new processes to expand the productivity of individual members in work groups. Related to the preceding is the inability or lack of desire on the part of management to create a work environment that

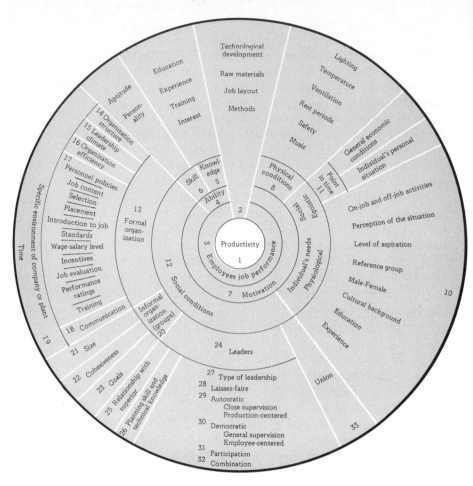

Figure 4-5
Sutermeister's Productivity Wheel. Source: Robert A. Sutermeister, *People and Productivity*, 2nd ed., McGraw-Hill Book Company, New York, 1969, p. i.

encourages technological and social growth. A more complex view of productivity determinants was developed by Robert A. Sutermeister.[17] Figure 4-5 shows the complex variables that make up the productivity equation as well as some examples of how employees restrict output in all organized work endeavors.

Employees restrict output because they are stultified by their work environment. Again, the complexity of employee productivity presents an excellent opportunity for management to exert formal and informal influence to gain the support of human assets in all organized work environments.

A study, similar to that of Sutermeister, that considered productivity in relation to a work group's environment, motivation, satisfaction, and absenteeism was made by James V. Clark in 1961.[18] The results of his research are reflected in Figure 4-6. The first section shows the conditions in the work group's environment. The second section shows the

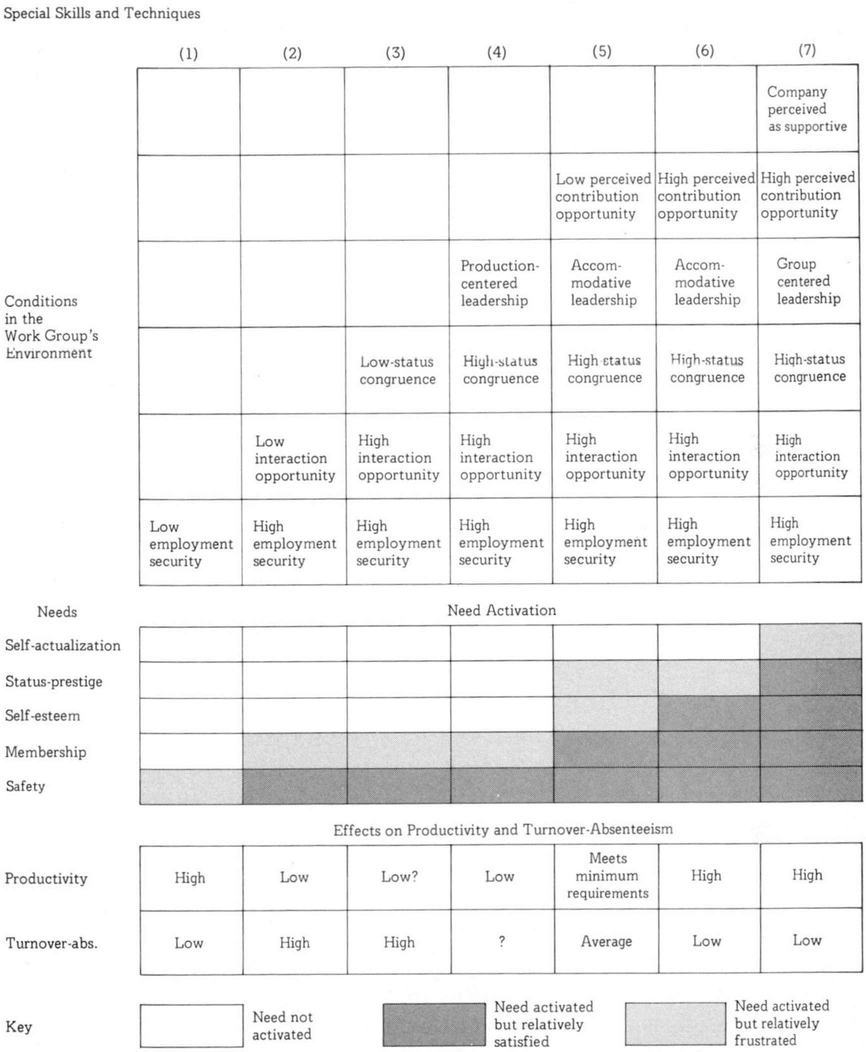

Special Skills and Techniques

	(1)	(2)	(3)	(4)	(5)	(6)	(7)
							Company perceived as supportive
					Low perceived contribution opportunity	High perceived contribution opportunity	High perceived contribution opportunity
Conditions in the Work Group's Environment				Production-centered leadership	Accommodative leadership	Accommodative leadership	Group centered leadership
			Low-status congruence	High-status congruence	High-status congruence	High-status congruence	High-status congruence
		Low interaction opportunity	High interaction opportunity	High interaction opportunity	High interaction opportunity	High interaction opportunity	High interaction opportunity
	Low employment security	High employment security	High employment security	High employment security	High employment security	High employment security	High employment security

Needs — Need Activation

Needs	(1)	(2)	(3)	(4)	(5)	(6)	(7)
Self-actualization							
Status-prestige							
Self-esteem							
Membership							
Safety							

Effects on Productivity and Turnover-Absenteeism

	(1)	(2)	(3)	(4)	(5)	(6)	(7)
Productivity	High	Low	Low?	Low	Meets minimum requirements	High	High
Turnover-abs.	Low	High	High	?	Average	Low	Low

Key: Need not activated | Need activated but relatively satisfied | Need activated but relatively frustrated

Figure 4-6
Some relations between conditions in the work group's environment, motivation, satisfaction, productivity, and turnover-absenteeism. Source: James V. Clark, "Motivation in Work Groups—A Tentative View," *Human Organizations*, vol. 19, no. 4 p. 202, Winter 1960–1961. Reproduced by permission of The Society for Applied Anthropology. *Human Organization* 19 (4) 1960–1961.

needs of each person and degree to which each need is satisfied. The third section shows the impact of each activity on productivity and turnover. As you view Figure 4-6, you can see that as the chart goes from point 1 to point 7, work conditions improve, a greater number of needs are satisfied, and the rate of employee productivity increases while the rate of labor turnover declines.

The significance of such research is depicted in a 1974 public service advertisement of the Department of Labor. The point of this advertisement is to increase productivity in the world of work in order to increase jobs as well as improve the competitive position of this country in world markets. Additional impetus for increasing productivity is provided by an annual inflation that in recent years has varied from 6% to 13%.

Training and Production Restrictions

The restriction of employee productivity can in some cases be traced to a lack of proper personnel training. New techniques, for example, may be introduced without giving employees adequate instruction for their use. Again, low productivity can be traced to the inability to carry out managerial duties effectively. To overcome training deficiencies requires a coordinated effort by management, workers, and supervisors to increase productivity through proper training of all personnel. The degree of training personnel may need shows in their experience level, their previous personal and professional development, and their education.[19] Figure 4-7 gives an example of this relationship.

This grid in Figure 4-7 provides a way to evaluate the interest of management in developing the abilities of personnel. Only position (9,9) provides a maximum opportunity to expand the abilities of all personnel beyond the daily routine. Stretching the ability of people beyond today is basic to the continued growth and vitality of all organized work. A managerial philosophy that deals only with the present will use the (1,1), (9,1), (5,5), and (1,9) style of management and may survive in the short run, but in the long run this could mean no enterprise to manage. The implications of this managerial philosophy are reflected in a training system designed to change as the developmental needs of all personnel changes within the work environment.[20] Figure 4-8 shows the degree of managerial interest in the total development of all personnel.

The integrated style of management seeks to inform all personnel of their responsibilities and their relationship to the whole organization. In many cases a person has technical skills but does not understand his or her place in the internal workings of the firm. A related need is to keep updating this information because organizational relationships normally do not remain static. People enter and leave firms at a faster rate today because of increased employee mobility and changing work habits of those entering the labor market. To assume a person need only be

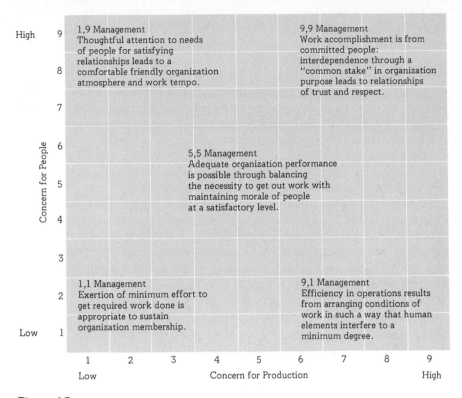

Figure 4-7
The Managerial Grid. Source: Robert R. Blake and Jane S. Mouton, Managerial Facades," *Advanced Management Journal,* July 1966, p. 31.

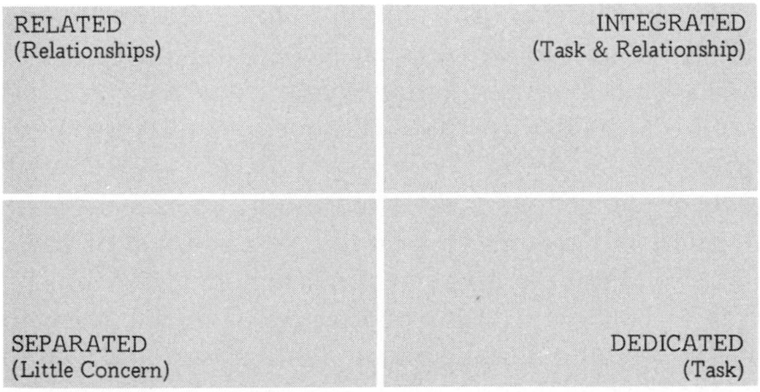

RELATED (Relationships)	INTEGRATED (Task & Relationship)
SEPARATED (Little Concern)	DEDICATED (Task)

Figure 4-8

trained once is to invite economic and personnel obsolescence. For example, what programs are designed in most firms to encourage employees with five years of tenure to upgrade their skills or acquire new skills to meet changing job requirements? The establishment of a training system is not enough to overcome productive restrictions unless an analysis of existing training methods is made to determine the effectiveness of all training methods to the organization. In today's cost-conscious world, a major area of cost cutting is in training and developing personnel because there appears to be no tangible results for the investment in dollars, time, and management skills. However, to overcome this trend, reeducation efforts should be launched to identify existing training needs and to design an effective training system to meet these needs.[21] A comparison of desired changes along with the training method to bring them about is provided in Figure 4-9.

As with solving the problem of restrictive employee output, the design of training techniques to overcome restrictive behavior is a continuous managerial process. Although education and training do not eliminate all restrictive behavior, they can reduce friction among various groups and can provide greater understanding of the desirability of effectively utilizing all assets of the corporation.

Conformity and Norms

Conformity involves uniformity, cooperation, common beliefs, and conventional behavior. Although this reflects a desire to receive approval from external forces, it also reflects a conflict between internal belief and external behavior. Contrary to general belief, conformers have no universal traits. For example, a cognitive conformer seeks answers to problems in the opinions and information of the group. On the other hand, the expedient conformer feels he or she has the right answer but goes along with the wishes of the group. A third type of conformer lacks self-confidence and accepts the group's opinion as correct.

The extent to which a person is influenced by group pressures is determined by the (1) meaning of the situation to the person, (2) strength of personal conviction, (3) person's need for group acceptance, and (4) individual's expertness. Again, individual needs alter behavioral patterns in terms of predicting the willingness of a person to conform to group norms.

A variable related to the preceding is the situation a person is in at a given time. Several situational factors that influence the issue of conformity are (1) the nature and importance of the issue, (2) how important is it for the person to be right, (3) how conspicuous or anonymous the individual is, (4) how unanimous the group opinion is, and (5) the intensity of the change to take place.[22]

Objectives of Development

		I	II	III	IV	V
		Change in Knowledge	Change in Attitude	Change in Ability	Change in Job Performance	Change in End-Operational Results
Conditions for Development			(Conditions in Col. I + II)	(Cols. I & II + III)	(Cols. I, II, & III + IV)	(Cols. I, II, III, & IV + V)
	Participant Characteristics	Sufficient IQ	Flexible attitudes on part of participants	Non-conflicting habits or personality traits		
		Sufficient motivation	Agreement with spirit of the material to be to be learned			
	Learning Effort	Direct method of instruction (programmed learning, lectures, films, reading, and so on)	Discussion of on the job applications and personal benefits	Practice of desired abilities	Opportunity for on-the-job practice of newly acquired abilities	
				Corrective training (therapy) to correct undesirable habits and behavioral patterns		
		Competent instruction				
	Leadership Climate		Neutral or positive attitude of superior toward development	Superior's attitude and example consistent with desired change	Coaching, counseling, and periodic performance review by superior consistent with desired performance	Performance appraisal by the superior based on practices taught in the learning phase
	Organizational Climate		Goals, top-management philosophy, and policies consistent with learning phase		Philosophy, practices, and precedents of the policy-making executives consistent with desired manager performance	Top management active support and interest in development
						Incentive system designed to reward practices taught in the learning phase
	Organizational Culture		Cultural conditions and social beliefs consistent with desired attitudes		Informal group rules and standards consistent with desired change	Positive employee and informal group attitudes toward desired change

Figure 4-9
Conditions required to induce change through management development.
Source: Robert J. House, *Management Development: Design, Evaluation, and Implementation,* University of Michigan: Ann Arbor, 1967, p. 18.

Social scientists have examined these situational differences and have drawn the following conclusions on their role in conformity behavior. Generally stated, these are as follows:

1. Support for a position by group members tends to decrease individual conformity.
2. Expert opinions tend to reinforce conformity rather than reduce it.
3. Attraction to a group can increase conformity but is no guarantee of absolute conformity.
4. Conformity increases when people work on group tasks, whereas work on individual tasks reduces conformity. (See Figure 4-10.)
5. Feelings of rejection increase a person's willingness to conform to group norms.[23] (See Figure 4-10.)

Norms are accepted ways of behavior that set a pattern governing the actions of individual group members. This pattern of behavior is en-

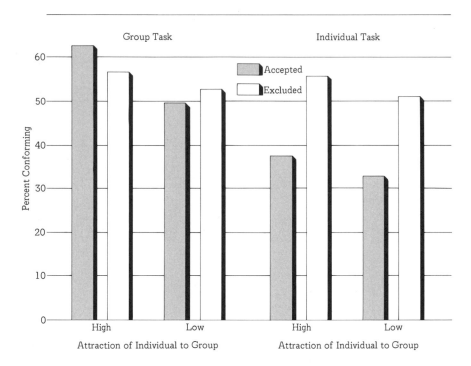

Figure 4-10
Conformity of excluded persons. Source: "Creativity and Conformity: A Problem for Organizations," Foundation for Research on Human Behavior, Ann Arbor: Braun & Brumfield, March 1965, p. 21.

forced through penalties or rewards to obtain the desired behavior from group members. A common example is the informal agreement to set a production quota for an eight-hour work period. For example, a quota of seventy units of production is set by the informal group as an accepted level of individual output per hour. A few months later a new employee enters the group and after several months on the job produces eighty units of output per hour. A verbal warning by other group members does not change the behavior of the new employee. Additional verbal and physical pressure fails to alter the behavior of the new worker. The final action is to remove the employee from the group by transfer, by dismissal, or by creation of an unbearable situation that causes the new employee to quit. Although this example is oversimplified, it does show the practices used to enforce informal standards of unit output as well as to govern the actions of individual members.

Norms like conformity can be enforced to the extent that the group is attractive as well as cohesive in terms of its members. An individual with no real intent of being part of a group would not be influenced to any extent by group pressure to follow accepted norms of behavior for group participants.

Conformity and norms are recognized as elusive components of an ever-evolving organizational style. How can we measure the degree of conformity in a firm as well as determine when conformity is a liability? One way is to identify the managerial style of the firm in terms of formal influences that require employees to adjust their life-styles to meet a prescribed pattern of behavior. Rensis Likert has developed Figure 4-11 to help business people analyze the management style of their companies.[24] Using these data, let us carry the system a step further by showing the effect of systems 1–4 on conformity and the establishment of norms in work groups.

Functions	System 1	System 2	System 3	System 4
Leadership	A	B	C	D
Motivation	A	B	C	D
Communications	A	B	C	D
Decisions	A	B	C	D
Goals	A	B	C	D
Control	A	B	C	D

Work group's ability to influence individual actions are reflected in the following scale as shown in the previous chart.
A—Work groups work without management input to set norms.
B—Work groups work with limited management input to set norms.
C—Work groups use management input to set norms.
D—Work groups work with management to set norms.

		SYSTEM 1 Exploitive Authoritative	SYSTEM 2 Benevolent Authoritative	SYSTEM 3 Consultative	SYSTEM 4 Participative Group
Leadership	How much confidence is shown in subordinates?	None	Condescending	Substantial	Complete
	How free do they feel to talk to superiors about job?	Not at all	Not very	Rather free	Fully free
	Are subordinates' ideas sought and used, if worthy?	Seldom	Sometimes	Usually	Always
Motivation	Is predominent use made of (1) fear, (2) threats, (3) punishment, (4) rewards, (5) involvement?	(1), (2), (3), occasionally (4)	(4), some (3)	(4), some (3) and (5)	(5), (4), based on group set goals
	Where is responsibility felt for achieving organization's goals?	Mostly at top	Top and middle	Fairly general	At all levels
Communication	How much communication is aimed at achieving organization's objectives?	Very little	Little	Quite a bit	A great deal
	What is the direction of information flow?	Downward	Mostly downward	Down and up	Down, up and sideways
	How is downward communication accepted?	With suspicion	Possibly with suspicion	With caution	With an open mind
	How accurate is upward communication?	Often wrong	Censored for the boss	Limited accuracy	Accurate
	How well do superiors know problems faced by subordinates?	Know little	Some knowledge	Quite well	Very well
Decisions	At what level are decisions formally made?	Mostly at top	Policy at top, some delegation	Broad policy at top, more delegation	Throughout but well integrated
	What is the origin fo technical and professional knowledge used in decision making?	Top management	Upper and middle	To a certain extent, throughout	To a great extent, throughout
	Are subordinates involved in decisions related to their work?	Not at all	Occasionally consultated	Generally consulted	Fully involved
	What does decision-making process contribute to motivation?	Nothing, often weakens it	Relatively little	Some contribution	Substantial contribution
Goals	How are organizational goals established?	Orders issued	Orders, some comment invited	After discussion, by orders	By group action (except in crisis)
	How much covert resistance to goals is present?	Strong resistance	Moderate resistance	Some resistance at times	Little or none
Control	How concentrated are review and control functions?	Highly at top	Relatively highly at top	Moderate delegation to lower levels	Quite widely shared
	Is there an informal organization resisting the formal one?	Yes	Usually	Sometimes	No—same goals as formal
	What are cost, productivity, and other control data used for?	Policing, punishment	Reward and punishment	Reward, some self-guidance	Self-guidance, problem solving

Figure 4-11

Source: Reprinted with permission of Macmillan Publishing Co., Inc., from *The Corporation as a Creative Environment* by Dan Fabun. Copyright © 1969 by Macmillan Publishing Co., Inc.

Why People Follow an Informal Leader

The informal leader, to be effective, must meet the expectations of the group members and also show the ability to handle the requirements of various situations. The traits that produce informal leaders are the following:

1. Technical competence
2. Seniority
3. Age
4. Work location
5. Mobility within a given work area
6. A responsive personality

Technical competence is the knowledge necessary to answer questions as well as the ability to complete a given task. Seniority refers to the length of service an employee has in a particular firm or job assignment. Seniority in union or nonunion firms is a major variable that determines the acceptance or rejection of leadership from an informal leader. Age in years as well as in job experience is another vital factor in determining the acceptance of an informal leader. As discussed earlier, the work location of a job can have a direct impact on the development of informal leaders. For example, the job design, number of people doing similar tasks, and attitude of people toward the formal leader influence the role an informal leader has in directing the group's activities. Closely related to job location is the informal leader's mobility to assure daily contact with all group members. Without communication or interaction the group and leader cease to function with any degree of success. Finally, a leader that fails to respond to the needs of individuals or the group at large will be replaced by a new leader. To avoid this loss of leadership an informal leader must (1) poll the group constantly for a consensus, (2) follow the accepted norms of the members, (3) use informal influence in a positive manner, and (4) govern the actions of individual members in a democratic manner.

Informal leaders have no direct representation within the formal structure but can provide information useful to decision makers within the formal structure. For example, major job changes that significantly alter the content of existing positions or require the acquisition of new job skills should receive some input from an informal leader to increase the acceptance of such changes by group members. Additional input from an informal leader is essential to set policies properly regarding promotions, transfers, and wages. Management should recognize that an informal leader is effective only to the extent that the leader accomplishes the goals of the group without selling out to the formal structure. To manipulate the leader or the group is to court hostility, friction, and noncooperation from all informal parts of the enterprise. Informal leaders and members can exercise a positive influence in all work efforts if they are given general guidelines to follow and if they become real participants in the activities of the firm. The challenge for management is to build a partnership of purpose that encourages formal or informal groups to achieve their respective goals within a climate of cooperation and mutual trust.

Summary

Work groups are an ever-present force in the life of organized work endeavors. To build a partnership of purpose is to recognize the common desires that exist in all group structures, to identify the functional relationships of each work group, and to recognize the traits that produce effective group results. Another component in this partnership of purpose is the impact of informal groups as they seek an identity, perpetuate the goals of the group, and set norms of behavior for group participants. Similarly, management should not view group loyalty as a negative force but should channel this element into a creative force to expand the knowledge and physical efforts of formal and informal entities. Moreover, an understanding of the behavior patterns in groups will further enhance the effectiveness of formal elements in obtaining the cooperation and participation of work groups and informal groups. The purpose of our discussion of production restrictions was to acknowledge the existence of nonproductive behavior, to suggest possible alternative solutions, and to identify wasteful organizational practices created by negative group pressures. A challenge of management is to overcome nonproductive behavior through positive leadership and cooperation with all organizational entities.

A major tool of management in overcoming production restrictions is training people to do the task of today as well as preparing them at company expense for the task of tomorrow. Present trends indicate an increased desire to train existing personnel, but little real concern is shown in designing systems to measure the effectiveness of existing training programs. Related to the preceding is the requirement of upgrading training so as to meet ever-changing technical, social, and developmental needs of all personnel. Again, training is a useful tool in overcoming production restrictions but should not be viewed as a cure-all for all managerial problems relating to productivity. Another area where management needs to think positively is in the attitude it takes toward conformity and group norms. The issue is not one of conflict or antagonism but should be one of influencing conformity and group norms to achieve the outcomes desired in the establishment of formal objectives. Similarly, a positive view of informal leaders and the contribution they can make in reaching formal objectives should be taken by a progressive manager. Work groups can build a partnership of purpose only if management provides the proper atmosphere.

Discussion Questions

1. Discuss the reasons that people belong to informal groups.
2. What are group norms and how can they affect production?
3. How does an informal leader attain that position?
4. Give some advantages that can accrue to an employee from membership in an informal group.
5. Define the role of the informal group in the accomplishment of change within an organization.
6. Discuss the informal group as it affects the supervisor.

Chapter Case 4

The ABC Company manufactures dishwashing machines. In the assembly section five men worked together assembling these machines. They were a closely knit group and morale was high in the section. Even though informality prevailed and there was a certain amount of horseplay among the men, production was at an acceptable level.

A team of methods specialists was working in the plant, and they determined that production could be raised if the assembly methods were changed. The cabinet containing the washing unit was put on a belt that moved it through the department and each worker was given a specialized operation to perform as it moved to his position.

Since the line was installed, production has fallen off and several members of the group are threatening to quit or ask for transfers. When questioned, they say that they do not like the assembly line and they want to return to the way they are used to working.

1. *What is the principal problem?*
2. *Was the change introduced properly?*
3. *What has happened to the relationships between the workers?*
4. *What has happened to the relationship between the workers and their jobs?*
5. *How would you have handled this change?*

Notes

1. Sexton Adams. *Personnel Management.* Columbus, Ohio: Grid, 1972, pp. 161–168.
2. Hanafi M. Soliman. "The Informal Group: A Potential Partner," *Industry Week,* June 12, 1972, pp. 53–54.

3. Keith Davis. *Human Relations in the World of Work*. New York: McGraw-Hill, 1969, p. 252.
4. Ibid., p. 270.
5. Adams, op. cit., p. 167.
6. Davis, op. cit., p. 254.
7. Ibid., p. 257.
8. Carol Ludington, ed., "Creativity and Conformity: A Problem for Organization," *Foundation for Research on Human Behavior*, 4th ed. Ann Arbor, Michigan: Foundation for Research on Human Behavior, 1958, p. 17.
9. Ibid., pp. 27–29.
10. Gordon L. Lippitt and Edith W. Seashore. *The Leader Looks at Group Effectiveness*. Washington, D.C.: Leadership Resources, 1961, pp. 3–7.
11. *Foundation for Research on Human Behavior*, pp. 5–8.
12. Ibid., pp. 9–12.
13. Ibid., pp. 20–26.
14. Herbert G. Hicks. *The Management of Organizations: A Systems and Human Resources Approach*, 2nd ed. New York: McGraw-Hill, 1972, pp. 413–428.
15. Ibid., pp. 432–438.
16. Robert M. Fulmer. *The New Management*. New York: Macmillan, 1974, pp. 357–360.
17. J. D. Dunn, Elvis Stephens, and J. Roland Kelley. *Management Essentials: Resource*. New York: McGraw-Hill, 1973, pp. 74–75.
18. Ibid., p. 322.
19. Ibid., p. 183.
20. Ibid., p. 185.
21. Ibid., p. 207.
22. *Foundation for Research on Human Behavior*, p. 17.
23. Ibid., p. 19.
24. Dan Fabun. *The Corporation as a Creative Environment*. Beverly Hills, Calif.: Glencoe Press, 1972, p. 29.

CUSTOM FURNITURE CASE: ALICE

Alice is the newest member of the stenographic pool. Her tests and interviews show that she is capable of doing as well as or better than the other people in the pool. She has been on the job about three weeks and has been turning out more work than many of the more experienced people. At a coffee break on Wednesday the following conversation occurs:

Mary: "Well, Alice, how do you like working here so far?"

Alice: "I like it very much but I do regret that I have been so snowed under with work that I haven't gotten to know everyone as well as I would like to."

Joan: "Yes, we've all noticed how much work you're turning out."

Alice: "Well, I like to carry my part of the load."

Mary: "You do realize, don't you, that you are making the rest of us look bad?"

Alice: "No, I didn't. I just want to make a good impression; I really need this job."

Karen: "Don't you know that they will expect you to keep up the pace once you have set it? And they'll also expect the rest of us to turn out as much as you do."

Alice: "Well, I guess that is your problem. I've gotta get back to work."

For the next several days Alice noticed that none of the members of the pool joined her for coffee or lunch and when she attempted to sit with them, it was as if she was not even there. Finally she confronted Mary:

Alice: "Mary, what is the matter? Have I done something to offend you and the other girls?"

Mary: "Well, no, not really."

Alice: "Then why is everyone avoiding me?"

Mary: "You made it clear last Wednesday that you didn't care what we thought. That you were going to break all the production records around here no matter how much the rest of us suffered."

Alice: "I don't understand what you are getting at."

Mary: "Well, dummy, we've got a pretty good thing going here as long as none of us tries to outdo the others. We know that we can all turn out a lot more work, but until you came, all of us were doing as little as we could and still not be ashamed to take our checks. Understand, the company was getting its money's worth, but we weren't killing ourselves like you have been doing from the beginning. As it is now, we are already starting to hear remarks about why we can't do more if you can."

Alice: "You mean that you want me to goof off and maybe lose my job?"

Mary: "You won't lose your job. And I don't think that you are going to like being ostracized the way you will be if you keep on with this speed of yours. Think it over."

Within a few days, Bill Jones notices that Alice's production is falling off; she is turning out about as much work as the other members of the steno pool.

1. How do you account for the downturn in Alice's work?
2. If you were Bill Jones, what action would you take?
3. Why are group pressures strong enough to cause such actions as restriction of productivity?

COMMUNICATION

5

For the full story, turn to the case on page 103.

GENERAL PURPOSES
OF CHAPTER 5

1. To examine proper methods of issuing orders
2. To look at the role of the grapevine in communication
3. To examine some barriers to effective communication
4. To probe the role of the supervisor in the communication process
5. To consider semantics as a major barrier
6. To investigate the role of feedback and the need for listening
7. To see the need for guidelines in a communication system
8. To survey the need for management information systems within the organizational structure

LEARNING OBJECTIVES

1. To list four guidelines to be considered in giving orders
2. To consider the reasons for a grapevine and give at least five methods for effective use of this communication tool
3. To name three barriers to communication
4. To explain the role of the supervisor in the communication process
5. To define *semantics* and explain why it is a barrier to communication by listing at least five semantic obstacles
6. To demonstrate the importance of feedback
7. To give at least six guidelines for the proper use of a management information system

The art of communication is as old as the human race, but no other area of interpersonal relationships has created more frustration, misunderstanding, and trouble. An avenue for communication requires a knowledge of what you want to say, a recognition of the interest of the person in receiving the message, and a willingness to use the right medium to gain a positive response to a given communication source.

How to Communicate

The successful supervisor is able to get through to subordinates, fellow supervisors, and superiors. This art implies a willingness to accept the fact that not all communications are clearly understood by a worker or by other supervisors or superiors. Thus, communication requires a clear message that is not open to personal interpretation. Directions must be stripped of ambiguity to prevent guesswork or misunderstanding of exactly what is expected of an employee. A special effort should be made to put in writing instructions that are detailed or highly technical.

Implicit in the art of communication is the need to establish an environment that encourages all employees to ask questions. This questioning process increases two-way communication, clears up misunderstandings, and enhances feedback from all personnel. As will be mentioned later in this chapter, an essential part of knowing how to communicate is the ability to develop a personal art of listening. Closely related to listening is the responsibility to keep people fully informed about all matters affecting the performance of their job. In summary, the ability to communicate implies the ability to make the message clear, remove ambiguity from directions, make written instructions concise, and encourage questions and feedback from all personnel.

How to Give Orders

In an age that tends to resist authority and resent autocratic decisions, there is a need to develop a cooperative climate that will enable a supervisor to direct the activities of workers through suggestions, mutual participation, and, in critical or emergency situations, direct command. Such a climate reduces internal friction and enhances the self-development of each employee. The mechanics of giving orders are based on four guidelines. Orders should (1) be clear and complete in content, (2) be designed for the person doing the task, (3) spell out in detail the facts needed to complete a given task, and (4) be attainable in light of an employee's work experience.[1]

A closer look at these guidelines for giving orders reveals several implications for all supervisors. First, orders should spell out the who, what, when, where, and why for a given task to all employees involved. Second, orders should identify (1) the experience of the employee, (2) the employee's ability to understand directions, (3) the willingness of each employee to cooperate, (4) the morale level of each employee, (5) the ability of each employee to work without direct supervision, and (6) the ability of each employee to complete a given assignment. Third, orders should contain all pertinent data to complete a task in the absence of a supervisor. Likewise, the supervisor and the employee should be aware of personalities when an order is issued. Fourth, orders should promote a feeling of respect for and confidence in the supervisor on the part of all employees.

As you can see, giving an order or directive does not necessarily imply compliance or agreement on the part of an employee, a supervisor, or a supervisor's superior. However, the ultimate task is to create a cooperative spirit in the organization that will let the individual, as well as the enterprise, achieve a sense of accomplishment, satisfaction, and mutual responsibility for the growth of the firm.[2]

The Grapevine

Up to this point in our discussion of the communication process we have dealt with the formal aspects of communication in an organization. However, an element that cannot be ignored is the informal communication channels that exist in every organization. This informal aspect seeks information on company policies on advancement, working conditions, changes in job status, financial structure of the enterprise, and actions affecting labor-management relations.

The grapevine in the organization is a communication tool that if properly utilized will improve employee morale as well as the operating efficiency of the enterprise. To take an antagonistic view of the grapevine is a sure way to increase rumors, encourage divisive behavior, and add to the anxiety level of all personnel. It is the supervisor's responsibility to use every management tool to increase the working harmony of employees. The grapevine is no exception, but unlike other management tools it does not follow a set pattern, nor does it respond immediately to corrective actions by the formal organizational structure. Consequently, the ultimate goal of all supervisors should be a positive attitude toward the grapevine as well as utilization of it to accomplish the objectives of the enterprise.

To use the grapevine effectively the following guidelines should be followed:

1. Inform all employees on matters that relate directly to their position.
2. Provide correct information in all communications with company personnel.
3. Announce changes in advance and tell how these changes will affect all employees.
4. Prevent internal friction by not concealing data available to sources outside the firm.
5. Announce decisions promptly to reduce false rumors.
6. Get more information on issues you cannot explain and report your findings as quickly as possible.
7. Remember that rumors start when information stops.[3]

The use of the grapevine in the communication process is not easy. It requires constant effort by supervisors to know what the grapevine is saying, to correct erroneous ideas, and to supply the grapevine with positive data to increase the effectiveness of all personnel.

Barriers in Communications

Mental Set
Mental set is actually a pattern of thinking and development that determines how a person interprets a word or statement. Attitudes developed over a period of years sometimes become so rigid that it is almost impossible to introduce changes or new ideas. Frequently differences in the mental set between management and workers make communications, even on noncontroversial subjects, complicated.[4] For example, suppose you, as a supervisor, have been told that a particular job is part of a rush order. You tell your group that they must push and complete this job by a certain time. This simple situation can easily produce three distinct interpretations:

1. To an executive it represents an opportunity to satisfy a customer and open up possibilities for more sales and greater profit.
2. To a supervisor it represents an opportunity to demonstrate the effectiveness of his department.
3. To the employees it represents an attempt to achieve more production for the same amount of pay.[5]

Upward Communications
Another area where barriers to communication can exist lies in the supervisor's function of reporting data to superiors in the organization. For example, several questions must be answered by a supervisor in reporting information to higher-level officials. Some questions follow:

1. What constitutes promptness in upward communications?
2. What constitutes accuracy in upward communications?
3. What constitutes completeness in upward communications?
4. What constitutes precise logic in upward communications?[6]

Horizontal Communications

Barriers to communication can also exist between departments on the same level. In some ways, communication between departments is more difficult than upward or downward communication. Upward communication is the flow of information from front-line or middle managers to the decision makers at the top of the organization. Upward flows of data serve as input upon which decisions or changes in policy are made to enhance the effectiveness of the enterprise at large. Without an upward flow of ideas top management tends to work in a vacuum, which in the long run will produce an organization unable to meet the challenges of today or tomorrow.

Unlike upward communication, downward communication comes down the communicator links from upper to middle to front-line supervisors. It is a known fact that this one-way system of communication is alive and well in most companies. For example, this form of assimilating data is reflected in order, directions, and memoranda designed to implement the decisions made by upper management. A well-balanced enterprise will encourage upward as well as downward communication. Both systems are essential to the vitality of all organizations.

Major areas of conflict are (1) lack of formal communication channels between departments, (2) intense loyalty of workers to a department, and (3) negative competition that seeks to take advantage of another department.[7]

A belief that all personnel have the right to be heard as well as to receive information is the best way to remove all communication barriers. Further, communications at all levels in the enterprise should be viewed as an exchange of information instead of a selling or conversion process.

The Supervisor

In the process of communication the supervisor plays a major role in determining the success or failure of a communications network within an organization. As a representative of management, the first-line manager has direct contact with employees. To ensure communication up and down the structure of the enterprise requires the exchange of ideas, complaints, questions, and problems. Moreover, it is not enough to give the facts alone. Understanding is essential for effective communication. An essential element of understanding is the ability to listen to the thoughts of all individuals as workers, managers, executives, and employers.

To obtain a clear picture of what the employee thinks requires building a bridge of mutual trust, respect, and consideration by a supervisor. If this bridge is built it will create a constructive avenue for the exchange of information essential to effective operation. If this bridge is not built because of management timidity, pride, arrogance, or indifference, the result will be one-way communication. Therefore, management must insist that all supervisory or executive personnel build this bridge of mutual cooperation with all workers to ensure the continued existence of the organization.[8]

To illustrate how to build this bridge, let us look at several examples from industry. First, Interstate Steel, in 1967, instituted informal management-labor discussions to overcome the rejection of a contract by union employees. These discussions were continued and have helped to remove misunderstandings and to communicate the views of labor and management. Second, PPG Industries, Inc., has set up ten-minute pre-shift meetings of first-line supervisors and their workers to review assignments, relay news from other departments, and talk about upcoming employee activities. Plant manager-employee sessions, in which management explains its problems and labor brings up grievances and suggestions, are conducted weekly. Third, a telephone communication system for Armco's Middletown works' 6000 employees has resulted in better job safety, quality, production, and service to the customer. Several unions have recommended this avenue as a means of reducing grievances as well as improving employee morale. However, it would be a mistake to rely solely on management-labor discussions for total communication with all employees.[9] The bridge toward mutual trust, respect, and cooperation can be built only if all interested parties work together toward this goal.

Rumors in Communication
As discussed earlier, the grapevine is part of the communication process but receives a bad name because it often spreads rumors. Rumor is unverified information communicated without a definite source of origin and lacking in factual evidence. It is passed without discretion and sometimes distorts the truth of a situation. Since much of the information is incorrect in the grapevine, it is presumed to be of little value to the organization.

Most rumors are based on partial information and tend to reflect the interest of the individual or individuals passing the rumor. Essential data are lost in transmission to other employees, for people have a tendency to remember details that reflect their view of themselves, other employees, or the organization.

To reduce the negative impact of rumors a supervisor should strive to identify the causes of the rumor instead of trying to extinguish it. This approach will prevent further conflict as well as remove personalities from the process of controlling rumors. Rumors are a symptom of workers' frustrations, mistrust, and dislike for being left out of the communication system. The best way to eliminate rumors is to keep all workers informed of events that have a direct bearing on their contribution to the organization.[10]

Semantic Barriers

There is a close parallel between communication and the science of semantics. Semantics strives to determine exactly what a person really means rather than merely what that person is saying. The goal of semantics in business is to provide a manager with a better understanding of the surrounding environment and help in relating to the thoughts of others. One aspect of semantics involves the ability to make a rational decision without clouding the issue with an emotional response. Another major concept is the skill of relating words in a message with the past experiences of the receiver. This assumes the presence of a common thread binding sender and receiver together. For example, employees, supervisors, and superiors are not stupid, but each position exhibits a variety of experiences in relation to the formal organizational structure.[11]

Recognizing the existence of semantic barriers in communication networks in an organization is a major step in improving the effectiveness of all forms of interpersonal communications. Moreover, semantic barriers usually follow the patterns outlined below.

One semantic barrier is the tendency to confuse words with objects. In interpersonal relationships it is assumed that every word reflects a physical point of reference. To illustrate this idea let us consider the word *unemployment*. To some it implies that a person has lost a job and is trying to find another one. To others it implies not having a job and at the same time being physically unable to obtain one. Yet another group would view unemployment as involving a temporary layoff resulting from changes in plant production schedules. A supervisor should realize that words are not objects but are interpreted according to the perspective of the individual sending or receiving a message.

A second semantic barrier is caused by the use of abstract terms in a careless manner. This barrier is similar to the one immediately preceding. Abstract terms should not be used loosely in interpersonal communications. The limitations of abstract terminology should be recognized by every supervisor. For example, *productivity* in the field of management is an abstraction because to a supervisor it can imply reducing unit cost but to the employees it can imply more work for less pay. Remember, as a supervisor in sending a message you know what you are talking about, but the key question is "Will the receiver view your message in the same light?"[12]

A further semantic barrier is caused by confusing facts with opinions. We see this barrier in every thought process. For example, suppose we survey 200 people and ask what they think of the color black. In this fictitious survey let us assume that the majority give a negative response. Note that a negative opinion on the word *black* is given without any factual basis. The proper way to gather evidence is to obtain the relevant facts, reach a logical conclusion, and if the situation warrants, issue your personal opinion.

A fourth semantic barrier derives from the assumption that all issues are either black or white. This barrier represents the viewpoint that all issues have only two possible solutions. However, most personal, economic, and social issues do not readily lend themselves to a clear choice between two courses of action. An example is a supervisor's view that all unions are bad. To take this position is to box oneself into a managerial corner. However, if the manager assumes that only *some* unions are poorly led or *some* union members are not cooperative, this is a more realistic view of unions. Thus, the multivalued view incorporating an understanding of semantics is essential if a supervisor is to prevent one-way communications.[13]

The mistaken judgment about a person based solely on one or two behavioral traits is a further semantic barrier. Simply stated, this is the tendency to take one characteristic shared by two individuals and then jump to the conclusion that all their traits are the same. Since all people have many character traits, it is very easy to find one trait shared by two people or an individual and an enterprise. Using this common trait, mistaken guilt or innocence can be stated. Based on illogical reasoning, an individual can be proved guilty or innocent of anything. To illustrate this idea, consider the number of grievances filed each year by workers and the number of warnings issued by supervisors. In many cases, these conflicts are the result of poor judgment, mistaken interpretation of facts, and a desire to place all workers or supervisors in one neat mental category. Again, the key to overcoming this tendency is to keep an open mind and realize that we all have mental blind spots that if not corrected will produce organizational conflict. Moreover, it should not be assumed that mistaken judgment is just a managerial problem; instead this problem should be viewed from a personal, a professional, an organizational, and a social aspect. If we are to eliminate personal bias and prejudice from our thinking, the semantic barrier of mistaken identification by one behavioral trait must be overcome.[14]

A final semantic barrier involves a tendency in written or spoken communications to cloud the issue with statements irrelevant to the situation at hand. Such actions are an attempt to avoid the real issue or to defer the unfavorable consequences of a poor decision. Also, this technique is used to soften the shock of turning down a promotion or pay raise or of firing an employee. Similarly, there is a tendency to cover up such facts with unrelated excuses and issues. Clear, precise, and direct instructions will prevent misunderstanding, frustration, and costly waste of material and human resources. Again, in communication the aim is to express or exchange ideas instead of selling a viewpoint to others in the enterprise.[15]

It should be apparent that to avoid confusing words with objects, using abstract terms, confusing facts with opinions, assuming all issues are black or white, using one trait to mark a person or group, and clouding issues with irrelevant facts requires a concentrated effort. Semantics, if used properly, can be a valuable managerial tool in improving all forms of communication.

Feedback

To find out how a firm is progressing toward a given objective requires feedback from all parts of the enterprise. Feedback occurs every day in our association with all other people and institutions. For example, we all want to know where we stand in relation to our work, our family, our associates, and our personal aspirations. In our culture we demand a reading on our actions to measure success or failure in pursuing a given objective. A world without feedback would be frustrating.

One form of feedback is negative. It records deviations from a predetermined standard. For example, in the school room, a student's failure to attend class is considered a deviation from the required class attendance. In the world of work, all must meet a standard of quality, but it is unrealistic to view these standards as absolutes because goals change over time. Also, because of changing environmental conditions, feedback systems created by organizations are not automatic. A given product inventory is altered by sales above expectations, thus requiring an increase in inventory levels, but sales below expectations require a reduction in inventory levels. Thus, negative feedback is part of our world, but it is not necessarily automatic in providing an immediate solution to a particular situation.[16]

In most discussions of feedback, little attention is given to the impact of positive feedback on individuals or organizations. Positive feedback encourages change, whereas negative feedback only indicates deviations from a prescribed course of action. To give greater meaning to positive feedback, look at the fields of business and education. Assume, as a supervisor, that an employee exceeds production standards by 30 percent. Should this deviation be corrected or should a positive view be taken to encourage others to follow the example of this exceptional employee? A student who has been failing a course may at mid-term begin to make a passing grade in the same subject. It would be illogical for an instructor to discourage the change in behavior of this student.

All information retrieved from a system of feedback in personal, professional, or social life is negative or positive in content. The trick is to use both types of feedback to improve the effectiveness of all communications.[17]

Listening

The real issue in communication is not what we say but the way others accept our ideas. For good communication, the art of listening must be developed if we expect others to pay attention. Further, in our busy lives we often show apathy, indifference, or hostility to ideas from others that could enhance our ability to cope with a changing environment. On the other hand, a good listener exhibits concern, appreciation, and receptiveness toward new ideas, methods, and opinions.

A problem in communicating with people is not listening to what is being said. For example, how often do we strive to gain new ideas from people we come in contact with each day? What is the physical attitude we take while listening to others in a conversation? It may be a smile, a yawn, or a faraway look. All these actions indicate interest or lack of it. Listening is a skill to be developed, but it requires self-discipline and concentrated effort.[18]

Realizing the need to develop good listening techniques in our communications with others, let us look at several suggestions. First, two-way communication encourages good listening habits. Second, it is essential for good listening that both parties understand each other. Third, a good listener exchanges ideas instead of selling them. Fourth, to encourage good listening habits, comments should be brief and to the point. Fifth, reasons for your news should be given in a positive manner without emotional overtones.

To evaluate your listening habits, study the following questions:

1. Do I have a tendency to call a subject unimportant?
2. Do I have a tendency to criticize a speaker's delivery?
3. Do I have a tendency to overreact to personal biases?
4. Do I have a tendency to listen only for facts?
5. Do I have a tendency to filter out parts of a presentation?
6. Do I have a tendency to fake attention?
7. Do I have a tendency to create distractions?
8. Do I have a tendency to avoid technical presentations?
9. Do I have a tendency to overreact to emotional terms?
10. Do I have a tendency to get ahead of the speaker and the real issue?[19]

All of us at one time or another could probably answer yes to one or more of these questions. We must try to develop the personal skill of really listening to others in our daily conversations. Remember, good listening takes practice and concentration.

Guidelines for Communication

The principal responsibility of a supervisor is to accomplish organizational goals with the assistance of all employees. The following are some guidelines for communication:

1. Anticipate the impact of a message on the receiver by planning communications to meet a precise need
2. Identify the purpose for each message and limit the message to that goal or objective
3. Consider the environment of a communication in terms of working relationships
4. Use group participation in creating a message to increase employee involvement in the decision-making process
5. Recognize the impact of emotions, tone of voice, and language on a receiver
6. Make a message reflect the interest of the employee, the supervisor, and the enterprise
7. Use feedback from previous messages to measure the effectiveness of earlier instructions
8. Make sure that communications in an organization reflect short-term and long-term goals
9. Do not fail to support communications with positive actions.
10. Recognize the value of developing a personal art of listening in any communication system[20]

Management Information Systems

With the coming of the computer, the technology to store and process large amounts of data has become a reality in business. Many firms have discovered that the assimilation of data is a source of frustration because they are not capable of using a vast amount of data effectively. Moreover, falsely assuming that a management information system will cure the communication ills of an enterprise can be a costly mistake in terms of money, manpower, and management talent. Another error is to acquire an expert with only computer knowledge, because limited or nonexistent knowledge of the world of business will result in a working management information system with no relationship to the communication needs of the firm. Another costly mistake is to assume that management and computer sciences speak the same language in the exchange of business data. To design, operate, evaluate, and improve a management information system requires the cooperation, trust, and mutual exchange of information between management, computer specialists, and all personnel within the firm. To conclude our look at management information systems, a suggested method of using it effectively is presented.

A management consultant has suggested the following guideline in using a management information system in any organization.

1. Look at the big picture.
2. Hold the reins on monetary expenditures.
3. Pick the right staff.
4. Understand the system.
5. Be certain it's fast enough.
6. Know how the system is linked up.
7. Know what's available.
8. Audit the system's value first.[21]

Summary

Communication is as old as humankind but is still a major source of frustration, misunderstanding, and adversity. Communication is the ability to make the message clear and concise, as well as to encourage questions and feedback from all persons in the organization. For a supervisor, proper use of the grapevine can enhance leadership skills and the economic effectiveness of the enterprise. Mental set, upward communication, and horizontal communication can involve barriers a supervisor should overcome in order to communicate successfully. Related areas of concern are the rumors present in a firm and the presence of semantic barriers that also must be overcome to ensure success in communicating with others. Similarly, a supervisor should encourage feedback from all sources and develop a personal art of listening to others. A management information system is an excellent management tool if understood and applied correctly to the firm's communication needs.

Discussion Questions

1. *Define the term* communication.
2. *Explain why it is important to encourage questions and feedback.*

3. Why do words have different meanings for different people?
4. What are the attributes of a proper order?
5. Why should supervisors take a positive attitude toward the grape-vine?
6. In what ways can the grapevine be used effectively by manage-ment?
7. What factors can contribute to barriers in horizontal communica-tion?
8. How can a supervisor reduce the negative impact of rumors?
9. Explain the value of feedback to successful communication.
10. Why is listening important in the communication process?

Chapter Case 5

Bill Eastling is a manager of the training section of the Calumet Company. He supervises twelve employees whose duties are to train new employees in the various sections of the firm. Bill prides him-self on the fact that he keeps his people informed on all matters that pertain to their jobs. Basically, he does a good job passing on information to them.

His door is always open to the employees and there is free dis-cussion about almost any matter, but everyone knows that in the end Bill will always make the final decision. Individuals have the habit of dropping into Bill's office and discussing all sorts of prob-lems of the section with him. During these discussions certain policies are discussed and decisions are reached that affect the entire department. Sometimes the information is passed along to all employees about the changes, but many times it is not.

When Bill sees that one of his people is not going along with the new procedures, he often questions another trainer about the rea-sons for this failure to comply and tells this person to "straighten out" the offender.

There are no job descriptions and no policy manual to use as guidelines. People are expected to know what Bill expects and to do it without question. Morale is very low in the section, especially among some of the new employees who are having great difficulty deciding what it is that will please Bill.

1. What is Bill doing wrong?
2. What would you do to improve communication in this depart-ment?
3. How can employee morale be improved?

Notes

1. *National Foreman's Institute.* Waterford, Conn.: Bureau of Business Practice, 1965. Sec. 7, Portfolio 3, p. 1.
2. Ibid., p. 2.
3. Ibid.
4. Ibid.
5. Ibid.
6. Ibid.
7. Ibid.
8. William E. Parker, Robert W. Kleemeir, and Beyer W. Parker. *Front Line Leadership.* New York: McGraw-Hill, 1969, p. 98.
9. ———. "Fireside Chats Kindle Understanding," *Industry Week,* October 5, 1970, pp. 46–50.
10. Keith Davis. *Human Behavior at Work.* New York: McGraw-Hill, 1972, pp. 268–269.
11. Stuart Chase. "Executive Communications: Breaking the Semantic Barrier," in Herbert G. Hicks (ed.). *Management, Organizations, and Human Resources: Selected Readings.* New York: McGraw-Hill, 1972, p. 210.
12. Ibid., pp. 212–213.
13. Ibid., pp. 213–214.
14. Ibid., pp. 215–216.
15. Ibid., p. 216.
16. Don Hellriegel and John W. Slocum. *Management: A Contingency Approach.* Reading, Mass.: Addison-Wesley, 1974, pp. 71–72.
17. Ibid., p. 73.
18. George R. Terry. *Supervisory Management.* Homewood, Ill.: Irwin, 1974, pp. 42–43.
19. Ralph G. Nichols. "Listening Is Good Business," in Max D. Richards and William Nielander (eds.). *Readings in Management.* Cincinnati: South-Western, 1974, pp. 105–110.
20. American Management Association. "Ten Commandments of Good Communication," in Harold Koontz and Cyril O'Donnell (eds.). *Management: A Book of Readings.* New York: McGraw-Hill, 1968, pp. 495–496.
21. Frederick Freelander. "Making a MIS Work in Real Life," *Industry Week,* April 2, 1973, pp. 41–43.

CUSTOM FURNITURE CASE: A BREAKDOWN IN COMMUNICATIONS

Bill Jones reached for the phone. It was a call from the sales representative in Denver, Colorado.

"Hello, Bill, I'll get right to the point. The Town House Motel has just informed me that they are ahead of schedule on construction and that they will be ready to open thirty days earlier than we thought. They will be ready to accept delivery on their furniture thirty days from today. That means the 25th of June instead of July."

"Oh no, David," answered Bill. "Everyone is trying to push up orders all of a sudden. A few weeks ago we didn't have enough business to keep everybody busy and we laid off a few people. Now we are swamped and the boss doesn't want any overtime."

"Well, you are going to have to help me somehow," David replied. "This customer has located a competitor who has enough of the most important pieces in stock for immediate delivery to enable them to open on that date. I'm sure they'll cancel the order if we can't ship. Think what that will do to our reputation in this part of the country."

"Well, David, we sure don't want that to happen," answered Bill. "Tell your people that we will do something. I'm leaving on my vacation at the end of this week, but I'll take care of it before I leave."

Bill hung up the phone and thought to himself, "These salespeople think everything is a crisis and that their customers are the only ones the company has." He turned back to the report that he was working on.

Friday afternoon, just as he was about to leave on his vacation, Bill remembered the phone call from David. He called the factory superintendent on the intercom. "Sam, David Webb called earlier this week. That order for the Town House Motel in Denver must be shipped to arrive there by the 25th. Can you get it out?"

"I think that we can just about make it if we can put in a little overtime," Sam said.

"Better not start that kind of talk. You know what the boss has said about overtime."

"He should have thought about that when he laid off those guys a few weeks ago. Get on with your vacation. I'll take care of it," Sam replied.

On the 18th, the factory superintendent received a call from David in Denver. "Hi, Sam. Has that order for the Town House gotten on the trucks yet?"

"What do you mean 'on the truck'? That order is not scheduled to be shipped until the 18th of next month, and we will ship it then, right on schedule."

"Didn't Bill tell you that the order had to be pushed up thirty days ahead of the original schedule?" asked David.

"Just before he left on vacation he told me that it had to be in Denver by the 25th and I thought that he was just checking on the original shipping date because we have been falling a little behind," answered Sam.

"Oh, brother, I'm afraid we are going to get a cancellation and a very angry customer out of this, but I'll call and see if I can do anything about it. Boy, we really get a lot of support from the home office," retorted David.

An hour later David called Sam and informed him that the order has been cancelled and the people at the Town House are furious and considering the possibility of a lawsuit against the company for delaying their opening.

1. *Comment on David's handling of the first phone call changing the delivery date.*
2. *What do you think of Bill's handling of the matter?*
3. *What blame can be placed on the factory superintendent?*
4. *How can this problem be avoided in the future?*

CHANGE

6

For the full story, turn to the case on page 122.

GENERAL PURPOSES
OF CHAPTER 6

1. To examine certain difficulties involved in altering or changing attitudes
2. To consider employee resistance to change
3. To look at some methods of gaining support for change
4. To see how change can be effected through the group structure
5. To consider the role of the supervisor in effecting change
6. To realize the value of participation in bringing about change

LEARNING OBJECTIVES

1. To realize that people do not resist change because it is change; rather, they resist the ways that change is implemented
2. To list four difficulties encountered in trying to change attitudes
3. To name seven reasons that change is often viewed as a threat to the employee's security
4. To give five courses of action that a supervisor can take in effecting change in a procedure
5. To name and briefly explain four overall approaches that may be used in gaining support for change
6. To cite four guidelines to be considered in initiating change through the work group
7. To describe six characteristics of planned change
8. To list seven prerequisites of effective participation in decisions regarding change
9. To name five avenues for building group participation in decisions that result in change
10. To give six advantages of group participation in discussions of change
11. To write voluntarily a short paper describing some change you recently resisted because of the way it was implemented

Change in people and organizations is essential for growth, technical progress, and adjustment to environmental circumstances. Change requires an understanding of personal attitudes toward the process, a willingness to let people have some say on changes affecting them, and a positive outlook toward change by all agents seeking to alter existing organizational relationships. In this chapter, we consider these topics: (1) dealing with attitudes toward change, (2) not resisting change, (3) gaining support for change, (4) initiating change through the group, (5) seeing the supervisor as the agent of change, and (6) participating in decisions regarding change.

The subject of change is enormous, but these several points should provide a basic understanding of what change is all about. These ideas may suggest to all supervisors and future supervisors ways to bring about change successfully in their organizations.

Attitudes

Attitudes are the views held by a person or group toward something, such as an idea, a project, or a new boss. These views reflect the willingness of people to act or refrain from acting to accomplish a given objective. A supervisor reinforces the views of people by ignoring attitudes or tries to alter attitudes through education, information, and concern for the views of each employee.

An attitude is positive if the individual has a positive relationship with his or her supervisor, job, and personal aspirations. On the other hand, a negative attitude is developed through a poor relationship with the supervisor or other organizational entities. Moreover, attitudes are contagious and can result in organizational dysfunctions. Thus, it is in a supervisor's best interest to recognize that attitudes exist, whether positive or negative, in all institutions. The person who can do most to modify attitudes is the supervisor in a daily relationship with all personnel.[1]

Modifying attitudes is difficult because we all have different personal values, experiences, and aspirations. Another difficulty is the impact of upper-management decisions that produce a positive or negative response in the mind of the supervisor. A supervisor will reflect this treatment in establishing departmental policies, procedures, and goals. A related consideration is the willingness of a supervisor to implement and receive organizational changes without feeling threatened or intimidated. Further, the more intense an attitude is, the harder it is for a supervisor to alter it.

Recognizing that not all negative attitudes can be fully eliminated is the first step in altering these attitudes. Also, willingness to accept a person for what he or she can contribute to the firm enhances a supervisor's influence on attitudes. Similarly, ability to listen, show personal concern, and offer alternatives is essential in modifying the attitudes of personnel.[2]

Lack of Resistance to Change

At first glance it might seem to be untrue that people do not resist change, but let us look at several facts. (1) Uncertainty underlies change and results from management's failure to state the impact on key people. (2) Individuals' perceptions of change tend to reflect the worst. (3) People like to have a certain degree of control over their environment but feel threatened when they have no voice in changes that affect them. (4) Change is resisted if it is based solely on personal rather than business requirements. (5) Changes usually alter working habits, requiring workers to acquire new skills. This event, if unexplained, is seen as a personal threat to job security. (6) Most changes alter social patterns and create uncertainty until new social patterns develop. (7) Change without an indication of the benefits for all personnel is viewed as a threat to the security of the individual or the group. Notice that all these reactions are not against change itself; instead, they reflect uncertainty, fear, insecurity, and hostility on the part of affected personnel.[3]

Realizing that resistance to change is a mirror of personal or group feelings rather than an all-out hostility toward change as such is a key step in making effective changes in organizations. For example, in our private lives we like to travel, to see new things, to acquire new possessions, and to enjoy new experiences. However, in the world of work we usually take a more negative view because we cannot see the value of change to our position, our activity, and our ability. Thus, a supervisor must realize that negative feelings about change do exist but are not always directed against a person or an enterprise. Moreover, these insecure feelings can be overcome through a desire to understand them and to educate people about the positive side of organizational change. Similarly, we need to recognize that change does not affect all personnel in the same way. Many firms have overreacted, attempting to remove resistance to new ideas without taking individual views into account. The result of such overreaction is to alienate a larger group of personnel than would have been the case if individual attitudes toward change had been considered.[4]

We have discussed attitudes toward change and the fact that people do not resist change but the effects of change. Another aspect of individual reaction to change is the inherent desire of us all to be accepted by our peers. Such acceptance tends to pressure us to conform to accepted behavioral patterns. As individuals we change behavior slowly, because of our desire to repeat and continue a basic life-style as long as possible. This slow change in behavior can produce conformity in values, beliefs, and individual aspirations. Likewise, pressure to conform may prevent capricious changes.

We all tend to reflect the values, beliefs, and expectations of the culture in which we grew up. This alone produces a diversity of views, which in turn makes introducing change a challenging undertaking. A supervisor is encouraged to be objective, but in reality any personal views influence an ability to introduce change successfully. Consequently, instead of resisting change, people may only be demonstrating differences in opinions, values, aspirations, and behavioral patterns.[5]

A final area in our discussion of why people do not necessarily resist change lies in the recognition of the need for change. For example, external environmental considerations such as markets, technology, and competition force enterprises to adjust to changing situations. This can encourage organizational adjustments by showing managers, workers, and stockholders the need for change. Another example is the creation of an organizational climate that encourages change by increasing enterprise and friendliness, reviewing such items as responsibilities of all personnel, quality and production standards, reward and penalty systems, and leadership styles of supervisors, managers, and executives.

Recognizing the need to change means a proper understanding of organizational issues. These issues can be identified by asking these questions: What issues need to be corrected? What caused these issues to surface? What must be changed to resolve them successfully? What forces will enhance or deter the success of implemented changes? What will be the result of such changes? How can the firm measure the impact of these changes?

The creation of a positive outlook toward change comes from a concentrated effort of all personnel to accept, review, anticipate, and initiate change. Such actions prevent organizational dry rot, dysfunctions, and inefficiency. Moreover, this creative climate can encourage organizational growth, technological progress, and adjustment to changing environmental circumstances.[6]

Gaining Support for Change

To gain support for change, you, as a supervisor, can use your understanding of employee attitudes to realize that people do not resist change but react favorably if prepared for change in advance. Let us assume that you are a supervisor of a machine assembly system for aircraft components. As a supervisor you introduce a new process to reduce material waste and to improve the productivity of your section. After a week you receive a complaint from industrial engineering that quality and quantity of aircraft components in your section are below standard. Moreover, in interviewing people in operations you find that some like the new procedures but that most do not feel comfortable with them. As a supervisor, there are several courses of action you can take. First, identify the issue, in this case a new procedure introduced by a supervisor. Second, take a positive attitude: listen to workers' views and reorient them in the new methods. Third, explain again the benefits of the new procedures, both to the employees and to the company at large. Fourth, allow more time to adjust to the new procedures and then offer incentives for the adoption of the new methods at a pace beyond the normal expectations of industrial engineers, supervisors, and management officials. Finally, provide personnel with data to justify the changes to the new procedures. Modify the new procedures if they do not show dramatic improvement over previous operating techniques.[7]

Gaining support for new techniques is a mutual process of exchanging ideas, altering operating methods, and removing the doubts of personnel. The importance of frankness is seen in its ability to lessen negative behavior, reduce turnover, and cut down on rumors. Adequate information is vital if changes are to produce positive results, and this information must include more than statistics showing how change will bring economic progress. It must also relate to the individual concerns of the workers. If it does not, conflict will surely result.

Dispensing the right information is an excellent way to soften blind resistance to change. When this is done, confidence, based on realistic data, replaces a feeling of insecurity. As stated earlier, change in itself does not create conflict, but the manner in which change is implemented often produces misunderstandings. Basically, information on change should include its effect on working conditions, job status, and personal life-styles. Remember, change affects the social, psychological, and economic position of all personnel.[8]

Gaining support for change involves constantly explaining and exchanging ideas about the planned changes. Closely related to the need for adequate information is the need to recognize the reaction of personnel to various approaches to the implementation of change. First, there is the dictatorial approach, which demands unquestioning compliance to change. This approach produces partial compliance but in the long run creates hostility and results in lower job performances. Second is the manipulative approach, which gives lip service to employee suggestions but ends by ignoring them all. This approach results in frustration, greater resistance to future changes, and a one-way exchange of information. The explanation approach, as mentioned earlier, is an effective avenue to introduce change. However, its major danger is the tendency to use superficial facts without outlining the specific steps needed to accomplish a given change in organizational relationships. A third approach involves consensus, which is designed to consider input from all personnel affected by changes, allowing them freedom to say how the changes will be accomplished. Although this approach can remove most employee objections, it is unrealistic, because of time, cost, and environmental considerations. A fourth approach, that of participation, is designed to facilitate the exchange of ideas between supervisors and employees on pending changes in working relationships. Its major limitation is the inefficiency that may result from suggestions at variance with the organization's objectives.[9]

Recognizing the strengths and weaknesses of each approach is important if a supervisor is to implement successful change in working relationships. However, to say one approach is best is to ignore organizational personalities, managerial styles, and operating procedures in today's companies.

Gaining support for change involves advanced planning, exchanging information, and knowing how to implement change in organizational relationships. A final consideration is managerial attitude, as reflected in the policies and procedures of an enterprise. In this discussion, three examples will show the *wrong* way to gain support for change in organizational relationships.

One attitude says that to initiate change is to risk defeat. Such an attitude perpetuates the status quo, helping those who profit from the way things are and encouraging those who would benefit from change to sit on the fence. The final result of such an attitude is at best a compromise that satisfies neither interest. This organizational inertia can only produce loss of jobs, profits, and taxes. For example, man's ability to travel to the moon began with the flight of the Wright brothers in 1909, when the concept of flight was considered an idle dream.[10]

Another negative managerial attitude is to try to produce conformity in all organizational actions. To make this concept work requires constant effort to select universal goals acceptable to all personnel without the need for individual commitments. A continuous effort to reduce people's confidence in their own abilities and to make the norm attractive is essential to perpetuate conformity. The major casualties of this attitude are the human elements of initiative, self-direction, and self-identity.[11]

A final negative managerial attitude is embodied in the use of technological changes to flatten the organizational structure. Such a change tends to centralize decision making, thus isolating lower-level supervisors and reducing their satisfaction with top management. A technological change in plant operations, for example, can result in dissension, resentment, and refusal to accept change. It also reflects a supervisor's feeling of having lost direct control over a department. Technological improvements can improve economic efficiency but they can also destroy the effectiveness of personnel.[12]

Initiating Change Through the Group

Closely related to gaining support for change is the need to initiate change through the group structure. The group represents a positive source of help for a supervisor making changes. We reflect the views of our peers, so a logical conclusion is that to alter an individual's viewpoint one should change the direction of his or her peer group. This statement implies that groups as well as supervisors can act as agents for change. Moreover, a mutual endeavor by groups and supervisors makes initiating change a group endeavor rather than a management endeavor. The ability to influence the actions of group members is based on how closely a person is associated with the group. For example, a group in which you have little interest would not alter your behavior significantly. As another example, consider a group that you think has definite value but that in its actions reflects a viewpoint contrary to your personal interest. In this case, you remain in the group but play a neutral role in influencing the group's actions or else you risk being ostracized from the group by voicing your opposition to its course of action. Consequently, groups are change agents to the extent that they can directly alter the behavior of their members. A supervisor should determine in advance the group's influence on its members before soliciting its support in changing organizational relationships.[13]

Initiating change through a group requires thoughtful consideration of several guidelines. Actions to be encouraged are (1) participating through open criticism and discussion of ideas without cutting off weaker group members; (2) thinking creatively, which can be fostered by brainstorming sessions, rewarding unusual ideas, and avoiding criticism of new and unconventional ideas; (3) venting possible interpersonal conflicts through individual counseling, group counseling, exchange of personal fears, and creation of an activity outside the firm to enhance the removal of interpersonal conflicts; (4) using deadlines to reduce procrastination, loss of time, and vacillation in group decisions (avoid the use of deadlines, however, as the *only* way to control a group); (5) coordinating group decisions by spelling out plans, decisions, conclusions, and personal costs in detail.[14] Initiating change through a group is complex. To use a group effectively takes time, planning, coordination, and a willingness to let the group control the environment. However, this attitude does not imply the abolition of managerial prerogatives. Remember, a supervisor is always accountable for the changes implemented in the subordinate group.

Supervisor as Agent

Because of daily interaction with subordinates, the supervisor has the greatest impact on the attitudes employees assume toward an organization. Change is a major area where employees reflect the supervisor's viewpoint. The acceptance of change is enhanced when a supervisor creates a climate of mutual respect, trust, and cooperation in relationships with all personnel.[15]

Change, like the passing of time, is an inevitable process in human lives. Some changes are gradual and others are fast, but regardless of their speed, they have a definite impact on all organizational relationships. Moreover, change tends to alter the philosophy and constraints under which a supervisor carries out obligations to the organization. Thus, every supervisor must develop a personal style of introducing change effectively. Also, a supervisor should view change as a dynamic, not static, process in working to meet managerial obligations.[16]

Although internal personnel can act as change agents, forces outside the firm can also effect change. But the supervisor is the final person to introduce, implement, and accomplish change in organizational relationships. Likewise, it is essential for upper management to support lower- or middle-level supervisors if a firm is to change without economic, humanistic, or managerial reversals. Thus, a forward-looking executive staff brings about change with the direct involvement of all supervisors responsible for implementing technical, social, or managerial changes.[17]

Supervisors should try to bring about orderly change. The orderly approach will make organizational change a total part of management development, which in turn can provide a pattern for growth in economic, humanistic, and managerial assets. According to Warren Bennis, "Organizational development is a planned process to bring about changes that enhance the ability of a firm to prosper and survive."

Easing a supervisor's task requires the use of organizational development guidelines such as these: (1) Planned change is brought about through educational strategy. (2) Planned change is a total organizational effort, not merely the job of a supervisor or upper management. (3) Planned change employs the experiences of all personnel to implement change effectively. (4) Planned change employs the use of change agents as consultants in or outside the firm to bring about change in a constructive manner. (5) Planned change is a collaborative organizational process of jointly determined objectives, methods, and influences. (6) Planned change is not economic in nature alone but embodies a humanistic philosophy in all organizational relationships.[18]

Participation in Decisions Regarding Change

Participation is a concept that requires advanced planning if it is to be implemented in the decision-making process of change. Like many managerial concepts, participation is based on several key prerequisites that are needed to make it a reality in the organizational process. These prerequisites follow:

1. There must be time to participate before action is required. Participation is hardly appropriate in emergency situations.
2. The financial cost of participation should not exceed the values, economic and otherwise, that come from it. Employees cannot spend all their time participating, to the exclusion of all other work!
3. The subject of participation must be relevent to the participant's organization or something in which he is interested, or he will look upon it merely as busy work.
4. The participant should have the ability, such as intelligence and knowledge, to participate. It is hardly advisable, for example, to ask the janitor in a pharmaceutical laboratory to participate in deciding which of five chemical formulas deserves research priority; but he might participate in other problems related to his work.
5. The participants must be able mutually to communicate—to talk each other's language—in order to be able to exchange ideas.
6. Neither party should feel that his position is threatened by participation. If a worker thinks his status will be adversely affected, he will

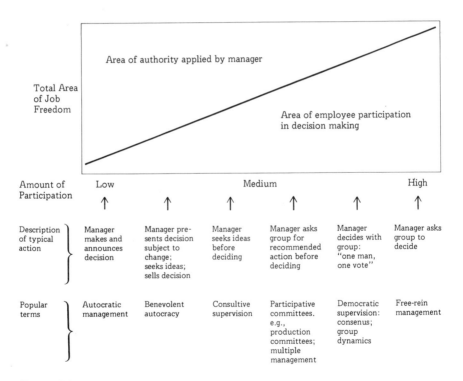

Figure 6-1
Development of participation. The amount of participation in a department along a continuum. Source: Adapted from Robert Tannenbaum and Warren H. Schmidt, "How to Choose a Leadership Pattern," *Harvard Business Review*, March–April 1958, p. 96.

116

not participate. If a manager feels that his authority is threatened, he will refuse participation or be defensive.

7. Participation for deciding a course of action in an organization can take place only within the group's area of job freedom. Some degree of restriction on subunits is necessary in any organization in order to maintain internal unity.[19]

Figure 6-1 is designed to show the impact of participation on choosing a leadership pattern. Figure 6-2 shows the impact of employee participation on productivity.

Earlier we dealt with three negative aspects that tend to discourage group participation in changing working relationships. Now let us consider five managerial avenues that build group participation in decisions regarding change. One managerial avenue that helps to build group participation is consultative supervision, which is a conscious effort by a supervisor to hear the ideas of all personnel affected by change. Such an approach tends to enhance the informal authority of a supervisor. The understanding of grievances is facilitated because each side is made aware of the other's viewpoint. Thus, two-way communication is developed through consultative supervision.

Another managerial bridge that helps to build group participation is democratic supervision. Democratic supervision uses group decisions to implement change. It is based on a one-man, one-vote concept of equal participation by all group members. However, in many cases this ap-

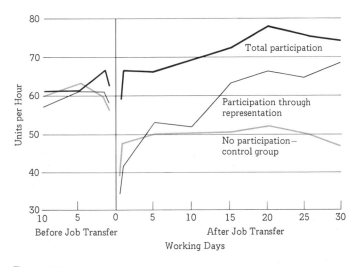

Figure 6-2
Employee participation in a job change in relation to productivity after the change. Source: *Leadership Patterns and Organizational Effectiveness,* Ann Arbor, Mich.: Foundation for Research on Human Behavior, 1954, p. 4. From the experiment of Coch and French.

proach does not work well in our present organizational structure, since it is based on a hierarchy of relationships. A lack of awareness on the part of managers, supervisors, and workers of the benefits of democratic supervision often poses a problem. Another issue is the group's tendency to pursue personal goals rather than to relate its decisions to organizational objectives.[20]

Another positive effort at group participation is the use of production committees. Production committees can often make genuine improvements in the working conditions surrounding them. This technique, however, requires the support of upper management, and it too has disadvantages. It is often made ineffective through abnormal group diversity. The group is sometimes unable to pursue a common sense of direction.

Suggestion systems can help to build group participation in decisions regarding change. Most are presented in writing, which eliminates face-to-face exchange of ideas. Employees sometimes distrust suggestion systems because they fail to receive credit for their ideas, and supervisors tend to view suggestions as criticisms of their ability. Conformity is attacked through suggestions, thus increasing the hostility of the old order, for suggestions tend to upset socially accepted patterns of behavior.[21]

A final vehicle used to employ the creativity of middle managers is the multiple management concept. This concept uses a junior board to create, screen, and develop managerial skills and to broaden the experiences of middle managers. Moreover, middle management can alter the trend to flatten the organizational structure to respond to technological changes.

People's desire to have a voice in the decision-making process of change is increased through the multiple management concept. For example, allowing workers, supervisors, managers, and outside personnel to inject their views into organizational discussions is a major step in making participation an integral part of the organization's internal fiber.[22]

As previously stated, participative techniques are an effective way to create a team spirit of mutual cooperation, development, and consideration for the views of all team members. An underlying premise is that all personnel have individual rights that can enhance the economic and humanistic growth of the firm. Related to this is the recognition that employees today do not want to lose their identity when they become part of an organization. Another premise reflects a positive view that each employee can make a worthwhile impact on the enterprise. Like any managerial skill, group participation will not cure all organizational ills, but if used properly it will (1) identify the objective the organization wishes to accomplish; (2) provide the facts with which to make a sound decision; (3) increase mutual responsibility for decisions that are made; (4) provide a time frame in which to use participation effectively; (5) educate all personnel on operating constraints; and (6) remove the fear of adverse effects on changing organizational relationships.[23]

Participation in the decision-making process or changes in internal relationships constitute a complex, continuous, and creative way of viewing manager-employee relations. In our discussion, we have (1) outlined five supervisory styles to enhance group participation; (2) demonstrated the use of team spirit to enhance group participation; and (3) illustrated the benefits of group participation in the decision-making process. In summary, participative decision making should recognize the psychological assumptions of a participative style of management.

From a supervisor's or manager's view, we assume that (1) the supervisor accepts the risk of being accountable for the group's decisions; (2) the supervisor accepts the role as consultant to group decisions; (3) the supervisor states an authority relationship in regard to the group; and (4) the supervisor increases the significance of each decision in light of the group's past achievements. These views suggest a value system, a confidence in the group's ability to act, a participative leadership style, and a feeling of personal security that encourages group action to reach organizational goals.[24]

The supervisor should analyze the group to determine if it has the following characteristics:

1. A high degree of independence
2. A willingness to accept responsibility for its actions
3. A willingness to work in a nondirective environment
4. An identity with the objectives of the organization as well as views that these objectives are important to its success
5. The skills and experience to handle issues entrusted to it
6. A willingness to share the authority and power derived from a group decision-making process[25]

The supervisor, in using participative decision techniques in regard to change, assumes that the organizational hierarchy wants group participation in the decision process. Policies, job descriptions, and public statements encourage group participation techniques. The organization is secure enough in its ability to develop group decision techniques to mold into a constructive pattern such variables as group cohesiveness, cooperation, acceptance of each member, and semantic differences in communication networks.

For a supervisor, participative decision-making techniques involve a never-ending task of group leadership, measurement, reorganization, and direction. It is essential to organizational success that participative decision-making techniques be an integral part of the decision-making process. However, they should not be used to the extent that they destroy the effectiveness of humanistic, economic, social, and political endeavors of an enterprise.[26]

Summary

Introducing change becomes a process of leading, directing, and influencing individuals to plan, accept, and participate in the change making. The attitudes of managers, supervisors, and workers can enhance the process of change or, in a hostile climate, can make it impossible. Supervisors or managers must recognize the role they play in molding and fixing the attitudes of personnel within the organization. Without a creative environment based on an attitude of mutual respect, a change agent will fail to bring about change in any organizational relationship. Moreover, people tend to resist change when it evokes uncertainty, fear, insecurity, and hostility. To overcome these negative feelings requires education, understanding, knowledge of group processes, and willingness to recognize the need for change in organizational relationships. Similarly, the effort to gain support for change is a continuous process that requires advanced planning, factual information, and anticipation of the effect of change on organizational relationships. The ways to bring about change are reflected in these approaches: dictatorial, manipulative, explanatory, consensus, and participative. However, the benefits and limitations of each approach must be weighed before it is used in the organizational environment. Further, negative attitudes of managerial defeatism, managerial conformity, and managerial misuse of technological change must be overcome. Ways of overcoming these negative influences are positive group interactions, positive group participation in decisions regarding change, and forceful use of a supervisor's managerial style to encourage change. Managerial styles that enhance change include consultative methods, democratic styles, production committees, suggestion systems, and multiple management. Finally, all change agents should recognize that workers, supervisors, managers, and corporations all have rights that should be respected.

Discussion Questions

1. *What is the importance of attitudes to a supervisor attempting to make changes?*
2. *Why is it so difficult to alter or modify attitudes?*
3. *What is your reaction to the statement "People do not resist change, they resist the way in which it is handled"?*
4. *What methods would you use to gain support for changing the time for this class to one hour later?*

5. *Why is it important to know the norms of a group before attempting to initiate change in its structure?*
6. *Explain why a change agent is so valuable to the management of an organization.*
7. *In what types of decisions should lower-level employees be allowed to participate?*
8. *In what areas of management can group participation be especially effective?*
9. *What characteristics should a group have for maximum participation in decisions?*

Chapter Case 6

You have recently been appointed supervisor of a production department. The supervisor you are replacing was an easygoing person who outlined the work to be done and to a great extent left it up to the workers to decide how it would be done, as long as production stayed at a level that seemed acceptable. Management has made it clear to you that it believes more work can be pushed through this department, and you are expected to get production up. You have read a great deal about Frederick W. Taylor and his principles of scientic management concerning the best way to do a job. You also have had some training in work simplification and time-and-motion studies.

One of the first things that you do is to take a stopwatch to the various jobs being performed and time the operations involved. From this information you arrive at certain standards for production on all jobs. These are posted on the bulletin board with instructions that the company expects these standards to be met in the future. You feel sure that these steps will increase production. You spend the next couple of days trying to familiarize yourself with the files and records involved in the job. Friday, when you see the production report, the figures are down from those your predecessor had been achieving.

1. What is your opinion of the manner in which the changes were introduced?
2. What are the reasons for the drop in production?
3. What will you do to rectify this situation?

Notes

1. Lester R. Bittel. *What Every Supervisor Should Know.* New York: McGraw-Hill, 1974, pp. 55–62.
2. Don Hellriegel and John W. Slocum. *Management: A Contingency Approach.* Reading, Mass.: Addison-Wesley, 1974, pp. 430–431.

3. "You're the Leader Change Attitudes," *Industry Week,* June 26, 1972, p. 51.
4. Theo Haimann and Raymond L. Hilgert. *Supervision: Concepts and Practices of Management.* Cincinnati: South-Western, 1972, p. 302.
5. George R. Terry. *Supervisory Management.* Homewood, Ill.: Irwin, 1974, pp. 14–16.
6. Hellriegel, op. cit., pp. 432–434.
7. "How to Introduce Change," *National Foreman's Institute,* Bureau of Business Practice, 1965. Section 1, Portfolio 8, pp. 1–2.
8. Haimann, op. cit., p. 303.
9. Clayton Reeser. *Management: Functions and Modern Concepts.* Glenview, Ill.: Scott, Foresman, 1973, p. 331.
10. Keith Davis and William G. Scott. *Human Relations and Organizational Behavior: Readings and Comments.* New York: McGraw-Hill, 1969, p. 284.
11. Ibid., p. 285.
12. Ibid., pp. 292–293.
13. Keith Davis. *Human Behavior at Work.* New York: McGraw-Hill, 1972, pp. 167–170.
14. William R. Dill, Henry B. Eyring, and Harold J. Leavitt. *The Organizational World.* New York: Harcourt Brace Jovanovich, 1973, p. 151.
15. Haimann, op. cit., p. 305.
16. Terry, op. cit., pp. 29–30.
17. Reeser, op. cit., p. 333.
18. Davis, op. cit., p. 190.
19. Ibid., p. 139.
20. Ibid., p. 146.
21. Ibid.
22. Ibid., p. 147.
23. Terry, op. cit., pp. 20–21.
24. Robert Tannenbaum and Warren H. Schmidt. "How to Choose a Leadership Pattern," *Harvard Business Review,* May–June 1973, pp. 170–173.
25. Ibid., pp. 175–178.
26. Ibid., pp. 179–181.

CUSTOM FURNITURE CASE: "EFFECTIVE IMMEDIATELY. . ."

It had been the practice for many years at Custom Furniture for the local salespeople to work out deliveries with Sam Crittenden, one of the delivery people for the company. Although Sam had no title, just about everyone looked to him as the unofficial leader in the warehouse. Sam was an intelligent man who always had the interests of the company in mind in everything he did on his job. The salespeople consulted with him when they needed deliveries and worked out schedules for the week. The system worked well and there was a minimum of bickering within the sales force concerning priorities on deliveries. Sam took great pride in being fair in working out these priorities. One day Bill Jones happened to be in the warehouse and heard the following conversation between two of the salespeople.

"You've been getting all of your orders shipped first lately and mine have been sitting in the warehouse while my customers complain," said Bryan Holmes to Jane Bryant. "You must have been turning on the charm for Sam."

"That isn't it at all," answered Jane. "It's just that all my orders lately have been concentrated downtown and yours have been out in the sticks. Sam has been trying to conserve fuel by making deliveries in as small an area as possible. He told me yesterday that he was going to start on some of your shipments tomorrow."

Bill returned to his office to work and did not hear the rest of the conversation.

"I know that, Jane. Sam and I have worked out mine for the next two or three days. I thought I'd just try to get a rise out of you about equal rights for women. I was just kidding," said Bryan.

After Bill finished his report, he went into the office of John Taylor, the general manager.

"John, I need to talk to you about something. We've got some problems about deliveries and the sales force is arguing among themselves about whose orders should go out first," said Bill.

John answered, "Bill, that really surprises me. I thought Sam [Crittenden] was doing a great job of working these things out. What do you think we should do about it?"

"I think all salespeople should check with me first and then I will schedule all the deliveries. Anyhow, Sam has enough to do driving the truck."

"Well," said John, "if you think it is necessary, go ahead. But be sure that Sam and the sales force understand this."

Bill immediately had one of the secretaries type the following notice and post it on the bulletin board:

EFFECTIVE IMMEDIATELY NO DELIVERIES ARE TO BE SCHEDULED OR MADE WITHOUT THE APPROVAL OF BILL JONES.

Signed
John Taylor

Within the next few days Sam was noticed sitting at his desk between deliveries studying the manuals for an air conditioning course that he was enrolled in at night in a local technical school.
1. What do you think of Bill's handling of this situation?
2. What mistakes did John make?
3. Explain the change in Sam's behavior.
4. If you were John, how would you have handled this matter?

MOTIVATION AND MORALE

THREE

This tea room is certainly a relief from the greasy spoons that we end up in when I'm out with one of the sales force.

That leads right into something I've been wanting to talk to you about.

Yes, what is that?

I've been noticing lately that you ar the other designe have been extend your lunch perioc

MORALE

John, we figure what's good for one
employee is good for the others.
No one makes the sales people
account for their time.

You should realize that's a whole
different ball of wax.

For the full story, turn to the case on page 159.

GENERAL PURPOSES OF CHAPTER 7

1. To attempt to define morale
2. To examine some of the factors that affect morale
3. To examine some of the methods commonly used in attempts to measure morale
4. To investigate job satisfaction and its effects on productivity
5. To inquire into the relationships of goals and morale

LEARNING OBJECTIVES

1. To define *morale*
2. To name four major components of morale
3. To list and briefly describe at least four broad factors that affect morale in an organization
4. To cite at least ten indicators of morale in a company
5. To designate three benefits of morale surveys to firms
6. To list by title the seven psychological levels of development and work values cited by Scott and Susan Meyers. Give a brief description of each level
7. To form an opinion of the relationship of morale to productivity
8. To give six traits necessary for effective goals
9. To account for the variances in what subordinates seem to want in a job compared to what their superiors believe they want

The word *morale,* as commonly used in business, refers to the positive or negative view taken by an employee toward an assigned task. Implied in this definition is the willingness of a person to accomplish group goals without letting personal goals dominate. Such a relationship is positive in that this cooperative spirit allows the formal group to reach its objectives. A negative relationship reveals itself when an individual is uncooperative, uninvolved, and unconcerned with personal needs or the needs of the formal group. The complexity of morale as a concept is reflected in this statement: "Morale equals the attitude toward work, environment, management style, and enterprise objectives." Good morale is not the result of manipulation, human relations campaigns, or motivational techniques. It is the result of an organizational philosophy that respects the dignity of the individual, using a leadership style that allows the accomplishment of individual and group goals. Morale is often viewed as consisting of four major components:

1. Group feeling: a type of togetherness that reflects a dedication to accomplish a common end.
2. Goal-directed behavior: group actions must be toward a specific task before the group can function effectively.
3. Shared value: shared values should exist within the group in the form of knowledge and expectations thus allowing the group to achieve its objective.
4. Worthwhile objective: the attractiveness of the goal should be universal in nature and offer rewards induced by group effort![1]

Morale is a measurement of managerial effectiveness in the development of human assets. Positive morale is a continuous process that cannot be purchased with money or bought with favors. Both positive and negative morale are contagious within an organized work environment. Low morale is a cancer. If allowed to grow unchecked within an organization, it will greatly reduce effectiveness.

Factors Influencing Morale

Group morale is a function of the relationships of individual members with each other. For example, in economics the term *psychological influence* is widely used. It refers to the belief that attitudes of a minority adversely affect the attitudes of the whole population. To apply this concept in the world of work, consider the development of rumors. Rumors are spread by a person or group because of fear, distrust, or disagreement with the objectives of the formal organization. Another factor that affects morale is the work inherent in a job assignment. If the work flow is not steady over an assigned work period, the uncertainty will mean frustration, errors, and delays in production schedules. The view a supervisor takes toward the company, its employees, and the job to be done is yet another factor that influences morale.

In contacts with supervisors in various industries, the authors have found a direct relationship between the attitudes of supervisors and their subordinates. A student working in a retail firm for two years had developed a negative attitude because of poor supervision; this was caused by constant managerial turnover and a lack of proper implementation of company policies and procedures. The tragedy of such a situation is that supervisors do not recognize the impact of their attitudes on the morale of their workers. The tendency is to blame poor

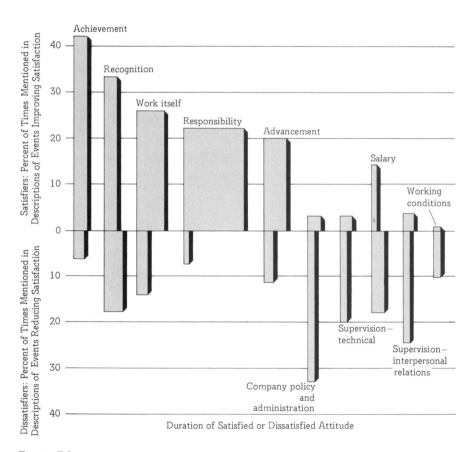

Figure 7-1
Factors affecting job satisfaction. Source: Theo Haimann and William G. Scott, *Management in the Modern Organization,* Boston: Houghton Mifflin, 1974, p. 357.

morale on worker indifference, on external influences, and in severe cases on the decisions of higher management. This is not to say that personal problems do not adversely affect morale. An enlightened supervisor will help identify the causes of personal problems and work through professionals in an effort to help the employee cope with obstacles.

Internal morale factors are present in the issues of wages, recognition, nature of the work, work conditions, and job security.[2] A highly sensitive point with all personnel is the pay they receive. If the compensation provides a fair rate of return in relation to the effort put forth, the employee will feel adequately rewarded. Experience tells us that managerial failure to justify wage rates and to apply them consistently results in internal friction. In reviewing the research of Herzberg and other behavioral scientists, it is apparent that recognition in a nontangible manner is essential for good employee morale on the job.

Nature of work refers to job tasks, repetitiveness, and physical stress. Recent articles in the press about boredom on automobile assembly lines provide a case in point. A related influence on morale is the presence of good or bad working conditions. Job security has a definite impact on morale. If a person feels the job is temporary, there is little incentive to identify with the goals of the firm. For example, repeated layoffs reduce employee confidence in management and in severe cases may result in theft and destruction of company property. The psychologist Frederick Herzberg has done significant research on job satisfaction. Figure 7-1 shows the result of this research.

A final factor that influences morale is the attitude of supervisors and employees toward internal working conditions. An example of the variances in perception among supervisors and employees is seen in Table 7-1. Morale is adversely affected when supervisors view money as the

TABLE 7-1
Mean ratings given by immediate superiors and by self ($N = 117$)

Scale	Superior rating	Self-rating
Ability to work with others	8.9	10.7
Amount of work done	9.4	10.5
Quality of work done	9.5	10.4
Leadership potential	5.9	8.9
Ability to do complicated jobs	8.5	10.4
Ability to work with minimum supervision	9.2	11.6
Conscientiousness	8.9	10.4
Overall performance	9.8	10.5
Average of 8 scales	8.8	10.4

Source: Personnel Psychology, Vol. 12, 51, 1959.

source of job satisfaction and employees view recognition for a job well done as more satisfying. Such a contrast can only lead to conflict, distrust, and low morale.

Measuring Morale

The following are morale indicators present in most organizations.

1. Labor turnover
2. Productivity
3. Waste and scrap
4. Quality records
5. Absenteeism and tardiness
6. Reports of counseling services
7. Grievances
8. Exit interviews
9. Accident reports
10. Medical records
11. Suggestions
12. Training records[3]

Trends in each of these provide a continuous barometer of organizational morale. Managerial follow-up through surveys or interviews may broaden management's understanding of these indicators.

Two examples may be helpful. Labor turnover is very costly to a firm. Assume that you are president of a firm. All human assets are eliminated, and you must estimate the cost of replacing all present human resources. Estimates of the costs of replacing the personnel range from *three* to *five times* the current annual payroll of the firm. A related example is the comparison of two businesses with identical traits. One firm produces a greater return on all investments because of highly motivated people, better internal structure, and greater teamwork. The difference between the two firms is made by the contribution of human assets.[4]

A further value of the investment in human assets is reflected in the statistics of Barry Enterprises, a maker of women's house slippers, pillows, bathrobes, and other items. In 1972, Barry has pegged replacement costs or investment in managers at $4000 for a frontline supervisor, $10,000 for engineers and other professionals, $16,000 to $18,000 for middle managers, and $35,000 and over for top-level management.[5]

Texas Instruments, in research on hiring a college graduate with a master's degree, stated that salary, benefits, and other employment costs are straight expense for twelve to eighteen months. The break-even point comes only after a period of two years. The replacement cost after this time is $15,000 to $20,000. A related study on clerical personnel placed the replacement cost at $1800 and a break-even point of three to six months.[6] Figure 7-2 illustrates the high cost of hiring and replacing personnel.

Although we recognize that rapid labor turnover is not the only indicator of poor morale, it does increase material waste, reduce productivity, reduce product quality, and increase the number and severity of accidents. To measure employee morale adequately, an enterprise must identify the factors that influence morale as well as recognize the cost of each to the organization.

Morale surveys, if properly conducted, provide several benefits. A major benefit is identifying how employees feel about their jobs. Morale surveys can also increase communication through interviews or questionnaires that reveal the interest of the employees. Morale surveys can

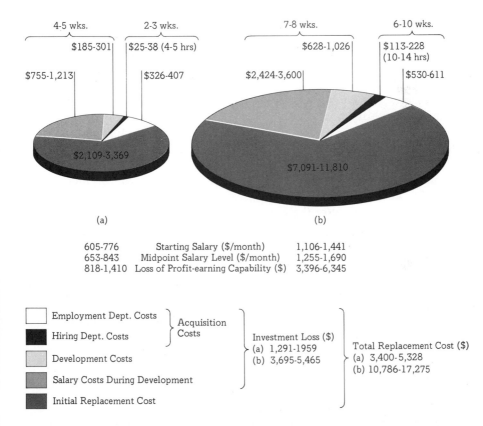

605-776	Starting Salary ($/month)	1,106-1,441
653-843	Midpoint Salary Level ($/month)	1,255-1,690
818-1,410	Loss of Profit-earning Capability ($)	3,396-6,345

☐ Employment Dept. Costs } Acquisition
■ Hiring Dept. Costs } Costs
☐ Development Costs
▨ Salary Costs During Development
■ Initial Replacement Cost

Investment Loss ($)
(a) 1,291-1959
(b) 3,695-5,465

Total Replacement Cost ($)
(a) 3,400-5,328
(b) 10,786-17,275

Figure 7-2
The high cost of hiring and replacing. Source: Based on material from Thomas M. Rohan, "Who's Worth What Around Here?" *Industry Week*, November 6, 1972, pp. 34–35.

provide an outlet for emotional pressures and improve the human relations attitude of management. Training needs for personnel at all levels can be identified through morale surveys. In areas with a formal bargaining unit, these surveys provide an avenue for the increased understanding of employees by management and unions.[7] A word of caution to all managers: morale surveys are not absolute cure-alls for personnel problems. The effective use of morale surveys is part of a managerial philosophy that seeks to build a partnership of purpose with the human assets of the organization.

The easiest way to destroy the effectiveness of morale surveys is to use them to threaten, remove, or downgrade the contribution of a person to the organization. Morale surveys should not be a managerial weapon but a means of improving the effectiveness of personnel. In the final analysis, the measurement of morale is a cooperative process between management and employees. Such cooperation can remove obstacles, hostility, distrust, and barriers to communication among organizational members. Moreover, the benefits of morale surveys are not without an investment in time, money, personnel, and follow-up actions from management. Notice that the term *investment,* not *cost,* is used because such an attitude reflects a positive view of morale surveys in the world of work. An offshoot of this positive viewpoint is the willingness of management to change any situation that has reduced the morale of personnel within the enterprise.

Once the need for morale surveys has been recognized, a system must be designed to collect data from personnel. One such is that of observation. Supervisors can observe the state of internal relationships of personnel in their jurisdiction. However, this technique will be ineffective without proper training of supervisors, so that they can analyze what they see, as well as alter their observations after morale changes. Survey forms constitute another source of morale data used widely in industry. A sample attitude survey questionnaire form is shown in Figure 7-3. A related example of a morale survey form is a multiple-choice opinion questionnaire shown in Figure 7-4.

Survey forms normally follow three general formats.
Objective surveys—uses a set of true or false questions or multiple choice questions to obtain the views of employees. Its major limitation is that of forcing people to make a choice that may or may not reflect the real views of the person answering the questionnaire.
Description surveys—uses a series of key questions to obtain a response from employees in their own words. An example of this technique is the use of interview surveys. While such techniques provide greater employee input, it requires more training for the person who conducts the interview as well as increases time and money costs to the firm.
Projective surveys—uses an abstraction that is incomplete or meaningless. It requires a person to complete the project by describing the

134

meaning of the project. Such instruments are used in the professional counseling of individuals with special morale problems.[8]

The survey form used to obtain morale data has a direct bearing on the depth, interpretation, and use of such data by management. Implementing morale surveys is tricky and complicated. The failure of morale surveys has in many cases been the result of poor managerial planning in designing a procedure to conduct them. For example, one instrument cannot adequately identify the morale concerns of office, managerial, and operative employees. Each work level reflects different job knowledge, job content, and job demands. Such variances must be reflected in instruments to provide adequate, statistically reliable data. A related concern is the mechanics of morale survey administration in terms of physical environment, number of people interviewed, and compiling the results for future distribution to employees. Again, the best instrument becomes useless when administrative safeguards are disregarded by management.[9]

An excellent study of job satisfaction was conducted by Xerox field managers in 1967. As a basis for their study they used Herzberg's concepts of *motivators* and *hygiene factors*. These concepts are outlined in Figure 7-5. To increase the validity of this morale study Xerox looked at three levels and types of managers. One group represented front-line foremen supervising technical representatives who install and maintain Xerox equipment. Another group represented marketing team managers whose function was that of front-line sales managers. A third group was represented by managers of sales and service administration whose function was that of branch office supervisors. The results of the Xerox study representing satisfying experiences are shown in Tables 7-2, 7-3, and 7-4. Dissatisfying experiences are found in Tables 7-6, 7-7, and 7-8. Table 7-5 shows a comparison of key factors appearing in satisfying experiences. Table 7-9 shows a comparison of key factors appearing in dissatisfying experiences.

As can be seen, the subject of morale, when broken down into job satisfaction and dissatisfaction, is complex. We cannot ignore the following conclusions:

1. There is a direct relationship between leadership style and subordinates' satisfaction or dissatisfaction with their jobs.
2. The challenge to management is that of structuring jobs so that employees can achieve, advance, and receive recognition.
3. The placement of an individual is a major influence in determining acceptable job performance.
4. Supervisors must plan and organize work to allow individuals to meet their basic human needs as well as meet their psychological and ego needs.

AJAX CORPORATION

PERSONNEL OPINION SURVEY

We are all interested in maintaining sound personnel policies and practices.
You can help by contributing your opinions by means of the attached questionnaire.

We would appreciate your frank, straight-from-the-shoulder answers. There
are no right or wrong answers. Please read each question carefully. Then
check the one answer which most nearly reflects your personal opinion.

This survey is completely anonymous. Questionnaires will be key punched
and analyzed by an outside firm. Please do not put your name anywhere on the
questionnaire. When you have finished, please return the questionnaire in
the enclosed envelope addressed to George Smith, Personnel Director.

Thank you for taking the time to give us your opinions.

(1) How much information do you receive about what is going on in your
department?

    1. __ I get more than enough information.
    2. __ I get all the information I am interested in.
    3. __ I get almost as much information as I am interested in.
    4. __ I get almost half the information I am interested in.
    5. __ I get very little of the information I am interested in.

(2) How well do you know what is expected of you in your job?

    1. __ I have only a very vague idea.
    2. __ I have a somewhat vague idea.
    3. __ I have a pretty good idea.
    4. __ I have a very good idea.
    5. __ I know exactly.

(3) When your supervisor makes decisions and commitments about your work, how
does he do it?

    1. __ He almost always talks with me about them.
    2. __ He usually talks with me about them.
    3. __ He talks with me about half the time.
    4. __ He sometimes talks with me about them.
    5. __ He rarely or never talks with me about them.

5. A key ingredient in employee satisfaction was their perception of managerial decisions in terms of fairness to all personnel concerned.
6. In-depth managerial development and training at all management levels are essential to maximize satisfaction of workers.
7. Xerox's research showed no clear relationship between job satisfaction and productivity.
8. Dissatisfaction increases an employer's costs. Such costs are reflected in increased employee turnover. A study of Ross and Zabder in 1957

(4) Does your supervisor ask for your advice about changes which will affect your job?

1. __ He always asks for my opinion.
2. __ He usually asks for my opinion.
3. __ He asks for my opinion about half the time.
4. __ He rarely or never asks for my opinion.
5. __ This does not apply to me.

(5) How sincere an interest do you believe your supervisor has in getting your opinions and suggestions?

1. __ He has a very sincere interest in getting them.
2. __ He has considerable interest in getting them.
3. __ He has some interest in getting them.
4. __ He has little or no interest in getting them.
5. __ I don't know whether he is interested in them or not.

(6) What attention or emphasis is given to the following by your supervisor?

	Too Much Attention	About Right	Too Little Attention	Doesn't Apply
The quality of your work	_____	_____	_____	_____
Costs involved in your work	_____	_____	_____	_____
Meeting schedules	_____	_____	_____	_____
Getting your reactions and suggestions	_____	_____	_____	_____
Giving you information	_____	_____	_____	_____
Making full use of your abilities	_____	_____	_____	_____
Safety and housekeeping	_____	_____	_____	_____
Development of his subordinates	_____	_____	_____	_____
Innovations, new ideas	_____	_____	_____	_____
Effective teamwork among his subordinates	_____	_____	_____	_____

Figure 7-3
Ajax Corporation Personnel Opinion Survey. Source: Theo Haimann and Raymond L. Hilgert, *Supervision: Concepts and Practices of Management*, Cincinnati: South-Western Publishing Company, 1972, pp. 317–318.

Confidential:
Do Not Write Your Name Anywhere

**Opinion and Idea Survey
Instructions**

For each question place a check
mark (✓) in front of the opinion
which comes closest to your opinion.
Read the whole question before
marking your opinion.
This is not a test. There are no right
or wrong answers. We merely want
your frank opinion. Your answer will
be your vote to tell us how you feel
about your job and your Company.
Be sure to answer each question.
An extra page at the back is provided
for any comments you have about
your job.
First, in order to arrange your opinions into groups, we need answers
to three questions.

1. In what age group are you now?
   1. ___ Under 20.
   2. ___ 20-24.
   3. ___ 25-34.
   4. ___ 35 and over.

2. How long have you worked for
   American States?
   1. ___ Less than 6 months.
   2. ___ 6 months to 2 years.
   3. ___ 2 years to 5 years.
   4. ___ 5 years and over.

3. In what division do you now work?
   1. ___ Claims and legal.
   2. ___ Operations.
   3. ___ Underwriting.

General Company Opinions

4. What does your family think about
   American States as a place to work?
   (Please check only one answer.)
   1. ___ They are happy I'm on the
      American States team.
   2. ___ They think it's an O.K. place
      to work.

3. ___ They don't care one way or
   the other.
4. ___ They don't like the Company.

5. What do your friends, neighbors, and
   business associates think of American States as an employer?
   1. ___ One of the best companies to
      work for in this area.
   2. ___ Better than the average
      company.
   3. ___ Just another place to work.
   4. ___ One of the poorest places in
      town to work.

6. What do you think of the insurance
   industry, compared to other industries, as a place to work and build
   your career?
   1. ___ I'd rather work in this indus-
      try than any other.
   2. ___ The insurance industry is one
      of the better ones.
   3. ___ It is below average.
   4. ___ The insurance industry is at
      the bottom of my list as a
      place to work.

7. How optimistic are you about American States future growth?
   1. ___ Looks like we have unlimited
      prospects for growth.
   2. ___ The future looks encouraging.
   3. ___ Our growth will probably be
      below average.
   4. ___ The future looks poor.

8. When you have a complaint or gripe,
   is it fairly heard and satisfactorily
   handled by the Company?
   1. ___ I never have any complaints.
   2. ___ My complaints are handled
      well.
   3. ___ Some effort is made, but not
      enough.
   4. ___ Complaint handling is unsat-
      isfactory.
   Do you have any comments?

Figure 7-4
First page from a multiple-choice opinion questionnaire; cover page not shown.
Source: Keith Davis, *Human Behavior at Work*, New York: McGraw-Hill, 1972,
p. 72.

138

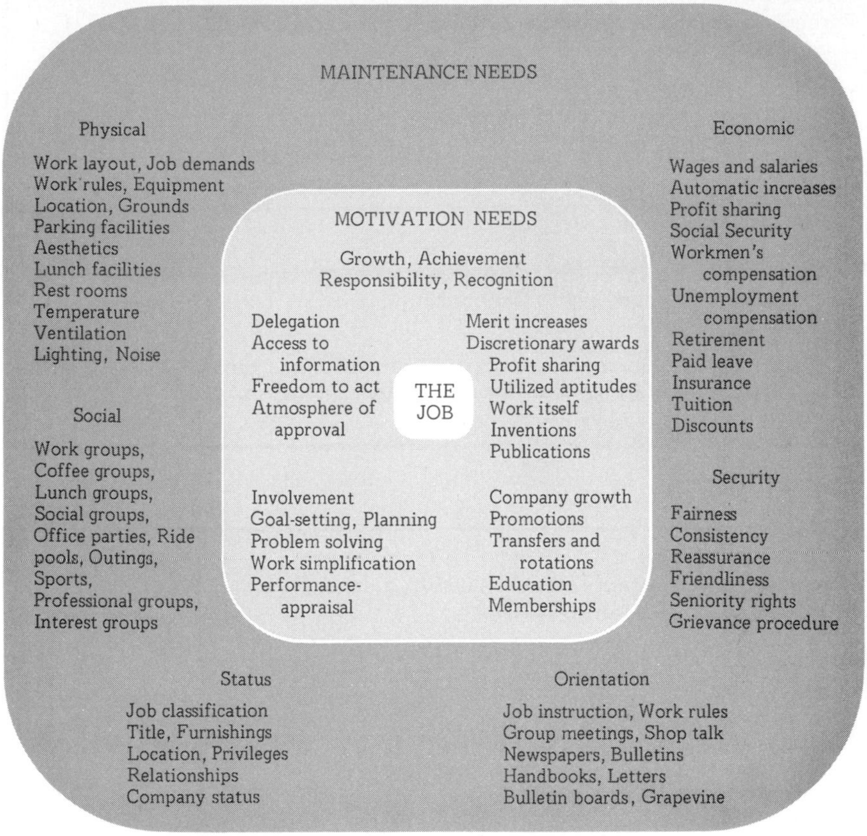

MAINTENANCE NEEDS

Physical

Work layout, Job demands
Work rules, Equipment
Location, Grounds
Parking facilities
Aesthetics
Lunch facilities
Rest rooms
Temperature
Ventilation
Lighting, Noise

Social

Work groups,
Coffee groups,
Lunch groups,
Social groups,
Office parties, Ride
pools, Outings,
Sports,
Professional groups,
Interest groups

MOTIVATION NEEDS

Growth, Achievement
Responsibility, Recognition

Delegation
Access to
    information
Freedom to act
Atmosphere of
    approval

THE
JOB

Merit increases
Discretionary awards
Profit sharing
Utilized aptitudes
Work itself
Inventions
Publications

Involvement
Goal-setting, Planning
Problem solving
Work simplification
Performance-
    appraisal

Company growth
Promotions
Transfers and
    rotations
Education
Memberships

Economic

Wages and salaries
Automatic increases
Profit sharing
Social Security
Workmen's
    compensation
Unemployment
    compensation
Retirement
Paid leave
Insurance
Tuition
Discounts

Security

Fairness
Consistency
Reassurance
Friendliness
Seniority rights
Grievance procedure

Status

Job classification
Title, Furnishings
Location, Privileges
Relationships
Company status

Orientation

Job instruction, Work rules
Group meetings, Shop talk
Newspapers, Bulletins
Handbooks, Letters
Bulletin boards, Grapevine

Figure 7-5
Employee needs: Effective job performance depends on the fulfillment of both motivation and maintenance needs. Motivation needs include responsibility, achievement, recognition and growth, and are satisfied through the media grouped in the inner circle. Motivation factors focus on the individual and his achievement of company and personal goals. Maintenance needs are satisfied through media listed in the outer circle under the headings of physical, social, status, orientation, security and economic. Peripheral to the task and usually group administered, maintenance factors have little motivational value, but their fulfillment is essential to the avoidance of dissatisfaction. An environment rich in opportunities for satisfying motivation needs leads to motivation seeking habits, and a job situation sparse in motivation opportunities encourages preoccupation with maintenance factors. Source: William A. Boothe, "Job Satisfaction," an original study of Xerox field managers. December 19, 1967.

TABLE 7-2
Percentage of factors appearing in satisfying experiences,
manager of sales & service administration ($N = 80$)

Factor	Total*
1. Recognition	65
2. Achievement	56
3. Advancement	19
4. Responsibility	15
5. Work itself	6
6. Status	6
7. Interpersonal relationship—superior	5
8. Interpersonal relationship—subordinate	4
9. Salary	3

* The percentages total more than 100 percent since more than one factor can appear in any single sequence of events.

TABLE 7-3
Percentage of factors appearing in satisfying experiences,
marketing team managers ($N = 60$)

Factor	Total*
1. Achievement	73
2. Recognition	47
3. Status	18
4. Advancement	15
5. Responsibility	5
6. Work itself	3
7. Interpersonal relations—subordinate	2
8. Salary	2
9. Interpersonal relations—superior	2

* The percentages total more than 100 percent since more than one factor can appear in any single sequence of events.

showed a positive correlation between need satisfaction and employee turnover.[10]

Management must restructure jobs so that workers can find greater personal satisfaction instead of following the recent trend of reducing job content to the lowest possible level. Future developments toward a meaningful relationship between productivity and morale, human needs and their method of satisfaction, is the responsibility of management.

An excellent article by Vincent S. Flowers and Charles L. Hughes

140

TABLE 7-4
Percentage of factors appearing in satisfying experiences,
marketing team technical managers ($N = 156$)

Factor	Total*
1. Achievement	55
2. Recognition	53
3. Responsibility	12
4. Advancement	8
5. Status	4
6. Work itself	4
7. Salary	2
8. Interpersonal relations—subordinates	2
9. Interpersonal relations—superiors	1
10. Interpersonal relations—peers	1
11. Job security	1
12. Company benefits	1
13. Supervision	1
14. Company policy	1

* The percentages total more than 100 percent since
more than one factor can appear in any single sequence
of events.

TABLE 7-5
Comparison of key* factors appearing in satisfying experiences

Factor	MSSA**	MTM†	MTTM†
1. Achievement	56%	73%	55%
2. Advancement	19	15	8
3. Recognition	65	47	53
4. Responsibility	15	5	12
5. Status	6	18	4
6. Work itself	6	3	4

* Those appearing in at least 4 percent of the sequences.
† MSSA = manager of sales and service administration, MTM
= marketing team manager, MTTM = marketing team technical manager.

entitled "Why Employees Stay" appeared in the July-August issue of
Harvard Business Review in 1973. The purpose of their research was to
discover why employees stay—motivational reasons, hygiene reasons,
and environmental reasons.

Figure 7-6 shows the relationship between job satisfaction and environmental factors for four types of employees. It also explains why
each type stays. The turnovers dislike their job, have few internal en-

TABLE 7-6

Percentage of factors appearing in dissatisfying experiences, managers of sales & service administration ($N = 80$)

Factor	Total*
1. Lack of recognition	31
2. Interpersonal relations—superior	19
3. Working conditions	15
4. Company policy	15
5. Supervision	15
6. Lack of achievement	10
7. Lack of responsibility	8
8. Interpersonal relations—peers	8
9. Salary	5
10. Too much responsibility	4
11. Lack of advancement	4
12. Work itself	4
13. Job security	4
14. Interpersonal relations—subordinate	1
15. Loss of status	1

* The percentages total more than 100 percent since more than one factor can appear in any single sequence of events.

TABLE 7-7

Percentage of factors appearing in dissatifying experiences, marketing team managers ($N = 60$)

Factor	Total*
1. Supervision	35
2. Lack of achievement	20
3. Lack of recognition	15
4. Lack of advancement	10
5. Interpersonal relations—superior	8
6. Salary	8
7. Company policy	7
8. Work itself	5
9. Interpersonal relations—subordinate	5
10. Interpersonal relations—peers	3
11. Job security	3

* The percentages total more than 100 percent since more than one factor can appear in any single sequence of events.

vironmental pressures to keep them in the company, and will leave at the first opportunity. The turn-offs also dislike their job but stay because they are financially dependent on company benefit programs and feel unable to obtain employment with other firms. The turn-ons like their

TABLE 7-8

Percentage of factors appearing in dissatisfying experiences, marketing team technical managers ($N = 156$)

Factor	Total*
1. Supervision	43
2. Lack of achievement	13
3. Lack of recognition	12
4. Lack of advancement	8
5. Company policy	8
6. Interpersonal relations—superior	8
7. Working conditions	7
8. Too much responsibility	4
9. Salary	4
10. Personal failure	4
11. Lack of responsibility	2
12. Personal life	1
13. Loss of status	1
14. Interpersonal relations—peers	1
15. Interpersonal relations—subordinates	1
16. Work itself	1

* The percentages total more than 100 percent since more than one factor can appear in any single sequence of events.

TABLE 7-9

Comparison of key* factors appearing in dissatisfying experiences

Factor	MSSA*	MTM†	MTTM†
1. Lack of recognition	31%	15%	12%
2. Lack of achievement	10	20	13
3. Supervision	11	35	43
4. Lack of advancement	4	10	8
5. Interpersonal relations—superior	19	8	8
6. Company policy	15	7	8

* Those appearing in at least 7 percent of the sequences.
† MSSA = manager of sales and service administration, MTM = marketing team manager, MTTM = marketing team technical manager.

respective jobs and are not forced by internal or external environmental factors to remain with the firm. However, continual job satisfaction is essential to the continued employment of such persons with the company. The turn-ons-plus like their respective jobs and stay with the firm because of adverse external environmental considerations. Permanent job dissatisfaction will cause these employees to become turn-offs. Such a gradual change will increase employee productivity and employee relations problems.[11]

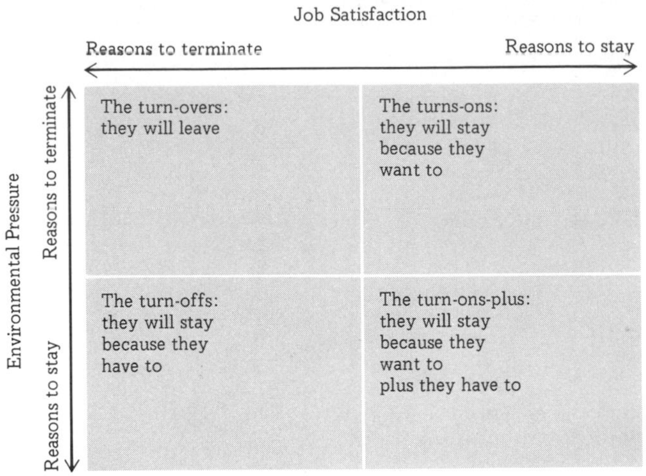

Job Satisfaction

Reasons to terminate ← ——————————————→ Reasons to stay

	Reasons to terminate	Reasons to stay
(top)	The turn-overs: they will leave	The turns-ons: they will stay because they want to
(bottom)	The turn-offs: they will stay because they have to	The turn-ons-plus: they will stay because they want to plus they have to

Environmental Pressure (vertical axis: Reasons to terminate ↑ / Reasons to stay ↓)

Figure 7-6
Job satisfaction and environment. Source: Vincent S. Flowers and Charles L. Hughes, "Why Employees Stay," *Harvard Business Review*, July–August 1973, p. 51.

The general conclusions reached from a review of Table 7-8 are as follows:

1. Low-skill manufacturing personnel stay because of fringe benefits and job security (maintenance reasons).
2. Managerial and professional personnel stay because of job satisfaction and company environment (motivation reasons).
3. Moderately skilled manufacturing and clerical personnel also stay because of job satisfaction and company environment (motivation reasons).
4. Employees with shorter service stay for internal environmental reasons, whereas longer-service people tend to be influenced by external environmental conditions.
5. People with higher educational achievements stay because of maintenance and motivational concerns. Similarly, people with noncollege experiences were influenced by maintenance and environmental concerns to remain with their present employer.[12]

Figure 7-7 shows the motivational, maintenance, and external reasons for staying among twelve employee classifications. The key symbols are defined as follows: motivational reasons, factors in company environment that motivate a person to stay with a firm; maintenance reasons, factors that provide tangible benefits for staying with a firm; external

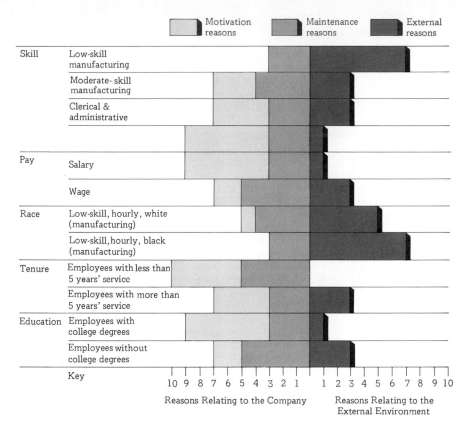

Figure 7-7
Number of motivational, maintenance, and environmental reasons for staying, among twelve employee classifications. Source: Vincent S. Flowers and Charles L. Hughes, "Why Employees Stay," *Harvard Business Review*, July–August 1973, p. 53.

reasons, influence from factors outside the organization that cause a person to stay with the firm.

Table 7-10 shows the effects of environmental factors on employees at various skill and job satisfaction levels. Low-skill employees feel bound principally by benefits, family responsibilities, the difficulty of finding another job, personal friendships with co-workers, company loyalty, and simple financial pressure. Moderate-skill employees feel the same, but tend to be less sensitive to environmental concerns. Managers stay because of job considerations and community ties. However, less influence was exerted on managers by company loyalty, family responsibilities, and the task of finding another job to stay with an enterprise.[13]

TABLE 7-10

The effects of environmental factors on employees at various skill and job satisfaction levels

Reasons for staying	Skill level			Job satisfaction level		
	Low	*Moderate*	*Manager*	*Very low*	*Low*	*High*
I wouldn't want to rebuild most of the benefits that I have now if I left the company.	72%	64%	26%	76%	63%	44%
I have family responsibilities.	69	55	46	76	73	44
I have good personal friends here at work.	57	45	34	35	45	38
The company's been good to me and I don't believe in jumping from company to company.	57	59	41	24	39	58
I'm working to make ends meet and I don't want to take the risks in a new job.	57	36	8	59	52	21
I wouldn't like to look for a job on the outside.	52	29	13	35	39	20
I'm a little too old for starting over again.	46	25	14	41	34	20
I wouldn't like to start all over learning the policies of a new company.	39	30	3	35	27	17
I like to live in this area.	30	31	58	35	28	37
Difficult to find a job.	58	42	47	59	53	42

Source: Vincent S. Flowers and Charles L. Hughes, "Why Employees Stay," *Harvard Business Review*, July–August 1973, p. 55.

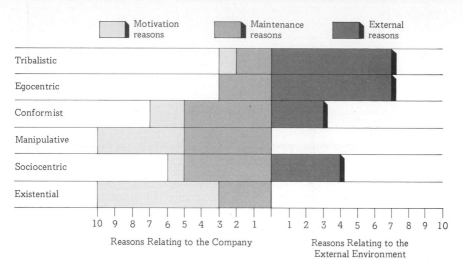

Figure 7-8
Number of reasons why employees stay, for different levels of work values.
Source: Vincent S. Flowers and Charles L. Hughes, "Why Employees Stay,"
Harvard Business Review, July–August 1973, p. 57.

Figure 7-8 shows the reasons why employees stay with a firm in relation to their different levels of work values. Figure 7-8 produced ten reasons why employees stay with a firm in relation to their various psychological levels. Environmental reasons were the main reasons for tribalistic or egocentric value people to say. Individuals with existential values tended to stay with the firm because of an internal climate that provided positive motivational influences. Further research tended to show that people working in areas with low skill manufacturing functions reflected tribalistic or egocentric values. In contrast, managerial, research, and other professionals demonstrated the values of manipulative or existentialism.[14]

Table 7-12 shows value systems and environmental factors that influence people to stay with the firm. People reflecting the traits of levels 5 and 7 tend to place less emphasis on external environmental concerns. People reflecting the traits of levels 2, 3, and 4 show concern for job benefits, family considerations, and new job requirements. Further research will increase our understanding of value systems and their impact on labor turnover and job satisfaction. One thing that stands out in Table 7-12 is that a manager or supervisor must acknowledge the presence of environmental and value influences in his or her own decisions, in the decisions of employees, and in the decisions of upper management. Such variances should be respected by all organizational entities in setting formal objectives for the enterprise.

TABLE 7-11
Values for working

The following categorizations of psychological levels of development and work values are based on Scott and Susan Myers' adaptation of Clare Graves's theory.

Level 1—Reactive. This level of psychological development is restricted primarily to infants, people with serious brain deterioration, and certain psychopathic conditions. For practical purposes, employees are not ordinarily found at Level 1.

Level 2—Tribalistic. These employees are best suited to jobs that offer easy work, friendly people, fair play, and, above all, a good boss. An employee at this level believes that he may not have the best job in the world, but he does as well as others with jobs like his. He likes a boss who tells him exactly what to do and how to do it, and who encourages him by doing it with him.

Level 3—Egocentric. The two major requirements of a job for this employee are that it pay well and keep people off his back. He does not care for any kind of work that ties him down, but he will do it if he must in order to get some money. Because of the raw, rugged value system of this employee, he needs a boss who is tough, but allows him to be tough too.

Level 4—Conformist. This employee likes a job which is secure, where the rules are followed, and no favoritism is shown. He feels that he has worked hard for what he has and thinks he deserves some good breaks. Others, he believes, should realize that it is their duty to work. He likes a boss who calls the shots, isn't always changing his mind, and sees to it that everyone follows the rules.

Level 5—Manipulative. The ideal job for this employee is one which is full of variety, allows some free wheeling and dealing, and offers pay and bonus on the basis of results. He feels he is responsible for his own success and is constantly on the lookout for new opportunities. A good boss for this employee understands the politics of getting the job done, knows how to bargain, and is firm but fair.

Level 6—Sociocentric. A job which allows for the development of friendly relationships with supervisors and others in the work group appeals to this employee. Working with people toward a common goal is more important than getting caught up in a materialistic rat race. He likes a boss who gets people working in close harmony by being more a friendly person than a boss.

Level 7—Existential. This employee likes a job where the goals and problems are more important than the money, prestige, or how it should be done. He prefers work of his own choosing that offers continuing challenge and requires imagination and initiative. To him, a good boss is one who gives him access to the information he needs and lets him do the job in his own way.

Source: Vincent S. Flowers and Charles L. Hughes, "Why Employees Stay," *Harvard Business Review,* July–August 1973, p. 56.

The implications of the research by Flowers and Hughes on the maintenance of positive morale within an enterprise are broad and dramatic.

1. The complexity of building morale in a positive nature is reinforced by their research.
2. In reviewing Figure 7-7, it is apparent that positive morale will in-

fluence the turn-ons but will have little effect on the turnovers, turn-offs, and the turn-on-plus employees.

3. From Figure 7-8, motivational reasons will be influenced by a greater extent by morale than maintenance or external reasons for staying with a firm.
4. The greatest challenge to management from a morale standpoint is to deal with individuals that feel locked in, alienated, and who display a great deal of job dissatisfaction.
5. A similar challenge reflected in Figure 7-9 and Table 7-11 is that of building morale in an environment that exhibits different values for working.
6. Table 7-12 shows the impact of internal and external forces on morale. Such data will help management to identify controllable and uncontrollable environmental forces that affect the morale of all personnel in the organization.

Relation to Productivity

Research on the relationship of morale to productivity has not always been conclusive, but substantial evidence suggests that in the long run, high morale is associated with increased employee productivity. As stated earlier, building a partnership of purpose requires a positive work environment. Such an atmosphere can increase the contribution of each organizational member. The complexity of this relationship is reflected by Victor H. Vroom, who states that low morale and high productivity, high morale and low productivity, high morale and high productivity, low morale and low productivity can all be present within an organization.[15]

A contrasting view of the general relationship of morale and productivity is reflected in the viewpoint of Keith Davis, who states that high productivity is a result of emphasizing scientific management that uses methods study, time study, and close supervision to achieve its objectives. The opposite of this view is one that stresses employee happiness without regard to the goals of the formal organization. An enlightened supervisor recognizes the need to integrate the goals of formal and informal members so that employees work together with high morale and high productivity. These three relationships are shown in Figure 7-9. Similar studies by Likert at the University of Michigan's Institute for Social Research have suggested a pattern of behavior that leads to high productivity and high employee morale. This relationship is reflected in the following: "The leadership and other processes of the organization must be such as to insure a maximum probability that in all interactions and all relationships within the organization each member will, in light of his background, values, and expectations, view the experience as supportive and one which builds and maintains his sense of personal worth and importance."[16]

TABLE 7-12
Value systems and environmental factors

Reasons for staying	Value system					
	Tribalistic (Level 2)	*Egocentric* (Level 3)	*Conformist* (Level 4)	*Manipulative* (Level 5)	*Sociocentric* (Level 6)	*Existential* (Level 7)
I wouldn't want to rebuild most of the benefits that I have now if I left the company.	67%	63%	61%	45%	70%	22%
I have family responsibilities.	72	65	59	45	60	37
I have good personal friends here at work.	50	52	46	15	58	29
The company's been good to me and I don't believe in jumping from company to company.	47	32	71	38	58	39
I'm working to make ends meet and I don't want to take the risks in a new job.	67	52	41	10	47	7
I wouldn't like to look for a job on the outside.	42	27	39	13	56	12
I'm a little too old for starting over again.	45	32	39	7	30	7
I wouldn't like to start all over learning the policies of a new company.	47	38	29	10	28	2
I like to live in this area.	45	30	32	45	40	49
Difficult to find a job.	40	47	56	40	56	49

Source: Vincent S. Flowers and Charles L. Hughes, "Why Employees Stay," *Harvard Business Review,* July–August 1973, p. 58.

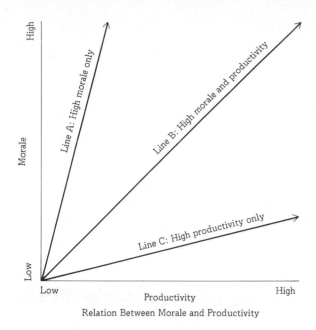

Relation Between Morale and Productivity

Figure 7-9
Morale information and its use. Source: Keith Davis, *Human Behavior at Work,*
New York: McGraw-Hill, 1972, p. 66.

Likert's principle of supportive relationships implies that (1) the supportive supervisor is sensitive to the needs and feelings of subordinates; (2) the supervisor respects and trusts subordinates; (3) the supervisor is receptive to their ideas and suggestions; (4) the supervisor has a sincere interest in the welfare of the employees.[17] Another outcome of Likert's research was to identify an effective supervisor as an individual who plans, directs, and coordinates the tasks of subordinates without being directly involved in the tasks of the work group. Table 7-13 illustrates this relationship from a study of railroad workers.

In reviewing the relationship of morale to productivity, we have discussed the views of Vroom, Davis, and Likert. Their research tends to support the belief that in the long run positive morale is essential for an organization to operate effectively in a changing world. Dr. Hanafi M. Soliman has developed a concept called an *operative theory of organization.* This approach implies the following:

1. Organization differences make it inappropriate to speak of a universal theory.
2. Grouping similar organizations enhances our ability to understand, to learn, and to identify the organizational theory that produces high morale and high productivity.

TABLE 7-13

Relation to section productivity of what foreman reports doing on the job

	Planning; skilled tasks	Providing materials to men; watching men	Same things men do	Keeping up track	Number of duties mentioned*	N
Foremen of	42	41	8	7	98	36
high sections	83		15			
Foremen of	25	42	15 ′	14	96	36
low sections	67		29			

* Responses total more than 72 because many foremen gave more than one answer.

Source: D. Katz, N. Macoby, G. Gurin, and Lucretia Floor. 1951/*Productivity Supervision and Morale Among Railroad Workers.*

3. Organizational theories of management change to reflect changing environmental conditions.
4. This approach identifies assumptions regarding nature of man, the nature of the organization, and the nature of prevailing technology.[18]

Soliman's operative theory of organization is outlined in Table 7-14.

Recognizing the impact of positive morale on productivity is the first step in building a partnership of purpose between management and labor. The issue is not that of questioning a relationship between morale and productivity but rather whether or not management's philosophy recognizes the impact of individual, supervisory, and organizational attitudes on employee productivity. Management should not leave it to labor unions, informal groups, environmental factors, and managerial prejudices to set productivity standards or adversely affect the morale of organizational members. Management should accept the responsibility of guiding the development of and should remove obstacles to positive morale and productive attitudes. Notice that the term *guide* is used because morale is not a result of manipulation, monetary rewards, or managerial directives. Morale and productivity are the end products of a managerial belief in the value of individual needs, organizational goals, and cooperation. Moreover, morale and productivity are continuous challenges to managerial creativity.

Goals as Factors

Morale becomes negative when employees receive no clear indication of what is expected of them, what resources they are to use, what proce-

TABLE 7-14

Classes of organization

Elements of organization	Class (A) Military organizations	Class (B) Industrial organizations	Class (C) Research and educational institutes	Class (D) Peace Corps and nonprofit organizations
Work	Generally speaking, work is highly structured, where every job has a clearly defined beginning and end. Communication flows from the top down. Decision-making powers are held in few hands, and at the highest level.	Work ranges between highly structured (assembly line work) to highly nonstructured (managerial work) depending on the size of the organization and the state of technology prevailing. Many times, both types of work exist in the one organization.	Generally speaking, work is highly nonstructured.	Generally speaking, work is highly nonstructured.
Participants	Participants are expected to follow orders precisely. No deviation due to human needs, feelings, perception, and so on, is to be allowed.	On the "freedom to act" continuum, participants are expected to be located at almost every point ranging from low to high depending on the nature of their work. More participants are expected to fall at the low end of the continuum and only a few are expected at the high end of it.	Participants are expected to have more freedom of action at almost all levels within the organization.	Participants are expected to have more freedom of action at almost all levels within the organization.

Source: Hanafi M. Soliman, "Making the Formal Organization More Productive," *Industry Week,* June 19, 1972, p. 46.

dures they are to follow, and what time is needed to accomplish a given task. For goals to be effective they should reflect the following traits:

1. Goals should evolve from participation of those responsible for achieving them.
2. Goals should challenge the talents of the individual to give a person a sense of achievement and self-development.
3. Goals are unrealistic if they fail to relate to the knowledge, skill, and environment of organizational entities.
4. Goals, like any managerial tool, become obsolete because of changes in managerial and organizational needs.
5. Individual goals should be limited in scope to prevent confusion or neglect in areas of responsibility of an employee.
6. Goals should be ranked in order of importance to provide guidelines for prospective employee actions.[19]

The attitude of a supervisor toward the role of goals in employee development is seen in Table 7-15.

Morale is enhanced under the new managerial style because of employee self-direction and employee satisfaction gained from achievement motivation. Morale under the traditional viewpoint was ignored

TABLE 7-15
Our viewpoint of management is changing

Old and traditional management	*New and emerging management*
A. Management is a system of authority.	A. Management is a resource.
B. The supervisor is authoritative, has power over people.	B. The supervisor serves as a co-ordinative stimulus, has power through employee participation.
C. Activities emphasized.	C. Results emphasized.
D. Rational thinking (deductive and inductive) utilized	D. Causative thinking utilized.
E. Supervisor	E. Supervisor
1. Decides goals in terms of activities sought.	1. Gives overall objectives in broad terms to employees.
2. Prescribes activities to perform.	2. Permits employees to set their own goals.
3. Checks activities achieved against standards.	3. Discusses, evaluates, and modifies, if necessary, the employee-set goals.
4. Rewards or punishes based on activities.	4. Checks performance against results-oriented goals.
	5. Encourages employee satisfaction gained from achievement motivation.

Source: George R. Terry, *Supervisory Management.* Homewood, Ill.: Richard D. Irwin, 1974, p. 90.

because the employee is a passive participant in management endeavors.

Goals that outline a person's job responsibilities should reflect a high degree of agreement between a supervisor and employees. The results of "fuzzy" goals to the area of job content are reflected in Table 7-16.

Goals also serve as a means of evaluating the existence of two-way communication between managers and employees. The outcome of one-way communication reflects a disregard of employee input in setting organizational goals. The results are seen in Table 7-17.

TABLE 7-16
Comparative agreement between superior-subordinate pairs on basic areas of the subordinate's job. (Percentages based on study of 58 pairs.)

	Agreement on less than half the topics	Agreement on about half the topics	Agreement on more than half the topics
Job duties	15.0%	39.1%	45.9%
Obstacles in the way of subordinate's performance	68.2%	23.6%	8.1%

Source: N. R. Maier, L. R. Hoffan, J. J. Hoover, and W. A. Read, "Superior-Subordinate Communications in Management." American Management Association.

TABLE 7-17
Extent to which superiors and subordinates agree on aspects of communication between them

	% Top staff say about foremen	% Foremen say about themselves	% Foremen say about the men	% Men say about themselves
Feel very free to discuss important things about the job with superior	90	67	85	51
Always or nearly always tell subordinates in advance about changes which will affect them or their work	100	63	92	47
Always or almost always get subordinates' ideas	70	52	73	16

Source: F. G. Mann, "A Study of Work Satisfactions as a Discrepancy Between Inferred Aspirations and Achievement." Survey Research Center, Ann Arbor, Michigan, 1953.

Goals may have a negative influence on morale when there is broad disagreement among all organizational entities as to what produces job satisfaction. These variances in employee and supervisory estimates are reflected in Table 7-18.

Goals may have a negative influence on morale when they are handed down by management in the form of written directives, policies, and procedures. Such statements set a general course of action for employees to follow but fail to match the needs of people with the needs of the organization. Effective goals are the product of exchanging ideas, be-

TABLE 7-18
What subordinates want in a job, compared with their superiors' estimates

	As men	As foremen		As general foremen	
	Rated the variables for themselves	Estimated men would rate the variables	Rated the variables for themselves	Estimated foremen would rate the variables	Rated the variables for themselves
Economic variables:					
Steady work and steady wages	61%	79%	62%	86%	52%
High wages	28	61	17	58	11
Pensions and other old-age-security benefits	13	17	12	29	15
Not having to work too hard	13	30	4	25	2
Human-satisfaction variables:					
Getting along well with the people I work with	36%	17%	39%	22%	43%
Getting along well with my supervisor	28	14	28	15	24
Good chance to turn out good-quality work	16	11	18	13	27
Good chance to do interesting work	22	12	38	14	43
Other variables:					
Good chance for promotion	25%	23%	42%	24%	47%
Good physical working conditions	21	19	18	4	11
Total	*	*	*	*	*
Number of cases	2,499	196	196	45	45

* Percentages total over 100 because they include three rankings for each person.

Source: R. L. Kahn, "Human Relationships on the Shop Floor," *Human Relations and Modern Management.* North-Holland Publishing Company, 1958.

liefs, and attitudes among managerial, supervisory, and operative personnel. A spirit of mutual cooperation will make implementing organizational goals an effective economic and social process. Likewise, goals can serve as a means of developing the existing talents of all personnel to a point of individual growth and participation.

Goals, when properly designed, give a clear sense of direction to all by making all organizational members, not just management, responsible for their accomplishment. Fuzziness, poor communication, and disagreements over the meaning of job satisfaction are reduced or eliminated.

Summary

Morale is an elusive concept to define but not to discuss as a managerial philosophy. As a philosophy, it reflects the dignity of the individual through a leadership style and provides for the accomplishment of individual and group goals. Poor morale is often blamed on worker indifference, external influences, or managerial directives. However, an enlightened supervisor will respond to the challenge of building positive morale instead of relinquishing the task to the union, to the employee, or to other managerial personnel. Furthermore, supervisors will recognize that their personal source of job satisfaction may or may not be the same as that of the employees working in the same organization.

The measurement of morale within an organization is also elusive because it is nonquantitative. Also, the factors used as indicators are often misinterpreted by managerial personnel. One measurement of poor morale is high employee turnover, which increases the operating cost of the firm. Morale surveys are designed to identify how employees feel about their job. To carry out morale surveys in an efficient and effective manner requires advanced managerial planning as well as safeguards to prevent the misuse by organizational entities. The Xerox study showed there is a relationship between leadership styles and employee satisfaction. A challenge from the Xerox study for management is to structure positions so that employees can advance and receive recognition on the job.

A study by Flowers and Hughes dealt with the relationship between job satisfaction and environmental factors for four types of employees. Also examined were motivational, maintenance, and external reasons for people staying with a firm. Another factor influencing morale is the various skill levels at which people work in an organization. A related variable affecting morale is that of work values inside a firm. This research helps to increase our understanding of the complexity of positive morale and identifies the variables that make its continued presence a challenge to management.

The relationship of productivity to morale has not been proved in all behavioral research. The work of Davis, Herzberg, Likert, and Soliman could indicate that in the long run high morale is essential to the continual effective operation of a firm. The issue is not whether a relationship exists between productivity and morale, but whether a managerial philosophy can be developed that recognizes the impact of individual, supervisory, and organizational attitudes on employee productivity. Morale is not the result of a human relations campaign, manipulation, or monetary rewards.

Goals are vital to the success of an organization. However, their effectiveness depends on management's ability to define them clearly, to outline definite results, and to identify the resources needed to accomplish the organizational tasks. Goals in a participative climate serve as an avenue for enhancing employee development, self-direction, and employee satisfaction. Goals can eliminate controversy over job content, can increase two-way communication, and can create agreement on the causes of job satisfaction. Morale equals the attitude toward work, environment, management style, and enterprise objectives.

Discussion Questions

1. *Compare the morale as shown on a football team to that in a business enterprise.*
2. *Discuss the statement "Positive morale is a continuous process that cannot be purchased with money or bought with favors."*
3. *What are some factors that contribute to high morale?*
4. *If you were manager of a firm, what are some of the factors that you would want to examine in an attempt to measure morale in your organization?*
5. *What are some of the benefits that may result from the use of morale surveys? What are some of the pitfalls?*
6. *According to the research of Flowers and Hughes, do you consider yourself a turn-on, turn-off, or turnover?*
7. *Based on Meyers's adaptation of Graves's theory in Table 7-11, describe your own working level at the present time.*
8. *What effects might these values for working have on attempts to improve morale?*
9. *In what ways is setting goals important to the maintenance of the positive aspects of morale? Is it possible for goals to have a negative influence?*

Chapter Case 7

You have several jobs that you need to fill. According to values for working, which level would you consider appropriate for the following jobs.

Research scientist	Marketing specialist	Secretary
Accountant	Food checker	Warehouseperson
Salesperson	Female assembler	File clerk
Security guard	Draftsman	Truck driver

Notes

1. Theo Haimann and William G. Scott. *Management in the Modern Organization*. Boston: Houghton Mifflin, 1974, p. 359.
2. Theo Haimann and Raymond L. Hilgert. *Supervision: Concepts and Practices of Management*. Cincinnati: South-Western, 1972, p. 311.
3. William A. Boothe. "Job Satisfaction," an original study of Xerox field managers, December 19, 1967.
4. Thomas M. Rohan. "Who's Worth What Around Here?" *Industry Week*, November 6, 1972, p. 29.
5. Ibid., p. 32.
6. Ibid.
7. Keith Davis. *Human Behavior at Work*. New York: McGraw-Hill, 1972, p. 69.
8. Ibid., p. 73.
9. Ibid., pp. 73–74.
10. Boothe, op. cit., pp. 14–15.
11. Vincent S. Flowers and Charles L. Hughes. "Why Employees Stay," *Harvard Business Review*, July–August 1973, p. 51.
12. Ibid., p. 53.
13. Ibid., p. 55.
14. Ibid., p. 56.
15. Haimann and Scott, op. cit., pp. 361–362.
16. Arnold S. Tannenbaum. *Social Psychology of the Work Organization*. Belmont, Calif.: Brooks/Cole, 1966, p. 73.
17. Ibid., p. 74.
18. Hanafi M. Soliman. "Making the Formal Organization More Productive," *Industry Week*, July 19, 1972, pp. 43–45.
19. George R. Terry. *Supervisory Management*. Homewood, Ill.: Irwin, 1974, pp. 82–83.

CUSTOM FURNITURE CASE: DESIGN VS. SALES

There have always been some problems between the salespeople and the designers at Custom Furniture. The designers consider themselves to be professionals. They all have college degrees and belong to professional organizations such as the National Association of Interior Designers. They consider the sales personnel as people to figure prices, see that proposals are prepared, and take care of any problems that may arise with delivery and installation.

Everyone in the sales department considers the designers a necessary evil, temperamental and much less interested in profits than in their own reputations. Most salespeople realize but will not admit that the designers actually do much of the selling for them. Sales personnel are paid on a commission on sales; designers receive a salary.

Lately some of the designers have been taking long lunch hours and leaving early, saying that they are going to go by the Decorative Center, where many manufacturers have showrooms. Although these visits are part of their duties, John Taylor believes the visits are excessive. He remembers when he himself used this excuse to leave early on a Friday afternoon when he was designer.

One day he suggests to Cecil Mooney that they have lunch together. This is the way the luncheon progresses:

Cecil: "Wow, this restaurant is certainly a relief from the greasy spoons that we end up in when I am out with one of the sales force."

John: "Funny you'd say that. It leads right into something I've been wanting to talk to you about."

Cecil: "Yes, what is that?"

John: "I've been noticing lately that you and the other designers have been extending your lunch period quite frequently."

Cecil: "John, we figure what is good for one employee is good for the others."

John: "What do you mean by that remark?"

Cecil: "No one makes the salespeople account for their time. They take as long as they want for lunch and leave early every afternoon."

John: "You should realize that is a whole different ball of wax."

Cecil: "You mean that because they are paid a commission, they don't have to keep any regular hours? There are some who think the designers should be receiving some of that commission money. Anyhow, we do most of the work and I'd like to see some of those people sell anything without our selection of furnishings, colors, and well, really the whole package. All they have to do is take our work, put prices on the individual items, get a proposal typed, and take it to the customer. The presentation that we prepare does most of the work for them."

John: "I knew there was some animosity between you and them, but I didn't realize that there were such strong feelings."

Cecil: "Well, I can tell you that there are, and morale is pretty low in my department. None of the designers has had a raise in a year. And when business is good, the salespeople automatically make more money. It just isn't fair."

John: "Cecil, I think that you are underestimating the worth of our sales force. It is very difficult these days to get people to spend money and you must admit that your people do not pay much attention to price when you are planning a job. Many times the salespeople have long lunches with clients, trying to make friends with them. And as for leaving early, it is difficult to do much selling after four o'clock when people are trying to wind up the day and get home themselves."

Cecil: "I might have known that you would take their side."

John: "I don't believe you should make that accusation. And the fact remains that you and your people were hired to put in an eight-hour day."

John observed the habits of the designers for the next couple of weeks and there was no improvement in their observing of rules concerning hours and John notices many arguments taking place in the design department between the salespeople and the designers. There have been some complaints from sales that design is taking too much time on jobs and that a few orders have been lost because the customers would not wait for their presentations.

1. How do you feel about John's attempts to excuse the salespeople?
2. Is Cecil correct in his estimate of the situation?
3. What action should John take to clear up this problem and see to it that no more orders are lost because of delays?

MOTIVATION

8

I certainly agree that what we need is a little more motivation and a lot less goldbricking.

For the full story, turn to the case on page 246.

GENERAL PURPOSES
OF CHAPTER 8

1. To analyze the role of motivation in work
2. To examine the role of money as a motivator
3. To distinguish between manipulation and motivation
4. To look at the role of individual differences among people
5. To identify some defense mechanisms used by individuals to combat frustration
6. To investigate the relationship of subordinates to authority figures

LEARNING OBJECTIVES

1. To name three traits that a study of motivation assumes to be present in any organized endeavor
2. To list and briefly describe four views of the basic motives of mankind
3. To define the equity theory of wages
4. To name three deceptive qualities of human traits
5. To define manipulation and give three examples of its use in a work setting
6. To give the names of and define nine defense mechanisms used by individuals to protect themselves and to combat frustration
7. To differentiate between impulsive subordinate and compulsive subordinate
8. To define masochistic behavior and distinguish it from withdrawn patterns
9. To name three factors upon which the motivation of a manager is dependent

Asociety dominated by organizations affords an excellent opportunity to analyze the role of motivation in work. People spend over half of their waking hours in work organizations, a fact that shows the need to study motivation and its relationship to the behavior of individuals in society. Over the years we have used many motivational techniques to direct the efforts of people in all types of organized endeavors. However, we have used many of the motivational tools blindly because of our failure to recognize different educational, ethnic, and socioeconomic backgrounds. Moreover, to have effective organizations we must know how to encourage effective individual performance. The complexity of motivation is reflected in personal differences, but the size, shape, task, and functions of diverse enterprises increases the complexity of motivational tools and their implementation in the world of work.

A study of motivation assumes the presence of at least three traits in any organized endeavor. One trait is the financial ability to attract, retain, and reward the organization's members. This trait implies the ability to use the available financial assets effectively. Also, the use of money influences employee motivation, either positively or negatively. A second trait is the presence of a hierarchy of relationships to carry out the goals of the organization. This trait implies a supervisor-subordinate relationship, as well as varying degrees of status and power, that influences motivation in work. A third trait is the assignment of an individual task that is essential to the completion of various mangerial functions. This trait implies the need to bring together a broad diversity of talents to accomplish the organization's goals.[1]

Just as organizations differ in what they can do to influence motivation, people differ in what motivates them to work. People work hard because of companionship, money, and/or a pay-incentive system that rewards their work behavior positively. The challenge to management is to recognize and understand the impact of various motivational systems on individual and group behavior within an organized work endeavor. The success or failure of motivation rests not on the technique itself but on management's ability to match the needs of people with appropriate incentives.

Needs

As individuals, we spend a great deal of energy to reach a desired goal, to satisfy a given need, or to complete a given task. This effort tends to reflect physical, psychological, and social needs that enhance our own personal well-being. A variety of individual backgrounds, hopes, ambitions, and psychological makeups determines the desires of a person and how she or he hopes to satisfy these desires.[2]

The needs of people are reflected in four views of the basic human motives. The sociological view states that human behavior is the result of people and events in their social sphere. The values and customs of a society determine the actions of people in that society. The biological view states that human actions are determined by physical and biological needs and drives. The physical needs of people become the motivation for the actions of people in society. The psychoanalytic view states that our motives are mostly unconscious, hidden under the surface. Such a view believes that motivators of human action are unknown to conscious reasoning. The behaviorist view is result oriented. It states that human actions are the result of various inputs over time. A more recent approach is the humanistic theory, which gives credit to biological drives but also honors sociological causes. Also, the humanistic theory recognizes the place of behaviorist stimuli and psychoanalytic stimuli in motivating human behavior. Accepting the humanistic theory will cause a manager to view the motivation of people in the world of work as a complex, complicated, and multifaceted phenomenon.[3]

From this brief look at needs, it is apparent that a simple definition fails to reflect the varying degree of what needs are, what satisfies a need, and whose need takes priority. In an organized endeavor, these issues are answered through goal-directed activities, but such efforts require a personal identification of human needs with those of the formal organization. Managers face the challenge of satisfying multiple needs in a socioeconomic environment by building a positive relationship between human, social, economic, and organizational needs.

Money as Motivator

Money is an important incentive in society because it represents the power to save or the power to spend. Money buys things that people value, thus providing a psychological lift through the acquisition of economic goods. A survey by Gwin, Veroff, and Feld in 1960 revealed:

Economic and material matters figure in the sense of happiness and unhappiness which Americans experience. Contrary to the tendency of the romantic to depreciate the importance of money for happiness, people attach primary importance to economic and material considerations as they think about happiness and unhappiness. Happiness is expressed in terms of having "enough" money; being free from debt; having a nice home. Similarly the complaints refer to such things as debts, bills, and inadequate housing.[4]

The elusiveness of permanent monetary satisfaction is reflected in the previous statement. Also, the way we exchange in rapid succession cars, houses, recreational interests, and family ties further illustrates the elusiveness of permanent monetary satisfaction. In the film *Future Shock* a little girl goes into a toy store and trades her doll for a new one. She receives a $1 bill for her old doll and walks out of the store with a brand new doll. Such instant exchange and gratification further explodes the view of human beings as only economic entities. Money in the short run provides satisfaction, but in the long run people tend to seek higher goals to meet their complex innate needs. The inability of money to provide long-term satisfaction is reflected in Figure 8-1, which shows the relationship between absenteeism and satisfaction with wages for white-collar workers.

Monetary compensation usually involves wages, salaries, and fringe benefits in the form of insurance, retirement, and similar employee benefits. To an organization, monetary compensation reflects a firm's ability to attract and to hold the personnel necessary to accomplish the tasks of the enterprise. Pay increases, if given in small increments, tend to discourage employee satisfaction. As labor costs increase as a percentage of all costs, management should review the effectiveness of monetary compensation in meeting financial, social, and achievement needs of employees. Monetary rewards are significant to the extent that the expenditure of human effort does not exceed the anticipated level of satisfaction desired by the employee.[5]

David McClelland, in his research on achievement motivation, concluded that people with a low desire for achievement seek monetary rewards, whereas people with high achievement drives use monetary rewards as a maintenance factor. Moreover, monetary incentives are seen as carriers of social values to achievement-driven workers. A survey of Israeli executives and union leaders showed that 86 percent of union

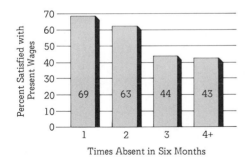

Figure 8-1
Relationship between absenteeism and satisfaction with wages. Source: F. C. Mann and H. J. Baumgartel, "Relationship Between Absenteeism and Satisfaction with Wages," *Absences and Employee Attitudes in an Electric Power Company.* Copyright © 1952 by the University of Michigan. Published by the Institute for Social Research, the University of Michigan.

leaders and 64 percent of executives believed that extra pay for extra work is the best way to get more output from workers.[6]

It is clear that money has reward value in a purely economic sense and that people expect to be paid for the contributions they make to achieve the organization's goals. One view of wages is embodied in the expectancy theory, which states that people expect certain outcomes from their behavior and will work to achieve a desired outcome. Such research tends to associate pay with such motives as security, psychological gratification, status, esteem, and recognition. For job performance to be affected by pay policies, good performance must be associated with high pay. Likewise, an employee must associate the achievement of high performance with personal efforts.

A second theory of wages is the equity theory. The issue is to maximize the rate of pay as well as receive a fair rate of return for the contribution to the firm. This evaluation reflects a comparison between an employee's input and pay received in relation to other individuals

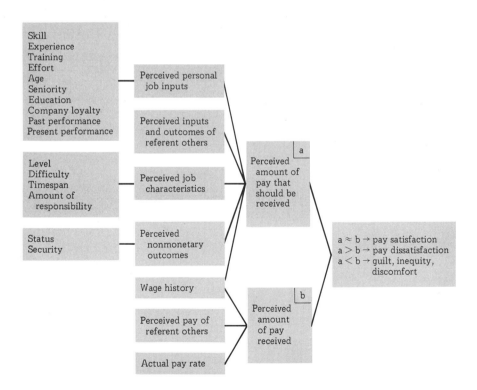

Figure 8-2
Model of the determinants of pay satisfaction. Source: E. E. Lawler, *Pay and Organizational Effectiveness,* New York: McGraw-Hill, 1971, p. 215. Copyright 1971 by McGraw-Hill. Used by permission of McGraw-Hill Book Company.

doing similar work. This perception of pay relates directly to the degree of satisfaction a person receives from the completion of an assigned task.[7] Figure 8-2 reflects the elements that affect a person's perception of wages in terms of producing job satisfaction.

The significance of pay in determining job satisfaction is reflected in a survey of 300 manual workers. In this survey, pay was ranked sixth below steady employment, working conditions, fair adjustment of grievances, safety insurance, and pensions. A similar study of 150 office workers placed pay as second and steady work as first in determining job satisfaction.[8] Table 8-1 contrasts the results of these two surveys.

The results of each survey could alter significantly the motivational tools management would use to motivate these two diverse work groups. To be effective a motivational system has to consider the varied interests of each group. Such a system implies that many universal tools of motivation must be shelved for a custom approach to meet a specific need. Management has often failed to reflect the human, organizational, and managerial needs of the firm. Programs that have worked for one firm are not always the answer to another firm's motivational problems. For example, the use of participative management requires an open environment of mutual trust among managers, supervisors, and employees. However, participative management will not work unless employees are trained to be self-motivated, self-directed, and responsible for their individual assignments. Such a managerial style alters

TABLE 8-1
Average ranking of relative importance assigned to job factors by two different groups of workers

Job factors	300 manual workers	150 office workers
Steady employment	1	2 (*tie*)
Working conditions	2	5
Fair adjustment of grievances	3	6 (*tie*)
Safety	4	11 (*tie*)
Insurance systems and pensions	5	10
Amount of pay	6	2 (*tie*)
Type of man in charge	7	6 (*tie*)
Chance for promotion	8	1
Medical and dental services	9	13
Method of pay	10	14
Chance to show initiative	11	4
Voice or share in management	12	8
Hours of work	13	9
Employee stock subscription	14	11 (*tie*)

Source: William E. Parker, Robert W. Kleemeier, and Beyer W. Parker, *Front Line Leadership,* New York: McGraw-Hill, 1969, p. 98. After Table 9, (p. 198) in *Zest for Work* by Rexford Hersey (Harper & Row, 1955).

traditional relationships, which may be disturbing to a manager who is accustomed to an authoritative managerial style. Emloyees cannot implement a motivational system unless they are trained in advance concerning what is expected of them.

Likewise, monetary systems of pay must reflect the specific needs of a firm to compensate employees adequately for the contributions they make to the firm's success. Many firms striving to provide a competitive system of monetary incentives have overlooked the financial and managerial limitations of their own enterprise. Such a drastic error inflates wage and salary costs without motivating personnel to perform at a higher level of efficiency. For example, wage settlements in 1974 averaged 11.2 percent, and there was no growth in employee productivity. An excellent example of this phenomenon is the settlement of the coal strike in 1974, which produced the largest settlement ever in the eighty-four-year history of negotiations in the industry.

Establishing a cause-and-effect relationship between methods of compensation and employee behavior is a constant challenge to all managers. Base pay is used to bring personnel into the organization as well as to reward employees for long-term service. Variable pay has been used to reward higher levels of performance for individuals performing the same job, but this has been weakened by collective bargaining agreements, government regulation, and managerial failure to reward superior performance. Supplementary pay provides tangible and intangible benefits, such as pensions, insurance, sick leave, and recreational programs.[9]

An excellent example of the use of base, variable, and supplementary pay is the General Motors program of compensation. In 1973, the average employee's base pay was $15,000. Total compensation averaged $18,000 with fringe benefits. The collective bargaining agreement of 1973 raised the total average pay in 1975 to over $20,000. If pay motivates workers, then why were over 3 million national grievances filed in the 1970 national collective bargaining negotiations? If pay motivates workers, then how do we explain the sixty-seven-day company-wide strike in 1970 and the protracted walkout at the Lordstown and Norwood, Ohio, assembly plants in 1972?

Similar complaints are found among white-collar workers and middle managers. Nor is dissatisfaction absent from the executive suite. For example, John Z. DeLorean, a $500,000 a year vice-president, left GM in 1973 to operate a Cadillac dealership and serve as president of the National Alliance of Businessmen. The inability of pay alone to motivate people was reflected in a turnover of 44,000 out of 100,000 workers at Chrysler in 1969.

General Motors, having recognized the need to use more than just "the carrot" to motivate personnel, has started a worker's involvement program at the Lakewood, Georgia, plant. GM's Fremont, California plant has implemented an orientation program for 750 salaried personnel to focus on worker motivation. A related program at Fremont is "planned time off," which gives an employee a day off from Tuesday through Thursday with two days advance notice. A 1969 absenteeism level of 9.4 percent was reduced to 5.4 percent in 1973.[10]

General Motors, with 808,000 employees, is not alone in placing too much reliance on a compensation program to produce committed, motivated, and creative assemblers, supervisors, managers, and corporate executives. As participants in the American economic experience, we have created similar programs in government, education, and related business enterprises. Yet these tremendous strides in economic rewards have not produced a simlar increase in productivity, product quality, or employee commitment. For example, Cadillac called back 324,000 of its 1974 cars because of one defective steering mechanism. Why was this defect not identified before January of 1975?

Uniroyal, in building a new plant in Kennett, Missouri, implemented a 9.9 managerial style to direct the efforts of all employees. After three years, the plant operated at 120 percent of its projected capacity with a 1.7 percent rate of absenteeism plant-wide. Uniroyal pays all employees a salary, has machine operators participate in the decision-making process, and places the responsibility for product quality on individual machine operators. After an initial orientation session, all operators are expected to function with no direct supervision, as well as to meet quality standards with reduced levels of in-process inspection. To further increase employee motivation, the company does not provide traditional status symbols such as executive parking areas, rest rooms, or a caste system of benefits. Although this approach has significantly increased the commitment of all personnel, there have been workers fired for falsely reporting output as well as for excessive absences. However, the success of this program has encouraged management to try a similar approach at the Red Oak and Maryville plants. Uniroyal altered its method of compensation to machine operators by paying salaries, but unlike many firms it went on to change its managerial style to increase employee commitment, responsibility, and participation in accomplishing the success of the Kennett plant.[11]

In reviewing the relationship of money to motivation, we have discussed the elusiveness of monetary compensation, the relationship of achievement motives to compensation, the impact of company compensation programs, the role of pay in producing job satisfaction, and the danger of overextending capital resources by adopting the wrong system of compensation. In our review of several compensation programs we stressed that pay alone will not motivate personnel to a higher level of performance. However, pay coupled with an altered managerial philosophy will be more likely to produce positive results, as shown in the Uniroyal experience.

To close our review of monetary rewards in relation to productivity on a positive note, let us look at some general guidelines that should enhance the effectiveness of compensation programs. Burt K. Scanlan has produced an excellent set of guidelines to measure the effectiveness of a wage payment system.

1. The general level of wage for any given type of labor must be kept consistent with what others are paying.
2. If dissatisfaction is to be prevented and harmony maintained, it should provide for periodic lump-sum adjustment to prevent discrepancies between the newly hired and those who joined the organization at an earlier point in time.
3. If wages are to act as a motivator to any degree at all, then any increases which are gven beyond some very minimum level must in fact, not just in theory, be based on merit.
4. Also, if the wage system is to have some motivational value, and not cause dissatisfaction, the dollar differential between what the average versus the superior performance gets must be significant.
5. If wages are to be used to induce higher-level performance, the amount offered in terms of increases must also be significant.
6. Where the wage level is already relatively high, as would typically be the case with professional employees, the real issue or crux to motivation may well be in the areas of job design or managerial leadership, not wages.
7. There is a need for a great deal more upward communication with respect to wages.
8. As long as industry is concerned about motivating people to perform to the full level of their capability and since wages can and do play a role in this process, perhaps a different approach than that historically used is needed.[12]

Traits

Traits are "attitude bench marks" that give each person a distinct identity. The trait of affiliation is reflected in the human desire to have social contact with others. Power traits are distinguished by a person's being either a leader or a follower in various social endeavors. Curiosity traits reveal the human need to seek answers to the new and unknown. Traits pertaining to security stress the human determination to seek to satisfy important needs, thus avoiding anxiety caused by negative economic, social, and psychological factors. Emotions reflect a variety of human traits because of the different ways we as individuals express our emotions. All these traits give people a distinct profile that becomes an identification mark in their associations with others.[13]

Traits are not limited to people; organizations display traits in setting up operating policies and procedures. A motivational checklist provides

172

a way to judge the success of a firm in responding to the personality traits exhibited by people and organizations.

Motivation Checklist

1. Do I try to provide a work atmosphere that is open and encourage new ideas?
2. Have I taken the time to study each job situation and tried to see if each member of my work team is matched to a job consistent with his ability and growth potential?
3. Have I tried to insure that each worker feels a part of the work team?
4. Am I careful to insure that I play no favorites in my supervisory capacity?
5. Where possible do I encourage flexibility so that the worker may become more nearly matched to his ability?
6. Do I attempt to have the physical surroundings both on the job and at break time as pleasant as possible?
7. Am I as highly motivated toward top job performance as I should be?
8. Have I taken the time to make certain that every worker feels that he is an important part of the work team?
9. Have I tried to see to it that every worker has been encouraged and given every opportunity for personal success?
10. To the extent possible, do I involve each worker in the decision-making process?[14]

Although this checklist can increase organizational success in identifying and meeting the issues of human traits on organizational resources, it overlooks three deceptive human qualities. First, individuals tend to mask their real desires by using objects, actions, money, or relationships to reflect intangible motives such as prestige or achievement. As a result management uses superficial traits to guide its thinking in striving to motivate personnel to action. However, the real issue does not surface in influencing managerial actions. Symptoms of hidden motives are turnover, absences, and systematic wage demands. A second deceptive aspect of traits is the tendency of people to substitute an immediate obtainable goal, such as a raise or promotion, to satisfy an intangible need such as accomplishment. For example, an individual who is bored with a job because it has no challenge may seek to overcome this frustration by demanding an exorbitant raise or a lavish fringe benefit package, or he or she may develop a negative psychological association with the need of the organization. A third deceptive aspect is the concept of maturation of human traits over time. For example, the traits that influence younger employees' actions are not the traits of older employees. The danger of most motivational systems is the belief of universality that ignores the fact that all age levels do not possess the same traits.[15]

Manipulation

Manipulation is the managerial art of fraudulently directing the activities of personnel in an organization. In the past, many firms have used human relations gimmicks to obtain the cooperation of employees. One such technique is to fake a personal interest in people while failing to have genuine concern for the problems of subordinates. A similar manipulative technique is to provide information to personnel on company activities in company publications. Like the company unions of the past, such publications tend to be suspect because of questionable contents, slanted articles, and overemphasis on issues unrelated to the needs of all employees. Another gimmick used is the status symbol, which is designed to give the employee a feeling of importance but in reality has little or no relation to the job performed. For example, to classify a dishwasher as a sanitary engineer does not increase the importance of the job to other personnel. Campaigns to obtain employees' viewpoints are often meaningless because managerial actions fail to implement meaningful changes in the working climate of many firms. Listening without action is a form of manipulation prevalent in many enterprises today. A final example of manipulative techniques is the game of employee participation. Such participation is real to the extent that it increases employee responsibility, employee decision making on real issues, and employee direction in shaping the structure and technology of the organization.[16] As managers, we recognize the presence of these manipulative techniques. More enlightened managers are striving to take a true interest in people by using two-way communication between managers and personnel. Such endeavors increase job value through redesign rather than through superficial status symbols. A nonmanipulative approach uses employees' ideas to meet changing environmental concerns and makes employee participation a reality in shaping organizational relationships.

Louis Fried, in an article entitled "Games Managers Play," has provided an excellent outline of the way managers manipulate an organization to their personal advantage. The techniques are as follows:

1. The *"stone tablets"* policy—assumes policy decisions should not be changed to meet new circumstances. Such an attitude provides a sense of security as well as allowing a person to evade accountability for personal behavior.
2. The *"crash"* program—a manager deliberately avoids action to create a crisis situation. Using this false crisis, the manager seeks to become a hero by doing the task to cover up previous negligence or

error. Such actions increase operating costs and reduce morale through internal managerial confrontations.

3. *"Hot Potato"*—is the game of passing the buck as well as placing the blame for failure on the other managers. Such actions place personal advancement first over the well-being of the organization.

4. *"Consensus"*— surveys the views of a select group to gain a consensus answer on an issue. Such actions are an attempt to avoid personal responsibility by stating decisions in terms of a group statement.

5. *"The delayed reaction decision"*—is the game of forcing a subordinate to act because of inaction by a supervisor. The result is to adopt positive policies and to blame the subordinate for failures. Such actions protect an inept manager while allowing an ambitious person to exercise undue influence on company operating procedures.

6. *"Musical Chairs"*—an executive ploy used to blame poor organizational performance on realignment of supervisory responsibilities. Such actions gain time but do not solve immediate problems. Also, such actions produce a high state of supervisory anxiety due to constantly changing job assignments.[17]

All these forms of managerial maniuplation are costly, unproductive, and produce undesirable attitudes in terms of intraorganizational relationships. Manipulation has no place with an enlightened managerial style of mutual respect, trust, and cooperation.

Individual Differences

Heredity and environment, along with learning experiences, unite to produce a personality. Personality is

the way a man looks and talks and thinks and feels, the things he likes and the things he hates, his abilities and interests, his hopes and desires, the way he wears his hat or whistles a tune or throws a ball. . . . The fact that a man is fat is as much a part of his personality as the fact that he has a deep voice. If his greatest desire is to play big-league baseball, that's as much a part of his personality as his politics. If he's always suffering from headaches, if he loves sweet, rich desserts, if he hates his mother-in-law—these things are also his personality. Personality simply means the total person. . . .[18]

Personality and emotions are reflected in complexes that affect individual and organizational behavior. A complex is composed of interrelated feelings, memories, impulses, and emotionally charged ideas. The "self" complex expresses emotions about oneself. It is made up of feelings of anger, pride, fear, amusement, disgust, and self-assertion. The "sex" complex expresses feelings of love, affection, tenderness, mating instincts, and parental impulses. The "herd" complex exhibits feelings of loneliness, sympathy, trust, attachment, imitation, and appeal. These feelings unite an individual with society. As individuals we express these emotions in our dealings with people, organizations, and ideas in life. The variety of complexes and the emotions associated with each complex illustrates the complexity of understanding, recognizing, and motivating individuals in the world of work.

Although human beings are individuals in many respects, they exhibit common traits. For example, they possess an intellect that determines cause-and-effect relationships as well as adapts to changing environmental influences. They can set an objective and determine how to obtain the result desired. They can design tools to increase productivity in making, selling, and consuming goods. As discussed in Chapter 5, they can communicate ideas, feelings, and strategies in the oral and written word. As a final trait, they can pass present knowledge to future generations.

To use these common traits as building blocks in motivating individuals requires an understanding of how people learn. Managers should reinforce proper responses through rewards that relate to individual aspirations. They should show the results of a response and alter improper work procedures through coaching and additional guidance. Training activities need to be related to individual and organizational needs. Managers should space learning activities to provide time for assimilation of ideas as well as to receive feedback as to what the trainee has gained from all training activities.[19]

To identify individual differences requires a review of personnel records, observation on the job, and a review of social settings. Personnel records provide a historical review of employment in terms of length of service, absenteeism, and levels of satisfactory performance. To use a person effectively requires a review of that person's training and educational history. This helps determine the strengths of personnel in light of organizational manpower requirements. Personnel records show health trends that might affect the assignment of a person to a particular job.

On-the-job observation can also increase a supervisor's understanding of the personnel under supervision. For example, the relationship of a worker to other workers is exhibited in group and individual contacts at work. How well does the employee relate to other people? A related benefit of observation is the direct feedback concerning the speed with which a person completes an assigned task and the level of work quality. A vital area for understanding is the attitude of employees toward authority. The way a supervisor uses authority will increase employee cooperation or in negative cases will increase supervisor-employee conflicts. At the same time, employees must adhere to the decision-making power of management to provide a consistency of direction to ensure

TABLE 8-2

Personnel records	Job observation	Social settings
1. Past employment	1. Worker relationship	1. Family relationships
2. Training and education	2. Speed of work	2. Particular skills
3. Health record	3. Job quality	3. Total social interaction
4. Family pattern	4. Attitude toward authority	
	5. Creative ideas	

Source: Victor B. Ficker, *Effective Supervision.* Columbus, Ohio: Charles E. Merrill, 1975, p. 118.

the continued profitability of the enterprise. On-the-job observation provides an avenue for encouraging creativity by providing avenues for employees to express their ideas on ways to improve operating procedures. The need for creative ideas is critical to the continued growth of a vibrant, innovative, and creative enterprise.

In our organized industrial setting, the social setting of each employee is regarded as a private concern unrelated to the world of work. However, employees bring their social values to work and exhibit them in performing their assigned tasks. A supervisor must balance an interest in the personal life of employees to avoid the appearance of meddling, indifference, or hostility.[20] Table 8-2 summarizes several techniques to use in observing individual differences.

In summary, several key points are suggested for effectively understanding individual personalities.

1. Personality is a product of heredity, environment, and learning experiences in life.
2. Complexes are an interrelated system of charged emotional ideas.
3. Humans possess several common traits such as intellect, goal setting, tool design, and communication skills.
4. Training activities should use these common traits to enhance the learning experiences of personnel in terms of motivation and supervisory effectiveness.
5. Observing individual differences through personnel records, job observation, and social contacts enhances a supervisor's ability to utilize all personnel in relation to human and organizational aspirations.

Defense Mechanisms

Defense mechanisms are employed by individuals to protect themselves. They are an excellent example of the individuality of people and prove a challenge to managers. Some of the defense mechanisms that people project are

1. *Identification*—the trend of adopting the behavior of the group, the boss, or the society at large. Unions and management stereotype members of respective groups.
2. *Projection*—the trend of seeing in other people the undesirable traits of ourselves. Distrust of people leads to a conclusion that the firm cannot be trusted.
3. *Compensation*—the trend to accept a secondary goal to gain satisfaction. Employees dislike their job environment but demand excessive wage and fringe benefits to gain satisfaction.
4. *Overcompensation*—the trend to use earlier achievements to cover current failures. This is an application of the "Peter principle" of being effective at one managerial level but ineffective at a higher managerial level, thus using past achievements to hide present weaknesses.
5. *Fantasy*—the trend to escape reality by dreaming of imagined successes. A production worker carrying out a routine task may dream of a promotion, future retirement, etc. to relieve the monotony of the job.
6. *Regression*—the trend of retreating from responsibility. Refusal to take a promotion or refusal to assume more responsibility for personal actions are cases in point.
7. *Denial*—the trend of refusing to accept the reality of a situation. Blaming others for not receiving a promotion when the person refuses to gain the skills essential for promotion is a form of denial.
8. *Starting rumors*—the trend to enhance the ego of a person or group. In slow economic times rumors of layoffs seek to hide feelings of insecurity.
9. *Rationalization*—the trend to justify actions by placing the blame for results on other people. A salesman fails to meet his monthly quota and blames the failure on production, delivery, or his boss's lack of support rather than on his own weaknesses such as laziness or lack of attention of customer demands.[21]

To motivate people, supervisors must understand defense mechanisms as expressed by groups and individuals. Such an understanding prevents rash action and enhances the supervisor's ability to deal with personality differences at work.

Individual differences are further reflected in the development of the human personality and add new dimensions to a manager's desire to motivate people to achieve a common goal. Consequently, all enterprises seek to achieve their objectives, maintain internal stability, and adapt to their external environment. To identify the motivational problems of people employed in an enterprise requires an awareness of the demands people make upon the formal organization. These demands by people result from several basic development trends expressed by a large majority of the population in a given place of employment. It is assumed that human beings in our culture exhibit the following development trends:

1. People tend to move from a passive state as infants to an active state as adults. For example, people become more self-determined in achieving a given objective.
2. People tend to move from dependence on others to a state of relative independence as adults. Economic security becomes a matter of personal action instead of reliance on others.
3. Behavior patterns become broader, complex, and varied in our relationships with people. A child deals with family members but adults deal with a wide range of human personalities.
4. Interest in events becomes a challenge to examine, to analyze, and to interpret the impact of events in adult experiences. People no longer accept human behavior at face value but seek to identify cause-and-effect relationships.
5. People tend to move from a state of instant gratification as infants to a variety of foresight practices to secure their future. The acquisition of wealth, influence, position, and power becomes a matter of personal commitment, not family relationships.
6. People develop a position equal to their peers to supercede their peers as their life experiences continue over time. Children as adults become income producers, family heads, and leaders in their professions, thus reversing their role as subordinate members of a family or society.
7. People develop a feeling of self-worth and integrity. Identity as an infant is with the family unit but as an adult identity becomes a personal self-concept.[22]

The development trends noted previously comprise only one aspect of the total human personality. These development trends are a continuum based on new life experiences. Such new experiences shape and alter human personalities. Likewise, these trends assume that healthy personality growth will continue and that the growth of any individual in our culture may be described and measured. Cultural norms, individual limitations, and defense mechanisms prevent maximum expression of development trends. Finally, expression of such developmental trends requires a supervisor to separate superficial from genuine trends to measure accurately the motivational mode for a given human personality.

To the extent that employees are inclined to develop mature relationships, they will want to express their desires at the adult end of each specific developmental continuum. To obtain optimum personality expression requires the creation of careers that permit people to be active, to be independent, to have longer time perspectives, to occupy a high position, to have control over their environment, and to express many of their inner abilities.[23]

As managers, supervisors, and employees, we can expect people to act on the mature adult developmental level or we can expect them to act at a lesser degree of maturity. The point is that managerial policies, procedures, and actions set the direction for all human relationships. From a motivational view, the more mature perspective enhances the effectiveness of physical and human assets. This effectiveness is achieved at less cost in terms of money, materials, and human casualties than would be the case under a negative view of human maturity. Thus, developmental trends remain a basic property of the human personality.

Dynamics of Subordination

Successful motivation of subordinates is partly a result of identifying the subordinates' relationship to authority figures. For example, a potential source of conflict is an individual's desire to dominate authority figures as well as be dominated by these same authority figures. A similar source of conflict is an individual's desire to alter the environment or to react to stimulus in that environment. These individual traits of dominance, submission, activity, and passivity help to describe four types of subordinates found in many organizations.

1. The impulsive subordinate strives to dominate authority figures by active rebellion against symbols of authority. Such behavior leads to superior-subordinate conflict and in extreme cases results in the termination of the employee. On the other hand, a constructive rebel uses the urge to dominate as a way to change authority relationships to influence events as well as improve the working environment for all personnel. A destructive rebel uses the urge to dominate as a way to gain real or imagined victories over authority figures. Such actions produce internal conflicts and usually end in the removal of the subordinate from the organization.

2. The compulsive subordinate seeks to dominate authority figures through passive behavior. For example, a compulsive subordinate makes a decision but reverses his or her course of action because of a feeling of uncertainty. A similar example of compulsive behavior is that of indecisiveness. Such reverses in behavior reflect a desire to control authority figures, but this desire is overcome by feelings of guilt that produce hesitation, doubt, and rigidity as a defense against the wish to dominate others. The following example reflects a sense of doubt, attitude reversal, hidden aggression, and denial of responsibility.

Dr. Richard Dodds, a newly hired physics research worker in a company laboratory, entered the office of his superior, Dr. Blackman, and showed him a letter. This letter was from Professor Wilkin of another research institution, offering Dodds a position. Blackman read the letter.

Dodds: "What do you think of that?"

Blackman: "I knew it was coming. He asked me if it would be all right if he sent it. I told him to go ahead if he wanted to."

Dodds: "I didn't expect it, particularly after what you said to me last time. I'm really quite happy here. I don't want you to get the idea that I am thinking of leaving. But I thought I should go and visit him. I think he expects it, and I wanted to let you know that just because I was thinking of going down, that did not mean I was thinking of leaving here, unless, of course, he offers me something extraordinary."

Blackman: "Why are you telling me all this?"

Dodds: "I didn't want you hearing from somebody else that I was thinking of leaving here, because I was going for a visit to another institution. I really have no intention of leaving here, you know, unless he offers me something really extraordinary that I can't afford to turn down. I think I'll tell him that, that I am willing to look at his laboratory, but unless there is something unusual for me, I have no intention of leaving here."

Blackman: "It's up to you."

Dodds: "What do you think?"

Blackman: "Well, what? About what? You've got to make up your mind."

Dodds: "I don't consider this job too seriously. He is not offering anything really extraordinary. But I *am* interested in what he has to say, and I would like to look around his lab."

Blackman: "Sooner or later you are going to have to make up your mind where you want to work."

Dodds: "That depends on the offers, doesn't it?"

Blackman: "No, not really; a good man always gets offers. You get a good offer and you move, and, as soon as you have moved, you get other good offers. It would throw you into confusion to consider all the good offers you will receive. Tell me, isn't there a factor of how stable you want to be?"

Dodds: "But I'm not shopping around. I already told you that. He sent me this letter; I didn't ask him to. All I said was I think I should visit him, and to you that's shopping around."

Blackman: "Well, you may choose to set aside your commitment here if he offers you something better. All I am saying is that you will still be left with the question. You've got to stay some place, and where is that going to be?"

Dodds: (*after some discussion of how it would look if he changed jobs at this point*) "Look, I came in here, and I want to be honest with you, but you make me feel guilty, and I don't like that."

Blackman: "You are being honest as can be."

Dodds: "I didn't come in here to fight. I don't want to disturb you."

Blackman: "I'm not disturbed. If you think it is best for you to go somewhere else, that is OK with me."

Dodds: (*after another lengthy exchange about what he really wants and how his leaving would look to others*) "I don't understand you. . . . All I wanted was to show you this letter, and let you know what I was going to do. What should I have told you?"

Blackman: "That you had read the letter and felt that under the circumstances it was necessary for you to pay a visit to Wilkin, but that you were happy here and wanted to stay at least until you had got a job of work done."

Dodds: "I can't get over it. You think there isn't a place in the world I'd rather be than here in this lab. . . ."[24]

3. The masochist seeks to evoke aggressive actions from an authority figure by an active attempt to be controlled by an authority figure. A common example is deliberately performing below accepted levels of output in order to invite criticism. Such behavior attracts attention and invites control from others and removes any personal responsibility for one's actions. Such behavior is illustrated in quadrant C of Figure 8-3.

4. The withdrawn person exhibits a passive effort to turn all interests toward self. Such an attitude reflects distrust, noncommitment, and disinterest in organizational objectives. This individual will complete all routine tasks but contribute little in terms of creativity or innovative contributions to the enterprise. Passive-submissive behavior is often mistaken for loyalty or acceptance of the status quo.[25] The following case history describes a type of career adjustment similar to the withdrawn pattern.

In a current study of professional scientists and engineers in a research and development center, some colleagues and I discovered a type

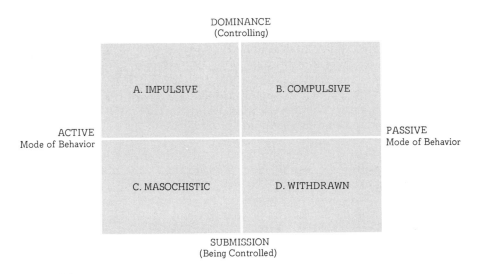

Figure 8-3
Patterns of subordinacy. Source: Abraham Zalexnik, "The Dynamics of Subordinacy," *Harvard Business Review*, May–June 1965, p. 122.

of career adjustment with features very similar to the withdrawal pattern described above. Over an interval of about two years during which we collected data, no individual of this type left the company. All other types of career adjustment showed a small, but readily apparent, turnover, including some individuals who left because they were dissatisfied with their work and others who left for better opportunities elsewhere.

The apathy evident in the absence of any turnover was supported by further evidence. There existed, for example, an interesting contradiction in response. On the one hand, the withdrawn type expressed personal disappointment in his career, a feeling of fatigue presumably neurotic in origin, some anxiety, and depression. On the other hand, individuals in this group tended to evaluate favorably their company, supervisor, and work colleagues. They expressed little desire to move elsewhere or to seek opportunities in other types of work.[26]

The four patterns of subordinacy are a result of personal inner motivation as well as the impact of external stimulus on personal attitudes, actions, and reactions. The four subordinacy patterns—impulsive subordinate, compulsive subordinate, masochistic subordinate, and withdrawn subordinate—are not fixed absolutes but reflect four processes in the development of supervisor-subordinate relationships. Again, the issue in motivating people is to relate motivational techniques directly to individual needs. To use the wrong approach in dealing with these four subordinates is to fulfill their individual needs for aggression, removal from responsibility, persecution, and nonalignment with organizational goals. All such actions are nonmotivating as well as self-destructive in terms of human and organizational assets. For a supervisor, motivation requires an awareness of (1) whom to motivate, (2) how to motivate, (3) when to motivate, and (4) when to use alternative motivational tools. Failure to deal with these issues is reflected in the following case history:

The president of a large, aggressive company came to me one time with an experience that had left him stunned. He had undertaken a program to select and train promising juniors for promotion to supervisory and staff jobs. He talked personally with many men and helped in the selection and preparation for promotion. The promotions were announced and followed almost immediately by a wildcat strike led by dissatisfied subordinates who felt they had been overlooked.

What shocked the president was the fact that his intention to open new opportunities, to help people design a future for themselves in his organization, had misfired. He wondered where he had miscalculated the motivations of subordinates. He was on the verge of disillusionment with the younger generation.[27]

Final suggestions in dealing with impulsive, compulsive, masochistic, and withdrawn personnel are presented in the following reflection on supervisor-subordinate relationships:

A supervisor and a subordinate employee should have a clear understanding on work issues and areas of personal conflict. Such an understanding implies a knowledge of where each person stands as well as a tentative view of what each person would like to see happen in the future. Using this technique helps to build a positive working relationship between supervisors and subordinates.

A supervisor should realize that his or her actions evoke a response from subordinates that is either positive, neutral, or negative. For example, a compulsive doubter evokes doubt and guilt in others. This subordinacy requires a firm and decisive stance to remove doubt as a motivational factor.

Likewise, the masochistic subordinate seeks punishment as a motivational factor. This type of subordinacy requires a supervisor to use earned rewards or nonpunishing actions to alter such negative behavior. Impulsive behavior in subordinates requires a supervisor to maintain control and direct the course of the supervisor-subordinate relationship. To maintain a balance in human relationships is a constant effort of reading and understanding human behavior. A good place to start is to analyze our own behavior in dealing with others.

In our dealings with people we tend to express the feelings of others in ourselves. For example, feelings of empathy, fear, anger, and hostility tend to evoke a similar response from ourselves when we are confronted with such emotions in human relationships. The issue is to identify the source of such feelings and respond in terms of what is needed to improve the situation.

Conflict is a positive force when placed in an objective setting without emotional overtones. Such actions require a supervisor and subordinate to dissolve an issue into components and design a method for resolving the issue to the satisfaction of all parties concerned.

Objectivity is further enhanced when practical issues and realities are addressed. Such actions move an organization closer to a goal by solving problems through positive supervisor-subordinate relationships.

Positive interaction and contact with subordinates is essential to understanding the motivational mode of people. A state of withdrawal is necessary in forming new ideas but permanent withdrawal leads to conflict, misunderstanding, and suspicion in superior-subordinate relationships.[28]

Motivation as viewed by the supervisor requires (1) an identification of human needs, (2) a determination of the role of money in motivating people, (3) an identification of traits that induce motivated behavior, (4) an avoidance of manipulative actions, (5) an awareness of individual differences, (6) an awareness of personal development trends, and (7) an understanding of the dynamics of subordinacy. To conclude our discussion of motivation, we will attempt to outline the conditions for manager motivation. Managers, like subordinates, reflect the motivational complexities reviewed earlier in this chapter. Consequently, the organizational need to motivate managers is a critical factor in determining the development of positive human relationships.

Conditions for Manager Motivation

Scott Meyers, in his research on managerial motivation, obtained the following results in a study of 1344 managers at all levels of Texas Instruments. The motivation of a manager is dependent on (1) interpersonal competence, (2) the opportunity to work toward meaningful goals, and (3) the existence of appropriate management systems.

Interpersonal Competence

Interpersonal competence reflects a managerial style of human development designed to give expression to higher motivational levels, self-realization, and creativity. Meaningful goals incorporate human and organizational goals to achieve a common objective by removing irrelevant objectives. Managerial systems create an environment conducive to achieving organizational goals through positive reinforcement. This survey at Texas Instruments found that 30 percent, or 403 managers, had high motivational traits; 40 percent, or 538 managers, exhibited partial motivational traits; and 30 percent, or 403, displayed low motivational traits. Managerial levels and levels of motivation are described in Figure 8-4. Eighty-seven percent of all highly motivated managers were below

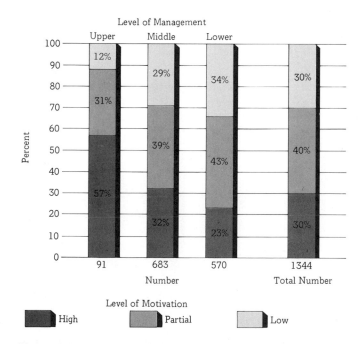

Figure 8-4
Relationship of motivation to level of management. Source: M. Scott Myers, "Conditions for Manager Motivation," *Harvard Business Review*, January–February 1966.

the upper management level, thus indicating the relatively minor role of organizational levels as a motivator.

Styles of supervision were labeled developmental, traditional, and reductive. Figure 8-5 shows the relationship of motivation to these three supervisory styles. For example, 30 percent, or 403 managers, rated their supervisor as being developmental; 40 percent, or 538 managers, rated their supervisor as traditional; and 30 percent, or 403 managers, rated their supervisor as reductive.

Most highly motivated managers had developmental bosses, whereas only 8 percent had reductive bosses. On the other hand, two-thirds of the poorly motivated managers had reductive supervisors. Further, the placement of developmental supervisors was not limited to upper levels of management but was distributed throughout the firm, as depicted in Figure 8-6.

As would be expected, managers were more objective in describing the bosses' managerial style than they were in appraising their own effectiveness. Developmental supervisors produced a higher level of motivation in reductive and developmental managers. Likewise, reductive managers accurately described their managerial style but failed to see the negative influence of their supervisor on subordinates. Figure 8-

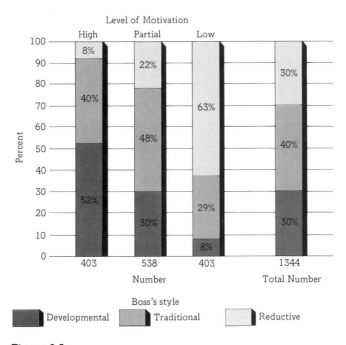

Figure 8-5
Relationship of motivation to boss's style. Source: M. Scott Myers, "Conditions for Manager Motivation," *Harvard Business Review*, January–February 1966.

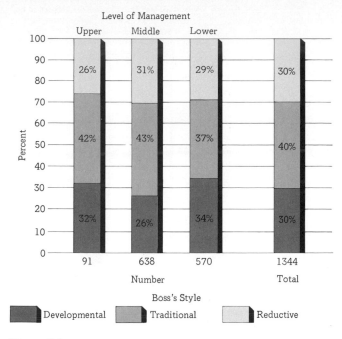

Figure 8-6
Distribution of style of supervision. Source: M. Scott Myers, "Conditions for Manager Motivation," *Harvard Business Review*, January–February 1966.

7 shows the manager's view and the superior's view of their ability to stimulate people toward positive work attitudes.

A composite description of 403 highly motivated managers and 403 poorly motivated managers is reflected in Figure 8-8. Highly motivated managers described their supervisors as open-minded, having high expectations, providing easy access to company data, and encouraging managers to learn from mistakes. Poorly motivated managers described their supervisors as authority oriented, failing to accept conflicting views, discouraging creative activities, failing to recognize job achievement, and stressing failures.[29]

Meaningful Goals
Closely related to interpersonal competence is the need for managers to face the challenge of achieving meaningful goals. To set goals effectively requires (1) the ability to relate personal and organizational goals, (2) the ability to design a means of setting and achieving goals, and (3) a willingness to respond favorably to organizational goals.[30] Moreover, an effective managerial system is built on these principles: (1) Individuals and organizations achieve their goals together. (2) People direct activities to accomplish a given goal. (3) A developmental

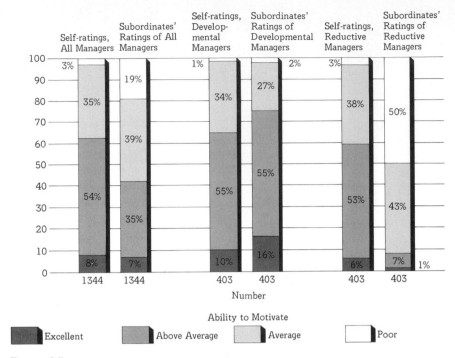

Figure 8-7
Ability to motivate—self-ratings vs. subordinates ratings. Source: M. Scott Myers, "Conditions for Manager Motivation," *Harvard Business Review*, January–February 1966.

philosophy of supervisory management, in contrast to a reductive philosophy that restricts managerial growth, helps to create a positive working environment.

Figure 8-9 shows the cyclical relationship of supervisory style, goal setting, and management systems. The developmental cycle produces in a manager a feeling of growth that influences personal attitudes toward life, work, and company operating procedures. Job success is a consequence and cause of the various stages in the development cycle. A reductive cycle that breeds interpersonal conflict produces conditions of failure, disapproval, or punishment. Managerial defenses show up as cynicism, hostility, and aggression unrelated to organizational goals. Managers seldom stay in one cycle or another. Movement from traditional, reductive, and developmental cycles is a product of personal growth, learning experiences, and managerial supervisory experiences.

Management Systems
The need has been stressed for organizations to encourage positive interaction between the personal competence of managers and organiza-

188

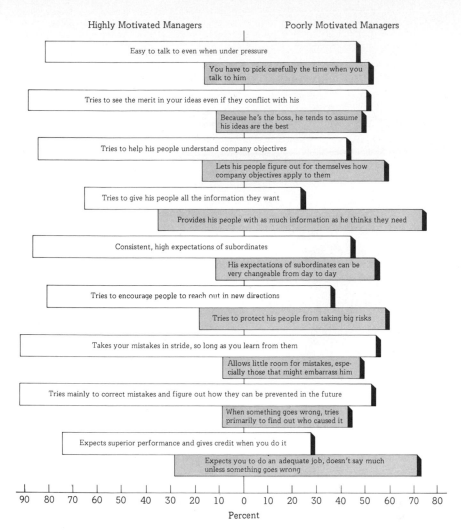

Highly Motivated Managers — Poorly Motivated Managers

Easy to talk to even when under pressure

You have to pick carefully the time when you talk to him

Tries to see the merit in your ideas even if they conflict with his

Because he's the boss, he tends to assume his ideas are the best

Tries to help his people understand company objectives

Lets his people figure out for themselves how company objectives apply to them

Tries to give his people all the information they want

Provides his people with as much information as he thinks they need

Consistent, high expectations of subordinates

His expectations of subordinates can be very changeable from day to day

Tries to encourage people to reach out in new directions

Tries to protect his people from taking big risks

Takes your mistakes in stride, so long as you learn from them

Allows little room for mistakes, especially those that might embarrass him

Tries mainly to correct mistakes and figure out how they can be prevented in the future

When something goes wrong, tries primarily to find out who caused it

Expects superior performance and gives credit when you do it

Expects you to do an adequate job, doesn't say much unless something goes wrong

90 80 70 60 50 40 30 20 10 0 10 20 30 40 50 60 70 80

Percent

Figure 8-8
How the manager sees his boss. Source: M. Scott Myers, "Conditions for Manager Motivation," *Harvard Business Review*, January–February 1966.

tional goals. This leads to a review of the third aspect of managerial motivation—a management system that allows a manager to achieve a given objective. Moreover, such a system exhibits the personality of a manager and demonstrates a developmental, traditional, or reductive style of supervision. A brief description of five managerial systems used by Texas Instruments provides an overview of the role of the systems in satisfying the needs of company, customer, and employee. A planning conference in December is designed (1) to increase employee input in

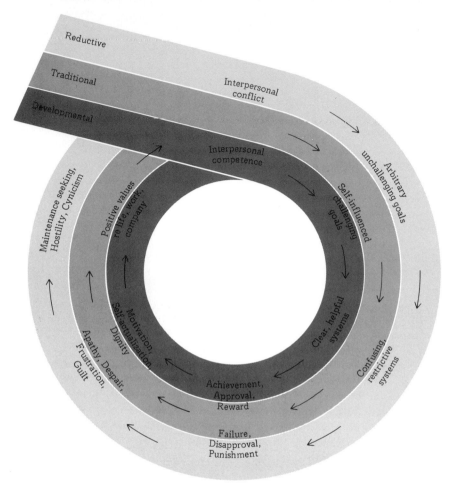

Figure 8-9
The motivation cycle. Source: M. Scott Myers, "Conditions for Manager Motivation," *Harvard Business Review*, January–February 1966.

setting goals, (2) to increase an awareness of company goals in communications, (3) to increase professional growth of all personnel, and (4) to increase earning recognition. Performance reviews twice each year set objectives, review achievements, and determine pay status of an employee. Likewise, attitude surveys measure managerial effectiveness. Working committees analyze problems and design remedial action. Work simplification stresses training to harness employee creativity as well as return cost savings to employees through profit-sharing programs. Such individual efforts involve job design based on supervisor and associate planning and lead to professional development in terms of earnings, attitudes, and identification with company goals. Inventory control systems seek to balance demand for assembly line parts with considerations for inventory costs, insurance, and part obsolescence.

A manager's motivation is a function of interpersonal competence, meaningful goals, and helpful systems to produce effective job performance. A positive result is based on the continued growth of managers in using developmental strategies in designing a work environment. A negative result is based on a reductive strategy that lacks positive motivational influences. The end result of the reductive strategy is that employees react badly, which in turn places management in a defensive position, and leads to manipulation of employees. In extreme cases, such behavior brings the loss of managerial rights through unionization. This is the result of the employees' desire to control their destiny, to have a sense of accomplishment, and to overcome a real or imagined social injustice.

Interpersonal incompetence, failure to provide meaningful goals, and misuse of management systems are due to a lack of sensitivity or inability to relate to the motivational needs of all employees. Consequently, a managerial style reflects the personality of all managers, their mental health and their ability to create a developmental climate that seeks to maximize the achievement level of all human assets.[31]

Summary

The complexity of motivation is reflected in personal differences but size, shape, tasks, and functions of diverse enterprises increase the complexity of motivational tools and their use in the world of work. An organization must be able to hire personnel at a reasonable level of wages, must be able to establish supervisory subordinate relationships, and must assign individual tasks to carry out various managerial functions. The challenge to management is to recognize and understand the impact of various motivational systems of individual and group behavior within an organized work endeavor. As individuals, we extend a great deal of energy to reach a desired goal, to satisfy a given need, or to complete a given task. Human needs can be defined as biological, sociological, and psychoanalytical. The humanistic theory recognizes the place of these three needs in striving to motivate people in business enterprises. In an organized endeavor, these issues are answered through goal-directed activities, but such efforts require a personal identification of human needs with those of the formal organization.

Money is an important incentive in society because it represents the power to save or the power to spend. In the short run, money provides satisfaction but in the long run, human beings tend to seek higher goals to meet their complex innate needs. Many firms striving to provide a competitive system of monetary incentives have overlooked the financial and managerial limitations of their own enterprise. Such a drastic error inflates wage and salary costs without motivating personnel to perform more efficiently. The experience of General Motors and other companies in placing too much reliance on compensation to motivate employees is evident in their failure to achieve motivation. Such economic rewards have not produced a similar increase in productivity, product quality, or employee commitment. To be effective, compensation should follow the guidelines of Charles D. McDermid, who associated human needs with various wage incentive systems.

Traits are "attitude bench marks" that give each person a distinct identity. Traits can be those of affiliation, curiosity, security, or emotion. Traits are not limited to people; organizations display traits in setting up operating policies and procedures. Although traits provide an idea regarding human aspirations, they are not universal enough to be an absolute guide to managerial action. Manipulating people to direct their activities in an organization is total disregard of human traits. Manipulation is seen in the form of false interest in subordinates' needs, status symbols, and false employee participation in organizational decisions. More enlightened managers try to take a genuine interest in people by using two-way communication between managers and personnel.

Personality and emotions are reflected in complexes that affect individual and organizational behavior. The variety of complexes and the emotions associated with each complex illustrate the complexity of understanding, recognizing, and motivating individuals in the world of work. To identify individual differences requires a review of personnel records, on-the-job observation, and social settings.

Closely associated with individual differences are defense mechanisms that people project to protect themselves. Some of the defense mechanisms that people project are (1) identification, (2) projection, (3) compensation, (4) overcompensation, (5) fantasy, (6) regression, (7) denial, (8) rumors, and (9) rationalization. To motivate people, supervisors must understand defense mechanisms as expressed by groups and individuals. To identify the motivational problems of people employed in an enterprise requires an awareness of the demands people will make on the formal organization. As managers, supervisors, and employees we can expect people to act on the mature adult developmental level or we can expect them to act at a lesser degree of maturity. The point is that managerial policies, procedures, and actions set the direction for all human relationships.

Successful motivation of subordinates is a result of identifying subordinates' relationship to authority figures. Four relationships to authority are that of dominance, submission, activity, and passivity. Individuals exhibit these traits as impulsive subordinates, compulsive subordinates, masochistic subordinates, or withdrawal subordinates. The four patterns of subordinacy are a result of personal inner motivation and of the impact of external stimuli on personal attitudes, actions, and reactions. To use the wrong approach in dealing with these four subordinates is to fulfill their individual needs for aggression, for removal from responsibility, for persecution, and for nonalignment with organizational goals. Again, the issue in motivating people is to relate motivational techniques directly to individual needs.

The motivation of a manager depends on interpersonal competence, the opportunity to work toward meaningful goals, and the existence of appropriate management systems. Interpersonal competence reflects a managerial style of human development designed to give expression to higher motivational levels, self-realization, and creativity. A positive result is based on the continued growth of managers in using developmental strategies in designing a work environment. A negative result is based on a reductive strategy that lacks positive motivational influences. The end result of the reductive strategy is the reactive behavior of employees, which in turn places management in a defensive position, thus leading to manipulation of employees. Interpersonal incompetences, failure to provide meaningful goals, and misuse of management systems are due to a lack of sensitivity or inability to relate to the motivational needs of all employees.

Discussion Questions

1. *What is motivation? How does it relate to the needs of individuals?*
2. *What are some of the major factors or influences that seem to motivate people?*
3. *In what ways may acceptance of the humanistic theory affect the way in which a supervisor approaches motivation?*
4. *Surveys have shown that employers tend to list money high on the list of items most important to employees, whereas workers often rank it as low as sixth on their list. How do you account for this discrepancy?*
5. *Why do you think that in many instances it is more important to an employee to know that he or she is being paid fairly in relation to other individuals in the firm than to consider the actual monetary value of wages received?*
6. *Why do you think that planned time off, which gives workers their choice of days off (with sufficient notice) would reduce absenteeism?*
7. *If pay alone does not motivate employees to higher productivity, what additional benefits are needed to accomplish this motivation?*

8. *Why is it important for management to have knowledge about the deceptive aspects of traits shown by employees?*
9. *What are some of the problems that may be caused by manipulation of workers by their managers?*
10. *Why is it important for a manager to pay attention to the individual differences of subordinates? How can these differences be detected?*
11. *When you become frustrated, which of the defense mechanisms do you resort to in an effort to protect yourself?*

Chapter Case 8

The union contract in effect at Adams Company states that if any employee's job is done away with because of automation or subcontracting, the employee will be trained in another job with no reduction in pay. John Austin has been a welder for the company for several years. Recently a new machine has been purchased that makes spot welds automatically. John has been told that he is to be trained for a new job and today his supervisor has asked John to meet him in the machine shop.

When John arrives, his supervisor is waiting for him beside what looks like a drill press. He explains to John that operating this machine is very simple and that all he has to do is to place a piece of sheet metal on the table of the press, press an electric switch, and, when the machine has drilled all the necessary holes simultaneously, remove it and place it on the moving belt to his left. The supervisor's parting remark to John is, "There's nothing to it. I'll wager that my twelve-year-old could be doing this job with ten minutes of training."

1. *If you were John, how would you feel about the job, the company, and the supervisor?*
2. *How can the supervisor get John to motivate himself to have any real pride in his work?*

Notes

1. Edward E. Lawler, III, "The Mythology of Management Compensation." Dale S. Beach. *Managing People at Work Readings in Personnel.* New York: Macmillan, 1971, pp. 430–432.
2. George R. Terry. *Supervisory Management.* Homewood, Ill.: Irwin, 1974, p. 175.
3. Robert M. Fulmer. *The New Management.* New York: Macmillan, 1974, pp. 94–96.
4. "Comparison of Sources of Happiness and Unhappiness" from *Americans View Their Mental Health:* A Nationwide Interview Survey, by Gerald Gurin, Joseph Veroff, and Sheila Field. Joint Commission on Mental Illness and Health. Monograph Series 1, no. 4, © 1960 by Basic Books, Inc.

5. J. D. Dunn, Elvis Stephens, and J. Roland Kelley. *Management Essentials: Resource.* New York: McGraw-Hill, 1973, p. 91.
6. Keith Davis. *Human Behavior at Work.* New York: McGraw-Hill, 1972, p. 476.
7. John B. Miner and Mary Green Miner. *Personnel and Industrial Relations: A Managerial Approach,* 2nd ed. New York: Macmillan, 1969, pp. 376–379.
8. William E. Parker, Robert W. Kleemeier, and Beyer W. Parker. *Front Line Leadership.* New York: McGraw-Hill, 1969, p. 98.
9. Edwin B. Flippo and Gary M. Munsinger. *Management,* 3rd ed. Boston: Allyn & Bacon, 1975, p. 349.
10. ———. "G M Zeroes in on Employee Discontent," *Business Week,* May 12, 1973, pp. 141–142.
11. ———. "A Plant Where Workers Like Their Jobs," *Business Week,* September 8, 1973, pp. 64–65.
12. Burt K. Scanlan. "Is Money Still the Motivator?" Herbert J. Chruden and Arthur W. Sherman, Jr. (eds.), *Readings in Personnel Management.* Cincinnati: South-Western, 1972, p. 433. Reprinted by permission of the International Personnel Management Association, 1313 East 60th Street, Chicago, Illinois, 60637.
13. Tannenbaum, op. cit., pp. 26–30.
14. Victor B. Ficker. *Effective Supervision.* Columbus, Ohio: Merrill, 1975, pp. 63–65.
15. Saul Gellerman. "Dynamics of Motives," *Motivation and Productivity,* American Management Association, 1963.
16. William F. Whyte. "The Manipulation Problem," Earnest Dale. *Readings in Management: Landmarks and New Frontiers,* 2nd ed. New York: McGraw-Hill, 1965, p. 291.
17. Louis Fried. "Games Managers Play," in Herbert G. Hicks (ed.), *Management, Organizations, and Human Resources: Selected Readings.* New York: McGraw-Hill, 1972, pp. 290–293. ("Games Managers Play" copyright 1967 by the American Institute of Certified Public Accountants.)
18. William C. Menninger and Harry Levinson. *Human Understanding in Industry.* Chicago: Science Research Associates, 1956, p. 18.
19. Herbert G. Hicks. *The Management of Organizations: A Systems and Human Resources Approach,* 2nd ed. New York: McGraw-Hill, 1972, pp. 125–131.
20. Ficker, op. cit., pp. 113–118.
21. Dunn, op. cit., pp. 136–138.
22. Chris Argyris. "The Human Personality." Robert A. Sutermeister, ed., *People and Productivity.* New York: McGraw-Hill, 1969, pp. 2–4.
23. Ibid., pp. 4–8.
24. Abraham Zaleznick. "The Dynamics of Subordinacy," *Harvard Business Review,* Special Publication, *How Successful Executives Handle People,* 1970, pp. 145–146.
25. Ibid., 142–146.
26. Ibid., 147–148.
27. Ibid., p. 141.
28. Ibid., pp. 152–153.
29. M. Scott Myers, "Conditions for Manager Motivation." *Harvard Business Review,* Special Publication, *How Successful Executives Handle People,* 1970, pp. 112–117.
30. Ibid., p. 116.
31. Ibid., pp. 118–125.

It might be a good idea to conduct some sort of survey to find out what's bothering them.

MOTIVATIONAL TECHNIQUES

9

You remember that suggestion box I put up a few months ago and how many "drop deads" and "turn blues" I fished out before I took it down?

For the full story, turn to the case on page 246.

GENERAL PURPOSES
OF CHAPTER 9

1. To identify some techniques that may prove to be helpful as motivation tools
2. To take a further look at the managerial grid
3. To examine Herzberg's dual-factor theory

LEARNING OBJECTIVES

1. To name three outcomes to be desired from training (*T* groups)
2. To differentiate between 9,1 task management and 1,9 country club management according to the managerial grid
3. To describe the 9,9 team management approach
4. To name and describe three general philosophies of personnel management
5. To cite the differences between horizontal job loading and vertical job loading
6. To distinguish between job enrichment and job enlargement
7. To name eight traits that Rensis Likert believes are displayed by supervisors whose work groups show the most favorable and cooperative attitudes
8. To name and describe the five needs as described in Maslow's hierarchy of human needs
9. To state the significance of Scott Myers's research into motivation at Texas Instruments

The climate in which a manager attempts to motivate personnel was discussed in the preceding chapter. A related need is to identify techniques that may help to motivate personnel. Limits on time and space prevent an exhaustive review of all motivational techniques available to managers. The techniques presented in this chapter, however, reflect a variety of approaches that have proved successful in actual use. These methods have been designed by researchers into management and incorporated into real systems. As with all managerial tools, the ideas presented here are not absolutes, nor are they intended as the answer to all problems related to motivating personnel. These motivational techniques are presented to help provide an awareness of several views and to challenge present or future managers to evaluate their effectiveness in motivating personnel.

Chris Argyris's Views on Training Groups

Corporate management tends to become sluggish and inflexible as the life of the firm is extended. Monetary rewards often replace personal initiative and interest in a job as the length of service increases. How does one instill in the managerial staff a continued desire to be self-directing and creative? Is motivation only a matter of crisis management, centralized controls, rewards and penalties, and static organizational structures? Chris Argyris believes that training groups can help expand managerial horizons beyond the traditional concepts of management.[1] In Table 9-1 a brief summary is given of the values of a traditional management structure.

Exposure to new management techniques can provide a manager with new strategies to govern future policy decisions. This requires providing a simulated experience designed to show a manager that past answers are not necessarily appropriate to today's issues. A similar need is to reeducate the manager to use new values. An example is the growth of authentic relationships that increase the esteem and self-awareness of all organizational members. Another example is psychological success, which is the ability to challenge the mental competence of managers through completing meaningful tasks. These two concepts are essential cornerstones in developing effective executive competence.

Training groups are an educational experience in which people analyze their behavior, analyze and review the behavior of others, and experiment with new behavioral concepts. The result should be greater awareness and acceptance of self and others. This training should also enable a group to complete a project with the least amount of human

TABLE 9-1
The pyramidal values

There are certain values about effective human relationships that are inherent in the pyramidal structure of the business organization and which successful executives (understandably) seem to hold. Values are learned commands which, once internalized, coerce human behavior in specific directions. This is why an appreciation of these values is basic in understanding behavior.

What are these "pyramidal" values? I would explain them in this way.

1. The important human relationships—the crucial ones—are those which are related to achieving the organization's objective, i.e., getting the job done, as for example:

We are here to manufacture shoes, that is our business, those are the important human relationships; if you have anything that can influence those human relationships, fine.

2. Effectiveness in human relationships increases as behavior becomes more rational, logical, and clearly communicated; but effectiveness decreases as behavior becomes more emotional. Let me illustrate by citing a typical conversation:

Have you ever been in a meeting where there is a lot of disagreement?
All the time.
Have you ever been in a meeting when the disagreement got quite personal?
Well, yes I have, but not very often.
What would you do if you were the leader of this group?
I would say, "Gentlemen, let's get back to the fact," or I would say, "Gentlemen, let's keep personalities out of this." If it really got bad, I would wish it were five o'clock so I could call it off, and then I would talk to the men individually.

3. Human relationships are most effectively motivated by carefully defined direction, authority, and control, as well as appropriate rewards and penalties that emphasize rational behavior and achievement of the objective.

If these are the values held by most executives, what are the consequences? To the extent that executives believe in these organizational values, the following changes have been found to happen.

(1) There is a *decrease* in receiving and giving information about executives' interpersonal impact on each other. Their interpersonal difficulties tend to be either suppressed or disguised and brought up as rational, technical, intellectual problems. As a result, they may find it difficult to develop competence in dealing with feelings and interpersonal relations. There is a corresponding decrease in their ability to own up to or be responsible for their ideas, feelings, and values. Similarly there is a dropping off of experimentation and risk taking with new ideas and values.

(2) Along with the decrease in owning, openness, risk taking, there is an *increase* in the denial of feelings, in closeness to new ideas, and in need for stability (i.e., "don't rock the boat"). As a result, executives tend to find themselves in situations where they are not adequately aware of the human problems, where they do not solve them in such a way that they remain solved without deteriorating the problem-solving process. Thus, if we define interpersonal competence as (*a*) being aware of human problems and (*b*) solving them in such a way that they remain solved, without deteriorating the problem-solving process, these values serve to decrease interpersonal competence.

(3) As the executives' interpersonal competence decreases, conformity, mistrust, and dependence, especially on those who are in power, increase. Decision making becomes *less effective*, because people withhold many of their ideas, especially those that are innovative and risky, and organizational defenses (such as management by crisis, management by detail, and through

200

fear) *increase.* So do such "protective" activities as "JIC" files (just in case the president asks), "information" meetings (to find out what the opposition is planning), and executive politicking.

If this analysis is valid, then we must alter executives' values if we are to make the system more effective. The question arises as to what changes can and *should* be made in these values.

But since executives are far from unknowledgeable, why have they clung to these pyramidal values? First, because they are *not necessarily wrong.* Indeed, they are a necessary part of effective human relationships. The difficulty is that alone they are not enough. By themselves they tend to lead to the above consequence. What is needed is an additional set of values for the executives to hold. Specifically there are three.

1. The important human relationships are not only those related to achieving the organization's objectives but those related to maintaining the organization's internal system and adapting to the environment, as well.

2. Human relationships increase in effectiveness as *all* the relevant behavior (rational and interpersonal) becomes conscious, discussable, and controllable. (The rationality of feelings is as crucial as that of the mind.)

3. In addition to direction, controls, and rewards and penalties, human relationships are most effectively influenced through authentic relationships, internal commitment, psychological success, and the process of confirmation. (These terms are clarified in the body of the article.)

Source: Reprinted with permission from Argyris, *Interpersonal Competence and Organizational Effectiveness* (Homewood, Ill.: Richard D. Irwin, Inc., 1962 c.).

---

costs. A further aim is to identify the role of leadership, the place of rewards and penalties, and the impact of information on structuring effective groups. In the final analysis a training group should have three desired outcomes:

1. Have members explore their values and their impact on others.
2. Have members determine the extent to which they wish to modify previous values as well as develop new values to guide their actions.
3. Show how groups can inhibit or facilitate human growth and decision making.[2]

The key to effective authentic relationships in any organization is a climate of trust. Such a climate makes leadership a group process that uses the expertise of each member as various problems are solved. Related to this is development of a decision-making forum based on a team approach that tests the learning experiences of the group. The ability of the group to function under stress in making a decision will test the authenticity of group relationships. Finally, additional learning experiences provide avenues for individual and group growth.[3]

In analyzing their educational experiences, training groups noted the tendency of members to ignore the views of others, to pressure others to accept a different viewpoint, and to place members in a win-lose position. People tend to learn from such organizational experiences when

TABLE 9-2
Who learns from T group experiences?

People who learn in T groups seem to possess at least three attributes:

1. A relatively strong ego that is not overwhelmed by internal conflicts.
2. Defenses which are sufficiently low to allow the individual to hear what others say to him (accurately and with minimal threat to his self), without the aid of a professional scanning and filtering system (that is, the therapist, the educator).
3. The ability to communicate thoughts and feelings with minimal distortion. In other words, the operational criterion of minimal threat is that the individual does not tend to distort greatly what he or others say, nor does he tend to condemn others or himself.

This last criterion can be used in helping to select individuals for the T group experience. *If the individual must distort or condemn himself or others to the point that he is unable to do anything but to continue to distort the feedback that he gives and receives, then he ought not to be admitted to a T group.*

To put this another way, T groups, compared to therapy groups, assume a higher degree of health—not illness—that is, a higher degree of self-awareness and acceptance. This is an important point. *Individuals should not be sent to the laboratory if they are highly defensive.* Rather, the relatively healthy individuals capable of learning from others to enhance their degree of effectiveness are the kinds of individuals to be selected to attend.

Source: Reprinted with permission from Argyris, *Interpersonal Competence and Organizational Effectiveness.* (Homewood, Ill.: Richard D. Irwin, Inc., 1962 c.).

they possess the traits expressed in Table 9-2. Another way to use training groups is to set up activities in which each member advises as well as receives guidance. These activities increase interpersonal competence through greater self-awareness and self-acceptance. A similar method for overcoming communication problems is to role-play these situations. Through role-playing the members can diagnose a problem, identify individual or group issues, and find more effective means of overcoming communication and organizational problems. Training groups offer an excellent way to test recommendations made by members in an organization. An effective way to reduce departmental rivalries is to set up training groups to role-play a real-life situation.

Chris Argyris, in writing about training groups and laboratory education, tried to overcome the following misunderstandings:

1. Training groups and lab experiences do not alter personal behavior without the awareness, cooperation, and participation of group members.
2. A lab exercise is open experience guided by the interaction of all members—not one staff member or educator.

3. A lab exercise seeks to use creative conflict to express differing views to increase the acceptance of other participants.
4. Lab experiences are not designed to create callous people with a dislike for others in society who do not adopt an open life style.
5. Training group experiences are not designed for psycho-analysis nor intensive group therapy.
6. Lab experiences involve risks but are not designed to destroy the feelings of participants.
7. Laboratory experiences seek to provide leaders—an awareness of the consequences and cost of their present leadership style. Moreover, alternatives are provided but their implementation is a personal process.
8. Like any educational process training groups and lab exercises do not result in guaranteed changes. For example, to adopt a trusting attitude in a hostile climate is unrealistic behavior for any individual.[4]

A similar issue in training group and lab exercises is the desire to develop a cause-and-effect relationship between educational and organizational experiences. A study of twenty executives revealed that the impact of lab education continued for a period of six months. However, adverse organizational circumstances at ten months meant a return to traditional relationships. Thus, the acceptance of new values requires a change in all organizational members. Moreover, pyramidal values are effective in routine operating procedures, but for innovative or creative actions the new values and leadership patterns are more effective. Table 9-3 presents the successes and difficulties of several participants thirty days after completing a lab experience.

Lab exercises and training groups are not a panacea for all organizational issues. However, ten years of use have produced positive results in solving some organizational problems. But not all firms can or want to use such experiences because they require changes in managerial policies, controls, and technology. A trend toward trust, commitment, and risk taking grows in a supportive organizational climate. The final results of laboratory education are individual because of the variation in personalities and organizational needs. Not all training groups cover the same material. Some exercises stress interpersonal experiences, others intellectual issues, or small-group concerns, or a varying combination of all these. The best way to evaluate training groups and lab exercises is personal experience.[5]

Blake's and Mouton's Views of the Managerial Grid

9,1 Task Management
People are seen by some as being lazy, apathetic, and indifferent to the needs of the enterprise. Using this premise, a manager many sacrifice

TABLE 9-3

The excerpt presented here mirrors the tone of the entire meeting. I have not purposely selected only that section in which the men praised the laboratory. If the men had criticized the laboratory, such criticism would have been included. As you may see, the researcher actually pushed the group for more negative comments.

Except for minor editing, these are direct quotes:

No. 4 [after reporting that his superior, a member of the experimental group, had made a decision which should have been left to him]: I was really fuming. I was angry as hell. I walked into his office and I said to myself, "No matter what the hell happens, I'm going to tell him that he cannot do that any more." Well, I told him so. I was quite emotional. You know it floored me. He looked at me and said, "You're right; I made a mistake, and I won't do that again." Well I just don't think he would have done that before.

No. 7: The most important factor in motivating people is not what you say or do; it's giving a person the opportunity to express his views and the feeling that one is seriously interested in his views. I do much less selling but it sure takes longer.

No. 2: I've had a problem. I now have a greater need for feedback than before, and I find it difficult to get. The discussion on internal commitment made much sense to me, and I try to see if I can create conditions for it.

The thing that bothers me is that I try to handle it correctly, but I don't get feedback or cues as to how well I'm doing, as I used to at the lab. The meeting is over, and you don't know whether you've scored or not. So after each meeting I've got 10 question marks. The things that before were never questions are now question marks.

You don't get feedback. You ask for something and they respond, "I know what you're trying to do." They think I've got something up my sleeve. All I want is to get feedback. It was obvious to me they were all waiting for me to make the decision. But I wanted them to make it. This was their baby, and I wanted them to make it. Two days later they made it. Fine, in this case I got feedback. The point was that their decision was a severe reversal, and I realize it was difficult for them to make. But they made it. Before, I simply would have pointed out the facts, and they would have "agreed" with the reversal, but down deep inside they would have felt that they could have continued on. As it is now, it's their decision. I think they now have a greater sense of internal commitment. People are now freer to disagree.

No. 11: My list of decisions to be made is longer. I am hoping that they will make some decisions. I now know how much they wait for me.

No. 11: [after telling how he wrote a note which in effect damned No. 2 and maintained his own correctness, then reread it and realized how defensive he was]: Before I wouldn't have even seen this.

No. 2: One of our most difficult jobs will be to write our feelings and to write in such a way that others can express their feelings.

No. 3: I have some difficulties in evaluating this program. What have we gotten out of this? What are we able to verbalize about what we got out of this? Do others of you have difficulty in verbalizing it?

No. 2: I have the same difficulty. I have been totally ineffective describing the experience.

No. 8: Each time I try I give a different answer.

No. 1: I don't have too much difficulty. One thing that I am certain of is that I see people more as total human beings. I see aspects of them that I had never seen before.

No. 9: I'm frustrated because I now realize the importance of face-to-face communication. I'm so far from the general managers that it is not so hot. Has anyone tried to write memos that really get feelings brought out?

I find myself questioning much more than I ever did before. I have a more questioning attitude. I take into account more factors.

No. 4: We've been talking about things as if we've slowed down a bit. We haven't. For example, remember you [No. 1] and I had a problem? I'm sure Arden House was very helpful. If I hadn't been there, my reaction to you would have been different. I would have fought you for hours.

No. 1: I know we can talk to each other more clearly. It's not a conscious way. It's spontaneous.

No. 3: I have to agree we can make some decisions much faster. For example, with [No. 2] I simply used to shut up. But now I can be more open. Before the laboratory, if I had an intuitive feeling that something was wrong, but I wasn't sure, I'd keep quiet until things got so bad that then I'd have a case to go to the boss. Now I feel freer to talk about it sooner and with [No. 2].

I now feel that we are going to say exactly how we feel to anyone. You [the president], for example, don't have to worry, and, therefore, question, probe, and draw us out.

President: Yes, and today I found [No. 1], who told me that he simply would not agree with me. And I said to myself, "God bless you. He really is open now."

No. 1: I agree. I would not have expressed this feeling before being in this group. It's obvious that one should but I didn't.

[No. 2 and No. 1 show real insight into how they are being manipulated by people outside and above the group. They are much more aware of the manipulative process. "This kind of manipulation is dynamite. It burns me up."]

No. 1: Yes, it's really horrible to see it and not be able to do anything about it.

No. 7: In this case it seems to me you've got to really hit hard, because you're dealing with an untrained man [laughter]. . . . I think I now have a new understanding of decision making. I am now more keenly aware of the importance of getting a consensus so that the *implementation* is effective. I am not trying to say that I do this in every meeting. But I do strive more to give opportunity for consensus.

No. 1: One of the problems that I feel is that the "initiated" get confused so they don't play the game correctly. Sometimes I feel walked upon, so I get sore. This is difficult. [Many others expressed agreement.]

No. 6: Does it help to say, "I trust you?" I think it does.

No. 11: For example, [No. 2], you went to a meeting where you admitted you had made a mistake. Boy, you should have heard the reaction. Boy, Mr. ——— admitted a mistake. Well, wonderful; it helped to get these guys to really feel motivated to get the job done.

No. 9: Yes, I heard that many took on a deeper feeling of responsibility to get the program on the right track.

No. 7: I'd like to come back to what [No. 6] said. I used to say to people that I trusted them, that I was honest, and so on. But now I wonder if people really believe me, or if they don't begin to think if I'm not covering that I'm not honest.

No. 3: Another example which I am now aware of is the typical way we write memos. We start off: "I have confidence in your judgment to handle this question," and so on. Few more paragraphs. Then fifth paragraph reads: "Please confirm by return mail exactly what you have done and what controls have been set up."

No. 2: I agree. We do an awful lot to control people. Although I think that we're trying.

[No. 7 gave examples of how he stopped making a few phone calls to exert pressure. Others agreed.]

Researcher: Aren't there negative comments?

No. 11: We have one man who has chosen not to be here. I wonder why?

No. 3: Well, really, to me that is a sign of health in the group. He feels he would still be accepted even if he didn't come. It certainly would be easy for him to come and just sit here.

No. 1: Yes, he wouldn't go to the trouble of avoiding a meeting that you didn't think was important.

No. 3: The only negative that I can think is: "What can you tell me that actually increases effectiveness?" I am not sure, but I must agree that there is a whale of a different climate.

No. 7: Well, I'd like to develop a list of things that we feel we have gotten out of this program so far. How do others of you feel? [All agreed, "Let's try."]

All group members reported they reached the following conclusions:

a) All of us begin to see ourselves as others see us . . . a real plus.
b) A degree of greater confidence in oneself in meetings and in interviews. Beginning to be more comfortable with self.
c) Greater confidence in associates. We feel more secure that you're telling what you think. . . . Greater feeling of freedom of expression to say what you really think.
d) Individuals have a greater understanding and appreciation of viewpoint of associates.
e) Greater appreciation of the opposite viewpoint.
f) An awareness of what we do and others do that inhibits discussion.
g) More effective use of our resources . . . getting more from them, and they feel this . . . patient to listen more.
h) Meetings do not take longer and implementation is more effective. Internal commitment is greater.
i) We have had a great realization that being only task-oriented, we will not get the best results. We must not forget worrying about the organization and the people.
j) We get more irritated to infringement of our jobs and unique contributions.
k) Fewer homemade crises.

No. 6: One of the difficult things about the list is that when you look at it, you wake up to the fact that you haven't really been using these principles. When you tell someone else who doesn't realize the gap between knowing something and actually doing it, he doesn't realize.

No. 7: But I think I really did learn and do care. Now when I think what I used to do, because that was the way. Today I realize that I could have had three times as much if I had known what I know now.

Source: Reprinted with permission from Argyris, *Interpersonal Competence and Organizational Effectiveness* (Homewood, Ill.: Richard D. Irwin, 1962, c.).

---

concern for people to obtain maximum output in goods or services. This attitude creates a work environment based on authority with no room to question the reason for completing a given task. Even at middle-management levels to challenge orders, ideas, or methods is to invite a charge of insubordination and lack of cooperation. Moreover, the economic view of human beings is the basis for motivation that uses rewards or penalties to direct work. The need to have meaningful work or personal worth is ignored in the exercise of power in an authoritarian model. Further, management is the only authority that decides the

TABLE 9-4
Supervisory style and personal characteristics: A 9,1 outlook

A 9,1 managerial outlook can be summarized in terms of how managerial responsibility for people is exercised to gain effective production. The following attitudes are typical:

Planning. "I do planning by setting goals and schedules to be followed by each subordinate. Then I work out procedures and ground rules and make individual assignments. I also establish check points so that I can assure myself that actions I have authorized are being taken as I intended them to be done."

Work execution. "I watch the work closely. I criticize as I see the necessity for it and authorize changes as needs for them arise."

Follow-up. "I have plans laid for the next assignments and move people on to them as operations dictate. Recognition and corrective action are extended to individuals on a one-by-one basis."

Managing mistakes by subordinates. "My immediate reaction is to find out who is responsible for the mistake and to mete out the appropriate disciplinary action in a swift and compelling manner."

When policies or procedures are violated. "Uniform policies are indispensible to orderly production. Policies and procedures should be well defined to cover all but emergency situations. They also should be continuously enforced whenever deviations from them arise."

Source: Robert R. Blake and Jane Srygley Mouton, *The Managerial Grid,* Houston: Gulf Publishing Company, 1964. Copyright © 1964.

means to be used to meet a person's physical needs at work. Social interaction is to be avoided at all cost because social relationships interfere with the accomplishment of enterprise objectives. Another issue in 9,1 management is that personal creativity is ignored by management as unimportant to the growth of the firm. The end result is that personnel turn their creativity toward efforts to defeat the system.[6] Table 9-4 shows the supervisory style and personal traits of a 9,1 managerial viewpoint.

1,9 Country Club Management
The 1,9 management style is a direct contrast to 9,1 management. The central issue is to build positive human relationships with little concern for completing organizational aims. This style of management is a way of life in a cost-plus operating environment. This managerial style may also be produced by a lack of competition that would force a firm to remain economically competitive. A manager in this climate maintains productivity at a level that avoids conflict as well as provides maximum satisfaction and security for organizational members. Moreover, in most cases group pressure forces a manager to retreat from any unpopular decisions that place additional responsibilities on employees. Similarly,

TABLE 9-5
Supervisory style and personal characteristics: A 1,9 outlook

In terms of managerial functions a typical 1,9 outlook can be expressed as follows:

Planning. "Little planning is done either by myself or with my subordinates. Rather, I tend to give broad assignments and to convey my confidence in subordinates by saying, 'I'm sure you know how to do this and that you will do it well.' "

Work execution. "I see my people frequently and encourage them to visit me as their work permits. My goal is to see that they are happy and that they are able to get the things they request. I rarely criticize but often compliment. That's the way to encourage people."

Follow-up. "I hold a meeting with those who are on the job where I place emphasis on congratulating the group as well as individuals. Our "wrap-up" sessions usually revolve around what did or didn't cause friction on the job and how we can help things go smoothly in the future. I try to minimize any mistakes and to smooth over conflicts so as to eliminate ill will. My people know that I feel I can only be helping myself when I am helping them."

Managing mistakes by subordinates. "My approach to errors is to avoid blaming or placing responsibility, but to support the person who was in the wrong by saying something like, 'Well, we all make mistakes, but I know you did the best you could. Maybe we'll have better luck next time.' "

When policies or procedures are violated. "Policies and procedures are intended as guidelines for action rather than as rigid requirements. When the deviation is slight or the policy not too important, it is best to wink. If the violation is more severe, the person will usually straighten up if he knows you want him to."

Whereas the 9,1 manager was described as an individual who placed high value on sound decisions in comparison with the value he places on good relationships the 1,9 manager places high value on good relationships in comparison with the value he places on sound decisions. He does so by accepting opinions, attitudes and ideas of others in preference to pushing his own. He rarely generates conflict, but when it does appear, he tries to soothe bad feelings to keep people together. He is patient and his temper is not easily triggered. When tensions between people do arise, many times his humor has the effect of reducing them.

1,9, then, is the "soft," "togetherness," or "human relations" approach to management. Being soft, it rarely confronts or challenges an individual to grow. Being soft, it also rarely aids an organization to become the kind of responsible agency needed in a society that, quite properly, demands performance and achievement.

Source: Robert R. Blake and Jane Srygley Mouton, *The Managerial Grid.* Houston: Gulf Publishing Company, 1964. Copyright © 1964.

a 1,9 manager strives to build loyalty through warmth, acceptance, and understanding. Creativity is nonactive because it would upset existing supervisor-subordinate relationships. This form of supervision is reported to be most effective in stifling creative ideas in an organization. Table 9-5 shows the supervisory style and personal traits of a 1,9 managerial philosophy.[7]

5,5 Middle-of-the-Road Management

The 5,5 management style pushes to obtain results but responds just enough to employee dissatisfactions to avoid low morale or hostility. The idea of success is a fair day's pay for a fair day's work. Moreover, planning is based on achievable goals in terms of persons of average abilities working under moderate pressure. The reason for a goal is explained and feedback from personnel is used to avoid conflict or resistance to company goals. Directing employees is a process of leading, motivating, and communicating company plans through formal rules, procedures, spans of control, and chains of command. However, a major difference from 9,1 or 1,9 managerial styles is that the 5,5 manager recognizes the existence of informal groups. By listening to what the informal group is saying, a 5,5 manager seeks to build a positive relationship between formal and informal groups. Further, a manager seeks to shape the thinking of informal groups by feeding confidential information to reduce conflict, correct false rumors, and relieve the tensions of members. Similarly, creativity is a superficial device used to release the creative energies of people through gimmicks. For example, a suggestion system is used to obtain employee ideas because immediate supervisors fail to listen to subordinates' ideas.[8] Table 9-6 gives a brief idea of the supervisory style and personal traits of a 5,5 managerial philosophy.

TABLE 9-6
Supervisory styles and personal characteristics: A 5,5 outlook

Typical ways the 5,5 manager handles managerial functions can be described as follows:

Planning: "I plan the work for each subordinate. After explaining goals and schedules, I make individual assignments. I insure that subordinates understand what I expect of them and that they feel free to come back if they need help in carrying out the assignments that have been made."

Work execution: "I keep up with each man's job and review his progress with him from time to time, or when he asks for it. I am always there to lend support if he gets into trouble or to give positive suggestions if he is having difficulty."

Follow-up: "I hold a meeting with those involved in the job to point up the group's good points as well as mistakes and to indicate how they can improve. Each individual gets the opportunity to discuss any reasonable suggestions he might have for improvement as I give the next assignments."

When policies or procedures are violated: "It is essential that policies and procedures be followed and it is my responsibility to "sell" my people on following them. If they understand that rules are for the *good* of all, they generally will follow them willingly."

Managing mistakes by subordinates: "This is the kind of mistake that can't be overlooked more than once. Next time, I'll have to take some action."

Source: Robert R. Blake and Jane Srygley Mouton, *The Managerial Grid.* Houston: Gulf Publishing Company, 1964. Copyright © 1964.

1,1 Impoverished Management

This style of management shows little or no concern for achieving organizational goals and no care about human relationships. The manager follows the rules but does not become personally involved. A person with this managerial view has often failed to receive a promotion and is stuck in a particular job. A similar view is sometimes taken in a bureaucratic environment where no one is ever fired. Creativity is avoided at all cost to further ensure the manager's ability to blend into the landscape. However, creative managers tend to express themselves through involvement in community projects.[9] Table 9-7 shows the supervisory style and personal traits of a managerial philosophy of 1,1.

9,9 Team Management

The 9,9 team management style seeks to build an effective group based on the efforts of each member to achieve success. Such an approach avoids a task-oriented method using people as tools of production, as in a 9,1 managerial style. Similarly, the team approach overcomes the human relations approach of 1,9 management, which reduces concern for organizational success to a minimum. Further, a team approach avoids yielding production levels to avoid conflicts with personnel.

Management seeks to build a climate of team effort under conditions of mutual trust. Such a climate seeks to maintain its effectiveness through individual accountability, self-direction, and acceptance of organizational goals. A team approach seeks feedback from all members

---

TABLE 9-7
Supervisory styles and personal characteristics: A 1,1 outlook

1,1 attitudes toward managerial functions can be described as follows:

Planning. "I give broad assignments but I don't tend to think in terms of goals or schedules. I do little planning. A way that you might describe my job is that I'm a message carrier. I carry the story from those above me to those below me and put as little embroidery or interpretation on it as possible."

Work execution. "I make the rounds, but take little on the spot action. I leave people to solve their own problems. They like it best that way and I do too."

Follow-up. "I talk to my boss to find out what is to be done next and to find out who he wants to do it."

Managing mistakes by subordinates. "Oh! *They* are always causing trouble, but what can you do?"

When policies and procedures are violated. "When policies and procedures are violated it's better to turn your head than to cause a furor unless the situation is one which is actually dangerous. Many rules are made to be broken, and most peple use good judgment when they do so."

Source: Robert R. Blake and Jane Srygley Mouton, *The Managerial Grid.* Houston: Gulf Publishing Company, 1964. Copyright © 1964.

TABLE 9-8
Supervisory style and personal characteristics: A 9,9 outlook

The 9,9 attitudes toward managerial functions can be summarized as follows:

Planning. "I get the people together who have relevant facts and/or stakes in the outcome to review the whole picture, get reactions and ideas. Then, I and my subordinates establish goals and flexible schedules as well as procedures and ground rules, and set up individual responsibilities."

Work execution. "I keep familiar with major points of progress and exert influence on subordinates through identifyng problems and revising goals and schedules with them as necessary. I lend assistance when needed by removing road blocks."

Follow-up. "I conduct a 'wrap-up' to evaluate how a job went and to find out what can be learned from it. If appropriate, I give recognition on a team basis as well as recognizing outstanding individual contributions."

Managing mistakes by subordinates. "Tough luck. It's embarrassing, but the thing is to study the problem and to learn from it. When can we get together?"

When policies or procedures are violated. "I discuss violations with those involved in order to diagnose what the problem is. If the procedure or policy is inappropriate, steps are taken to change it. If misconduct, what motivated it needs understanding before corrective action is taken.

Source: Robert R. Blake and Jane Srygley Mouton, *The Managerial Grid.* Houston: Gulf Publishing Company, 1964. Copyright © 1964.

in planning the direction the firm will take. Such an attitude tries to build sound interpersonal relationships designed to meld economic, social, and psychological needs for all team members. Such a view invites new ideas, initiates creative conflict, and provides alternative solutions to organizational problems. This managerial philosophy views subordinates as equals with the ability to direct their own activities without excessive controls, manipulative gimmicks, or indifference to human organizational concerns.[10] Tables 9-8 shows the supervisory style and personal traits of a manager using the team approach. Figure 9-1 shows the relationship of the five managerial styles to each other in terms of their concern for production or their concern for people.

Herzberg's View of Motivation

A traditional avenue for motivating people is the application of physical and psychological "KITA." Physical "kicks in the ass" are inelegant, destroy an organization's image of benevolence, and produce negative results. The more sophisticated form of "KITA" is psychological. Cruelty is invisible. The pain produced is felt internally. The system does the dirty work. Psychological "KITA" produces some ego satisfaction for

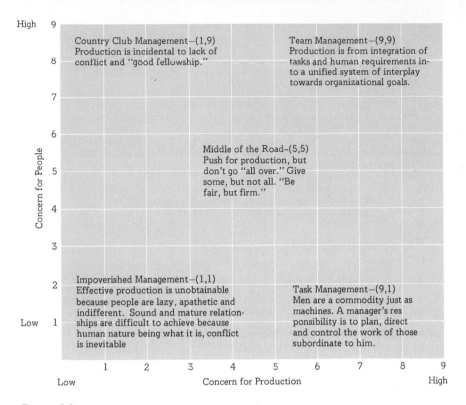

Figure 9-1
The Managerial Grid. Source: Robert R. Blake and Jane Srygley Mouton, *The Managerial Grid*, Houston: Gulf Publishing Company. Copyright © 1964.

those who use this technique. To kick a person physically or psychologically produces movement, but it does not produce motivation.

A related "KITA" approach is the use of positive rewards to achieve employee motivation. Money, status, promotions, and other rewards produce movement but do not produce motivation. The reason for this is that real motivation is internal—self-directing—and personally initiated. Positive "KITA" is the use of an external stimulus to produce a desired response in people. Thus, the manager is the motivating force who uses various stimuli to achieve movement of employees toward a desired result. In large, complex organizations a manager is physically, emotionally, and intellectually unable to provide an individual stimulus for all employees. Consequently, the goal should be to channel the creative motivational interests of people to achieve individual and organizational objectives.

Several myths regarding motivation are reflected in the following

212

positive "KITA" personnel practices used to instill motivation. They are as follows:

1. Reducing the time spent at work increases employee motivation.
2. Increasing wages is a sure way to achieve employee motivation.
3. Increasing fringe benefits will motivate personnel to achieve a management goal.
4. Human relations training will increase a manager's ability to motivate people.
5. Sensitivity training increases a manager's awareness of the feelings of others, which in turn increases a manager's ability to motivate people.
6. Communication is the answer to personnel motivational problems.
7. Two way communication motivates people through an exchange of ideas.
8. Job participation is the answer to employee motivation problems.
9. Employee counseling to increase understanding of employee concerns is an avenue to produce positive motivational results.[11]

All these practices produce short-term results but fail to give long-lasting results. Their failure increases operating costs and perpetuates the development of more expensive positive "KITA" approaches.

As long as motivation is a process of external stimulation, the employee moves without any clear understanding of why such movement is necessary. Several studies in recent years suggest that factors creating job satisfaction (and motivation) are distinct from factors creating job dissatisfaction. Moreover, the lack of satisfaction or dissatisfaction in a job is a result of the human need to satisfy biological needs as well as to achieve psychological growth. For example, a survey of 1685 employees in twelve investigations revealed several motivators that produce job satisfaction and several hygiene factors that cause job dissatisfaction at work. The personnel in this survey were from several firms representing managers, supervisors, and professional, trade, semiskilled, and unskilled employees at all organizational levels. The results of this survey are shown in Figure 9-2.

In personnel management three general philosophies of personnel management have developed to direct the work of employees. They are as follows:

1. Organizational theory holds that proper organizational design will produce positive job attitudes. Such a design seeks to overcome the irrational and varied behavior of the human element in an organization.
2. Industrial engineering views man as economically motivated through an incentive system that creates the most efficient use of the human machine. Thus, hygiene factors seen in Figure 9-2 are used to create the most efficient work process.

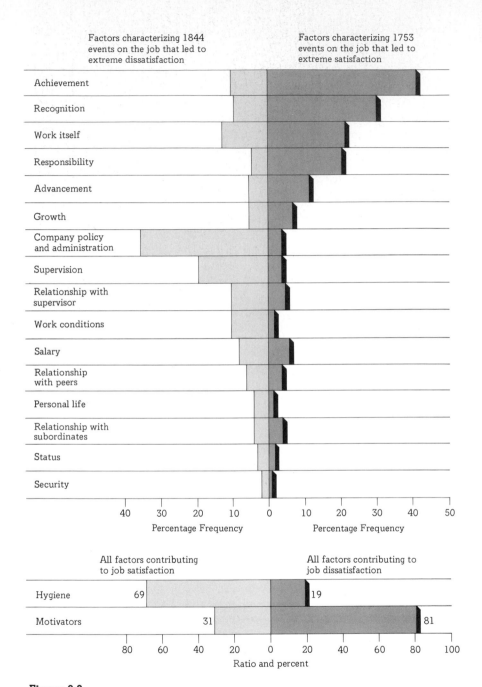

Figure 9-2
Factors affecting job attitudes as reported in investigations. Source: Frederick Herzberg, "One More Time: How Do You Motivate Employees?" *Harvard Business Review*, January–February 1968.

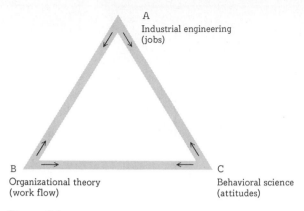

A
Industrial engineering
(jobs)

B
Organizational theory
(work flow)

C
Behavioral science
(attitudes)

Figure 9-3
"Triangle" of philosophies of personnel management. Source: Frederick Herzberg, "One More Time: How Do You Motivate Employees?" *Harvard Business Review,* January–February 1968.

3. Behavioral science seeks to build a positive social and psychological climate through attention to group interests and individual attitudes. Human relations education seeks to create positive employee attitudes in an organizational climate that leads to job efficiency.[12]

These three philosophies are viewed as a triangle in Figure 9-3. Thus, motivational-hygiene theory seeks to enrich all jobs to use all personnel effectively. All three personnel philosophies seek to alter motivational factors by manipulating the content of the employee's job. An example of such manipulation is *horizontal job loading.* One way to achieve this is to increase the production expected of an employee each day. Another way to load a job horizontally is to add more routine tasks to the same position. A final example of horizontal job loading is to remove difficult tasks to increase employee output.

An opposite trend is *vertical job loading* to provide motivation at work. Table 9-9 lists the principles and motivators involved. A study of stockholder correspondents employed in a large corporation showed that attitudes were poor and that the job provided no challenge. To overcome this situation a job enrichment program was initiated using the principles shown in Table 9-9. At the same time, a control group continued to use the traditional approach in handling stockholder correspondence. Similarly, two uncommitted groups were used to measure the Hawthorne effect (an increase in productivity caused by increased attention of managerial personnel, see Chapter 1). At the end of six months there was no change in the uncommitted and traditional groups in terms of productivity or improvement in job attitudes, but the unit applying the

TABLE 9-9
Principles of vertical job loading

Principle	Motivators involved
A. Removing some controls while retaining accountability	Responsibility and personal achievement
B. Increasing the accountability of individuals for own work	Responsibility and recognition
C. Giving a person a complete natural unit of work (module, division, area, and so on)	Responsibility, achievement, and recognition
D. Granting additional authority to an employee in his activity; job freedom	Responsibility, achievement, and recognition
E. Making periodic reports directly available to the worker himself rather than to the supervisor	Internal recognition
F. Introducing new and more difficult tasks not previously handled	Growth and learning
G. Assigning individuals specific or specialized tasks enabling them to become experts	Responsibility, growth, and advancement

Source: Frederick Herzberg. "One More Time: How Do You Motivate Employees?" *Harvard Business Review.* January–February, 1968.

job enrichment principles in Table 9-9 outperformed the other work units. There was a lower rate of absenteeism and members were promoted at a much higher rate. Figure 9-4 shows the changes in performance levels for the achieving unit. Figure 9-5 shows the improvement in the achieving group's attitudes toward their positions. Table 9-10 gives the suggestions of all participants and classifies them as horizontal or vertical loading techniques. The principles applied to vertical job loading are identified as items A to G in Table 9-9. In Table 9-10 the principles of vertical job loading outlined in Table 9-9 are related to the employees' suggestions on job improvement.

To conclude this overview of Herzberg, several suggestions for a supervisor seeking to implement a job enrichment program are presented as follows:

1. Select those jobs in which attitudes are poor, hygiene is costly, and motivation will make a difference in performance?
2. Approach any job with the conviction that it can be changed.
3. Brainstorm for ideas to enrich a job without concern for practicality.
4. Remove suggestions that are hygiene centered instead of motivationally oriented.

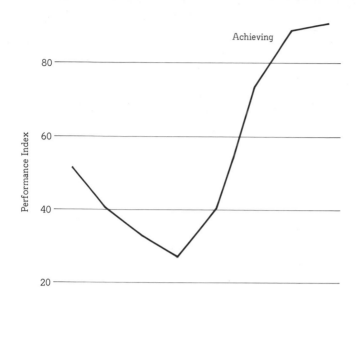

Figure 9-4
Shareholder service index in company experiment. Source: Frederick Herzberg, "One More Time: How Do You Motivate Employees?" *Harvard Business Review*, January–February 1968.

5. Strive to remove general terms and make suggestions relate to job requirements.
6. Screen the list to eliminate ideas that load a job horizontally.
7. Use employee's ideas but avoid direct participation to prevent the negative impact of human relations hygiene and manipulative practices.
8. Initial attempts should create a controlled experiment similar to the one used by the stockholder correspondence units. Such an experiment enhances the measurement of improvement by contrasting the work of traditional and achieving structured units.
9. Recognize that a job change reduces employee efficiency at first but increases as employee experience with new techniques increases.

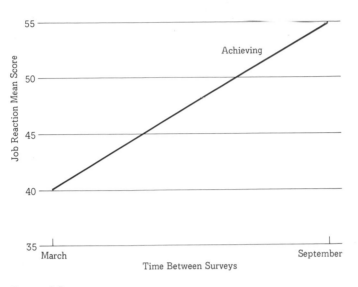

Figure 9-5
Changes in attitudes toward tasks in company experiment. Source: Frederick Herzberg, "One More Time: How Do You Motivate Employees?" *Harvard Business Review*, January–February 1968.

10. To overcome the anxiety and hostility of front-line supervisors requires the use of job enrichment concepts to change the jobs they do.[13]

Motivation and job enrichment involve a continuous managerial process. Likewise, job changes should create a positive relationship between job challenge and personal skill levels. Individuals with greater personal skills will show their ability and move to positions of greater challenge and psychological growth. Motivators as opposed to hygiene factors have a long-term impact on employee attitudes. Money and time used to create job enrichment incentives will produce greater economic, social, and psychological success than efforts at better personnel management through the use of hygiene incentives.

Rensis Likert's View of Motivators

As with all managerial trends, there exists a distinct outline of traits associated with high-producing managers. One such trait is a feeling of

TABLE 9-10
Enlargement vs. enrichment of correspondents' tasks in company experiment

Horizontal loading suggestions (rejected)	Vertical loading suggestions (adopted)	Principle
Firm quotas could be set for letters to be answered each day, using a rate which would be hard to reach.	Subject matter experts were appointed within each unit for other members of the unit to consult with before seeking supervisory help. (The supervisor had been answering all specialized and difficult questions.)	G
The women could type the letters themselves, as well as compose them, or take on any other clerical functions.	Correspondents signed their own names on letters. (The supervisor had been signing all letters.)	B
All difficult or complex inquiries could be channeled to a few women so that the remainder could achieve high rates of output. These jobs could be exchanged from time to time.	The work of the more experienced correspondents was proofread less frequently by supervisors and was done at the correspondents' desks, dropping verification from 100% to 10%. (Previously, all correspondents' letters had been checked by the supervisor.)	A
The women could be rotated through units handling different customers, and then sent back to their own units.	Production was discussed, but only in terms such as "a full day's work is expected." As time went on, this was no longer mentioned. (Before, the group had been constantly reminded of the number of letters that needed to be answered.)	D
	Outgoing mail went directly to the mailroom without going over supervisors' desks. (The letters had always been routed through the supervisors.)	A
	Correspondents were encouraged to answer letters in a more personalized way. (Reliance on the form letter approach had been standard practice.)	C
	Each correspondent was held personally responsible for the quality and accuracy of letters. (This responsibility had been the province of the supervisor and the verifier.)	B, E

Source: Frederick Herzberg. "One More Time: How Do You Motivate Employees?" *Harvard Business Review.* January–February, 1968.

trust and confidence in members, supervisors, the organization, and job aspects. Such a positive attitude reflects an identification with organizational objectives rather than the usual indifference reflected in most firms. People are viewed as more than economic beings to be controlled by authoritarian concepts. Concern for ego motives such as achievement, value, and identity is a primary factor in defining organizational relationships. This concern seeks to mobilize motivational forces, such as the desire for growth, self-fulfillment, acceptance, and completion of meaningful tasks. Security motives move beyond economic issues to curiosity, creativity, and a desire for new experiences. The end result is to produce an enterprise capable of realizing the goals of people and the goals of managers at all organizational levels.

Implied in the development of a high-producing group is the growth of a social system based on interlocking work groups. These work groups strive to perpetuate group loyalties, an awareness of other's needs, and high personal commitment to the achievement of individual, group, and organizational goals. Work groups formed on this social base use participation to make decisions to determine the direction of all enterprise activities. Mutual influence and communication become the avenue to coordinate the diverse activities of organizational entities. Measurement is a matter of self-guidance rather than initiated controls from external managerial influences. To use this managerial style reflects the manager's confidence in his or her ability to deal with subordinates as equals capable of making a positive contribution to their work environment. Leadership becomes a collective process of group interaction in contrast to the authoritarian style of traditional managerial systems.

Likert, in his research, discovered the following traits in supervisors whose work groups displayed the most favorable and cooperative attitudes.

1. He is supportive, friendly, and helpful rather than hostile.
2. He is aware of group needs but does not allow peer influence to alter in a negative way company objectives.
3. He views subordinates as people of integrity, self-worth, and achievement.
4. He views individuals with a realistic level of expectation designed to challenge the ability, the initiative, and the psychological growth of people.
5. He views subordinate training and development as essential measurements of his ability to direct the work of people.
6. Directing employees becomes a matter of setting goals, providing required resources, and initiating a work activity.
7. Technical competence becomes a matter of increasing subordinate qualifications instead of using knowledge as a measure of superiority.

220

8. Leadership is based on group leadership techniques designed to build a working team to reach a given level of human and enterprise achievement.[14]

Such research illustrates the impact of managerial assumptions on attitudes that subordinates develop at work.

Implied in the term *integrated* is a positive interaction of people and the work environment based on accomplishment, trust, and mutual respect. These general ideas form the basis of a leadership style used by high producing managers. Moreover, an individual interprets his interaction with managerial policies in three distinct ways. First, cultural and individual values influence people's attitudes toward managerial actions. Second, the greater a person's working experience the more that person expects managerial actions to produce results related to needs. Third, high-level expectations require management to build a highly supportive relationship with subordinates to accomplish enterprise objectives. All these views are essential ingredients a high-producing manager uses to build an effective working team in an enterprise.

The leadership and other processes of the organization must be such as to ensure a maximum probability that in all interactions and all relationships within the organization each member will, in light of his background, values, and expectations, view the experience as supportive and one which builds and maintains his sense of personal worth and importance.[15]

As an organizational concept supportive relationships enhance the effectiveness of economic motivators. Also, attitudes built on a supportive philosophy become reinforcing and cumulative in developing organizational relationships. Likewise, the full impact of each available motive will combine with similar motives to provide a coordinated, enthusiastic effort.

The principle of supportive relationships requires every individual to recognize the purpose of the enterprise as relatively important to the individual's and the enterprise's needs. Further, an individual must feel that job performance directly enhances the firm's ability to achieve its objectives. Implied in the performance of a task is a feeling of personal value reflected in the way management designs the content of a job. Supportive job structuring shows an awareness of human aspirations and expectations. An awareness of subordinates' experiences and expectations must go beyond superficial observation. Empathy can increase a supervisor's knowledge of subordinates' interest but often empathy tends to reflect personal, not group aspirations. Feedback on what a subordinate expects and how a subordinate sees the supervisor is vital to building truly supportive relationships. In a complex enterprise, surveys at regular intervals on many variables can provide data to guide

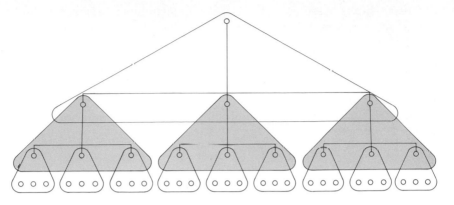

Figure 9-6
The overlapping group form of organization. Work groups vary in size as circumstances require although shown here as consisting of four persons. Source: Rensis Likert, *New Patterns of Management*, New York: McGraw-Hill, 1961.

managerial actions. Another avenue is the creation of work group relationships that provide ways to express, to stimulate, and to create supportive relationships.

We maintain a sense of personal worth by seeking approval from people we identify with and whose approval and support is vital to our psychological growth. A progressive manager seeks to create a work group climate that supports individual values, aspirations, and expectations. Further, interaction of people should expand beyond just one work group to produce group loyalty, effective interrelationships, and achievement of high performance goals.

Figure 9-6 shows the development of overlapping group memberships at all levels of the organization. The dark lines in Figure 9-6 show that interaction is part of individual and group relationships. All organizational members should reflect a linking process that permeates the hierarchical structure of any firm. Moreover, the supervisory process should facilitate the growth of supportive relationships. Such an organization provides a framework for a management system designed to strengthen group functioning at all organizational levels.

To create a supportive organizational structure requires individuals, supervisors, and managers to

1. Accept the decisions of a group based on mutually accepted objectives.
2. Influence decisions and goals of a group in light of personal values, experiences, and goals.
3. Communicate openly with all members to reveal interests, aspirations, and anxieties of all group members.

222

4. Accept the influence and ideas of other members to increase organizational effectiveness.
5. Implement the decisions of the group as part of a personal commitment to the group.
6. Recognize the achievement of individuals and groups in completing an assigned task.[16]

Maslow's Theory of Motivation

Abraham Maslow developed a hierarchy of needs that has withstood the critical analysis of other behavioral scientists. Figure 9-7 shows the need hierarchy of humans in terms of physiological needs, safety needs, social needs, esteem needs, and self-realization needs. As humans receive satisfaction at one level of needs, they move to the next level until they reach the ultimate need of self-realization. Several key propositions of Maslow's theory of motivation are

1. A person is a wanting being—he always wants, and he wants more.
2. A satisfied need is not a motivator of behavior.
3. Human needs are arranged in a series of levels—a hierarchy of importance.[17]

Physiological needs are at the lowest level of the hiararchy and at the bottom of the motivation theory. They are reflected in the human need to eat, to breathe, to rest, to drink, and to engage in active endeavors. Physiological needs tend to be independent of each other in satisfying physical needs. For example, a thirsty person needs water to satisfy this need while still breathing air. The need for water is not satisfied by the consumption of air. In our society of affluence, physiological needs are

Figure 9-7
Maslow's hierarchy of needs. Maslow views an individual's motivation as a predetermined order of needs. Physiological needs are the most imperative ones, but psychologically, the need for self-realization is highly important to each individual. Source: Herbert G. Hicks, *The Management of Organizations: A Systems and Human Resources Approach*, 2nd ed., New York: McGraw-Hill, 1972.

limited in their ability to motivate people. In contrast to this is the experience of underdeveloped areas where satisfaction of physical needs is a continuous fight for survival. Thus, cultural influences have a direct impact on the ability of physiological needs to dominate human motives. Physical needs are repetitive and span a short period of time. Consequently, to base motivation on physical needs alone is costly because of the limited satisfaction they provide. Such activities are taken for granted in our society. Our attention is turned to meeting higher needs such as security, social interaction, and respect from others. Historical evidence suggests that the dominance of physiological concerns tends to thwart the development or fulfillment of higher-level needs. Furthermore, the dominance of any need at any time shapes the individual's view of tomorrow. Utopia becomes the satisfaction of a need such as thirst, hunger, or rest.

Safety needs become dominant when physiological needs are fulfilled. Safety needs reflect the human desire to avoid physical dangers such as assault, fire, and accidents. A related desire is economic security—earning enough money to maintain a given standard of living. Another safety need is the desire for certainty in human, organizational, and environmental relationships. In a work relationship, security needs become evident as employees seek to identify acceptable behavioral patterns to guide their actions. A feeling of dependence tends to increase a person's insecurity because of the control exercised by another person in the same environment. For example, a supervisor can increase feelings of insecurity in employees through arbitrary decisions, favoritism, and discrimination in making job assignments. Thus, real and imagined threats to security can intensify feelings of hostility, distrust, and insecurity in employees.

The third need in Maslow's hierarchy of needs is the need for social interaction. Most of us desire a sense of belonging, a sense of acceptance by associates, and a sense of friendship with personal acquaintances. Managers, in taking a purely intellectual and economic view of people, tend to ignore their social needs. For example, fear of social interaction is expressed by supervisors who distrust the actions of informal groups. A lack of social empathy can produce a managerial style that is cold, elusive, and insensitive to noneconomic concerns. Social needs may also be overlooked in the organizational structure. If it is inflexible in responding to internal or external influences, policies, procedures, and strategies are required to define human relationships in the enterprise. After having worked within such a rigid structure, many managers become indignant when faced with the result: uncooperative, indifferent, and antagonistic employees.

Esteem needs involve self-esteem as well as the esteem of one's peers. Development of self-confidence requires the opportunity to use one's knowledge to solve issues, to gain independence, and to exhibit personal competence. Esteem from others is exhibited in status symbols, rewards for superior performance, and personal influence on actions taken by fellow employees. The ability in a manager to fulfill esteem needs produces a feeling of value, identity, purpose, and competence in employees. Unlike physical needs, esteem needs are almost insatiable. Therefore, there is a continuous search for further satisfaction in the life of an individual. The managerial trend of reducing most jobs to their lowest level of job content has removed many opportunities for the satisfaction of esteem needs in the world of work. Managers should create an organizational climate that provides avenues for all personnel to fulfill their esteem needs.

Self-realization needs become a dominant influence after physiological, safety, social, and esteem needs have been fulfilled to an acceptable level. Self-realization is the process of identifying one's potential, fulfilling that potential, and developing it to the highest possible level of achievement. The exact form needs take is a matter of personal expectation, attitude, and ambition.[18] An excellent illustration of how self-realization needs vary is the number of ideas people have in defining the term *success*. Success, like self-realization, is a relative concept based on the perception a person has of self, of personal abilities, and of the environment. Managers should stress the achievements of people and use their mistakes to aid in the development of personal competence to achieve human and organizational objectives. To assume that all employees have only physiological and safety needs is to limit substantially the contribution that they can make to the surrounding world. In a time of rising costs, the desire for satisfying social, esteem, and self-realization needs is paramount to the survival of human and nonhuman entities.

To comprehend fully Maslow's hierarchy of needs an individual must recognize their interdependence. Such an overlapping relationship is presented in Figure 9-8. For example, as safety needs are satisfied they do not disappear but instead exert less pressure in dominating an individual's behavior. The satisfaction of higher-level needs requires that a person reach a higher peak of satisfaction to fulfill that need. Before a person strives to fulfill the need for esteem, the physiological, safety, and social needs must be fulfilled.

Maslow's theory of human motivation reflects the development of a general level of maturity in individuals. Thus, several qualifications of Maslow's theory are given below to help those now serving as managers.

1. As noted in Figure 9-8, the lines between each need are not absolutes with clearly defined boundaries.
2. People do not all reach the same level of maturity. The general ranking of Maslow's need hierarchy is altered by personal interests, perceptions, and aspirations.

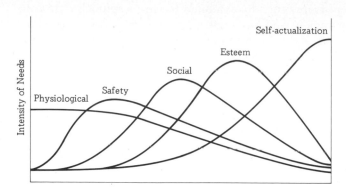

Figure 9-8
Level of attainment or personal growth. The peak of each level must be passed before the next level can begin to assume a dominant role. With self-development, the number and variety of wants increase. Note that in the esteem peak the different needs of an individual are simultaneously active. Source: David Krech, Richard S. Crutchfield, and Egerton L. Ballachey, *The Individual in Society*, New York: McGraw-Hill, 1962, p. 77.

3. People do not always relate a stimulus to a need and then follow a prescribed course of action based on a stimulus-response relationship.
4. People tend to act on the basis of several needs, not just a single need.
5. People seldom act in identical ways to solve a need in life. For example, the need for achievement is reflected in sports, in education, in business, and in individual relationships.
6. People often substitute secondary goals when direct fulfillment of a need is blocked.
7. People are unable to achieve instant gratification of all their needs. Thus, human behavior becomes a process of reaching short-range aims to reach ultimately a long-term objective.[19]

Mason Haire provides an excellent summary of the relationships of Maslow's theory of needs to motivation of people in a work environment.

Everyone is constantly striving for need-satisfactions. It is part of the situation that, at work, the superior controls many of the means to need-satisfaction. By the proper use of his control of the means of need-satisfaction, he can provide or withhold rewards at appropriate times. When we remember the principle of the Law of Effect—that behavior which seems to be rewarded tends to be repeated, while that which seems not to lead to reward or seems to lead to punishment tends to be eliminated—it is clear that the superior has a great opportunity for shaping behavior. Indeed, whether he is conscious of it or not, the superior is bound to be constantly shaping the behavior of his subordinates by the way in which he utilizes the rewards that are at his disposal, and he will inevitably modify the behavior pattern of his work group thereby.[20]

McGregor's Views on Motivation

Douglas McGregor, professor of industrial management at Massachusetts Institute of Technology, developed the Theory X and Theory Y concept of assumptions concerning employee behavior in the world of work. (See also Chapter 2.) McGregor labeled the following assumptions about human behavior as Theory X.

1. In the interest of economic ends management must organize the productive resources of an enterprise such as money, materials, and people.
2. To reach economic objectives requires the creation of a highly structured environment to modify or control the behavior of people to fit the needs of the enterprise.
3. The passive nature of people requires that management threaten, reward, punish, and praise employees to achieve organizational objectives.
4. The typical employee will do as little as possible to earn his pay.
5. The typical employee seeks to be led because he lacks ambition and refuses to accept responsibility for his own actions.
6. The typical employee will resist organizational changes because of his self-centered nature.
7. The typical employee is too dumb to direct his own work without adverse organizational results.[21]

Using this view of workers, a manager creates a working climate of policies, procedures, and programs designed to offset the negative influence of employees. A philosophy of management built on direction and control fails to relate to the higher needs. A person seeking social or ego needs at work will not receive satisfaction if provided only more financial security, such as pay or fringe benefits. In an age of affluence newer workers are motivated to a lesser degree by physical and security needs. New workers seek to fulfill social and ego needs through active participation in their work environment. Thus, yesterday's motivators of security and direction by control often fail to motivate new workers to achieve organizational objectives. According to McGregor, a manager using Theory X makes the following assumptions about human behavior.

To some extent industrial management recognizes that the human adult possesses capabilities for continued learning and growth. . . . In its basic conceptions of managing human resources, however, management appears to have concluded that the average human being is permanently arrested in his development in early adolescence. Theory X is built on the least common human denominator: the factory "hand" of the past. . . . Conventional managerial strategies for the organization, direction, and control of the human resources of enterprise are admirably suited to the capacities and characteristics of the child rather than the adult.[22]

Maslow, in writing about the Theory X view of motivation, made the following observation:

The belief [is often held] that some people are sheep and some people are shepherds, that only a small proportion of the population is capable of self-rule, [and] independent judgment . . . while the larger proportion of the population is stupid, suggestible, and is fit only to be led and taken care of. The fact of the matter is that when people are led, and when decisions are made for them, they steadily become less and less capable of autonomy, of leading themselves, of making their own decisions. In other words, this belief is a self-fulfilling prophecy.[23]

Consequently, the assumptions of Theory X are a reflection of managerial policies and procedures instead of a true picture of inherent human nature.

The inability of Theory X to motivate people positively has led to the development of a contrasting managerial view called Theory Y. Like Theory X, Theory Y makes several basic assumptions about human nature. Six views of people under Theory Y are

1. Management is responsible for organizing an enterprise to achieve economic ends.
2. The expenditure of physical and mental effort in work is as natural as play or rest.
3. Average people exercise self-direction and internal control toward the objectives to which they are committed.
4. Under proper conditions average people learn to accept responsibility.
5. Commitment to objectives comes as a result of the rewards associated with achieving the objectives. Ego needs and self-realization needs are the most significant rewards.
6. Imagination, motivation, creativity, and the potential for development are widely, rather than narrowly, spread throughout the population.[24]

Theory Y tends to criticize traditional management philosophies as well as ask all managers to alter their managerial style to achieve human and nonhuman objectives. Theory Y, to be used effectively by a practicing manager, requires an awareness of three major cautions. First, strong value judgments emphasize self-direction, freedom, and autonomy. Implied in such value judgments is the assumption that all employees desire total freedom and such freedom will not conflict with organizational objectives. However, research by Maslow and other psychologists shows that total freedom leads to anarchy, overindulgence, and irresponsibility in human and organizational relationships. Second, work dissatisfaction is not the result of job simplification, the industrial revolution, and job standardization, but reflects the conflict of person to person, person to society, and person to work organizations. Thus, human alienation is not a phenomenon of the world of work, but reflects the human inability to maintain identity in an ever-changing social, economic, and political environment. Third, increasing the availability of leisure time has reduced the role of a job in providing need satisfaction. Theory X and Y provide an excellent framework that a manager can use to evaluate managerial style and the impact of assumptions about people on organizational effectiveness.[25]

Theory Y can be introduced in the real world by using several innovative concepts. First, a manager can decentralize an organization to provide a degree of individual freedom, to increase personal responsibility for employee's actions, and to provide positive avenues for expressing ego needs. Second, job enlargement can enhance personal worth by providing a greater challenge to individuals. Third, under proper conditions participation and consultative managerial styles can satisfy social and self realization needs. Fourth, the use of managerial appraisal by objectives seeks to give an individual a larger role in measuring his contribution in reaching organizational objectives.[26]

Scott Myers' View of Motivation

Scott Myers, manager of personnel research at Texas Instruments and an industrial psychologist by training, conducted a six-year study of motivation while at Texas Instruments. This study sought to answer the question "Who are your motivated workers?" From this research three questions were identified and three distinct answers were provided to guide the thinking of all managers. They are as follows:

1. What motivates employees to work effectively? "A challenging job which allows a feeling of achievement, responsibility, growth, advancement, environment of work itself, and earned recognition."
2. What dissatisfies workers? "Mostly factors which are peripheral to the job—work rules, lighting, coffee breaks, titles, seniority rights, wages, fringe benefits, and the like."
3. When do workers become dissatisfied? "When opportunities for meaningful achievement are eliminated and they become sensitized to their environment and begin to find fault."[27]

All individuals selected for this project were from three salaried job categories—scientists, engineers, and manufacturing supervisors. Also two hourly paid positions of technicians and assemblers were used in this project. Each participant was asked to identify the favorable or

TABLE 9-11

Scientist—favorable
About six months ago I was given an assignment to develop a new product.
It meant more responsibility and an opportunity to learn new concepts. I had
to study and learn. It was an entirely different job. I always enjoy learning
something new. I had been in basic research where it's difficult to see the end
results. Now I'm working much harder because I'm more interested. I'm
better suited for this type of work.

Scientist—unfavorable
In the fall of 1961 my group would find problems which needed work. We
presented them to our supervisor, and he would say, "Don't bother me with
details; we are in trouble in this area and need one person for guidance and
I am this person." He assigns the problems. He said, "Do what I say whether
you think it will work or not." I wouldn't come in Saturday. Made me want
to go home and work on my yard. Negative attitude. Killed my initiative
because no matter what I came up with my supervisor wouldn't accept it. At
first we tried to convince him but finally gave up. Very few gains made in
this environment.

Engineer—favorable
In 1959 I was working on a carefully outlined project. I was free to do as I
saw fit. There was never a "no, you can't do this." I was doing a worthwhile
job and was considered capable of handling the project. The task was almost
impossible, but their attitude gave me confidence to tackle a difficult job. My
accomplishments were recognized. It helped me gain confidence in how to
approach a problem. It helped me to supervise a small number of people to
accomplish a goal. I accomplished the project and gained something
personally.

Engineer—unfavorable
In December 1961 I was disappointed in my increase. I was extremely well
satisfied with the interview and rating. I was dejected and disillusioned, and
I still think about it. I stopped working so much at night as a result of this
increase. My supervisor couldn't say much. He tried to get me more money
but couldn't get it approved.

Manufacturing supervisor—favorable
In September 1961 I was asked to take over a job which was thought to be
impossible. We didn't think TI could ship what had been promised. I was told
half would be acceptable, but we shipped the entire order! They had confidence in me to think I could do the job. I am happier when under pressure.

Manufacturing supervisor—unfavorable
In the fall of 1958 I disagreed with my supervisor. We were discussing how
many of a unit to manufacture, and I told him I thought we shouldn't make
too many. He said, "I didn't ask for your opinion . . . we'll do what I want."
I was shocked as I didn't realize he had this kind of personality. It put me in
bad with my supervisor and I resented it because he didn't consider my
opinion important.

Hourly male technician—favorable
In June 1961 I was given a bigger responsibility though no change in job
grade. I have a better job, more interesting and one that fits in better with my
education. I still feel good about it. I'm working harder because it was
different from my routine. I am happier . . . feel better about my job.

Hourly male technician—unfavorable
In 1962 I was working on a project and thought I had a real good solution. A
professional in the group but not on my project tore down my project bit by

bit in front of those I worked with. He made disparaging remarks. I was unhappy with the man and unhappy with myself. I thought I had solved it when I hadn't. My boss smoothed it over and made me feel better. I stayed away from the others for a week.

Hourly female assembler—favorable
About two weeks ago I wire-welded more transistors than anyone had ever done—2,100 in nine hours. My foreman complimented me, and I still feel good. Meant self-satisfaction and peace of mind to know I'm doing a good job for them. Once you've done it, you want to do it every day, but you can't. It affected my feelings toward everyone. My old foreman came and talked to me. I didn't think I could ever wire-weld.

Hourly female assembler—unfavorable
For a while the foreman was partial to one of the girls on the line. She didn't work as hard as the other girls and made phone calls. It got to the point where we went to the man over her foreman and complained. We were all worried since we are afraid of reprisals. . . . The girls don't act the same toward each other now because they are afraid. It affects everyone's work. It has been going on for such a long time it's uncomfortable. It is being stopped now by the foreman's supervisor and that girl has been moved.

---

unfavorable experiences associated with present or past job experiences. From 715 interviews, the interviewers were able to identify favorable or unfavorable job experiences for all five job classifications. A brief statement in Table 9-11 provides a sample of the experiences outlined by all five job areas at Texas Instruments. To increase the researchers understanding of various responses two factors were used to classify the views of each participant. First-level factors were defined as events that produced favorable or unfavorable feelings toward work experiences. A follow-up interview was conducted to determine "why" the first-level factor produced a favorable or unfavorable attitude toward present or past work experiences. Fourteen first-level factors were identified as receiving the greatest attention from participants in selecting favorable and unfavorable job experiences. Figure 9-9 shows the list of factors and classifies each item as favorable or unfavorable in shaping employee attitudes. Achievement received a two-to-one ratio of favorable to unfavorable responses from 235 interviews. On the other hand, company policy and administration procedures produced a negative four-to-one ratio from 101 interviews. Further analysis of respondents produced two distinct traits for "motivation seekers" and "maintenance seekers."

Maintenance seekers
Motivated by environment
Avoid motivation opportunities
Little satisfaction from accomplishment
Negative attitudes toward work
Little interest in quality work
Seldom profit from experiences professionally

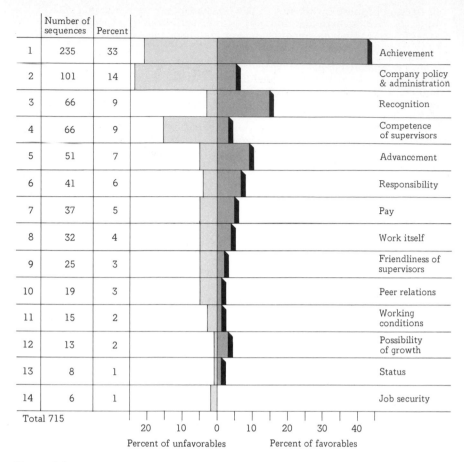

	Number of sequences	Percent		
1	235	33		Achievement
2	101	14		Company policy & administration
3	66	9		Recognition
4	66	9		Competence of supervisors
5	51	7		Advancement
6	41	6		Responsibility
7	37	5		Pay
8	32	4		Work itself
9	25	3		Friendliness of supervisors
10	19	3		Peer relations
11	15	2		Working conditions
12	13	2		Possibility of growth
13	8	1		Status
14	6	1		Job security
Total 715				

20   10   0   10   20   30   40

Percent of unfavorables   Percent of favorables

Figure 9-9
Factors that favorably or unfavorably shape employee attitudes. Source: Scott Myers, "Who Are Your Motivated Workers?" *Harvard Business Review*, January–February 1964.

Values blow with the wind
Motivation seekers
Motivated by the task
High tolerance for environmental factors
Great satisfaction from work
Positive attitudes toward work
Strive for quality work
Benefit from experiences professionally
Values self chosen and developed

People tend to remain permanent members of maintenance- or motivation-oriented groups. However, a maintenance seeker in an achievement environment tends to adopt the traits of motivation seekers. Likewise, motivation seekers in a nonachievement climate tend to adopt the traits of maintenance seekers.

Figure 9-10 shows the first-level factors that tended to motivate scientists in their work. Favorable responses are shown on the top side of Figure 9-10; unfavorable responses are shown on the lower side of Figure 9-10. Favorable responses were motivators that had little or no relation to the job itself. Unfavorable responses were maintenance needs that related directly to the job itself. The depth of feeling for each value is reflected in the length of the bar for each factor listed in Figure 9-10. For example, scientists obtained long-lasting positive feelings from work itself and long-lasting negative feelings from responsibility disappointments. Similarly, in Figure 9-11a engineers show a pattern of satisfaction similar to that of scientists in Figure 9-10. Moreover, Figure 9-11a adds the factor of friendly supervision and pay. Pay was less of a motivation and tended to be a greater source of dissatisfaction in directing the efforts of engineers. Likewise, friendly supervision was not a motivator but could produce dissatisfaction in adverse situations.

Manufacturing supervisors in Figure 9-11b tended to value advancement, growth, and responsibility as measures of success through advancement in administrative positions. Work itself was not mentioned by manufacturing supervisors but a desire for growth and peer

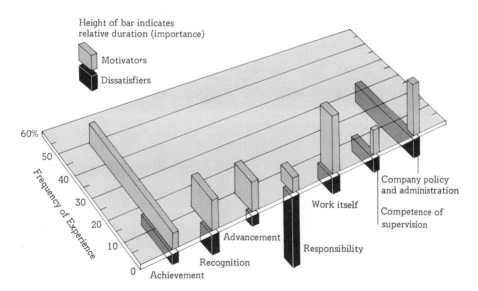

Figure 9-10
Factors affecting motivation of scientists. Source: Scott Myers, "Who Are Your Motivated Workers?" *Harvard Business Review*, January–February 1964.

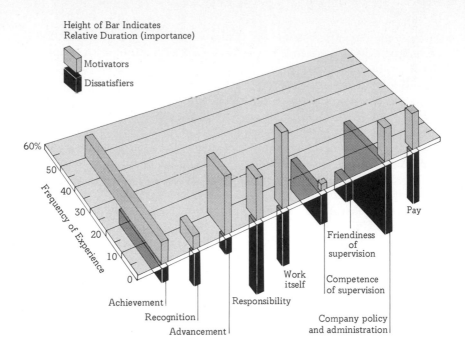

Height of Bar Indicates
Relative Duration (importance)

☐ Motivators
■ Dissatisfiers

60%
50
40
30
20
10
0

Frequency of Experience

Achievement
Recognition
Advancement
Responsibility
Work itself
Company policy and administration
Competence of supervision
Friendliness of supervision
Pay

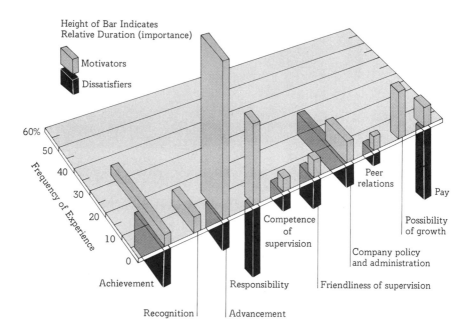

Height of Bar Indicates
Relative Duration (importance)

☐ Motivators
■ Dissatisfiers

60%
50
40
30
20
10
0

Frequency of Experience

Achievement
Recognition
Advancement
Responsibility
Competence of supervision
Friendliness of supervision
Peer relations
Company policy and administration
Possibility of growth
Pay

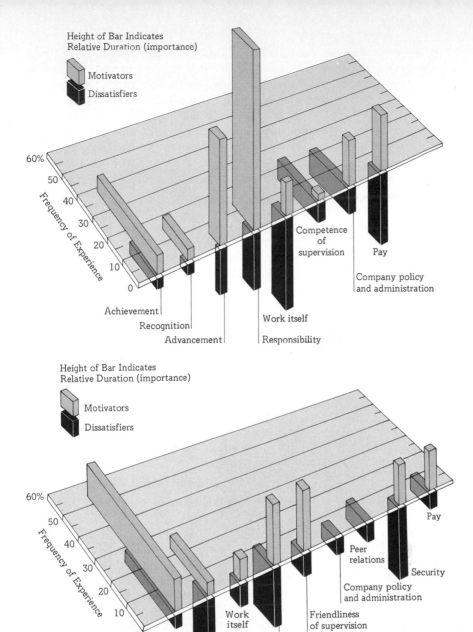

Height of Bar Indicates
Relative Duration (importance)

Motivators

Dissatisfiers

60%
50
40
30
20
10
0

Frequency of Experience

Achievement
Recognition
Advancement
Work itself
Responsibility
Competence of supervision
Pay
Company policy and administration

Height of Bar Indicates
Relative Duration (importance)

Motivators

Dissatisfiers

60%
50
40
30
20
10
0

Frequency of Experience

Achievement
Recognition
Work itself
Competence of supervision
Friendliness of supervision
Company policy and administration
Peer relations
Security
Pay

Figure 9-11
Source: Scott Myers, "Who Are Your Motivated Workers?" *Harvard Business Review*, January–February 1964.

relations appeared as new factors. Success was equated with job achievements, and failure was equated with lack of opportunities for career advancement. Likewise, company operating procedures could block advancement as a maintenance factor but could enhance advancement as a motivational factor. Peer relations were of limited influence except in cases where peer pressures blocked the advancement of a supervisor toward a career goal. Pay was the greatest source of dissatisfaction because managers equate pay with success and view company reimbursement programs as unrelated to the level of responsibility assumed by manufacturing supervisors.

Male technicians in Figure 9-11c produced the greatest contrast between motivators and dissatisfiers on the job. Technicians saw achievement, advancement, and responsibility as motivators in their work. Similarly, pay, work itself, competence of supervision, and company policy tended to be the greatest sources of dissatisfaction among hourly male technicians. Such a contrast in attitudes presents a supervisor with the challenge of providing creative ways to use a technician's desire for achievement, advancement, and responsibility. In a job environment that is highly restrictive in terms of job design a technician tended to be highly frustrated by the lack of job challenge provided by his daily assignments. Technicians, as their educational, experience, and aspiration levels increase, tended to suffer from the organizational malady of underemployment. Put another way, the individual was overqualified for the present job assignment. To remedy this situation would require limited direct supervision by superiors as well as the enrichment of the technician's position vertically in light of changing personal qualifications.

Female assemblers showed a more significant variance in their attitude toward work than did scientists, engineers, manufacturing supervisors, and male hourly technicians. In Figure 9-11d the factors viewed as motivators by female assemblers were achievement, competence of supervision, friendliness of supervision, and security. Failure to receive recognition for contribution to the firm was a major source of job dissatisfaction. Inadequate supervision was another major source of job dissatisfaction among female assemblers. A further source of job dissatisfaction was the threat, real or imagined, to continued employment. Pay was more of a dissatisfier than a motivator to most female assemblers. Peer relations were a major source of dissatisfaction when the job environment produced a high degree of friction in interpersonal relationships. Unlike the hourly technicians, female assemblers sought close supervision from supervisors to provide recognition, understanding, and approval in completing job assignments.[28]

The sources of favorable and unfavorable attitudes toward work have been described. However, to be clearly understood such attitudes need input from participants as to why they feel the way they do toward a

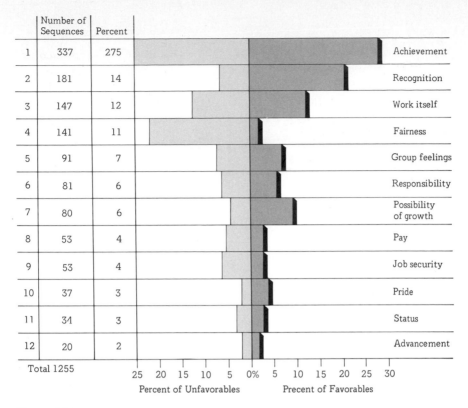

	Number of Sequences	Percent		
1	337	275		Achievement
2	181	14		Recognition
3	147	12		Work itself
4	141	11		Fairness
5	91	7		Group feelings
6	81	6		Responsibility
7	80	6		Possibility of growth
8	53	4		Pay
9	53	4		Job security
10	37	3		Pride
11	34	3		Status
12	20	2		Advancement

Total 1255

```
25  20  15  10  5  0%  5  10  15  20  25  30
   Percent of Unfavorables      Precent of Favorables
```

Figure 9-12
Second-level factors. Source: Scott Myers, "Who Are Your Motivated Workers?"
Harvard Business Review, January–February 1964.

particular event. Factors that produce meaning or tell the "why" of a decision are shown in Figure 9-12. These results were obtained from 1255 responses in 715 interviews. It is interesting to note that nine out of twelve second-level factors appeared as first-level factors. Pie charts identify factors that were motivators or dissatisfiers and show the relationship of first- and second-level factors to each other. Horizontal charts show the influence of first-level factors that shaped the development of secondary-level feelings.

Figures 9-13a and 9-13b show why achievement was a motivator and why failure was a dissatisfier. Likewise, Figures 9-14a and 9-14b show the factors that contributed to feelings of achievement or failure. Figure 9-15a shows the factors that made recognition a motivator in the life of several Texas Instruments employees. Figure 9-15b shows the factors that made recognition a dissatisfier in the work experience of several Texas Instruments employees. The role of pay in shaping positive or negative job attitudes is reflected in Figures 9-16a and 9-16b. Pay, as

A. WHY ACHIEVEMENT IS A MOTIVATOR

Recognition 24%
Pay 3%
Achievement itself 43%

Group feeling 7%
Work itself 8%

Pride 6%
Responsibility 2%

Growth 4%
Miscellaneous 3%

B. WHY FAILURE IS A DISSATISFIER

Failure itself 50%
Miscellaneous 9%

Lack of recognition 12%
Work itself 8%

Unfairness 8%
Shame 8%

Security 5%

Figure 9-13
Source: Scott Myers, "Who Are Your Motivated Workers?" *Harvard Business Review*, January–February 1964.

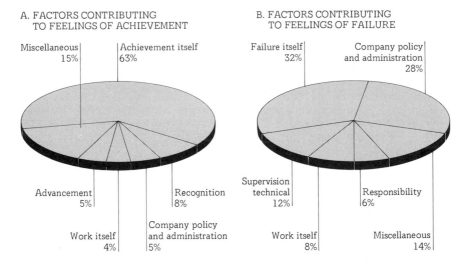

A. FACTORS CONTRIBUTING
   TO FEELINGS OF ACHIEVEMENT

Miscellaneous 15%
Achievement itself 63%

Advancement 5%
Recognition 8%

Work itself 4%
Company policy and administration 5%

B. FACTORS CONTRIBUTING
   TO FEELINGS OF FAILURE

Failure itself 32%
Company policy and administration 28%

Supervision technical 12%
Responsibility 6%

Work itself 8%
Miscellaneous 14%

Figure 9-14
Source: Scott Myers, "Who Are Your Motivated Workers?" *Harvard Business Review*, January–February 1964.

238

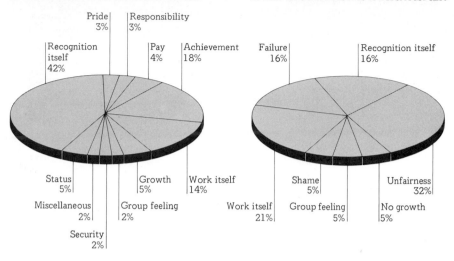

A. WHY RECOGNITION IS A MOTIVATOR   B. WHY RECOGNITION IS A DISSATISFIER

Figure 9-15
Source: Scott Myers, "Who Are Your Motivated Workers?" *Harvard Business Review*, January–February 1964.

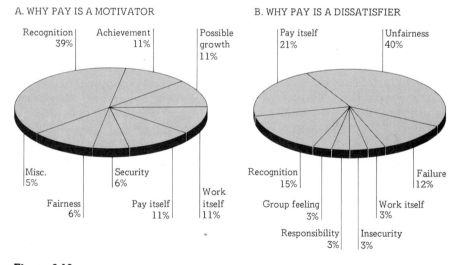

A. WHY PAY IS A MOTIVATOR   B. WHY PAY IS A DISSATISFIER

Figure 9-16
Source: Scott Myers, "Who Are Your Motivated Workers?" *Harvard Business Review*, January–February 1964.

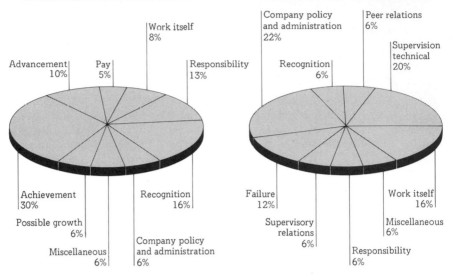

A. FACTORS CONTRIBUTING TO
SATISFACTION WITH WORK ITSELF

B. FACTORS CONTRIBUTING TO
DISSATISFACTION WITH WORK ITSELF

Figure 9-17
Source: Scott Myers, "Who Are Your Motivated Workers?" *Harvard Business Review*, January–February 1964.

stated earlier, is valued in terms of the purchasing power it represents and in terms of the recognition provided from receiving a high wage for the task performed. Closely related to pay is the degree of satisfaction or dissatisfaction with a job in the work environment. Figure 9-17 shows the distribution in percentages of factors that produce job dissatisfaction. Fairness in supervisor-employee relations was shown to be a maintenance factor in structuring positive supervisor-employee relationships. Sources of feelings of unfairness are shown in Figure 9-18. Note technical supervision and company policies were the greatest sources of negative employee feelings. Such feelings produced a negative attitude toward the enterprise.

Thus, a fitting close to the review of secondary factors that express the "why" of employee views is a brief look at the importance of good supervision. Figure 9-19b shows the factors that made supervision a dissatisfier in an employee's work experience. A supervisor's role should be that of providing conditions to motivate an employee's behavior without sacrificing the employee's desire to satisfy maintenance needs. Figure 9-20 presents a contrasting view of motivation and maintenance needs of employees in a work environment.

Having read Scott Myers's viewpoint on a maintenance-motivation theory of management, readers are inclined to ask, "How can I apply

240

FACTORS CONTRIBUTING TO FEELINGS OF UNFAIRNESS

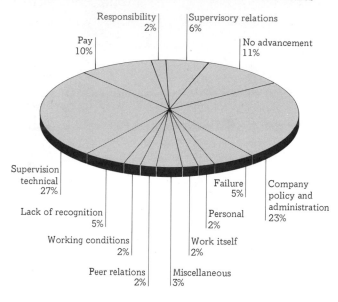

Figure 9-18
Source: Scott Myers, "Who Are Your Motivated Workers?" *Harvard Business Review*, January–February 1964.

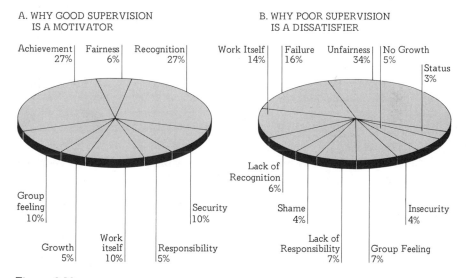

A. WHY GOOD SUPERVISION IS A MOTIVATOR

B. WHY POOR SUPERVISION IS A DISSATISFIER

Figure 9-19
Source: Scott Myers, "Who Are Your Motivated Workers?" *Harvard Business Review*, January–February 1964.

MOTIVATIONAL TECHNIQUES 241

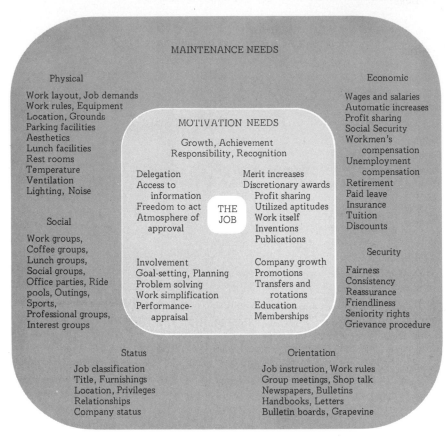

MAINTENANCE NEEDS

Physical

Work layout, Job demands
Work rules, Equipment
Location, Grounds
Parking facilities
Aesthetics
Lunch facilities
Rest rooms
Temperature
Ventilation
Lighting, Noise

Social

Work groups,
Coffee groups,
Lunch groups,
Social groups,
Office parties, Ride
pools, Outings,
Sports,
Professional groups,
Interest groups

MOTIVATION NEEDS

Growth, Achievement
Responsibility, Recognition

Delegation
Access to
information
Freedom to act
Atmosphere of
approval

THE
JOB

Merit increases
Discretionary awards
Profit sharing
Utilized aptitudes
Work itself
Inventions
Publications

Involvement
Goal-setting, Planning
Problem solving
Work simplification
Performance-
appraisal

Company growth
Promotions
Transfers and
rotations
Education
Memberships

Economic

Wages and salaries
Automatic increases
Profit sharing
Social Security
Workmen's
compensation
Unemployment
compensation
Retirement
Paid leave
Insurance
Tuition
Discounts

Security

Fairness
Consistency
Reassurance
Friendliness
Seniority rights
Grievance procedure

Status

Job classification
Title, Furnishings
Location, Privileges
Relationships
Company status

Orientation

Job instruction, Work rules
Group meetings, Shop talk
Newspapers, Bulletins
Handbooks, Letters
Bulletin boards, Grapevine

Figure 9-20
Employee needs—maintenance and motivational. Source: Scott Myers, "Who Are Your Motivated Workers?" *Harvard Business Review,* January–February 1964.

this concept?" To apply this concept to an organization, a supervisor must be willing to express these ideas in day-to-day contact with management and other supervisors. For effective supervisors, this managerial theory will provide additional insight into the reason employees act as they do. Another benefit for an effective manager is the further development of leadership skills. For supervisors using traditional supervisory techniques, the adoption of a motivation-maintenance theory of management depends on its total integration into the managerial philosophy of the enterprise. The adoption this theory is not a substitute for overcoming managerial deficiencies such as poor supervisory training, poor supervisory selection, or poor evaluation of supervisory effectiveness.[29]

Summary

Several motivational techniques have been identified in this chapter to provide an awareness of various ways to motivate personnel. Chris Argyris suggested the use of training groups as a means of motivating people. Through the use of training groups, a manager is able to evaluate present leadership style and the consequences of that leadership style. It should be understood that lab experiences are not a case of blind acceptance of new values or of the imposition of one viewpoint on lab participants. Although lab exercises have been used successfully for over ten years, it is unrealistic to state that training groups constitute a remedy for all organizational ills. Like any managerial tool, their effectiveness is determined by the support provided by upper management in altering traditional organizational concepts.

An alternative managerial style was developed by Blake and Mouton. This managerial grid presented five managerial styles and the consequences of each style in terms of human, organizational, and environmental relationships. The 9,1 style seeks to build an authoritarian climate to govern all company relationships. The 1,9 style takes a human relationship approach that expresses little, if any, concern for organizational aims. A 5,5 style seeks to walk a fine line between concern for organizational aims and concern for the development of positive human relationships. In this relationship the informal group becomes in effect a co-manager directing the efforts of the enterprise. A 1,1 style reflects a manager who is turned off by concerns relating to people or relating to the organization. Such a manager finds expression of inner feelings through involvement in community-related projects. A 9,9 team approach seeks to build a climate of effectiveness based on individual accountability, self-direction, and acceptance of organizational goals.

Frederick Herzberg has developed a motivational theory designed to provide greater job satisfaction in all organized business entities. A major point of Herzberg was that of removing the "carrot" and the "stick" as the only motivational tools to obtain employee cooperation. Likewise, motivation is more than job design changes, human relations training, communications, and employee counseling. The failure of such techniques rests on the fact that such approaches rely strictly on extrinsic motivation. Herzberg believes that extrinsic motivation produces movement but fails to generate any form of internal self-direction. Herzberg's study of stockholder correspondents shows the value of vertical job loading in enriching an employee's job. Motivation and job enrichment are continuous managerial processes that cannot be obtained through gimmicks, manipulation, or hygiene incentives.

Rensis Likert sought in his research to identify the traits of managers associated with high producing groups. Several of these traits reflect the development of supportive relationships based on the view of subordinates as people of integrity, worth, and achievement. Supportive job structuring shows an awareness of human aspirations, expectations, and goals in maintaining a person's sense of personal achievement. The key to developing supportive relationships is personal identification with the purposes of the enterprise.

Abraham Maslow developed a hierarchy-of-needs concept designed to show the motivational needs of human beings. Physical needs relate to body functions and to the need to be actively engaged in purposeful endeavors. Safety needs reflect the desire to avoid physical dangers, such as assault, fire, and accidents. Social needs reflect the desire for acceptance, for friendship, and for a sense of belonging. Esteem needs reflect a sense of confidence designed to gain peer approval or provide positive interaction with one's environment. Self-realization is the process of identifying one's potential, fulfilling that potential, and developing it to the highest level of achievement. To use Maslow's theory of human motivation, a manager should be aware of the qualifications that increase the validity of that theory.

Douglas McGregor presented two distinct approaches toward the motivation of people. Theory X, commonly viewed as the traditional approach, is designed to offset the negative influence of employees. Such a managerial style relies on external stimuli to direct, coerce, and control individual actions in completing organizational actions. A contrasting view, referred to as Theory Y, or the humanistic approach, seeks to achieve human and nonhuman objectives. Any manager desiring to use Theory Y should be aware of the value judgments that underlie this managerial concept. In the real world, Theory Y is based on a decentralized structure, job enlargement, consultative management, and evaluation by objectives.

Scott Myers, in six years of research at Texas Instruments, sought to identify the traits of motivated workers. Using several job categories and the use of interviews, he identified favorable and unfavorable job experiences. Based on this research, he classified employees as maintenance seekers and motivation seekers. First-level factors were defined as events that produced favorable or unfavorable feelings toward work experiences. Figure 9-9 identified fourteen first-level factors that influenced employee attitudes positively or negatively. Figure 9-10 showed the first-level factors that tended to motivate scientists in their work. Figure 9-11b showed the attitudes of manufacturing supervisors in their

244

work. Male technicians in Figure 9-11c produced the greatest contrast between motivators and dissatisfiers on the job. The viewpoint of female assemblers was reflected in Figure 9-11a. Figure 9-12 through 9-19a identified the secondary-level factors that produced job satisfaction or job dissatisfaction among all five employee groups. Figure 9-20 presented a contrasting view of motivation and maintenance needs of employees in work environment. The adoption of this theory is not a substitute for overcoming managerial deficiencies such as poor supervisory training, poor supervisory selection, or poor evaluation of supervisory effectiveness. These motivational techniques are presented to provide an awareness of several views and to challenge all present or future managers to evaluate their effectiveness in motivating personnel.

Notes

1. Chris Argyris. *Interpersonal Competence and Organizational Effectiveness*. Homewood, Ill.: Irwin, 1962, pp. 316–317.
2. Ibid., pp. 316–321.
3. Ibid., p. 325.
4. Ibid., pp. 326–331.
5. Ibid., pp. 333–338.
6. Robert R. Blake and Jane S. Mouton. *The Managerial Grid*. Houston: Gulf, 1964.
7. Ibid., pp. 7–10.
8. Ibid., pp. 11–15.
9. Ibid., pp. 16–17.
10. Ibid., pp. 17–20.
11. Frederick Herzberg. "One More Time: How Do You Motivate Employees?" *Harvard Business Review*, January–February, 1968, pp. 54–56.
12. Ibid., pp. 57–58.
13. Ibid., pp. 59–62.
14. Rensis Likert. *New Patterns of Management*. New York: McGraw-Hill, 1961, pp. 97–106.
15. Ibid.
16. Ibid.
17. Herbert G. Hicks. *The Management of Organizations: A Systems and Human Resources Approach*, 2nd ed. New York: McGraw-Hill, 1972, p. 283.
18. Ibid., pp. 284–286.
19. Ibid., pp. 287–289.
20. Ibid., p. 290.
21. Douglas McGregor. "The Human Side of Enterprise," in Dale S. Beach (ed.), *Managing People at Work*. New York: Macmillan, 1971, p. 218.
22. Hicks, op. cit., p. 296.
23. Ibid.
24. From *Management, the Individual, the Organization, the Process* by Gerald H. Graham. Copyright © 1975 by Wadsworth Publishing Company, Inc., Belmont, California 94002.
25. Hicks, op. cit., pp. 298–299.

26. McGregor, op. cit., pp. 223–225.
27. Scott Myers. "Who Are Your Motivated Workers?" *Harvard Business Review*, January–February, 1964, p. 73.
28. Ibid., pp. 73–80.
29. Ibid., pp. 81–88.

CUSTOM FURNITURE CASE:
THE CARROT AND THE STICK

Production is down in the plant at Custom Furniture and John Taylor is discussing this matter with Bill Jones, the office manager.

John: "Bill, you probably know that our production is slipping. I wanted to get your ideas on this problem before I talk to Sam. You know he thinks that I am too easy on our employees. We've just got to figure some way to get the production people motivated."

Bill: "Well, John, you know that I kind of go along with Sam about this handling workers with kid gloves. But I certainly agree that what we need is a little more motivation and a lot less goldbricking."

John: "I was thinking that it might be a good idea to conduct some sort of survey to find out what is bothering them—what it is that they really want out of their jobs."

Bill: "Boy, could that open a can of worms! You remember that suggestion box I put up a few months ago and how many "drop deads" and "turn blues" I fished out before I took it down?"

John: "That could have been because of the way it was introduced to them and also because no reward was offered if the suggestions were adopted."

Bill: "I still believe that the best way to get them motivated is with some more discipline—a few three-day layoffs, some letters in their personnel files, and they'll come around. After all, we have done everything in the world for them. We air-conditioned the plant, spruced up the washrooms, gave them coffee breaks in the morning and afternoon. Compared to some of the places that I have seen, this is like a country club. What is it they want? We've even simplified most of the jobs so that they don't even have to think, just perform the operations."

John: "You're right. But have all these things made them want to be better workers? What is it that motivates people? Is it money? Is it working conditions? Just what is it?"

1. What management concepts do you recognize in this situation?
2. What is the major problem?
3. What alternative courses of action are open to John Taylor?
4. Which alternative would you choose?

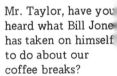

LABOR RELATIONS

10

For the full story, turn to the case on page 288.

GENERAL PURPOSES
OF CHAPTER 10

1. To gain an insight into the modern concerns of labor relations
2. To look at the behavior of contemporary union members
3. To examine the various stages in union-management relationships

LEARNING OBJECTIVES

1. To name four concerns that are relatively new to labor relations
2. To discuss the problems of age, both old and young, with management
3. To name nine factors to be considered in writing job descriptions that may be subject to bargaining
4. To state in general the five provisions of the General Electric affirmative action program
5. To describe recent changes in leadership patterns that increase opportunities to utilize women's leadership strengths
6. To formulate a reaction to the surveys concerning the relative position of men and women in industry
7. To construct a ten-step program for an effective affirmative action program for women
8. To define the term *disadvantaged individual*
9. To name three necessary attitudes to be adopted by firms employing ex-inmates of penal institutions
10. To describe at least five types of union members
11. To name and briefly describe four stages in union-management relationships

Labor relations has traditionally been concerned with wage patterns, fringe benefits, and internal management-labor issues. However, in the 1970s labor relations has become involved with new concerns such as minority employment, women in business, the socially disadvantaged in business, and the increasing role of employees under age twenty-five. Although collective bargaining remains a central issue in managerial and labor relations, it has lost its significance as the sole determinant of positive management-labor relations. This development reflects the fact that 75 percent of America's labor force is not union organized. Consequently, management must expand its horizons beyond collective bargaining to noneconomic issues relating to employment opportunities, advancement opportunities, and satisfaction of social issues. Management is not alone in feeling the influence of new employee concerns. Union leaders are faced with similar issues in developing a bargaining strategy.

The changing size and demographic distribution of the labor force is shown in Figure 10-1. A brief review shows an increase in older and

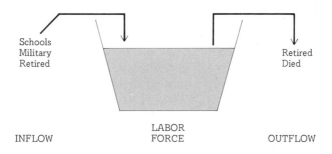

Changes in the labor force by age, 1960—75 (in millions)

	Actual		Projected	
Age	1950	1960	1970	1975
14–24	13.3	13.6	19.8	21.7
25–34	15.1	15.0	16.7	20.8
35–44	14.1	16.8	16.5	16.2
45–64	19.1	24.1	29.1	30.5
Total	64.7	73.1	85.7	93.0

Figure 10-1
The input-output of the labor supply. Source: U.S. Department of Labor, Bureau of Labor Statistics, *Interim Revised Projections of U.S. Labor Force, 1965–75*, Special Labor Force Report No. 24.

younger workers with a shortage of manpower in the group consisting of workers thirty-five to forty-five years old. The increase in younger workers without marketable skills is shown by the fact that 30 percent of the young people have not completed high school. Declining blue-collar jobs make future unemployment a definite fact of life. A related issue is the changing value structure of younger employees. This value structure often does not relate to traditional managerial concepts. For example, younger employees are less submissive to authority, so managerial styles must become more humanistic and participative.

A decline in upper-age groups will increase competition for managerial talent. Pay in financial and humanistic terms will become increasingly important in securing and retaining managerial talent. A shortage of older managers will force management to identify prospective managerial talent among the twenty-five- to thirty-five-year-old employees. A positive effect of this trend is the removal of "shelf-sitting" periods in the life of corporate managers. The economic impact of higher wage incentives is offset by an increased pay-back period of fifteen to twenty-five years.[1]

As stated earlier, union leaders are also feeling the impact of changing membership among minorities and younger workers. From 1964 to 1970 there was a general increase in contract rejections by rank-and-file members. Similarly, local demands have increased in the last few years to the point where the solution of economic demands marks the start of labor-management negotiations. For example, General Motors and the United Auto Workers settled economic issues in December of 1967 but local issues were not resolved until July of 1968. The youth explosion is seen in the Rubber Workers Union, where one-third of its 208,000 members are under the age of twenty-five. Forty percent of the UAW membership among hourly employees has less than five years of service. Younger workers are less disciplined. There has been a 50 percent increase in casual absenteeism at General Motors during the past five years.[2]

The black revolution is a second major force that is changing traditional union attitudes toward minority participation. A new body of case law is knocking down racial barriers and segregated seniority lines in the steel industry. The failure of unions to respond to minority demands has produced wildcat strikes at a Dodge plant in Hamtramck, Michigan. The refusal of trade unions in construction industries to remove discrimination barriers in Pittsburgh was responsible for a wildcat strike that stopped all construction. The rise in Equal Employment Opportunity complaints will also alter traditional union membership patterns.

A third force altering union views is the split between the AFL–CIO and the Alliance for Labor Action. George Meany remains the guiding force of the AFL–CIO, which represents the more traditional views of union leaders in this country. The ALA represents a collective membership of 2 million Teamsters and 1 million auto workers. This alliance is becoming socially active, expressing its concern for slum tenants, supporting private antipoverty programs, and attempting to attract younger workers.

The impact of these two diverse union giants will be seen in a competitive drive for membership, for wage settlements, and for influence over general economic conditions. Walter Maggiolo, a veteran federal mediator, showing his concern for such competitive actions, stated that local grievances will be forgotten in the struggle to gain national headlines. A related problem is that of convincing union members that wage settlements are fair in order to eliminate the danger of strikes and inflationary settlements. From this brief view of labor, it is apparent that management must face a younger, more aggressive labor force, a declining supply of managerial talent, minority demands for representation in higher-paying jobs, and splintered union representation of employee demands. Thus, labor relations has expanded from a focus on wages and fringe benefits to social and humanitarian concerns.[3]

Environmental Conditions

Trade unions have expanded membership to include teachers, secretaries, salespeople, and retail clerks. As trade union membership expands beyond blue-collar jobs, union influence in labor-management relations becomes greater. The growth of union representation among governmental and municipal employees will further alter traditional bargaining styles and philosophies. For example, since the early 1970s, we have seen increased union militancy among teachers, firefighters, police officers, and postal workers as they strive to increase their economic and social status. Whether future developments will be positive or negative will depend on the policies adopted by management and by labor in meeting employee demands.[4]

Another environmental factor is the managerial philosophy adopted by management and labor as they seek to create a constructive work environment. Table 10-1 illustrates two contrasting models of organization structure and the climate created by the adoption of such managerial techniques. Table 10-2 shows the personnel and labor relations policies adopted by liberal and conservative organization models.

In labor-management relations, a major area of concern is the work environment in which individuals perform a certain task. For example, in writing a job description there may be as many as nine traits to be considered that are defined in management-labor negotiations. They are as follows:

1. *Degree of physical exertion required.* Management has reduced the level of physical exertion through automation and the use of power

TABLE 10-1
Contrasting models of organization structure and climate

Liberal organizations	Characteristic	Conservative organizations
(Low degree of structure)		(High degree of structure or bureaucracy)
Broadly defined	Jobs	Narrowly defined
Either not used or very general	Job descriptions	Used, clear and specific
Structure		
Specialization by process; not too specialized	Horizontal division of labor (specialization)	Specialization by function; much specialization
Nonexistent or not used	Standardization of policies, procedures	Used, extensive
Nonexistent or not used	Formalization (degree to which documents and forms are used)	Used, extensive
Flat organization, few levels	Vertical division of labor (chain of command)	Tall organization, many levels
Communications		
Informal, multichannel communications "system"	General description of communications	Well-defined chain of command
Much communication encouraged in all directions (up, down, and lateral)	Amount and direction of communication	Little communication encouraged; mostly downward
Adequate; mostly accurate	Quality of communication	Needs supplementary system; somewhat inaccurate
Decision making		
Decentralized	General decision	Centralized
Wherever the knowledge necessary for good decisions is located	Location of most critical decisions	Toward the top of the hierarchy
Made by work groups and administrators	Goal-setting decisions	Made by individual administrators
Responsibility for decisions given to doers	Attitude toward decision-making responsibility	Responsibility for decisions is administrators'
Encourages doers to take reasonable risks	Risk taking	Discourages risk taking by doers
Encourages creative decisions by experimentation, cross fertilization, and rewards	Creativity (in decisions and tasks)	Expects creativity to come from administrators and filter down from there

254

Coordination

Informal, unprogrammed; performed by work groups	General description	Programmed by use of SOP's, individual coordinators, or hierarchy

Control/leadership style

Large	Span of control	Small
Determined by work group and administrator	Control standards	Determined by administrator
Goal oriented	Control orientation	Goal and procedures oriented
Flexible	Degree of control	Inflexible
General	Leadership style	Close
Supportive, warm, favorable, trusting, approving, rewarding	Attitudes toward subordinates	Control oriented, unfavorable, distrusting, disapproving, punishing

Conflict management

Conflict is normal and must be managed	General attitude	Conflict is abnormal and must be suppressed
Work it through after thorough discussion	Method of handling conflict with subordinates, peers, and superiors	Suppress by use of authority; competitive; try to win administrators' point of view

Source: William F. Glueck, *Personnel: A Diagnostic Approach.* Dallas: Business Publications, 1974, pp. 77–78.

tools. Unions have asked for higher wages, increased rest periods, and reduced hours of work for individuals involved in jobs requiring heavy physical exertion.

2. *Degree of environmental pleasantness or unpleasantness.* Management in responding to union pressure has improved the work environment for most employees. The impact of the Occupational Safety and Health Act of 1971 has also brought dramatic improvements in employee working conditions

3. *Location of work.* Location of work becomes a matter of personal preference in light of company job requirements.

4. *Time duration of work.* Time duration of work is determined by physical job requirements, by four- or five-day workweeks, and by the introduction of flexible working hours.

5. *Degree of specialization.* Degree of specialization provides an excellent contrast of management's and labor's views. For example, labor has sought to limit employees to a specific task so as to create an inflated demand for personnel. Management has sought to broaden

TABLE 10-2
Personnel policies of liberal and conservative organization models

Liberal organizations		Conservative organizations
Vague or not used	Job descriptions	Used detailed
Emphasis on output, not process of output	Working conditions	Time clocks, close check on hours and times
Worked out by work groups	Employment planning	Worked out by management
Human asset accounting	Human assets in accounting	Traditional accounting
Work groups and management	Recruiting responsibility	Management
Recruiting some risky candidates	Recruiting standards	Recruiting safe candidates
Informal procedures; primary interviewing by work groups	Selection	Extensive use of formal procedures, tests, interviews by management
Relaxed, social as well as technical	Orientation	Stressful, sink or swim
Planned by employee and management	Career development	Unplanned or planned by management
Voluntary by employees after management announces openings	Transfers	Transfer by management with no rewards for those refusing transfers
None	Employment contracts	For key positions
Planned by management and work group	Technical training	Planned by management
Integrated on-the-job and off-job experiences, with work-group input in planning	Management development	Not stressed or tenuously related to job
Jointly by superiors, subordinates and peers	Performance evaluation	By superiors; sometimes announced to subordinates
Management announces that positions are open, interviews all those interested	Promotion systems	Management initiates and decides
Multiple compensation systems, including group incentives	Compensation	Individual incentives
Employees have a voice in how benefit money is spent	Benefits	Management "giveth"
Used	Productivity schemes (Scanlon Plan, etc.)	Not used

Separates supervisor from discipline– independent channel	Discipline	Management both boss and judge
Cooperative fair play to both sides	Labor relations	Competitive zero-sum games

Source: William F. Glueck, *Personnel: A Diagnostic Approach.* Dallas: Business Publications, 1974, p. 79.

employee job requirements to reduce the size of the labor force as well as to increase the productivity of all employees.

6. *Educational requirements.* Educational requirements have reduced the demand for unskilled and semiskilled labor. A related result of higher education requirements is underemployment of people in positions that fail to challenge their abilities.

7. *Experience qualifications.* Experience qualifications present a contrast in management and labor views. Management seeks to hire people with a high level of experience because this reduces training costs and increases employee productivity. Labor sees excessive experience requirements as a barrier to hiring employees with little or no job experience. However, labor's apprenticeship programs are often excessively long in training people to be electricians, plumbers, and so on.

8. *Human interaction.* As people's aspirations and ambitions increase, the desire for social interaction has become a major concern in placing people in an organization. Employees vary in how desirable they find social interaction. For example, some people prefer to work alone and should be placed in jobs that limit their social interaction with people.

9. *Psychological dimensions.* Psychological dimensions include job freedom, job responsibility, and risk taking. Again personal preferences dictate the level of freedom, responsibility, and risk individuals are willing to accept.[5]

Figure 10-2 shows the relationship of these nine job traits to two job tasks. Work has value to the extent that the individual views that work as being useful to society and to the degree that the job relates to the individual's job potential.

Fair Employment

Title VII of the Civil Rights Act was amended in 1972 to prohibit discrimination in employment practices. This amendment has increased the legal complexities of management-labor relations. For example, the steel industry paid a settlement of $16 to $20 million over issues relat-

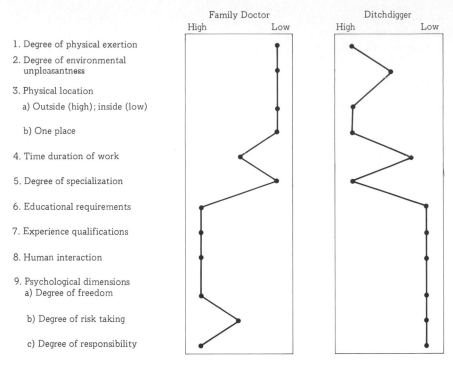

Figure 10-2
Characteristics of jobs, or task differences. Source: William F. Glueck, *Personnel: A Diagnostic Approach*, Dallas: Business Publications, 1974, p. 85.

ing to fair pay. A similar settlement on EEOC complaints provided $7 million in back pay and $23 million in wages for American Telephone and Telegraph's employees. Since 1965 the Equal Pay Act has awarded over $55 million to employees.

To bring a company into compliance with EEOC regulations requires the establishment of a voluntary program to provide guidelines for directing managerial action in meeting EEOC requirements. One way to accomplish this objective is to identify by geographic location, by department, and by job description the placement of minorities and women. This utilization analysis can provide a clear picture of the representation of minorities and women in a job category. Job descriptions that create barriers to employment because they exceed job requirements are suspect under Title VII regulations. Such a managerial audit should provide a timetable for increasing the representation of minorities and women in undcrutilized areas. Recruitment has become the central criterion in determining how effective companies are in attracting, hiring, and promoting minorities and women. A model affirmative

258

action program must have an updated inventory of employee job skills to implement an effective training and development program.

An EEOC program must have the support of top management in terms of budgets, staffs, rewards, and punishments to convince all personnel of management's serious commitment to EEOC regulations. Second, responsibility for meeting EEOC regulations should be given to an EEOC officer within the company. This individual should have the authority to establish, to maintain, and to direct the activities of an ongoing company affirmative action program. To be effective, a company's voluntary affirmative action program must influence all organizational entities to provide any legal protection.[6]

To encourage other organizations to improve their labor relations with minorities, the following program could serve as a model. This program was developed by General Electric in 1970 to guide managerial thinking in developing fair employment practices. The success of this program is seen in the fact that minority employment is up by 57 percent at all levels, and there has been a 6 percent increase in employment opportunities for women. A 250 percent increase in minority employment in higher-level positions is another accomplishment of this program. This program provides the following data:

1. It lists the components of an equal opportunity and minority relations program.
2. It provides a demographic overview of present and future population trends to identify the presence of all minorities as a percentage of the total population.
3. It provides a one- to five-year projection of minority hiring in relation to the makeup of the general population revealed in a demographic survey. The objective is to hire the same percentage of minority people as is available in the work force.
4. It presents a performance analysis to ascertain the hiring, promotion, and termination practices of the firm for the past year.
5. It states present and five-year goals for exempt minority and women work forces among twenty-eight General Electric salary levels.[7]

To implement General Electric's affirmative action program, its corporate management has designed four yardsticks to guide all managers. The first option states that minorities should represent the demographic traits of the area in which a plant is located. In other words, if minorities represent 10 percent of the city's population, they should represent 10 percent of the work force of that plant. Option 2 states that if minorities represent 10 percent of the national population, the company's goal should be to have 10 percent minority representation in the sales force, in professional jobs, and in all managerial areas. Option three says that minorities should be represented at each plant organizational level at the same percentage that they are represented in the plant's population.

TABLE 10-3
Participation of women and minorities, 1968 and 1973

Job categories	All employees			Women			Minorities		
	December 1968	December 1973	Percent increase	December 1968	December 1973	Percent increase	December 1968	December 1973	Percent increase
Officials and managers	23,024	26,486	15.0	119	473	297.5	195	678	247.7
Professionals	53,624	44,905	—16.3	1,289	2,020	56.7	1,068	1,902	78.1
Technicians	19,846	15,377	—22.5	1,742	1,473	—15.5	726	964	32.8
Sales workers	4,599	7,622	65.7	336	595	77.1	79	362	358.2
Office and clerical	40,807	36,301	—11.1	28,898	27,068	—6.3	1,844	3,558	93.0
Craftsmen	53,802	57,215	6.3	801	1,367	70.7	2,340	3,791	62.0
Operatives	88,910	101,099	13.7	41,869	46,856	11.9	11,182	18,703	67.3
Laborers	23,745	19,193	—19.2	8,663	8,869	2.4	3,489	3,385	—3.0
Service workers	3,689	3,011	—18.4	424	657	55.0	660	572	—13.3
Total	312,046	311,209	—0.3	84,141	89,378	6.2	21,583	33,915	57.1

Source: Theodore V. Purcell, "How GE Measures Managers in Fair Employment," *Harvard Business Review*, November–December 1974, p. 102.

For example, a plant located in an area where 15 percent of the population has Spanish surnames should have a 15 percent Spanish representation among plant officials, technicians, and managers. Option 4 is based on the representation of minorities in universities and professional trade schools. Seven percent of all college graduates are black; therefore, company positions requiring college education should be filled by blacks at a level of 7 percent or more. The progressive manager will use all four options in striving to meet the affirmative action goals. Table 10-3 shows the increased participation of women and minorities at G.E. from 1968 to 1973.

The General Electric EO/MR measurement format has proved to be an effective system for achieving greater minority participation in a large, decentralized company. Its success depends on the comprehensive measurement of performance at all levels and an attendant penalty/reward system. With extensive experimentation, measurement-incentive systems like this format could become important instruments for securing organizational change.[8]

Women in Business

Elizabeth Koontz, a prominent author, rebuts the view that a "woman's place is in the home." One reason is that in many instances homemaking is no longer a full-time job. Similarly, increased educational levels may lead women to need more intellectual stimulation than that pro-

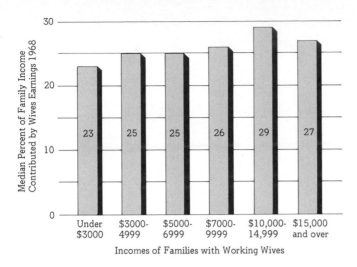

Figure 10-3
Income contributions by working wives, by family income levels. Source: U.S. Department of Labor.

vided by home, neighborhood, and supermarket. And contrary to traditional views, women are in the labor force because of pressing economic need. Figure 10-3 shows the contribution of working wives to family income levels. Many jobs are sexless in terms of the ability of females to carry them out. A shift from aggressive leadership styles to styles based on persuasion and understanding of human needs increases opportunities to utilize women's leadership strengths. Some negative attitudes toward women in the world of work do persist. Here are a few.

1. Women increase company costs because of illness and absenteeism.
2. Women steal jobs from men.
3. Women do not want increased job responsibilities and promotions.
4. Men are reluctant to work for women managers.
5. Women do not remain in the labor force as long as their male counterparts.

The impact of occupational segregation is shown in Figure 10-4. Income equality according to sex is reflected in Table 10-4. A male's median income is $9631, compared to a female's median income of $5701. Table 10-5 shows the relationship of occupational segregation and income inequality. Table 10-6 further illustrates the concept of occupational segregation by showing occupational areas in which women represent 69 percent or more of an occupational area. To overcome the difficulties faced by women at work, several developments

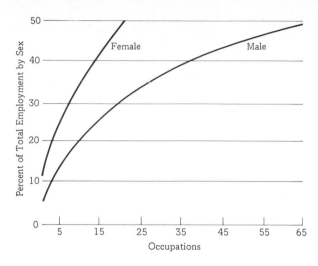

Figure 10-4
Concentration of male and female employment, 1969. Source: Hedges, *Monthly Labor Review*, June 1970, p. 19.

have taken place. The National Organization for Women, representing 35,000 members, has filed charges of discrimination against 1300 companies. In response to increasing EEOC complaints, the federal government's 1974 budget for this agency was increased to $44 million. An out-of-court settlement with the Bank of America raised women's salaries by

TABLE 10-4
Total income by sex, 1971; year-round, full-time workers

Total money income	Percent of males	Percent of females
$1 to $999	1.3	1.9
$1,000 to $2,999	3.0	8.2
$3,000 to $4,999	7.8	28.1
$5,000 to $6,999	13.7	30.3
$7,000 to $9,999	27.5	21.8
$10,000 to $14,999	29.6	8.1
$15,000 to $24,999	13.1	1.4
$25,000 and over	4.0	0.3
Median income	$9,631	$5,701

Source: Mary Hamblin and Michael J. Prell, "The Incomes of Men and Women: Why Do They Differ?" *Monthly Review of the FRB of Kansas City,* April 1973, p. 4.

TABLE 10-5
Median income by occupation and sex, 1971; civilian, year-round, full-time workers

Occupation	Median income in occupation	Male median income	Female median income	Per-cent of full-time male labor force	Per-cent of full-time female labor force	Female workers as per-cent of occupation group
Managers, Officials, and Proprietors	$12,192	$13,087	$6,970	15.8	6.4	14.6
Professional and Technical	11,395	12,842	8,515	15.7	18.6	33.4
Sales Workers	9,683	11,122	4,681	6.2	4.2	22.3
Craftsmen and Foremen	9,664	9,779	5,493	21.6	1.4	2.7
Operatives	7,274	8,069	4,884	17.7	13.9	25.0
Laborers (except farm)	6,932	7,063	4,486	4.8	.6	5.1
Clerical Workers	6,904	9,512	5,820	6.9	39.3	70.6
Service Workers	6,090	7,484	4,375	6.9	13.3	44.8
Farmers and Farm Managers	n.a.	4,915	n.a.	3.4	.2	2.2
Farm Workers	n.a.	3,806	n.a.	1.0	.3	10.8
Private Household Workers	n.a.	n.a.	2,323	n.a.	1.7	n.a.
	n.a.	9,631	5,701	100.0	100.0	29.8

Source: Mary Hamblin and Michael J. Prell, "The Incomes of Men and Women: Why Do They Differ?" *Monthly Review of the FRB of Kansas City,* April 1973, p. 5.

$10 million, established a $3.75 million trust fund for education and self-development programs, and increased the goal of the number of women to be employed by Bank of America to 40 percent by 1978.[9]

A recent survey of 1500 *Harvard Business Review* subscribers sought to identify the proper role for men and women in the work environment. This survey identified several subtle forms of differential treatment that adversely affects the career progress of female employees. Participants in this survey were presented with case incidents to identify the course of action they would take in dealing with male and female employees in an organization. A profile of the participants is presented in Table 10-7. One general conclusion reached is that males should sacrifice family obligations for career demands. On the other hand, female employees are expected to place family responsibilities first and career interests second. A second general conclusion is that managers are more likely to retain a male employee rather than a female employee when personal

TABLE 10-6
The jobs that women hold

Secretaries	2,922,000	99%	Real-estate agents	128,000	37%
Receptionists	423,000	97%	Cleaning-service		
Typists	980,000	96%	workers	680,000	33%
Child-care workers	341,00	96%	Restaurant workers	160,000	32%
Nurses, dietitians	879,000	96%	Writers, artists,		
Hairdressers, cos-			entertainers	284,000	32%
metologists	354,000	91%	College teachers	130,000	28%
Bank tellers	252,000	88%	Accountants	155,000	22%
Bookkeepers	1,393,000	88%	Bank, financial		
Cashiers	864,000	87%	officers	81,000	19%
Health-service			Sales managers	90,000	16%
workers	1,310,000	87%	Physicians		
File clerks	231,000	85%	and dentists	58,000	9%
Librarians	125,000	83%	Science		
Counter clerks			technicians	75,000	9%
(nonfood)	243,000	74%	Policemen, firemen	65,000	5–
Office-machine					6%
operators	480,000	71%	Lawyers	12,000	4%
Schoolteachers	1,988,000	70%	Engineers	9,000	Less
Health technicians	220,000	70%			than
Food-service					1%
workers	2,277,000	70%	Construction		
Retail clerks	1,600,000	69%	craftsmen	20,000	Less
Social workers	195,000	55%			than
Office managers	132,000	42%			1%

Source: U.S. Dept. of Labor unpublished survey.

TABLE 10-7
Characteristics of participating HBR subscribers

Relative size of organization		Age		Marital status		Sex	
Among		Under 30	18%	Married	85.0%	Male	94.7%
largest	56.7%	30–34	20	Single	11.3	Female	5.3
About		35–39	17	Other	3.7		
average	27.7	40–44	15				
Small	15.6	45–49	13				
		50–54	9				
		55–59	5				
		60–65	2				
		Over 65	1				

Source: Benson Rosen and Thomas H. Jerdee, "Sex Stereotyping in the Executive Suite," *Harvard Business Review*, March–April 1974, p. 47.

conduct threatens continued employment with the firm. A third general conclusion of the study is that managers favor males in selection, promotion, and career development decisions.

Three incidents dealt with the sacrifices expected of career men and career women in relation to their families. The first incident dealt with a career man or a career woman's attendance at a cocktail party. Figure 10-5 shows the response of participants in evaluating three alternatives. Such a survey reveals that wives of career men are expected to attend social activities but husbands of career women are not expected to attend. A second incident showed how sexual discrimination tends to work in favor of female employees. This incident provided three alternatives in response to a request for a leave of absence. Female employees received a more favorable response for a leave of absence than did their male counterparts. Figure 10-6 shows the response of survey participants in relation to this incident. A third incident involving family relationships was a clash between the professional careers of a husband and wife. Again, the participants were given four alternatives in determining the course of action they would take. Figure 10-7 reveals that organizations work harder to retain male employees than to keep female employees. All three incidents show a trend of managerial support for male employees and the greater demands placed on the families of male employees.

The next two case incidents dealt with disciplinary problems in rela-

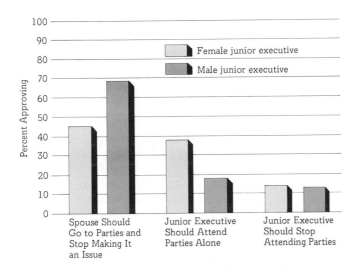

Figure 10-5
The cocktail party. Source: Benson Rosen and Thomas H. Jerdee, "Sex Stereotyping in the Executive Suite," *Harvard Business Review*, March–April 1974, p. 48.

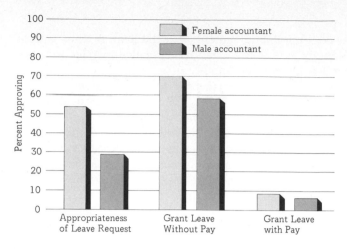

Figure 10-6
Request for leave of absence. Source: Benson Rosen and Thomas H. Jerdee, "Sex Stereotyping in the Executive Suite," *Harvard Business Review*, March–April 1974, p. 50.

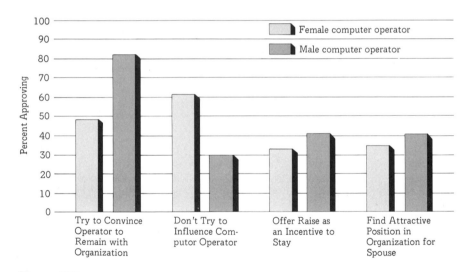

Figure 10-7
"Valuable" computer operator. Source: Benson Rosen and Thomas H. Jerdee, "Sex Stereotyping in the Executive Suite," *Harvard Business Review*, March–April 1974, p. 51.

tion to employee tardiness and a philandering junior executive. In Figure 10-8, the harshness of disciplinary action is greater for a female engineer than for a male engineer in the same circumstances. Figure 10-9 reveals a similar pattern of discrimination in dealing with a philandering junior executive because managers are more concerned about pre-

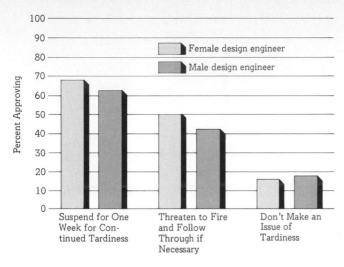

Figure 10-8
Chronically late design engineer. Source: Benson Rosen and Thomas H. Jerdee,
"Sex Stereotyping in the Executive Suite," *Harvard Business Review*, March–
April 1974, p. 52.

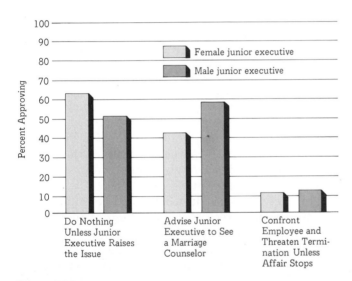

Figure 10-9
Philandering junior executive. Source: Benson Rosen and Thomas H. Jerdee,
"Sex Stereotyping in the Executive Suite," *Harvard Business Review*, March–
April 1974, p. 52.

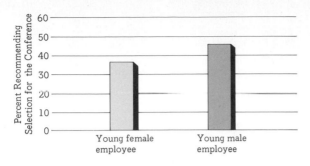

Figure 10-10
Training conference. Source: Benson Rosen and Thomas H. Jerdee, "Sex Stereo-typing in the Executive Suite," *Harvard Business Review*, March–April 1974, p. 54.

serving male employment than female employment. The reluctance of organizations to develop and train females for advancement is shown in Figure 10-10. Again, men received more favorable consideration than women in obtaining training for upper advancement. The last two incidents dealt with sex stereotyping in regard to the selection and promotion of males and females to managerial positions. The first incident involved the selection of a purchasing manager who is required to travel extensively throughout the country. Figure 10-11 shows how male and female candidates fare in the selection of a purchasing agent. Survey respondents feel that (1) women are less suitable for such a job, (2) women should not travel, and (3) women are less likely to remain with the organization. The last case incident dealt with the promotion of a male and female to the position of personnel director. A related issue in this decision is a conflict between family interests and job demands. Figure 10-12 shows the response of survey participants in hiring a personnel director. Again, male candidates received more favorable consideration than did their female counterparts.[10]

The significance of this research is reflected in current employment trends. Thirty-three million women represent 40 percent of the United States' work force. Sixty percent of the women in the work force are single, divorced, widowed, or married to men who earn less than $7000 per year. Thus, women, like men, work for money, self-satisfaction, and fulfillment of personal aspirations. To establish an affirmative action program for women requires the following:

1. Assign the responsibility of creating such a program to a male manager, to a woman, to a consultant, or to a task force.
2. Establish a statistical analysis of positions presently occupied by women in terms of salaries and level of responsibility.
3. Hold all operating managers accountable for successes and failures in striving to implement an affirmative action program for women.

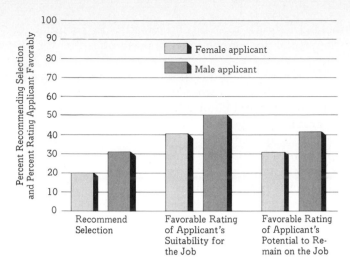

Figure 10-11
Selection of purchasing manager. Source: Benson Rosen and Thomas H. Jerdee, "Sex Stereotyping in the Executive Suite," *Harvard Business Review*, March–April 1974, p. 55.

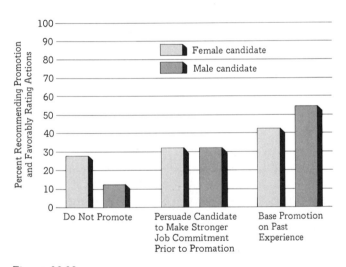

Figure 10-12
Promotion to personnel director. Source: Benson Rosen and Thomas H. Jerdee, "Sex Stereotyping in the Executive Suite," *Harvard Business Review*, March–April 1974, p. 56.

4. Establish a tracking network to identify women with potential to guide the developmental and promotional opportunities for women in the organization.
5. Restructure jobs to remove insignificant and unrelated job requirements that often prevent the use of women.
6. Have realistic, measurable, and challenging objectives to guide the thinking of all operating managers.
7. Obtain qualified female applicants for responsible managerial positions through competitive recruitment programs.
8. Develop special awareness and career-planning seminars to motivate women to seek more challenging positions.
9. Develop an awareness seminar for lower-level managers to overcome discrimination against women in promotion policies.
10. Review personnel policies that discriminate against the advancement of women to higher level positions.[11]

In 1973, 1998 college women were hired to work in 140 companies. A similar survey showed that 3068 women would be hired in 1974 from college graduating classes. To encourage women to broaden their career interests, the U.S. Department of Labor has produced a booklet entitled "Careers for Women in the '70's." This booklet encourages women to seek employment as system analysts, computer programmers, accountants, engineers, and in social service positions. Mary Janney, the co-director of the Washington Organization for Women, or WOW, stated that young women must break away from traditional woman-oriented jobs such as secretaries, bank tellers, and file clerks to higher-level positions. This change, however, will not occur without a struggle.[12]

The Disadvantaged in Business

Fair employment, women in business, and the disadvantaged in business are the new frontiers that will challenge the managerial talent of all managers working in labor relations. The term *disadvantaged individual* has been defined by the Manpower Administration of the U.S. Department of Labor to include

1. A school dropout
2. A member of a minority
3. Those under twenty-two years of age
4. Those forty-five years of age or over
5. The handicapped

The five basic combinations of the definition are

1. Poor school dropout without suitable employment
2. Poor minority member without suitable employment
3. Poor youth without suitable employment

4. Poor older worker without suitable employment
5. Poor handicapped worker without suitable employment[13]

Blacks
In 1966, 23 million blacks lived in the South and 80 percent lived in the central city. Figure 10-13 shows the concentration of black poor in central cities and suburbs in 1970. Moreover, the number of blacks aged sixteen to nineteen in the central city grew by 75 percent from 1960 to 1969. The black young adults aged twenty to twenty-four grew by 67 percent from 1960 to 1969. The result was that in 1970 the unemployment rate for black teenagers was 32 percent. Similarly, in the recessionary period of 1974, black unemployment for young adults was 24 percent.[14]

Spanish-Speaking Americans
Five million Spanish-speaking Americans are of Mexican origin or descent. Puerto Ricans make up 1.5 million. Six hundred thousand Cubans entered the United States in 1969, and over 2 million people of Spanish descent came from Central or South America. The geographic dispersion of Spanish-Americans is shown in Figure 10-14. Eighty-four percent of the Spanish-speaking people live in metropolitan areas. The economic situations of Spanish-speaking Americans are seen in examples of family incomes:[15]

1971	Spanish	$ 7,250 median income
1971	Anglo	10,300 median income
1971	Blacks	6,400 median income
1971	Puerto Ricans	6,200 median income

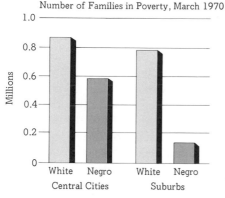

Number of Families in Poverty, March 1970

Most of the poor families in metropolitan area live in the central cities . . .

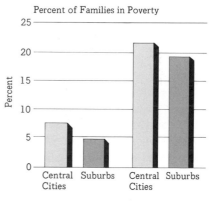

Percent of Families in Poverty

. . . but the proverty rate for Negro families is high even in the suburbs.

Figure 10-13
Concentration of Negro poor in central cities and suburbs. Source: U.S. Department of Labor, based on data from the U.S. Department of Commerce.

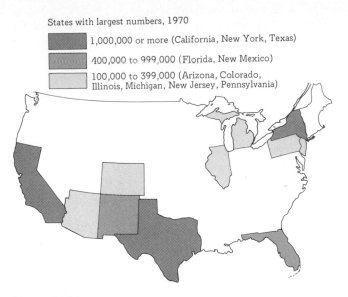

States with largest numbers, 1970

- 1,000,000 or more (California, New York, Texas)
- 400,000 to 999,000 (Florida, New Mexico)
- 100,000 to 399,000 (Arizona, Colorado, Illinois, Michigan, New Jersey, Pennsylvania)

Figure 10-14
Concentration of Spanish-speaking Americans. Source: U.S. Department of Labor, based on census date from the U.S. Department of Commerce.

American Indians

Unemployment on Indian reservations is 40 percent year round, and during the winter months it soars to 90 percent of the reservation's total labor force. Over half the Indian population lives in Oklahoma, Arizona, California, and New Mexico. Economic disadvantages are the result of broken treaties, dependence on bureaucratic programs, lack of industry to provide employment, and cultural shock. As a representative of American business, the labor relations expert should (1) recognize environmental factors that create a disadvantaged worker, and (2) recognize personal traits produced by environmental influences that shape a person's self-concept and place in the world. Like all workers, the disadvantaged person brings the influences of the world into the work environment. To hire, train, and maintain the services of disadvantaged people requires an alternative managerial approach. It is too easy to ignore problems in dealing with disadvantaged persons. The recent passage of OSHA and EEOC regulations should encourage managers in business to solve the problem of hiring and developing the abilities of all disadvantaged persons. Continuing to dismiss the problem invites further governmental action to induce business to complete its social obligation. Our recent experience with employment quotas in hiring personnel should further stimulate labor relations experts to take creative measures to identify and employ disadvantaged personnel.[16]

272

True, business is not a social agency designed to solve all the social ills of humanity. However, business profits are eroded by taxes that support counterproductive social programs such as poverty programs, correctional institutes, and related public-supported agencies. A similar counterproductive area is increased security expenditures to protect employees, property, and products. Gopal C. Pati, an educator and authority on training ex-convicts, designed a positive approach to training and developing ex-convicts in industry. In Chicago, Oscar Gitz and 100 fellow businessmen created PACE (Programmed Activities for Correctional Education) for inmates of the Cook County Jail. In contrast to a national rate of 75 percent recidivism, only 15 percent of the PACE trainees released from jail have returned there. McDonald's Corporation has contributed over $2 million to PACE to ready inmates for productive work when released from jail. Polaroid has employed 189 ex-convicts and is asking other businesses to employ former inmates. The views of Polaroid are given in Table 10-8.

Personnel people hire, train, and develop workers as members of an organization. However, it is the function of labor relations specialists to maintain a positive work environment for all personnel. A progressive labor relations director can aid in developing managerial guidelines for dealing with all disadvantaged employees. For example, ex-convicts are an excellent source of unskilled and blue-collar workers that are chronically in short supply. Likewise, the strong desire of many ex-convicts to work tends to reduce turnover costs for employers willing to employ former prisoners. As with other disadvantaged persons, ex-convicts are benefiting from EEOC regulations and affirmative action programs in opening new employment opportunities. Several business groups such as the National Alliance of Businessmen and Job Opportunities are encouraging employers on career day to visit prisons for prospective employees. In a study of 158 persons in twenty business enterprises several suggestions were made to employers desiring to secure the services of ex-convicts. Three major suggestions were as follows:

1. Even though in many ways they are no different from the hard-core unemployed, ex-convicts do have particular problems that make finding a job more difficult.
2. Companies are more likely to have a successful program with ex-convicts if the individual's problems are dealt with on a realistic and personal basis.
3. The companies that fail in this program are those that do not give the ex-convict active help in the form of concerned supervisors, training, and commitment at the top levels of management.[17]

All successful company programs for hiring and training ex-convicts display several key traits:

TABLE 10-8
Rehabilitation is the unkept promise

A number of years ago, Polaroid set up a policy of what is called "special effort." In other words, we agreed that the company must make a special effort to hire people who would normally have an extremely difficult time locating a job and getting hired. We set aside jobs which were then made available to people with handicaps. By handicapped, I do not mean simply the physically disabled. I mean minority members and the Spanish-speaking, as well as the physically disabled such as the blind and deaf. The policy also included the retarded and, beginning about eight years ago, the former prison inmate.

Both of our initial efforts failed, and I would like to describe them and the reasons for their failures.

We were first asked to put some of our subcontract work in one of the prisons, so that the men might learn how to make a product that was different from license plates and broom handles. We sent in one of our Polaroid personnel to train a half-dozen inmates to produce one of our accessory products. The training couldn't have been easier. Within only a few weeks the inmates were matching and, in some cases, surpassing both the quantity and the quality of our regular employees. The Polaroid member of course became interested in the men (as is always the case). He then discussed hiring the inmates at Polaroid when they became eligible for parole. Five were hired and all but one failed. We found that this was because of the change in the atmosphere between Polaroid and the institution. In the prison there was no time pressure, only one supervisor, and the atmosphere was controlled. Exactly the opposite was true within our company. This particular experience, incidentally, made a good case for the need of halfway houses, or at least of some form of support for the reentry of the inmate into the job world.

The second effort, which also failed, was applied to a program (that is, a formal one) bringing inmates into jobs within the company. The problem was so simple. We brought six former inmates into the company as part of an inmate-jobs program. The problem was that everyone knew who they were and they were continually pointed out as "the cons." It was like having each with a sign on his forehead saying "convict." They were not being protected from their failures as most of us are; rather they were being pointed to as something different.

Our success, if I may call it that, began shortly after these two experiences.

We began hiring ex-offenders on an individual basis in the mid-1960s. The inmate was met by a personnel man at the institution just before he was to be released on parole. He was accompanied when he came for his first visit to Polaroid. We asked him to fill out two applications. On one, we had him leave certain questions blank, such as "Have you ever been arrested for other than a minor traffic violation?" The application became his public record. The other was filled out in detail with all his background on it. This application was put in a locked vault and was known to only the hiring supervisor, the personnel manager, and the general manager.

The former inmate now entered Polaroid no different from anyone else. He was protected. It was left entirely up to him whether or not he told about his background. Many have and many have not. We believe that these choices, like all others, should be left to the individual. The real point is that by doing this quietly, on an individual basis, it has worked. There are now over 100 former inmates at Polaroid. We have failed in only two cases.

I do not believe that it will help get other businessmen interested, however, when the success of this effort is presented either in this way or when they are told, "You should hire because it's right."

There is another part to this story which is equally interesting and of particular interest to the businessman.

Former inmates may be ignorant—that is, many have an extremely limited education—but they are very bright and quick to learn. Our training costs are low. Their absenteeism is substantially under our regular rate. There has been almost no turnover.

What the businessman has to learn is that our archaic prison institutions cost $27 million a year, a cost that does not include the costs of families on welfare and millions of dollars of other costs related to this particular human misery.

He must understand that 90% of the incarcerated will be on the street at some point in the future—and, until recently, 70% were doomed to return. And they will continue to return as long as we encourage a system aimed at punishment rather than rehabilitation. Punishment by sentencing and incarceration is punishment enough. Rehabilitation is still the unkept promise.

—A statement by Robert Palmer, who is director of community relations at Polaroid Corporation, Cambridge, Massachusetts. Mr. Palmer is also chairman of the Governor's Advisory Committee for Corrections in Massachusetts.

Source: Gopal C. Pati, "Business Can Make Ex-Convicts Productive," *Harvard Business Review*, May–June 1974, p. 71.

1. *Careful placement,* which usually calls for in-depth interviews over several days to identify inmate needs as well as several ways to meet those needs. (See Table 10-9.)
2. *Comprehensive orientation program* deals with work rules, discipline procedures, social relationships, and values that enhance a person's adjustment to a new environment. (See Table 10-10.)
3. *Confidentiality* is essential to a program's success to avoid the negative influence of prejudicial views. Polaroid reveals the data to plant managers, personnel managers, and first-line supervisor when dealing with ex-convicts.
4. *Competent staff* is committed to the rehabilitation of disadvantaged employees.
5. *Supervisory training* is the major need of all programs because these individuals exert the greatest influence on the survival of ex-convicts. (See Table 10-11.)

TABLE 10-9

The employment manager of a trucking firm said, "The initial contact with an ex-con is very crucial. We have to make him feel that we are friendly, cooperative, and understanding. You cannot project the image of a 'tough cop.' You cannot give him false promises. We have eight drivers with serious criminal records. None of them have left, none of them have stolen, none of them have physically attacked anybody. Good human relations pay off."

Source: Gopal C. Pati, "Business Can Make Ex-Convicts Productive," *Harvard Business Review*, May–June 1974, p. 75.

TABLE 10-10

Mr. Anderson is a fine machinist. He's just been released from prison and is looking for a job. He has paid his dues to society, is willing to work hard, and has a positive job attitude. A job is available, and the employer is willing to hire him. If he had the normal things most people have, his life would be on a new tack, but he does not. He does not have a car for getting to the plant, which is located in a white suburb that does not have good public transportation. By accepting goudging interest rates, Anderson does manage a loan with which to buy a third-hand car. Predictably, because he lives in a poor, ghettolike neighborhood, within a week his car is vandalized. He is now not only in debt but also without transportation; and even though he tries he often gets to work late. After a week or so of consistent lateness he is discharged for not doing his job.

Now Anderson is in a hostile world. Not surprisingly he commits a crime and goes back to the cooler, where he knows his pals will welcome and understand him.

Source: Gopal C. Pati, "Business Can Make Ex-Convicts Productive," *Harvard Business Review*, May–June 1974, p. 74.

TABLE 10-11

Once supervisors complete the program, informal interview sessions are held with the particular supervisors under whom the ex-prisoners will be working. These supervisors are told not to tell their fellow supervisors or other employees about the background of the trainee. At least five companies send their supervisors and managers to visit prisons. The president of a small company once remarked, "Something amazing happens to some of our supervisors when they come back from visiting a prison; they are so understanding, cooperative, and sensitive that I don't believe it."

Source: Gopal C. Pati. "Business Can Make Ex-Convicts Productive." *Harvard Business Review*, May–June 1974, p. 77.

---

6. *Follow-up* is essential to provide an ex-convict with positive ideas to reinforce his desire to be a productive member of society. Job stability is enhanced through internal support and through external support from friends, relatives, and interested public agencies.[18]

Company rehabilitation programs often fail because of lack of commitment by upper management, lack of concern by supervisory personnel, lack of training and opportunity, and employer pessimism. The following incident is an excellent example of lack of concern:

An excellent trainee in a machine shop was fired because he was often late during his probationary period. After he was fired, it was discovered that he had a brother, and that between them, they had only one set of working clothes. One brother wore them on the day shift, and when he came home, the other brother put them on for the night shift. If one brother was held over, the other was late.[19]

A lack of training and opportunity is presented in the next example:

Frequently, ex-convicts are placed on meaningless jobs that nobody else wants, or they are given jobs, on a trial basis, for which they are not trained. For instance, a manufacturer hired a former inmate with two years of college to lift 50- to 100-pound bags of salt. The work was physically exhausting. Instead of giving the man a job that he could handle (and plenty were available), the company fired him. The official reason given was the employee's inability to satisfactorily do the job to which he was assigned.[20]

Employer pessimism is presented in the last example:

Perceiving ex-convicts as beyond help, the managers accept them into their shops grudgingly. There the ex-convicts are expected to make it on their own, and, of course, they do not. One manager told me, "In our department, the theft rate has gone up since we hired that ex-con." When it was later proved that the ex-convict in question had nothing to do with the thefts, the manager made no attempt to revise his opinion. He expects the ex-convict to do all the changing; he does not understand that unless he changes first, the ex-convict does not stand a chance at altering his life pattern.[21]

Young People in Business

The increase in the population under age twenty-five is radically altering traditional management-labor relations. Although older workers accept adverse working conditions, younger workers refuse to accept jobs that endanger their health, have a high degree of direct physical labor, and provide no challenge. Therefore, management must alter a job's design to make it attractive to younger workers. A major area of stress for young workers is their belief that they should have the same rights as their bosses. Thus, they may tend to challenge their bosses on all job aspects that are related to their personal area of responsibility. To avoid unpleasant jobs, some younger workers tend to exaggerate health and safety issues. Younger workers fail to recognize the difficulties in bringing about change in an organized work environment. The passage of time is often viewed as a managerial tactic to delay action or avoid making a decision.

Younger workers' educational experiences fail to identify the values that business and commerce bring to society. A related failure of their educational experience is a limited knowledge of how business operates. One symptom of this trait is the movement of younger workers through several jobs within a five-year period following graduation. Work that is repetitious or shows no promise in terms of advancement is challenged by younger workers. Younger workers have had a positive impact on industry by helping to bring automation to highly repetitive tasks and by providing added impetus for management to enrich the job content of all positions.[22]

Further insight into the views of young people toward the world of business is reflected in their concept of managers. In a survey of young people, 40 percent of the males and 20 percent of the females selected management as a career objective. Young people selected management as a career because it offers the opportunity for (1) leadership, (2) a good salary, (3) challenge, (4) responsibility, and (5) contact with people.

Young people's awareness of the makeup of a manager's task is shown in Table 10-12. The views expressed here were based on a survey of young people aged nine to seventeen. Such data should encourage business managers to influence educational planning at all grade levels to expand the student's exposure to the place of business in our society. In conclusion, young people mentioned six ways in which they believe a person becomes a manager. Twenty-eight percent felt a manager goes through an apprenticeship program. Twenty-three percent felt that a person becomes a manager by working hard. Nineteen percent felt a person becomes a manager through special education. Eighteen percent felt a person is appointed as a manager. Fifteen percent felt that technical competence is the road to becoming a manager, and 11 percent felt a person becomes a manager by demonstrating leadership capabilities.[23]

Union Relations

Union members exhibit different identities based on years of union membership, type of work performed, family influences, and direct association with union activities. Some union members are idealistic and view unions as a vehicle for bringing about social changes. Other members form a solid core dedicated to the traditional union principles of improving workers' conditions of employment. A third group supports union activities but perennially criticizes union leadership and policies. A fourth group uses unions to advance its own self-interest. A fifth group, composed of skilled craftsmen, accepts the union but adopts managerial views in criticizing union programs and practices. Many union members are merely card carriers who are totally indifferent toward union activities. A local union has two governments to direct the activities of union members. One government sets up bylaws and rules to guide member relationships under the direction of an executive board. The second governmental entity composed of stewards and grievance committee members carries on collective bargaining activities. Stewards establish an employee-employer relationship under the influence of union rules and regulations.[24]

A major area of conflict is the role of union and management rights

TABLE 10-12

Respondents' understanding of the facets of the managerial role

Finding	Facet	Number of items answered correctly (out of 3)
More than 80% of the respondents scored correctly on all items for each of these facets	1. Dividing work into parts and allocating them to different people.	3
	2. Matching job requirements with individual skills, or assigning jobs to the right people.	3
	3. Checking that the work gets done properly and on time.	3
	4. Seeing to it that people improve their work skills and develop new ones.	3
	5. Upgrading employees who are good at their work.	3
80% (or more) of the respondents scored correctly on *two* items for each of these facets	6. Securing people with the right skills for the jobs to be done.	2
	7. Reviewing the appropriateness of the company's current objectives, tasks, and activities.	2
	8. Encouraging collaboration and cooperation among employees.	2
	9. Hiring and firing employees, depending on the needs of the company.	2
	10. Keeping one's own superiors informed of one's progress	2
80% (or more) of the respondents scored correctly on *one* of the items for each of these facets	11. Formulating the tasks of the employees.	1
	12. Compensating employees on the basis of performance.	1
	13. Providing a satisfying and motivating environment for the employees.	1
Fewer than 80% of the respondents scored correctly on *any* of the items for this facet	14. Making sure that the company is profitable.	0

Source: Rosalind C. Barnett and Renato Tagiuri, "What Young People Think About Managers," *Harvard Business Review,* May–June 1973, p. 111.

in a collective bargaining agreement. James Phelps of Bethlehem Steel stated the rights of management as follows:

The job of management is to manage. The operation of the enterprise at its maximum efficiency is management's responsibility and obligation. If a management believes that, in order to discharge its obligations, it must retain in full measure the so-called prerogative of management, it has the right to refuse to agree in collective bargaining to restrict those rights. If the management should agree to limit its exclusive functions or even to delegate certain of its duties to a union, it can enter into an agreement that will clearly define how far it has agreed to go. To the extent the parties have not seen fit to limit management's sphere of action, management's rights are unimpaired by the contract.[25]

Arthur Goldberg of the Steelworkers Union stated:

A backlog of rights and practices and precedents does develop as the collective bargaining relationship continues, based not on pre-union history but based on the period of the collective bargaining relationship.

. . . the practices which grow up during decades of a collective bargaining relationship cannot be swept aside . . . inevitably represent the set of circumstances which formed the backdrop of the negotiation of the current agreement.

. . . to the extent that present conditions and methods for change are not revised, they are accepted. Therefore, each party has the right to assume that changes in wages, hours, or working conditions not provided for by contract can be made only by mutual agreement or by following practices for making changes which have existed during the collective bargaining relationship or by virtue of management's exercise of an exclusive right (such as the introduction of new products, new machines, new material, new methods of manufacture, etc.). To suggest that management can make changes at will unless the contract specifically bars it is unfair and can lead to placing so many bars in the contract as to make successful negotiation increasingly difficult and operations less and less flexible, with detailed consideration of the facts and merits of each case replaced by precise rules and regulations.[26]

Management and labor face the challenge of establishing a middle ground in which to resolve the conflict between managerial and union rights in collective bargaining. Fortunately, they are moving toward a more enlightened relationship in their dealings with each other.

In spite of union member differences and disputes over management-union rights, most contracts are settled without adverse consequences. The strategy and tactics used by both parties to reach a given objective not only bring immediate results but shape the climate for management-union relations in the months ahead. In the opening session each party seeks to establish its position on key issues under contract consideration. As a matter of common sense, money issues should be handled after noncost issues are settled. To reduce areas of conflict, management can trade off certain concerns in noneconomic issues to gain the support of union bargainers. In a climate of mutual flexibility, union and management representatives can resolve issues such as work rules, seniority rights, and stewards' roles.

The early stages of negotiations on monetary issues are designed to determine an acceptable level of settlement. For example, union members may ask for an increase of 14 cents per hour but be prepared to accept 9 cents per hour. Management counters with a zero hourly increase while setting a 6 cents per hour raise as their highest offer. After several meetings there exists a difference of 3 cents per hour in terms of management's position and labor's position. The union must decide whether to accept management's offer or to threaten to strike. An alternative is to compromise on 7 cents an hour with additional fringe benefits such as health care, retirement, or holiday pay. Thus, psychological pressure from both parties is used to enhance, influence, and alter the position of management or labor in contract negotiations. A skillful negotiator learns to read psychological messages to determine the real extent of a demand by management or labor. Each bargaining session presents new challenges to the creative abilities of all participants in reaching a positive settlement that does not adversely affect labor-management relationships.

In many adverse situations an arbitrator is needed to solve management-labor differences. Disciplinary cases provide an excellent example of management-labor conflict in interpretation of work rules. Arbitrators accept the right of management to give orders but management cannot issue orders that endanger the health or safety of employees. The use of physical force to carry out orders is another ground for grievances. Another area of friction arises when management fails to carry out its policies on absenteeism in accordance with prescribed procedures set forth in a negotiated contract. Similarly, arbitrators continue to support management in taking legal action to reduce the impact of walkouts, wildcat strikes, and similar disturbances that disrupt plant operations. On the other side of the issue, arbitrators have curtailed managerial rights to refuse to rehire employees who quit during periods of emotional stress. Discipline cases for theft and gambling on the job are two problem areas that are rarely solved to the ultimate satisfaction of both management and labor. Consider the following example:

Four employees were discharged after two warnings for shooting dice. When their case came to arbitration, each man was placed on the stand. The first one claimed he had taken up a collection for coffee for the group and was on his way out to get the coffee. The second maintained that he had just arrived for the second shift and was getting ready to change his clothes. He said he never gambled—didn't even know how to shoot dice. The third vowed sanctimoniously that he never gambled, and looked upon the practice as a vice. Finally, the arbitrator came to the fourth man, who had been caught with the dice.

"All these other men say they weren't gambling. But you—weren't you caught with a pair of dice in your hand?"

"Yes sir, I certainly was," was the amiable reply.

The arbitrator followed up quickly, "Then you were gambling, weren't you?"

The worker looked up, startled. "Gambling?" he exclaimed with indignation. "With whom, sir?"[27]

Although the examples given here do not answer all the questions a manager might have about arbitration, they provide a brief look at what a manager can expect if disciplinary measures are carried to arbitration by union representatives. Arbitrators can be a help in management-labor relationships. However, it should be the goal of management and labor to settle issues at the plant level. Arbitration is costly, time-consuming, and counterproductive in building sound labor-management relations.

A positive incident in union-management relations is the association between the International Union of Electrical Workers and several major electrical manufacturers. For example, 2200 employees in eight states have been upgraded to higher positions in the last three years. Most of the employees were high school dropouts, women, and minority individuals. One woman increased her weekly earnings from $50 to $120 per week. IUE has trained 3200 disadvantaged employees for higher-level jobs under four contracts with the Manpower Administration of the U.S. Department of Labor. A new contract will upgrade the job skills of 7000 IUE members in nine cities. The emphasis in recent contracts is to upgrade the skill level of present employees. For example, the Bendix plant in Franklin, Indiana, needed thirty-eight workers for a new product line. To obtain personnel for this operation the company agreed with the union to upgrade the skills of present personnel. As in any program there have been several failures. In one case, sixteen people were laid off because of a contract cancellation. In a second case, three people out of ten remained with a Brooklyn firm after being trained as television coil winders. The issue of job upgrading recognizes the need of people to receive a job challenge, to advance on that job, and to improve their economic status.[28]

Collective Bargaining

Collective bargaining has become the primary agent for designing organizational relationships between management and labor. This bargaining relationship can take several forms. Open conflict is a stage in union-management relations in which management refuses to accept the union as a bargaining agent or gives only token consideration of union demands. Containment is a management-union relationship in which management follows the guidelines of legal constraints. Accommodation is a union-management relationship based on avoidance of conflict between management and union interests. The danger in this relationship is its failure to provide real solutions to current or future problems. Cooperation provides a bargaining relationship built on consultation and action by managerial and labor representatives. The deal relationship is a trade-off arrangement in which management gives up an objective and the union responds by giving up a desired goal without the knowledge of its membership.[29] The consequences of union-management bargaining are seen in Table 10-13. Typical issues that brought about work stoppages in 1969 are shown in Table 10-14.

TABLE 10-13
Union and company alternatives in a bargaining situation and related consequences

Company	Union
Alternative 1: *Giving in to union demands*	*Alternative 1:* *Accepting company counteroffer*
Perceived *consequences:* 1. Lessening of investor return 2. Loss of competitive standing 3. Setting bad precedent 4. Avoiding costly strike 5. Avoiding government and public ill will	Perceived *consequences:* 1. Loss of membership support 2. Loss of status within union movement 3. Setting bad precedent 4. Avoiding costly strike 5. Avoiding government and public ill will
Alternative 2: *Refusing to accede to union demands*	*Alternative 2:* *Sticking to original demands*
Perceived *consequences:* 1. Due to potential strike, loss of investor return 2. Due to potential strike, loss of competitive standing 3. Loss of government and public good will 4. Maintenance of company prerogatives 5. Breaking union power	Perceived *consequences:* 1. Prove strength and determination of union to members 2. Due to potential strike, loss of member income 3. Due to potential strike, loss of member support 4. Loss of government and public good will 5. Teach company a "lesson"

Source: From *Psychology of Union-Management Relations*, by R. Stagner and H. Rosen. © 1965 by Wadsworth Publishing Company, Inc. Reprinted by permission of the publisher, Brooks/Cole Publishing Company, Monterey, California.

TABLE 10-14
Work stoppages by major issue, 1969

Issue	Stoppages (%)
General wage changes	49.6
Supplementary benefits	1.2
Wage adjustments	5.1
Hours of work	.1
Other contractual matters	1.5
Union organization and security	10.4
Job security	3.3
Plant administration	15.5
Other working conditions	4.0
Interunion or intraunion matters	8.8
Not reported	.4

Source: Bureau of Labor Statistics, U.S. Department of Labor, *Analysis of Work Stoppages, 1969*, Bull. 1687 (Washington, D.C., 1971), p. 19.

In the spring of 1974, a middle-management class at Richland College carried out a simulated exercise between management and labor representatives. The class of eighteen members was divided into two groups. Nine members of the class represented labor and nine members represented management. The period of negotiation was conducted for ten weeks. Actual face-to-face negotiations were conducted in five meetings that lasted approximately three hours each. The articles covered in the contract between REO and the United Furniture Workers of America were as follows:

Article I. Intent and Purpose
Article II. Recognition
Article III. Hours of Work
Article IV. Wages
Article V. Vacations
Article VI. Grievances
Article VII. Arbitration
Article VIII. Seniority
Article IX. Strikes and Lockouts
Article X. General Provisions
Article XI. Amendments
Article XII. Contract Dates
Article XIII. Training
Article XIV. Job Evaluation
Article XV. Union Shop Checkoff
Article XVI. Subcontracting
Article XVII. Pensions

The articles shown in this management-labor agreement provide an overview of the issues normally negotiated in union-management negotiations.

Summary

Collective bargaining has expanded its horizons to providing employment opportunities for the disadvantaged, for women, for minorities, and for youth. At the same time, labor relations must concern itself with wage patterns, fringe benefits, and internal management-labor relationships. The changing makeup of the labor population in terms of age is altering traditional managerial and union operating procedures. The impact of the black revolution will alter management's hiring practices as well as the membership patterns of most unions. The nature of work will be altered by adoption of a more open managerial philosophy. One aspect of this new philosophy is the voluntary compliance of companies with EEOC programs. An excellent example of an affirmative action program is the General Electric experience from 1968 to 1973.

A related new frontier in labor relations is the policy and procedure used to govern an organization's relationship to women employees. One area of concern among women is their high concentration in such positions as secretaries, receptionists, bank tellers, librarians, and related traditionally female occupations. A survey of 1500 subscribers to *Harvard Business Review* further illustrates the stereotyped roles given women in society. In this survey, female employees are expected to sacrifice career interests for family responsibility. A male is asked to sacrifice family obligations for career demands. Another finding of this study is a managerial trend to retain male employees over female employees when personal conduct threatens an employee's continued employment with the firm. A third finding of this study is that managers favor males in selection, promotion, and career development decisions. Case incidents were presented in the areas of career-family conflicts, disciplinary problems, and consideration for promotions. To encourage women to expand their occupational interests, the U.S. Department of Labor has produced a booklet entitled "Careers for Women in the '70's."

Closely related to women's struggle for equal employment opportunity is the struggle of the disadvantaged to find employment. Such people are designated as disadvantaged because of educational deficiencies, minority group affiliation, age, and physical or mental handicaps. The plight of blacks, Spanish-speaking Americans, and American Indians reflects the problems of disadvantaged persons. To continue to dismiss the problem of disadvantaged people is to invite further governmental action to induce business to identify and employ disadvantaged personnel. Another disadvantaged group in American society consists of ex-convicts. Programs such as PACE in Chicago have provided training and employment opportunities for inmates of the Cook County Jail. McDonald's Corporation has recognized the work of PACE by contributing over $2 million to fund operations. Polaroid has established a program for hiring ex-convicts and has encouraged other employers to do the same. A program for hiring ex-convicts requires careful placement, competent staff, supervisory training, and follow-up. Company rehabilitation programs may fail because of a lack of commitment by upper management, a lack of concern by supervisory personnel, a lack of training and opportunity, and employer pessimism.

Union members, like managers, are not stereotyped. Some union members are idealistic, some are highly dedicated, some are perennial critics, and some use the union to promote their own interests. A major area of stress in union relations is the concept of managerial rights as defined in a collective bargaining agreement. James Phelps and Arthur Goldberg have presented two opposing views of managerial rights. Fortunately, management and labor are moving toward a more enlightened relationship in dealing with each other. In adverse situations, an arbitrator is needed to settle disputes over interpretations of contract language as well as to settle grievances brought by union members against management. A positive example of union management relations is the work of the International Union of Electrical Workers to upgrade the job skills of its membership.

Collective bargaining has become the primary agent for designing organizational relationships between management and labor. Management-labor relations can take the form of conflict, containment, accommodation, cooperation, or a deal made without the knowledge of the union membership. Table 10-13 shows the consequences of union and managerial actions during a collective bargaining session.

Discussion Questions

1. *Why has collective bargaining turned away from exclusive attention to wages and fringe benefits in recent times?*
2. *Explain the role of young people in the shift in managerial styles toward more humanism and worker participation.*
3. *Do you believe that management itself in most instances has been responsible for the creation of such programs as the Equal Employment Opportunities Commission? Why?*
4. *What is your feeling about the negative attitudes toward women at work given in the chapter?*
5. *Describe your reaction as an employer to an applicant who has served a term in prison for burglary. For murder. For rape.*
6. *How do you account for the changes in attitudes of young workers toward jobs in which the duties are repetitive? Toward adverse working conditions?*
7. *Account for the drop in membership in unions of blue-collar workers.*

Chapter Case 10

A member of the work group for which Joe Jones is the supervisor has submitted a grievance stating that he is being discriminated against because he is black. You are the manager of this department and you know that Jones does not like Bill Brown because Bill has been associated with some movements working for equal opportunity for minority groups. Jones says that Brown is not leadership material and he has promoted several white workers who are not as good at their job as Brown. There is proof that Jones has told Brown that he does not like him and does not approve of his militancy. Employees are not represented by a union.
1. *Prepare a written answer to the grievance as you would if you were Joe Jones.*

2. *As manager of the department with a reluctance to lose the services of either person, how will you hande this situation?*

Notes

1. George S. Odiorne. *Personnel Administration by Objectives*. Homewood, Ill.: Irwin, 1971, pp. 186–188.
2. Richard Armstrong. "Labor 1970: Angry, Aggressive, Acquisitive." Reprinted with permission of *Fortune Magazine*, October 1969, pp. 1–6.
3. Ibid.
4. William G. Glueck. *Personnel: a Diagnostic Approach*. Dallas: Business Publications, 1974, p. 74.
5. Ibid., pp. 80–85.
6. Antonia Handler Chayes. "Make Your Equal Opportunity Program Court-Proof," *Harvard Business Review*, September–October 1974, pp. 81–89.
7. Theodore V. Purcell. "How G.E. Measures Managers in Fair Employment," *Harvard Business Review*, November–December 1974, pp. 100–103.
8. Ibid., p. 104.
9. Richard D. Steade. *Business and Society in Transition: Issues and Concepts*. San Francisco: Harper & Row (Canfield Press), 1975, pp. 86–90.
10. Benson Rosen, and Thomas H. Jerdee. "Sex Stereotyping in the Executive Suite," *Harvard Business Review*, March–April 1974, pp. 45–58.
11. M. Barbara Boyle. "Equal Opportunity for Women is Smart Business," *Harvard Business Review*, May–June 1973, pp. 88–95.
12. ———. "The Drive to Open Up More Careers for Women," *U.S. News and World Report*, January 14, 1974, p. 69.
13. Steade, op. cit., p. 214.
14. Ibid., p. 215.
15. Ibid., p. 218.
16. Ibid., p. 220.
17. Gopal C. Pati. "Business Can Make Ex-Convicts Productive," *Harvard Business Review*, May–June 1974, pp. 69–73.
18. Ibid.
19. Ibid., pp. 77–78.
20. Ibid., p. 78.
21. Ibid.
22. Lester R. Bittel. *What Every Supervisor Should Know*, 3rd ed. New York: McGraw-Hill, 1974, pp. 380–385.
23. Rosalind C. Barnett and Renate Fagiuri. "What Young People Think About Managers," *Harvard Business Review*, May–June 1973, pp. 106–118.
24. Bernard Karsh. "Union Traditions and Membership Apathy," *Labor Law Journal*, Vol. 9, No. 9 (September 1958), pp. 641–646. Copyright 1958, Commerce Clearing House, Inc.
25. James C. Phelps. "Management's Reserved Rights: An Industry View," *Management Rights and the Arbitration Process*, Proceedings of the Ninth Annual Meeting, National Academy of Arbitrators. Washington, D.C.: Bureau of National Affairs, 1956, p. 117.

26. Arthur J. Goldberg. "Management's Reserved Rights: A Labor View," reprinted by permission from *Management Rights and the Arbitration Process*, copyright © 1956 by The Bureau of National Affairs, Inc., Washington, D.C. 20037.
27. Lawrence Stessin. "Is the Arbitrator Your Friend?" *Supervisory Management*, Vol. 4, No. 8 (August 1959), pp. 9–16.
28. ———. "Union Connects Jobs and Workers," *Manpower*, Vol. 1, No. 11 (December 1969), pp. 26–30.
29. John B. Miner and Mary Green Miner. *Personnel and Industrial Relations: A Managerial Approach,* 2nd ed. New York: Macmillan, 1973, pp. 468–487.

CUSTOM FURNITURE CASE: THE COFFEE BREAK CRISIS

There has never been a written policy about coffee breaks at Custom Furniture. Everyone has just assumed that they were entitled to one in the morning and one in the afternoon for about fifteen minutes. There were vending machines close to all departments and employees selected their own times to take these breaks.

One afternoon John Taylor hears a ringing bell and loud voices in the area adjacent to the secretarial pool. He goes to the area to investigate the cause of the commotion and he sees Bill Jones ringing a large cow bell and announcing in a very loud voice "All right, everybody back to work. Break's over. Get back to work." Secretaries are looking at Bill as if he has lost his mind, but they are slowly filing back to their desks.

Taylor is on his way to an important appointment, so he decides to wait until the next day to talk to Bill about this incident. However, when he arrives the next morning two of the secretaries have asked permission to see him as soon as he comes in. He sends for them and they come into his office:

John: "Now girls, what is it that is so important?"
Nancy: "Mr. Taylor, have you heard what Bill Jones has taken on himself to do about our coffee breaks?"
John: "No, Nancy, to tell the truth, I haven't."
Nancy: "Well, look at this notice that he posted on the bulletin board."

John takes the notice and reads it. It states that all the office employees will take their coffee breaks between either 10:00 and 10:15 or 10:15 and 10:30 in the morning and between either 3:00 and 3:15 or 3:15 and 3:30 in the afternoon; that someone should be answering the phone in their department at all times; and that each person must be back at the desk by the end of the break.

Nancy: "We've always been allowed to take our breaks when we wanted to, not when someone told us to. He is getting to be a regular slave driver."

John: "Let me check into this, Nancy. I really can't say much until I've talked to Bill."

John goes back to Bill Jones's office and finds him busily working on one of his reports:

John: "Bill, what is all this ruckus about the secretaries and their coffee breaks?"

Bill: "Oh, they've been complaining to you, have they? I told them not to talk to you without going through me."

John: "That part is all right. I've always tried to keep an open-door policy for all employees."

Bill: "Well, that sort of undermines my authority. At any rate back to this break business. They have all been taking too much time on breaks, standing around the area gossiping while the phone rang off the wall and no work was being done. So I decided to restrict the breaks to certain times in the morning and afternoon. They can still take their breaks with their buddies. It will just take a little planning on their part."

John: "What was all the commotion yesterday with the bell ringing and the hollering?"

Bill: "Well, I was watching and some of them were not starting back to their desks in time to make it before break time was over. So I was just reminding them. Once they get into the habit, everything will be fine."

John: "Well, we'll try these rules of yours for a while but I don't want to hear that bell again. Do you understand?"

Bill: "Yes, sir!"

John forgot the incident until a few days later when he arrived at work a little early and saw a cluster of the people from the secretarial pool listening to a stranger on the parking lot. He later found out that the stranger was a union representative from the AFL-CIO.

1. Assuming that the secretaries had been overstaying their break, how would you have handled the situation if you were Bill Jones? John Taylor?
2. You are John Taylor. What will you do now?
3. Do you think that Nancy and the others have a legitimate gripe about Bill Jones's actions?

REWARDS AND PENALTIES

FOUR

INCENTIVES
11

I've made my number of parts for today. So I don't suppose there's any hurry.

Is that all you are interested in doing, Sally? Just making exactly the number of parts that standards call for in eight hours?

For the full story, turn to the case on page 336.

GENERAL PURPOSES
OF CHAPTER 11

1. To examine the role of money as a motivator
2. To contrast individual incentive with group incentives
3. To learn some of the effects of the Employee's Retirement Income Security Act of 1974

LEARNING OBJECTIVES

1. To name six guidelines in establishing an effective wage incentive system
2. To cite at least three ways in which firms have expanded their methods of compensation beyond mere wages and fringe benefits
3. To list the three major areas in which management strives to meet the financial needs of employees
4. To discuss the trend in granting of vacations during the period 1955 to 1970
5. To name four factors required to measure the impact of company benefits
6. To give your reaction to the rise in the extra costs of benefits from 1961 to 1971
7. To define *job* evaluation
8. To name and define three systems of job evaluation
9. To describe the Scanlon Plan of incentives
10. To discuss some advantages and disadvantages of placing all employees (including hourly workers) on a salary
11. To name four requirements of pension plans for the next thirty years
12. To list seven major provisions of the Employee Retirement Income Security Act of 1974
13. To name three preferences expressed by executives regarding compensation

Money as an Incentive

In many firms the payment of wages represents 50 percent or more of the expenses of operating the business. In this century scientific management has sought to motivate people through pay systems related directly to output. For twenty years human relations theorists viewed money as a minor issue in employee motivation. A recent survey in 1973 identified the job factors that produced employee dissatisfaction at work. Table 11-1 shows the results of this survey. E. E. Lawler, Jr., in his research on money as a motivator stated:

The data suggests that pay can be instrumental for the satisfaction of most needs but it is most likely to be seen as instrumental for satisfying esteem and physiological needs, secondarily to be seen as instrumental for satisfying autonomy or security needs and least likely to be seen as instrumental for satisfying social or self actual needs. . . . Thus, if a person at the time has strong self actualization or social needs, pay is not an important means to motivate him. If his needs are physiological, or esteem, then pay can be a useful motivator.[1]

Further research by Lawler suggests that socioeconomic conditions fail to influence an employee's attitude toward the importance of pay. Likewise, the value of pay to an employee is directly related to his or her efforts. Lawler presented several guidelines to managers constructing a wage incentive system. The guidelines are as follows:

1. Do not assume pay is necessarily the most important factor to all employees.
2. Do not believe it is sixth in preference either.
3. Pay is as important to those one level below you—maybe more so—as it is to you.
4. If employees complain about pay, see if the complaint has a non-economic cause.

TABLE 11-1

Reason	Percentage	Motivation
1. Poor wages	34	compensation
2. Boring job	20	self-actualization
3. Not doing what I want to	17	self-actualization
4. Have to work too hard	10	
5. Being held back	9	recognition
6. Hours too long	8	
7. Not many benefits	5	compensation

Source: William F. Glueck. *Personnel: A Diagnostic Approach.* Dallas: Business Publications, 1974, p. 406.

---

5. Tie pay to performance and make it a form of recognition if you want it to motivate.
6. Try to correlate importance of pay to people's backgrounds.[2]

A major point in Lawler's research is that not all wage incentive systems are effective. In order to motivate people, money must satisfy a need and must reward above-average performance.

The wages a person receives may be viewed from several levels of perception. For example, an individual who receives a 20 percent wage increase may gain a great deal of satisfaction. Another person receiving the same wage increase may feel alienated or cheated. Across-the-board raises do not have the same value for all members of the enterprise. Similarly, the value of a raise is viewed differently because of varying income levels, life-styles, and views of one's marketability. To be meaningful a raise must exceed guaranteed annual increases and relate directly to a person's contribution to the success of the enterprise. Thus, three ways to view a wage increase are as follows: (1) Wage incentives do not hold the same value for all personnel. (2) Wage incentives must significantly alter a person's economic well-being to have value. (3) Wage incentives should exceed annual or semiannual increases related to years of service.

If an employee is to be effective, he or she must not be asked to increase the level of productivity without additional compensation. To obtain a substantial wage increase, an employee must often leave present friends, incur greater risks, and lose present job security. Management must recognize that the greater the demand placed on the employee, the greater the financial expenditure needed to offset the psychological costs. The failure to offset psychological costs is a major reason why some companies fail to attract employees into front-line supervisory positions.

Receiving a raise below the employee's expectations tends to reduce his or her trust in the firm. Moreover, the failure to receive an expected raise does not alter the employee's desire for a future raise. A raise that meets an employee's expectations is viewed as a fair return for services given. Thus, the firm purchases an employee's continued employment, reassures the employee that the firm is responsive to employee needs, and reinforces feelings of security.

Limited salary scales tend to limit the growth of a firm. Failure to use financial incentives to overcome psychological costs of greater job responsibilities reduces the supply of managerial talent available to an enterprise. The greater an employee's task in relation to its impact on company policies, the greater are the adverse effects of failure or ineffective performance. To motivate an individual to move up the corporate ladder, money has to mean more than security. Because effective monetary incentives are not always economically feasible, management must use selectivity in granting substantial wage increases to corporate executives. Selectivity requires a firm to identify employees who respond in a positive, creative, and innovative manner. Thus, a wage incentive must overcome an employee's tendency to play it safe and provide motivation to implement creative ideas throughout the enterprise.

Money can bring about exceptional levels of achievement by offering the employee the chance to improve his or her financial position radically. The company must use selectivity to provide a significant return to the corporation, and this requires a system of measurement to identify exceptional services rendered. A major failure of most wage incentive systems is that they reward all personnel in the same manner. Rewards for mediocrity keep employees from leaving but do not motivate personnel to a higher level of commitment, achievement, or creativity.[3]

Role of Incentive Programs

People today are paid to do basic tasks but the impact of technocracy has required management to purchase the services of individuals with broad technological skills. Other influences on changing compensation programs are economic, social, and governmental regulations. To meet new compensation needs, enterprises must expand their methods of compensation beyond the scope of wages and fringe benefits. For example, firms are now providing day-care centers, time off for personal business, use of WATS lines for long-distance calls, and use of company copying equipment. One company has gone so far as to sell gasoline to employees in the company parking lot to help them avoid long waiting lines at gas stations. Each of these examples provides a brief look at the changing nature of employee compensation.[4]

To outline further the role of compensation in the world of work, it is wise to examine the traditional role of compensation. One of the first benefits provided employees was company housing and company stores. An excellent example of these benefits came in the expansion of the railroad across the country in the late 1800s. Major acts of legislation that altered compensation programs were the Social Security Act, the minimum-wage laws, and the Wagner Act. The right of unions to negotiate with management on wages, retirement, and other fringe benefits was established by the 1948 ruling of the National Labor Relations Board. The dramatic increase in employee benefits provided by business is shown in Table 11-2. In 1971, fringe benefits represented 31 percent of an employer's payroll. This represented an annual cost per year per employee of $2544. A breakdown of payments made by companies to support employee benefits is seen in Figure 11-1. The impact of Social Security payments is shown in Table 11-3.

TABLE 11-2

Comparison of 1951–1971 employee benefits: cents per payroll hour

Industry group	1951	1961	1971
All industries (137 companies)	34.5	71.6	143.5
Manufacturing (56 companies)	31.0	69.1	143.2
Nonmanufacturing (81 companies)	36.9	73.4	143.7

Source: Chamber of Commerce of the United States, *Employee Benefits 1971,* Washington, D.C., 1972, p. 27.

TABLE 11-3

Federal Social Security (old age, survivors, disability, and health insurance) provisions. Past and future financing provisions

Period	Maximum taxable earnings ($)	Combined employer-employee tax rate (%)			Self-employed tax rate (%)		
		OASDI	HI	Total	OASDI	HI	Total
1937–1949	3,000	2	—	2	—	—	—
1950	3,000	3	—	3	—	—	—
1951–1953	3,600	3	—	3	2.25	—	2.25
1954	3,600	4	—	4	3	—	3
1955–1956	4,200	4	—	4	3	—	3
1957–1958	4,200	4.5	—	4.5	3.375	—	3.375
1959	4,800	5	—	5	3.75	—	3.75
1960–1961	4,800	6	—	6	4.5	—	4.5
1962	4,800	6.25	—	6.25	4.7	—	4.7
1963–1965	4,800	7.25	—	7.25	5.4	—	5.4
1966	6,600	7.7	.7	8.4	5.8	.35	6.15
1967	6,600	7.8	1.0	8.8	5.9	.5	6.4
1968	7,800	7.6	1.2	8.8	5.8	.6	6.4
1969–1970	7,800	8.4	1.2	9.6	6.3	.6	6.9
1971	7,800	9.2	1.2	10.4	6.9	.6	7.5
1972	9,000	9.2	1.2	10.4	6.9	.6	7.5
1973	10,900	9.7	1.0	10.7	7.0	1.0	8.0
1974	12,000	9.7	1.0	10.7	7.0	1.0	8.0
1975–1977	*	9.7	1.0	10.7	7.0	1.0	8.0

* The 1972 amendments provide for automatic cost of living adjustments in the taxable wage base from 1975 on.

Source: Social Security Administration.

The most common method of employee compensation is that of an hourly wage. This hourly wage does not reflect overtime pay, shift differential pay, or premium pay for working on weekends or holidays. Most firms provide paid holidays, paid vacations, and personal leave to meet emergency needs. Again, the dramatic increase in paid holidays is

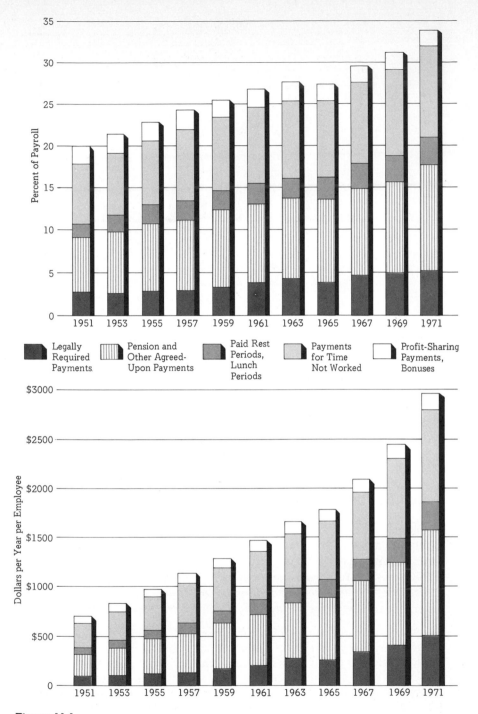

Figure 11-1
Comparison of 1951–1971 employee benefits for 137 companies. Source: Chamber of Commerce of the United States, *Employee Benefits* 1971, Washington, D.C., 1972, p. 28.

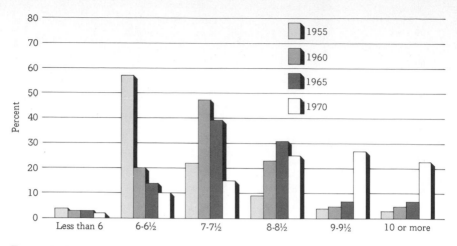

Figure 11-2
Trends in holidays and vacations. Source: Bureau of National Affairs, Inc., "Trends in Holidays and Vacations," *Bulletin to Management*, No. 1100 (March 11, 1971).

shown in Figure 11-2. Likewise, an increase in vacation time is reflected in Figure 11-3. A major increase in this area of compensation is seen in the increase in company programs to provide life, disability, and medical insurance for all employees. These programs are usually provided for employees at reduced rates. An increasing trend is for management to pay the total cost of financing these fringe benefits. Pensions and retirement programs represent the third major area in which companies strive to meet the financial needs of employees.

Benefits and Services

Employee benefits and services do not represent direct monetary payments to employees. Although benefits and services provided by various firms differ in content, they often provide similar fringe programs to employees. The following list by John B. Miner and Mary Green Miner, in *Personnel and Industrial Relations: A Managerial Approach,* gives a general overview of the services available to employees in an enterprise.

1. Services related to type of work performed, including subsidies for the purchase and upkeep of work clothes and uniforms, as well as for various types of tools used in connection with the work.
2. Eating facilities, including company restaurants, cafeterias, lunch rooms, and vending machines. Under certain circumstances meals may be provided free of charge. More frequently the charge is at cost or somewhat below.
3. Transportation and child care facilities, including parking lots, bus

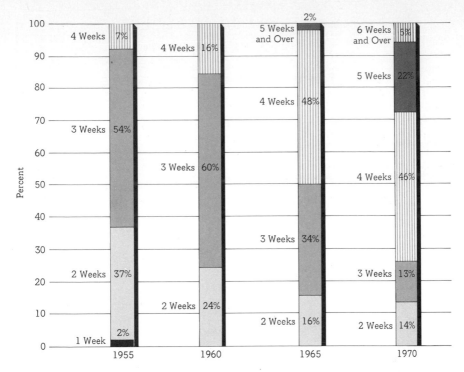

Figure 11-3
Vacation trends, 1955–1970: Percentage of collective bargaining agreements with specified maximum vacation allowances. Source: Bureau of National Affairs, Inc., "Trends in Holidays and Vacations," Bulletin to Management, No. 1100 (March 11, 1971), pp. 4–6.

service, company cars, assistance with arrangements for car pools, and day care centers for employees' pre-school children.

4. Housing services, including company-owned or -constructed housing projects, rental lists, assistance with home financing, guarantees on the purchase of homes owned by employees transferred to new locations, and payment of moving expenses.

5. Financial and legal services, including sponsorship of credit unions, help in preparing income tax forms, and many types of legal assistance available through the company legal department. In addition, a number of companies operate loan services for employees, although these are usually restricted to hardship cases. Group automobile insurance sometimes is offered on a payroll deduction basis.

6. Purchasing services, including company-owned or -operated stores and discounts on company products and services.

7. Recreational, social, and cultural programs, including sponsorship of company athletic teams, social clubs, summer camps, country clubs, recreational areas, orchestras, libraries, and discounts on tickets to cultural or sporting events.

TABLE 11-4

Employee compensation in the private nonfarm economy, 1970 (United States)

Compensation practice	All industries all employees		Manufacturing industries				Nonmanufacturing industries			
			Office		Nonoffice		Office		Nonoffice	
	Per-cent[1]	Dol-lars[2]	Per-cent[1]	Dol-lars[2]	Per-cent[1]	Dol-lars[2]	Per-cent[1]	Dol-lars[2]	Per-cent[1]	Dol-lars[2]
Total compensation	100.0	$4.54	100.0	$6.70	100.0	$4.24	100.0	$5.45	100.0	$3.66
Wages and salaries	89.0	4.04	89.1	5.97	87.4	3.70	90.2	4.91	89.1	3.26
Straight-time pay	79.8	3.63	78.1	5.23	76.2	3.23	80.9	4.41	82.3	3.01
Premium pay	2.1	.09	1.1	.07	4.0	.17	0.7	.04	2.3	.08
Overtime, weekend, and holiday work	1.7	.08	0.9	.06	3.2	.13	0.6	.03	2.2	.08
Shift differentials	0.3	.01	0.2	.01	0.8	.03	0.1	.01	0.2	.01
Pay for leave time	6.3	.28	8.2	.55	6.9	.29	7.0	.38	4.3	.16
Vacations	3.3	.15	4.2	.28	3.9	.16	3.5	.19	2.2	.08
Holidays	2.1	.09	2.7	.18	2.4	.10	2.3	.12	1.4	.05
Sick, civic, personal	0.8	.04	1.3	.09	0.5	.03	1.2	.06	0.6	.02
Nonproduction bonuses and severance	1.0	.04	1.7	.11	0.06	.03	1.6	.08	0.4	.01
Supplements[3]	11.0	.50	10.9	.73	12.6	.53	9.8	.53	10.9	.40
Social security[4]	3.4	.16	2.8	.19	3.7	.16	3.1	.17	3.8	.14
Unemployment insurance	0.7	.03	0.5	.03	0.8	.03	0.5	.03	0.9	.03
Workmen's compensation	0.9	.04	0.3	.02	1.0	.04	0.3	.02	1.5	.05
Life, accident, and health insurance	2.6	.12	3.1	.20	3.9	.16	2.0	.11	2.2	.08
Private pension plans	3.0	.14	3.6	.24	2.9	.12	3.8	.21	2.2	.08
Other	0.3	.01	0.6	.04	0.1	(z)	0.1	.01	0.3	.01

Z Less than $0.005.

[1] Of total compensation.

[2] Per hour of working time.

[3] Employer expenditures.

[4] Includes railroad retirement.

Note: Based on a sample survey. Covers employees in private nonfarm establishments having one or more paid workers.

Source: U.S. Bureau of Labor Statistics, *Employee Compensation in the Private Nonfarm Economy*, 1970.

8. Medical and community services, including plant infirmaries, clinics, and hospitals, with the more extensive facilities being found largely in isolated areas or foreign countries. In addition, companies provide physical examinations, visiting nurses, counseling services, and referrals to various community social service agencies.
9. Educational services, including sponsorship of off-hours courses, educational leaves, tuition refund plans, and scholarships or educational loans for employees and their children. Under certain conditions companies operate complete educational systems for the children of their employees.
10. Outplacement services, including making contacts with other employers in the area, help with writing up resumes, and secretarial assistance. Such services usually are provided only where large numbers of technical or professional employees are being terminated.[5]

The cost of these services is shown in Figure 11-4. For example, in 1970, 20 percent of all compensation was spent on benefits programs. Table 11-4 outlines the type of compensation provided employees in

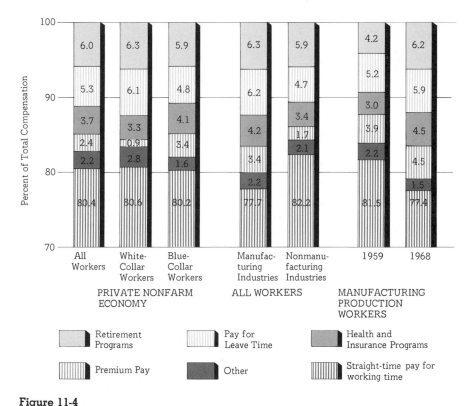

Figure 11-4
Structure of compensation for selected groups and industries, 1968, and manufacturing production workers, 1959 and 1968 (United States). Source: U.S. Department of Labor, Bureau of Labor Statistics.

TABLE 11-5
Cost of weekly employee benefits in industry, 1971 (United States)

	Per employee per week
All industries	$48.92
Manufacturers	
Petroleum industry	66.21
Chemicals and allied products	58.23
Transportation equipment	55.37
Primary metal industries	53.10
Food, beverages, and tobacco	51.31
Machinery (excluding electrical)	48.19
Stone, clay, and glass products	47.46
Instruments and miscellaneous products	46.71
Electrical machinery, equipment, and supplies	46.67
Fabricated metal products (excluding machinery and transportation equipment)	45.14
Rubber, leather, and plastic products	44.04
Printing and publishing	43.69
Pulp, paper, lumber, and furniture	42.87
Textile products and apparel	28.87
Nonmanufacturing	
Public utilities	58.42
Banks, finance and trust companies	52.08
Insurance companies	48.33
Miscellaneous industries (mining, transportation, research, warehousing, etc.)	45.83
Wholesale and retail (not department stores)	35.44
Department stores	25.90

Source: "Those Whopping Extra Benefits for Employees," *Nation's Business* 60 (August 1972).

1970 in manufacturing and nonmanufacturing industries. The weekly cost to industry in 1971 is shown in Table 11-5. From 1961 to 1971, the cost of benefits to employers went up 103 percent. This increase is outlined in Table 11-6.

To measure the impact of company benefits requires (1) a survey of employee attitudes, (2) a cost analysis on an annual basis, (3) a willingness to alter existing programs to meet changing needs, and (4) the recognition that financial solvency forces a firm to alter its benefit program in light of economic circumstances. Management should recognize its social responsibility in providing such services. However, to provide a benefit program that exceeds the financial capability of the firm is to invite economic and social disaster. A major source of inflation is the additional cost of benefit programs provided by firms as they compete for people. Companies should make available to the public figures revealing the cost of providing benefits and services to employees.

TABLE 11-6
Weekly extra benefit costs per employee (United States)

	1961	*1971*	*Percent increase*
Private pensions	$4.06	$7.73	+90
Paid vacations	4.06	7.69	+89
Old age, survivors, disability and health insurance taxes	2.58	7.15	+177
Insurance (life, sickness, accident, hospitalization)	2.62	7.10	+171
Paid rest periods, lunch periods, wash-up time	2.52	5.38	+113
Paid holidays	2.42	4.69	+94
Profit-sharing payments	0.77	1.65	+114
Workmen's compensation	0.77	1.58	+105
Paid sick leave	0.67	1.56	+133
Unemployment compensation taxes	1.46	1.15	−21
Employee meals furnished free	0.15	0.25	+67
Discounts on goods and services purchased from company	0.12	0.23	+92
Other fringe benefits	1.92	2.76	+44
Total fringe benefits	$24.12	$48.92	+103%
Average weekly earnings	$96.85	$158.85	+64%
Fringe benefits as percent of employee earnings	24.9%	30.8%	

Source: "Those Whopping Extra Benefits for Employees," *Nation's Business* 60, August 1972.

Employees tend to take company benefit programs for granted because they do not see the cost of such services in the products they produce or in the goods they purchase. These hidden costs must be identified to avoid excessive expenditures, excessive demands, and increased governmental pressures to finance social services. For example, a national health program is being proposed in the United States Senate that will be financed by a tax on the earnings of corporations and individuals. Such a tax will further aggravate a cost-push inflationary trend in the manufacture and distribution of goods and services. Management must constantly strive to obtain the greatest return possible from their financial support of employee benefit programs. Analysis of these factors can help in the continued success of present and future fringe benefit programs.

Setting Standards

One of the most difficult tasks for any manager is that of determining the wage scale for a given job. A common approach is the wage survey,

TABLE 11-7

Occupational earnings survey: sample of office occupations (average straight-time weekly hours and earnings of workers in selected occupations by industry division, St. Louis, Mo.–Illinois, March 1973)

Occupation and industry division	Number of workers	Average weekly hours (standard)	Weekly earnings (standard)			$60 and under 65	$65 70	$70 75
			Mean	Median	Middle range			
Men and Women Combined—Continued								
Secretaries—Continued								
Secretaries, Class C	1,747	39.5	$147.50	$143.50	$125.50–$169.50	—	—	—
Manufacturing	835	39.5	157.00	155.00	135.50– 177.50	—	—	—
Nonmanufacturing	912	39.0	139.00	131.00	118.00– 159 50	—	—	—
Public Utilities	247	39.5	172.00	174.50	156.50– 191.00	—	—	—
Wholesale Trade	126	39.5	140.00	138.00	119.00– 156.00	—	—	—
Retail Trade	71	39.5	129.00	128.50	117.50– 134.00	—	—	—
Finance	252	38.5	120.00	122.50	106.50– 129.50	—	—	—
Services	216	38.0	126.50	122.50	115.50– 137.00	—	—	—
Secretaries, Class D	1,323	39.0	132.00	130.00	115.00– 147.00	—	—	—
Manufacturing	797	39.5	134.00	133.00	119.50– 146.50	—	—	—
Nonmanufacturing	526	38.5	129.00	119.50	105.50– 150.50	—	—	—
Public Utilities	76	37.5	181.50	196.00	164.00– 200.00	—	—	—
Wholesale Trade	121	38.5	138.00	145.00	117.00– 154.00	—	—	—
Retail Trade	135	39.5	116.00	116.50	101.00– 124.50	—	—	—
Finance	152	37.5	111.50	108.50	100.00– 118.00	—	—	—
Stenographers, General	1,271	39.5	128.00	124.50	105.50– 148.00	—	—	1
Manufacturing	596	39.5	133.00	135.00	113.50– 149.50	—	—	—
Nonmanufacturing	675	39.0	123.50	114.50	98.50– 143.00	—	—	1
Public Utilities	183	40.0	153.00	154.00	129.00– 173.00	—	—	—
Wholesale Trade	80	40.0	146.50	133.00	114.50– 196.00	—	—	—
Retail Trade	69	39.5	103.50	104.00	92.00– 121.00	—	—	—
Finance	211	38.0	96.00	95.00	87.50– 102.50	—	—	—
Services	132	39.5	124.00	115.00	109.00– 133.00	—	—	1
Stenographers, Senior	1,275	39.5	133.00	128.50	112.00– 154.00	—	—	—
Manufacturing	564	40.0	134.00	131.00	115.00– 157.00	—	—	—
Nonmanufacturing	711	39.0	132.50	127.00	109.00– 148.00	—	—	—
Public Utilities	170	40.0	156.50	157.50	136.00– 184.00	—	—	—
Wholesale Trade	212	40.0	138.50	133.00	119.00– 156.00	—	—	—
Finance	208	37.5	114.00	111.00	104.00– 125.50	—	—	—

which identifies skill levels and wage rates associated with various job skills. In a union shop, prevailing wage rates become a critical yardstick in determining present and future raises. For example, national settlements in the auto, steel, and coal industries set the pattern for wage settlements in other organized industries. Management should provide employees with objective data to justify payment or nonpayment of existing wage rates in their industry. An excellent source of wage data is the U.S. Department of Labor's Occupational Earnings Survey as illustrated in Table 11-7.

To structure a wage payment system in industry requires the establishment of performance standards, evaluation methods, and a means of altering levels of compensation. One technique used to carry out these tasks is job evaluation. Job evaluation seeks to measure a person's

Table 11-7 (Continued)

	Number of workers receiving straight-time weekly earnings of—																
$75–80	$80–90	$90–100	$100–110	$110–120	$120–130	$130–140	$140–150	$150–160	$160–170	$170–180	$180–190	$190–200	$200–210	$210–220	$220–230	$230–240	$240 and over
—	17	36	92	181	266	218	191	179	139	129	114	106	33	22	12	7	5
—	—	8	20	27	92	106	134	102	73	79	77	56	30	13	9	5	4
—	17	28	72	154	174	112	57	77	66	50	37	50	3	9	3	2	1
—	—	—	3	3	12	9	19	24	44	38	31	47	3	8	3	2	1
—	—	—	10	26	6	28	15	21	2	9	6	3	—	—	—	—	—
—	—	—	5	16	21	19	2	7	—	—	—	—	—	1	—	—	—
—	17	23	35	38	83	30	7	17	—	2	—	—	—	—	—	—	—
—	—	5	19	71	52	26	14	8	20	1	—	—	—	—	—	—	—
—	35	75	157	212	180	214	168	120	59	25	18	41	6	4	9	—	—
—	2	24	65	116	137	172	134	79	23	20	12	12	1	—	—	—	—
—	33	51	92	96	43	43	34	41	36	5	6	29	5	4	9	—	—
—	—	—	4	—	4	4	2	3	10	1	3	27	5	4	9	—	—
—	—	7	14	14	—	15	16	35	20	—	—	—	—	—	—	—	—
—	12	20	24	29	26	13	—	—	2	4	3	2	—	—	—	—	—
—	18	20	44	40	2	6	16	2	4	—	—	—	—	—	—	—	—
10	89	128	183	173	123	134	133	109	49	36	52	40	6	3	2	—	—
—	9	37	81	74	61	89	99	76	21	8	37	4	—	—	—	—	—
10	80	91	102	99	62	45	34	33	28	28	15	36	6	3	2	—	—
—	—	1	9	14	25	11	26	25	22	12	15	14	6	1	2	—	—
—	—	—	8	22	2	16	2	2	2	2	—	22	—	2	—	—	—
3	11	16	15	5	15	3	1	—	—	—	—	—	—	—	—	—	—
7	66	71	41	17	5	3	1	—	—	—	—	—	—	—	—	—	—
—	3	3	29	41	15	12	4	6	4	14	—	—	—	—	—	—	—
—	35	69	188	192	171	196	80	98	73	57	62	51	1	1	1	—	—
—	17	26	60	108	62	88	30	45	55	52	19	1	1	—	—	—	—
—	18	43	128	84	109	108	50	53	18	5	43	50	—	1	1	—	—
—	—	—	8	32	8	15	44	14	3	36	8	—	1	1	—	—	—
—	7	7	21	20	40	40	23	4	3	2	3	42	—	—	—	—	—
—	11	15	75	40	28	39	—	—	—	—	—	—	—	—	—	—	—

Source: Bulletin 1775–69, U.S. Bureau of Labor Statistics, Department of Labor.

contribution to the enterprise and to set up a system for paying the person according to the level of performance. Several evaluation methods are as follows:

1. A point system usually takes a number of aspects of the job and assigns a point value to each. Table 11-8 provides an overview of a point system for clerical jobs.
2. The factor comparison system identifies key jobs and assigns a numerical value to each. The key jobs chosen should meet the following criteria:
   a. Must represent the entire range of jobs.
   b. Must be stable as to content.
   c. Must be well-recognized jobs.

TABLE 11-8
Evaluation points for clerical jobs

Factor*	Degree points					
	1st	*2d*	*3d*	*4th*	*5th*	*6th*
Education required	20	40	60	80	100	120
Experience required	25	50	75	100	125	150
Complexity of job	35	70	105	140		
Responsibility for relationships with others	15	30	45	60		
Working conditions	5	10	15	20		

* Weights assigned fit Kelly's weights of job aspects referred to above: e.g., education = 20%, experience = 25%, complexity = 35%, responsibility = 15%, working conditions = 5%.

Source: Robert Kelly, "Job Evaluation and Pay Plans: Office Personel," from *Handbook of Modern Personnel Administration.* Edited by Joseph Famularo. Copyright © 1972 by McGraw-Hill, Inc. Used with permission of McGraw-Hill Book Co.

    d. Must be clearly and exactly defined with respect to skills, responsibilities, and requirements.

    e. Must be acceptable to all evaluators in regard to description and rate of pay.

    f. Must stand out distinctly from other jobs so that there will be no misunderstanding among the raters.[6]

Eugene Benge, who developed the factor comparison technique, suggested the following job factors as an essential part of assigning wage rates in an organization:

    a. Mental requirements (mental traits such as intelligence, judgment, general knowledge of the job).

    b. Skill requirements (such as the ability to coordinate body and mind as needed for the job).

    c. Physical requirements (physical exertion needed on the job).

    d. Degree of responsibility for supervision of people, equipment, contact with the public, and so on.

    e. Working conditions (degree of disagreeable and hazardous conditions, such as noise, dirt, hours of work).[7]

Table 11-9 shows an example of the factor comparison technique.

3. The job ranking system ranks all jobs on the basis of their complexity and assigns a wage scale for each job. The simplest jobs have the lowest pay rate and the most complex jobs the highest.[8]

Regardless of the system used, management cannot view job evaluation as the total answer in determining wage rates. Economic, social,

TABLE 11-9

Example of factor comparison scales for physical requirements of jobs plotted against money paid for these requirements

$1.00 Key job 1	11.00	21.00	31.00 Key job 10
2.00	12.00	22.00 Key job 7	32.00
3.00 Key job 2	13.00	23.00	33.00
4.00	14.00 Key job 4	24.00	34.00
5.00	15.00	25.00 Key job 8	35.00
6.00	16.00	26.00	36.00 Key job 11
7.00	17.00 Key job 5	27.00	37.00
8.00	18.00	28.00 Key job 9	38.00
9.00 Key job 3	19.00	29.00	39.00 Key job 12
10.00	20.00 Key job 6	30.00	40.00

Source: William F. Glueck, *Personnel: A Diagnostic Approach.* Dallas: Business Publications, 1974, p. 413.

and technological influences force management to restructure the system of compensation. An example of structuring a compensation program is shown in the appendix at the back of the book.

Individual and Group Plans

The design of individual incentives in industry has become an area of contention between managers and their employees. Merit pay is a classic example of an individual incentive system. However, merit pay has lost some of its effectiveness because of favoritism, unequal wage rates for similar skills, and employee hostility. For example, assume a manager of a department consisting of fifteen people receives a directive that authorizes raises for only five of the people. As a result, five employees receive a raise and ten employees get no additional compensation. The issue is to justify failure to grant raises to ten employees as well as to justify the decision to management. Regardless of the outcome, morale is adversely affected and, more importantly, the organization may lose the continued support of the ten alienated employees. Moreover, in a mobile society like ours several, if not all ten, employees may choose to find employment with another firm. Thus, merit programs have been eliminated from many compensation programs.

The most common individual incentive in a manufacturing enterprise is the piece-rate system. Such a system provides an hourly wage rate in relation to a required level of output. For example, the garment industry has used this technique for years to pay its employees. The idea of the piece-rate system is to provide a basic wage level for all employees and at the same time offer all employees the opportunity to increase their level of earnings. An employee earning a base rate of $3.50 an hour could exceed the minimum standard of production and earn $3.60 or more per hour. Assume that an employee is expected to produce fifty garments per week to receive a base salary of $3.50 per hour. If that employee produces sixty garments, the rate of pay increases accordingly. To be effective, management must set a reasonable minimum standard that allows an employee the opportunity to increase earnings.

In service and retail industries, quotas, commissions, and gratuities are used to provide individual incentives for employees. For example, a shoe salesman may be guaranteed a base of $80 per week for selling 100 percent of his assigned quota. Given a quota of $40 per hour in sales, this man is expected to sell $1600 worth of shoes in one forty-hour week. Sales of $2000 might provide an employee with a commission of $180 (based on 9 percent commission on total sales). Employees in the food industry depend on gratuities to raise their level of income. A waitress in a restaurant might be paid $3 per hour but averages $5 per hour from customers' tips. Many sales organizations set up an individual incentive program using a straight commission arrangement. Such a person receives a commission of 15, 20 or 25 percent, or more, of the selling price of a product or service. This payment system provides a direct correlation between an individual's productivity and level of income. Individual incentives are harder to design, implement, and maintain than a group incentive system.

Group plans take the form of profit-sharing programs, bonuses, and related measures to reward the accomplishment of employees at work. American Motors was one of the first automotive manufacturers to implement a profit-sharing program for assembly line workers. The program was designed to increase company operating effectiveness as well as to share the results of this effectiveness with employees.

The Scanlon Plan represents one of the most successful group plans used to reward employees for outstanding performance. Committees composed of managers and employees seek to obtain suggestions for improving the operating effectiveness of the company. Management maintains the right to accept or reject ideas as well as the right to handle all negotiations with unions over grievances, wages, and working conditions. The Scanlon Plan provides a bonus to all employees based on a percentage of their gross earnings. Bonuses relate directly to the employee's wage rate and the level of job content. Bonuses are paid on a monthly basis and at the end of the year all funds in the reserve pool are divided among the employees. To provide a greater understanding of the Scanlon Plan three applications of this plan are presented to show its flexibility. Table 11-10 gives the make-up of three companies that have successfully used the Scanlon Plan. The three applications are as follows:

310

Atwood Vacuum Machine Company

This family-owned company, with its corporate headquarters located in Rockford, Illinois, has had the Scanlon Plan for 14 years. Six plants are covered. Total employment is in excess of 2,000 people. Everyone participates in the program, including the president of the company. At the time the Scanlon Plan was implemented, an individual incentive system was dropped.

Atwood is a supplier of automotive parts hardware to all of the major automobile manufacturers. It also has a general product division which manufactures proprietary products, such as trailer hitches, brake actuating systems, and trailer hot-water heaters. Each of the plants bargains individually with an independent union.

With a major share of its volume going to the automotive industry, the company is faced with the possibility of going out of business each model year. The fact that the company is making a certain component for the auto industry in 1969, for instance, certainly does not guarantee that it will be making it in 1970.

TABLE 11-10
Three companies using Scanlon Plans

	Atwood	*Parker*	*Pfaudler*
Number of employees	2,000	1,000	750
Number of plants	6	1	1
Union affiliations	3 (independent)	2 (AFL-CIO)	2 (AFL-CIO)
Product	Automotive hardware	Writing instruments	Project engineering, Glassteel equipment, stainless steel equipment, food-filling equipment
Type of production	High volume; competitive	High-volume consumer item	Custom as well as standard fabricating
Type of bonus measurement	Payroll/sales value of production	Payroll/sales value of production	Payroll/sales value of production
Frequency of reviewing measurement	Annually	Periodically	Periodically
Prior incentive plans	Individual incentive	Individual incentive	No incentives

Source: Fred G. Lesieur and Elbridge S. Puckett, "The Scanlon Plan Has Proved Itself," *Harvard Business Review,* September–October, 1969, pp. 109–118.

Each plant has its own Scanlon production committees. These committees are composed of employee, union, and management representatives. However, there are only two plants holding monthly screening committee meetings; the plants located within a 55-mile radius of Rockford attend the screening committee held there, while at the same time the other two plants, located over 200 miles away, join in holding a screening committee meeting. The company sends at least one executive from the main plant to attend the latter meeting.

Top management feels it is imperative that all of these plants operate under one plan. Depending on how severe the model change-over may be in a given year, one plant may very well be affected more than another is. Having them all together provides much-needed stability. It also facilitates the transfer of jobs from one plant to another.

Turning now to the record of incentive payments under the plan, the most important facts are these:

1. During the 14 years of the Scanlon Plan at Atwood, annual bonuses have ranged from a high of approximately 20% of the payroll to a low of approximately 5%.
2. In the 187 periods of operation (the company's accounting year consists of 13 four-week periods), bonuses have been earned in 163 periods.
3. The highest monthly bonus was approximately 26%.
4. There has been a close correlation between annual profits and bonuses paid.

In terms of suggestions received under the Scanlon Plan, Atwood has no peer. Over 25,000 suggestions have been turned in by employees.

A significant indicator of the efficacy of an incentive plan is whether sales or production grows in proportion to payroll. If payroll grows proportionately larger over the years, that is a sign (not necessarily an absolutely correct one) that incentives are not as effective as they should be. What is Atwood's experience in this connection? The measurement of performance used is total payroll to sales value of production; this ratio today is within 0.5% of the ratio at the time the plan was started 14 years ago. This is evidence of increased worker efficiency with willing acceptance of the technological changes introduced by management. Because of the volatility of the Atwood business, the method of measurement is evaluated every year.[9]

Parker Pen Company
In this company the Scanlon Plan is used solely in the Manufacturing Division, located in Janesville, Wisconsin. There are approximately 1,000 employees covered by the plan; it has been in operation for 14 years. There are two international unions involved; one is the United Rubber Workers of America, AFL-CIO, Local No. 663, covering the production workers, and the other is the International Association of Machinists, AFL-CIO, No. 1266, covering the tool room group. The company manufactures superior-quality writing instruments which are

sold domestically and exported throughout the world. The Janesville plant also supplies component parts to Parker subsidiaries located throughout the world.

Management installed the plan after disposing of an individual incentive system. That system had been in effect for many years, and both management and the union felt it had outlived its usefulness.

Under the system, the company had had trouble introducing automated or mechanical changes. Moreover, by 1954, costs had risen so that approximately 50% of the company product was being made outside of Janesville, and the Janesville plant was gradually becoming an assembly operation.

Probably one of the greatest benefits the company has received from the plan has been the acceptance of automation by the people involved. Partly as a result, the company now manufactures better than 80% of the product in the Janesville operation.

Unlike the other two companies described in this section, Parker makes a consumer product and hence gets locked in to certain price categories. For instance, the current Jotter ball pen, an important part of the company line, had a price of $1.98 established in 1955. The same price is in effect today. (How many other things can you buy today that have the same sales price as they had 14 years ago?)

As for bonuses paid, some of the salient facts are these:

1. The highest yearly average has been approximately 20%, and the lowest, 5½%.
2. During the 168 months of operation, bonuses have been paid in 142 months. The highest monthly bonus was approximately 30%.
3. The correlation between bonuses paid and division profits has been excellent.

If one were to ask management what it feels is the most important asset that the Scanlon Plan has brought to the company, the answer probably would be willingness to accept change. Out of this cooperative spirit have developed more jobs, whereas the trend was to fewer jobs prior to installation of the plan. As for the ratio of payroll to sales which is used for measuring bonuses, it is slightly in excess of one percentage point of what it was back in 1954. This fact is evidence of increased worker efficiency along with willing acceptance of technological changes introduced by management.[10]

Pfaudler Company
This company, a division of Sybron Corporation, is located in Rochester, New York. It produces chemical, pharmaceutical, food-manufacturing, and brewery equipment. The Scanlon Plan has been in existence at Pfaudler's for 17 years; the number of employees covered by the plan is approximately 750, and they work in the Manufacturing Division. There are two unions involved, the United Steelworkers of America, AFL-CIO, Local No. 1495, and the Coppersmithing Branch of Sheet Metal Trades, Local No. 356.

On many occasions we have heard executives at Pfaudler describe it as a "large job shop." By that they mean that much of its product is scientifically engineered and tailored to fit a specific application of a customer company in the chemical industry. Sales are highly volatile. For instance, because Pfaudler supplies in excess of 70% of the world's needs for glass-lines chemical equipment, it is faced from time to time with either a substantial backlog of orders or a pronounced lack of orders. The company's manufacturing cycle—the period from the time when an order is booked to the first delivery on the order—is generally 12 weeks.

The plan has been most effective in dealing with either an over-abundance of orders or a lack of them. As a result of the work of the various production committees and the screening committee, these ups and downs the company faces have been shortened on the downward cycle; the cooperation of the people involved has very often brought in work that otherwise would have gone to someone else.

The type of activity that the screening and production committees have engaged in has been very broad in range.

During each rebuilding and expansion program that the company has undertaken, production committees in the areas affected have had an opportunity, prior to the program getting under way, to pore over the blueprints of the work to be done. Committee members have raised questions concerning the layout of the equipment and recommended changes to ensure the best possible utilization of the new facilities.

As for the bonuses paid to employees participating in the plan, the highlights of the past 17 years are as follows:

1. The highest annual bonus year was 17½% of wages for the year, and the lowest was approximately 3% of wages.
2. Over the 204 months of operation, bonuses have been paid in 179 months.
3. The highest bonus earned during a given month was approximately 22%.

Blue-Collar Workers on Salary

Changing methods of employee compensation are reflected in the trend to place all employees on a salary. Gillette Safety Razor Company employs 1600 workers in their Boston plant. Time clocks are used to control lateness and absences as well as to provide data for accounting purposes. However, all regular employees receive a salary and suffer no loss in pay when absent from work. Gillette got the idea of an all-salaried work force from a review of its sick leave policy in 1955. To assist supervisors in evaluating justifiable absences, a twelve-day annual standard was established. Extensive absences without justifiable cause lead to dismissal. The result of this policy is that the absence rate of employees affected increased only 0.1 percent.

314

Polaroid, in Cambridge, Massachusetts, provides another example of the blue-collar worker on salary. The salary unification program began in 1966 and allows supervisors to use their judgment in determining payment for absences. An extensive orientation program was initiated to inform employees of their individual responsibility for job attendance. One side benefit of this program is that supervisors have greater authority to grant time off for personal reasons to employees. The absence rate for workers increased only 1 percent.

Kinetic Dispersion Corporation initiated a salary plan for blue-collar workers in 1962. To increase the program's effectiveness, a cooperative working relationship with local UAW officials was negotiated in a new contract. The first year was excessively expensive because of a high rate of employee absenteeism. With the cooperation of the UAW the contract was amended so that management could withhold pay for excessive absences without cause.

In 1971, Avon products introduced a weekly salary plan that provided automatic wage increases for production workers. Avon reduced absences by granting time off for personal reasons, which eliminated the employee trend of unnecessarily reporting sick for a full day. A side benefit of the salary policy was increased supervisory effectiveness in counseling and controlling unexcused absences. A unique result at Avon was the impact of peer pressure in controlling employee absences. Increased job responsibility added to the attractiveness of supervisory positions.

Black and Decker introduced in 1971 a weekly salary plan for employees that allows ten days of absence per year for acceptable reasons. Supervisors are given the task of determining payment or nonpayment for absences. The plan has not been implemented for every hourly employee because of a company policy of gradual implementation and the need to train employees and supervisors on procedures governing a weekly salary program. Black and Decker believes that the introduction of a salary compensation program has helped sustain a positive management-labor relationship. An 80 percent increase in output has resulted from improved work practices and technological developments. Table 11-11 identifies selected aspects of the five salary plans implemented by Avon Products, Gillette, Black and Decker, Kinetic Dispersion, and Polaroid. Table 11-12 shows the principal features of a typical salary plan. To implement a salary method of pay for all employees, management must find answers to several key questions:

1. What is the status of management-employee relations?
2. What is the nature of the present labor force?
3. How do front-line supervisors view their job?
4. Do present record-keeping techniques on absences provide a true picture of employee absenteeism?

TABLE 11-11
Selected aspects of salary plans

Company	Union status	Date of change-over	Objective of changeover	Treat-ment of time clocks	Absence rate for workers affected by plan*			Employee reaction	Employer appraisal
					Be-fore	After	Cur-rent		
Avon Products	Nonunion	1972†	Eliminate distinctions in treatment of office and factory employees	Removed	4.1%	4.4%	4.2%	Some preimplementation resistance from management; favorable postimplementation reaction, including that of supervisors	There were no specific gains, but management is satisfied that the approach is an essential part of its philosophy
Gillette	Nonunion	1955	Provide a logical alternative to improved sick leave	Retained	4.6	4.7	4.7	Generally favorable reaction, but initial minor concern about loss of status of clerical employees	Management is satisfied with the results
Black & Decker	Nonunion	1971	Improve employee relationships, with consequent benefits to operational effectiveness	Removed	1.5†	2.3	2.0	Introduction of plan a contribution to favorable attitudes; some supervisory concern over payment decisions	Response generated by the plan has enabled continued productivity improvements
Kinetic Dispersion	Union (UAW)	1962	Eliminate distinctions and provide security of income	Retained	§	§	§	Plan welcomed, but misused initially	Management is reasonably satisfied, although problems were far more severe than anticipated

| Polaroid | Nonunion | 1966 | Unify hourly and salaried employees | Retained until 1972 | 5.0 | 6.0 | 6.0 | Benefits of plan well accepted, but no fundamental change of attitude | Management is not unhappy and considers program now controlled |

* Basis of measurement may vary, so figures are not comparable between companies.

† Weekly salary plan was introduced in 1972, but 1968 changes equalized treatment in most cases.

‡ This applies for sickness only.

§ Rates were not measured; substantial increase occurred after changeover.

Source: Robert D. Hulme and Richard V. Bevan, "The Blue-Collar Worker Goes on Salary," *Harvard Business Review*, March–April 1975, p. 108.

TABLE 11-12
Principal features of a typical salary plan

Purpose of the plan
It provides for plant employees to be salaried; it represents a principal element in establishing uniform employee relations policies for everyone.

Eligibility
All employees are eligible after three months of service.

Time recording
Employees are no longer required to punch time clocks; supervisors will record lateness, absence, and sickness for control purposes.

Basis of payment
All employees will be paid biweekly, at a salary rate determined from their hourly rate prior to the changeover.

Payment for time not worked
No deductions will be made from salary for absence for any reason, unless absences other than sickness total more than 15 days in any 12-month period.

Sick pay
For absences after 15 days in any 12-month period due to sickness, payment will be made under the sickness and accident plan.

Timekeeping and attendance standards
Although salary will not be withheld unless an employee exceeds the limitations above, attendance records will be an important factor in evaluating performance for merit increases and promotion opportunities.

Probationary employees
Employees in their first three months of service will not be paid for absences of any kind, except for short periods of lateness at the supervisor's discretion.

Administration
Supervisors will be responsible for maintaining attendance records; any questions or comments should be directed to them.

Source: Robert D. Hulme and Richard V. Bevan, "The Blue-Collar Worker Goes on Salary," *Harvard Business Review*, March–April 1975, p. 110.

5. What is the status of union-management relationships?
6. Do two-way communication channels exist to communicate the purpose of a wage and salary plan?
7. Will management maintain its right to identify justifiable causes for employee absences?[12]

The experiences of these five companies suggest that a salary plan of compensation for hourly workers is economically feasible, personally rewarding, and a positive influence on management-employee relations.

Pensions

Today 30 million American workers are covered by 32,000 different pension plans with assets of $200 billion. Some 6 million retired individuals have received $10 billion a year from existing pension programs. The success, however, of present pension programs is being eroded by economic, social, and legal influences on corporate pension programs. For example, inflation at 10 percent per year has reduced the buying power of earlier pension programs. Legislation has been passed giving vesting rights to employees after seven years of service, thus increasing pension costs to employers. Expansion of benefits to widows and forms of termination insurance also increase administrative costs. Greater mobility among skilled and professional personnel means that procedures must be set up to transfer vesting rights between employers. An increased population of retired persons in relation to people employed and increased educational levels have altered the demands for future pension plans. All these factors increase the costs, the scope, and the administrative task of keeping pensions abreast of changing environmental factors.

Pension systems are a result of a psychological drive for security based partly on the experiences of the Depression and World War II. Earlier programs were funded out of regular income and as a result the fulfillment of promises was dependent on the economic health of the enterprise. Many company pension plans paid benefits in terms of income levels before retirement. Similar plans averaged the final several years of a worker's income to determine the payout. Pension reserves earn 5 to 8 percent return per year as investments but cannot meet inflationary rises in living costs of 9 to 12 percent a year. Thus, a firm faces the problem of increasing its level of financial contribution or seeking new ways to increase its yield on pension reserve funds. Figure 11-5 shows the impact of rising income levels on the amount a firm

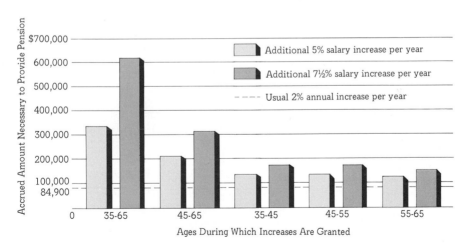

Figure 11-5
The effect of various salary increases on accrued amount necessary to provide pensions. Source: Robert D. Paul, "Thinking Ahead," *Harvard Business Review*, September–October 1974, p. 24.

must accumulate to provide a pension that maintains 50 percent of an employee's average salary for the last five years. A twenty-five-year-old employee earning $8000 per year with a 2 percent annual increase until age sixty-five will require a firm to accumulate $84,900 to fund that employee's pension program.

Shifts in population also alter pension planning for corporate planners. In 1973, there were 109 million people in the United States under thirty years of age. Also, there were 70 million people between the ages of thirty and fifty-nine. In an industrial society, the working span is usually from twenty-five to sixty-four years of age. Thus, the working population is a minority in relation to younger and older inhabitants. A declining birth rate will decrease the younger and working population during the next thirty years, but a rising population of those over sixty-five will increase pension costs. Social Security now faces the problem of increasing benefits to a larger population while the number of individuals paying the cost is declining. Consequently, in order to continue all Social Security programs, a dramatic increase in Social Security deductions or a decline in benefits to retired personnel will be required. Private pension programs face the same problem of increasing the costs of present workers in order to expand benefits to future and past retired employees. Figure 11-6 shows the changes in working and nonworking population in the United States from 1970 to 2020. To meet pension plans financial requirements for the next thirty years will require the following:

1. Increased financial contributions to pension programs so that the next generation will pay for its own pensions rather than paying for the pensions of employees working today.

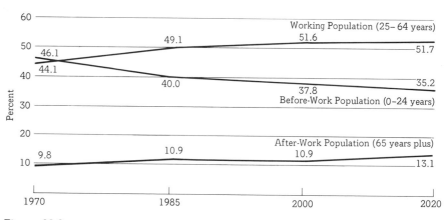

Figure 11-6
Percent of working and nonworking population 1970–2020. Source: Robert D. Paul, "Thinking Ahead," *Harvard Business Review*, September–October 1974, p. 28.

2. Setting realistic amounts for future pensions that balance individual needs to corporate assets and inflationary demands.
3. Seeking alternative funding avenues to finance future pension programs.
4. Setting up financial and legal safeguards to protect the pension rights of past, present, and future beneficiaries.[13]

Pension reform has been a major concern to labor and management since the establishment of pension programs after World War II. In 1962, the closing of the Studebaker automotive plants dramatized the lack of safeguards for company-funded programs. The passage of the Landrum-Griffin Act in 1959 was an attempt to regulate the use of pension trust funds. Further evidence of corporate and union abuse of pension funds led to the passage of the Employee Retirement Income Security Act of 1974. One goal of this legislation is to require adequate funding for pension programs. Table 11-13 provides an overview of this 1974 pension reform law. This law covers pension plans, profit-sharing plans, savings-thrift plans, stock bonus options, and employee welfare programs.

Major provisions of the Employee Retirement Income Security Act of 1974 are as follows:

1. *Eligibility.* Eligibility is based on one year of service but eligibility cannot be restricted by age limitations. For example, an employee reaching twenty-five years of age must be given up to three years credit for all previous employment. Programs that provide 100 percent vesting right upon employment can set a three-year eligibility requirement.
2. *Vesting standards.* Vesting standards give the firm three choices in establishing vesting rights. One option is 100 percent vesting after ten years of service. A second option provides a 25 percent vesting right after five years of service with gradual increase to 100 percent vesting rights after fifteen years of service. A third option provides 50 percent vesting when age and length of service equal forty-five, with 100 percent vesting rights incurred five years later. This option was open to employees with five years of service at the time the act was passed. The benefit of this program is that in a period of mobile employment, employees with five, ten, or fifteen years of service can carry their pension rights when changing employment.
3. *Funding requirement.* Employers must fund the full cost for current benefit accruals and amortize past benefits over thirty years for new plans and over forty years for existing plans. The aim of this requirement is to insure a constant level of funding to pay past as well as future pension demands.
4. *Plan termination insurance.* The law established a Pension Benefit Guarantee Corporation within the Department of Labor. The purpose of this insurance is to provide benefits to employees of companies

TABLE 11-13
The Pension Reform Law

Major provisions		Effective dates* Existing plans	New plans
Eligibility	Prohibits plans from establishing eligibility requirements of more than 1 year of service, or an age greater than 25, whichever is later.	January 1, 1976	Date of enactment (September 2, 1974)
Vesting	Establishes new minimum standards; employer has three choices: 1 100% vesting after 10 years of service, 2 25% vesting after 5 years of service, grading up to 100% after 15 years, 3 50% vesting when age and service (if the employee has at least 5 years of service) equal 45, grading up to 100% vesting 5 years later.	January 1, 1976	Date of enactment
Funding	Requires the employer to fund annually the full cost for current benefit accruals and amortize past service benefit liabilities over 30 years for new plans and 40 years for existing plans.	January 1, 1976	Date of enactment
Plan termination insurance	Establishes a government insurance fund to insure vested pension benefits up to the lesser of $750 a month or 100% of the employee's average wages during his highest paid 5 years of employment; the employer pays an annual premium of $1 per participant and is liable for any insurance benefits paid up to 30% of the company's net worth.	Benefits: July 1, 1974 Other provisions Date of enactment	Phased in over 5 years
Fiduciary responsibility	Establishes the "prudent man" rule as the basic standard of fiduciary responsibility; prohibits various transactions between fiduciaries and parties-in-interest, prohibits investment of more than 10% of pension plan assets in the employer's securities.	January 1, 1975	January 1, 1975
Portability	Permits an employee leaving a company to make a tax-free transfer of the assets behind his vested pension benefits (if the employer agrees) or of his vested profit-sharing or savings plan funds to an individual retirement account.	Date of enactment	Date of enactment

Individual retirement accounts (IRAs)	Provides a vehicle for transfers as noted above and permits employees of private or public employers that do not have qualified retirement plans to deduct 15% of compensation, up to $1,500, each year for contributions to a personal retirement fund. Earnings on the fund are not taxable until distributed.	January 1, 1975	January 1, 1975
Reporting and disclosure	Requires the employer to provide employees with a comprehensive booklet describing plan provisions and to report annually to the secretary of labor on various operating and financial details of the plan.	January 1, 1975	January 1, 1975
Lump-sum distributions	Changes the tax rules to provide capital gains treatment on pre-1974 amounts and to tax post-1973 amounts as ordinary income, but as the employee's only income and spread over 10 years.	January 1, 1974	January 1, 1974
Limits on contributions and benefits	1 Increases the maximum deductible annual contributions that can be made by self-employed people to H.R. 10 or Keogh plans to the lesser of $7,500 or 15% of earned income.	January 1, 1974	January 1, 1974
	2 Limits benefits payable from defined benefit pension plans to the lesser of $75,000 a year or 100% of average annual cash compensation during the employee's 3 highest paid years of service.	January 1, 1976	January 1, 1976
	3 Limits annual additions to employee profit-sharing accounts to the lesser of $25,000 or 25% of the employee's compensation that year.	January 1, 1976	January 1, 1976

* Applicable to single employer plans; multiemployer plans are given more time to comply with some of the new standards.

Source: Donald G. Carlson. "Responding to the Pension Reform Law." *Harvard Business Review.* November–December 1974, p. 134. © 1974 by the President and Fellows of Harvard College; all rights reserved.

whose pension plans fail. The annual premium is $1 per participant for single-employer plans and 50 cents per participant for multi-employer plans. This insurance covers vested benefits up to $750 per month or 100 percent of an employee's average wage for five years of employment—whichever is less. A major safeguard of this insurance is that an employer is liable for any insurance benefits paid by the insurance fund if the company's insurance plan fails. Its liability is limited to 30 percent of the company's net worth at the time the benefits are paid from the insurance trust fund.

5. *Fiduciary responsibility.* The purpose of the fiduciary responsibility safeguard is to establish guidelines for the financial management of pension trust funds. For example, managers of trust funds must diversify the investments of pension programs to reduce the risk of large losses. Likewise, an employer cannot invest over 10 percent of the pension trust fund in the employer's securities.

6. *Portability.* Portability allows an employee to leave a company and place vested benefits earned into a tax-qualified plan of his new employer. Table 11–14 shows the major types of tax-qualified plans under the 1974 act.

TABLE 11-14
Major types of tax-qualified plans

Profit-sharing	Savings or thrift	Fixed benefit pension	Money purchase pension
In effect, companies with profit-sharing plans share a fixed percentage of profits with employees each year. Typically, amounts are allocated to individuals (but held in trust) in direct proportion to their salaries. These amounts vest over time and are paid out, together with the investment earnings on the employee's accumulated amount, upon severance, retirement, death, permanent disability, or, in some plans, during employment. Amounts are taxable to the employee only when paid out. Employees may make voluntary contributions to the plan.	Participants in savings plans may contribute to individual accounts amounts usually ranging from 1% to 6% of salary. The company matches each employee's savings, generally on the basis of 50 cents to the dollar. Employer contributions vest, are paid out, and are taxed as under a profit-sharing plan.	This is the most common type of pension plan. The benefits payable from these plans are fixed relative to pay and service, and the cost of the benefits fluctuates.	These plans are similar to ordinary pension plans in all respects except that instead of fixing the benefit to be paid out (as, for example, an annual pension of 40% of the employee's final average salary), they fix the contribution the company will make each year on behalf of each employee (as, for example, 5% of the employee's salary that year). These contributions accumulate during the employee's service with the company and are translated into income at retirement at whatever rates prevail at the time.

Source: Donald G. Carlson, "Responding to the Pension Reform Law," *Harvard Business Review,* November–December 1974, p. 138. © 1974 by the President and Fellows of Harvard College; all rights reserved.

---

7. *Reporting and disclosure.* Employers are required to provide a detailed review of company pension programs every five years. On an annual basis, companies must notify all participants of material changes as well as show the financial condition of the pension program. Also an annual audit must be furnished to the secretary of labor detailing the soundness of the pension program in terms of assets, liabilities, and investment portfolios.[14]

It is evident that the cost of pension programs will increase dramatically in the years ahead. Inflationary pressures will increase employee demands to protect their future retirement benefits. Social and political forces will continue to increase employers' liability and responsibility for providing adequate pension benefits. The danger is that corporate assets may be stretched to the point that they will be unable to meet these new financial burdens. So management is faced with a financial dilemma of maintaining its solvency and of striving to respond to social, economic, and political influences. The Act of 1974 has increased significantly the regulatory power of the Department of Labor in the administration of corporate pension programs. Therefore, prudent management requires adherence to and an administrative policy designed to meet or exceed governmental guidelines to reduce the possibility of greater governmental controls over private pensions.

Executive Pay Preferences

A study of pay preferences of 300 executives at all managerial levels was conducted in seven large corporations. Sales for these companies in 1972 ranged between $500 million and $10 billion. Firms covered in the survey represented a food processor, a chemical producer, a grocery chain, an airline, a meat packer, an electronics firm, and an aerospace company. Table 11-15 gives a profile of the respondents. Views of the respondents cover a broad spectrum in terms of values, perceptions, and evaluations of present executive pay programs. One major conclusion reached was that standardized packaged pay programs are a major source of dissatisfaction. Thus, a firm should consider tailoring pay policies to permit some individual choice in computing executive compensation.

Figure 11-7 shows the value placed on various compensation arrangements for corporate executives. Pension benefits were highly prized as a major source of postretirement rewards. Traditional one-sum payments at retirement were viewed as having less value than a life annuity benefit. Such an annuity provides a supplement to normal pension programs.

Most executives sought noncash compensation in the form of additional vacation time. Other leisure time could be provided on a regular

TABLE 11-15
Profile of respondents

Age		
Mean	45.1	
Range	24 to 64	
Distribution	Under 35	15%
	35 to 44	30%
	45 to 54	39%
	55 and over	16%
Family status		
Married	99%	
Mean family size	4.2 persons	
Education		
High school or less	8%	
College training	13%	
Bachelor's degree	51%	
Graduate school	28%	
Service with employer		
Under 10 years	27%	
10 to 20 years	32%	
Over 20 years	41%	

Income		
Annual salary and bonus income		
Mean		$38,300
Range		$8,000 to $190,000
Distribution	Under $20,000	17%
	$20,000 to $29,999	34%
	$30,000 to $49,999	28%
	Over $50,000	21%
Average annual pension		$10,600
Mean company-provided life insurance		$78,000
Percentage of respondents receiving company-provided benefits		
Medical insurance		97%
Life insurance		94%
Pension		94%
Cash bonus and incentives		66%
Stock options and stock purchase		65%
Deferred compensation		21%
Use of company car		8%
Average outside income (investment, consulting, outside businesses, wife's income)		$6,100

Source: Wilbur G. Lewellen and Howard P. Lanser, "Executive Pay Preferences," *Harvard Business Review,* September–October 1973, p. 117.

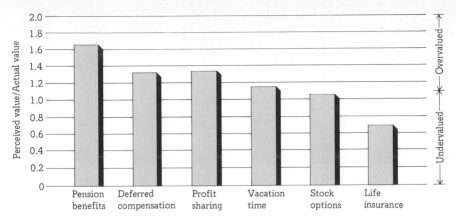

Figure 11-7
Ratios of perceived value to actual value, for selected compensation arrangements. Source: Wilbur G. Lewellen and Howard P. Lanser, "Executive Pay Preferences," *Harvard Business Review*, September–October 1973, p. 118.

basis to reward the success of corporate executives. In contrast to this, stock options were viewed as fifth in preference out of six compensation devices. Salary increases or bonuses of equal after-tax value were viewed as providing a greater financial reward to executives. Another item that executives viewed as of limited value was a paid life insurance program.

Further research determined that 75 percent of the executives studied preferred a "cafeteria" approach to executive compensation. Figure 11-8 shows the attitudes of various executives toward executive pay practices. Findings suggest that executives prefer 75 percent direct cash and 25 percent deferred or noncash items as a form of executive remuneration. Most executives were willing to reduce the amount of direct cash compensation in return for larger supplemental pay items.[15]

Malcolm S. Salter of the Indian Institute of Management in Ahmedabad has conducted several studies on executive compensation. One study covered fifty-three chief executives who were in office for at least six years between 1960 and 1974. Dominant in this study were companies with revenue from a single business. Related business companies in this survey were defined as companies with related technical, marketing, or other skills. Unrelated business companies were viewed as conglomerates whose parent company and subsequent acquisitions had no direct relationship to each other. The purpose of the study is to show that executive compensation is not related to a company's return on equity or the company's earnings per share. Table 11-16 shows the relationship between changes in top executive compensation and measures of corporate performance. Table 11-17 outlines the companies

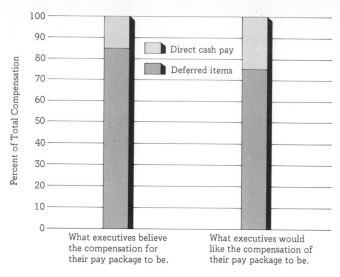

Figure 11-8
Perception of the total executive pay package. Source: Wilbur G. Lewellen and Howard P. Lanser, "Executive Pay Preferences," *Harvard Business Review,* September–October 1973, p. 120.

TABLE 11-16
Relationship between changes in top executive compensation and measures of corporate performance

	Return on equity		Earnings per share	
Nature of relationship	*Number of companies*	*Percent of companies*	*Number of companies*	*Percent of companies*
Significant and positive relationship	18	34%	32	60%
No significant relationship	35	66	21	40
Total	53	100%	53	100%

Source: K. R. Srinivasa Murthy and Malcolm S. Salter, "Should CEO Pay Be Linked to Results?" *Harvard Business Review,* May–June 1975, p. 68.

studied in the survey, the length of time each firm was studied, and how each firm was classified—dominant business, related business, or unrelated business. Table 11-18 shows that executive compensation varied to a greater extent in unrelated businesses than in dominant business organizations. Table 11-19 illustrates the type of companies in which

328

TABLE 11-17
Strategy classification and time period of companies studied

Dominant-business companies

Alcoa	1964–1972
American Smelting and Refining	1963–1969
Anaconda	1960–1966
B. F. Goodrich	1960–1971
Crown Zellerbach	1960–1967
Diamond International	1960–1969
Fibreboard	1964–1972
Firestone	1960–1971
Goodyear	1964–1972
Great Northern Nekoosa	1962–1971
Hammermill Paper	1960–1966
International Paper	1960–1965
Kimberly-Clark	1960–1966
Republic Steel	1960–1970
Reynolds Industries	1961–1972
Scott Paper	1962–1971
St. Regis Paper	1960–1971
Union Camp	1960–1971
U.S. Steel	1960–1968
Westvaco	1962–1971

Related-business companies

Abbott Laboratories	1960–1971
American Cyanamid	1960–1966
American Home Products	1961–1971
Borg-Warner	1960–1971
Bristol-Myers	1960–1966
Corning Glass Works	1962–1972
Dow Chemical	1964–1970
Eastman Kodak	1962–1969
Georgia-Pacific	1960–1971
Johnson & Johnson	1964–1971
Mead	1960–1968
Merck & Co.	1965–1972
Miles Laboratories	1965–1970
Minnesota Mining & Mfg.	1963–1970
Monsanto	1961–1968
Pfizer	1965–1971
Procter & Gamble	1960–1970
RCA	1960–1970
Smith Kline & French Laboratories	1960–1965
Sterling Drug	1960–1971
Upjohn	1963–1971
Warner-Lambert	1960–1966

(Continued)

TABLE 11-17   (Continued)

Unrelated-business companies

Airco	1965–1972
American Standard	1960–1966
Avco	1961–1971
FMC	1961–1969
W. R. Grace	1961–1974
ITT	1960–1972
Martin Marietta	1961–1971
Olin	1960–1963
Textron	1963–1971
TRW	1960–1969
USM	1963–1972

Source: K. R. Srinivasa Murthy and Malcolm S. Salter, "Should CEO Pay Be Linked to Results?" *Harvard Business Review,* May–June 1975, p. 69.

TABLE 11-18
Variability in total compensation of the top executive

	Dominant-business performance		Related-business performance		Unrelated-business performance	
Variability:	High	Low	High	Low	High	Low
Low (less than 15%)	45%	56%	23%	22%	0%	57%
Medium or high	55	44	77	78	100	43
Number of companies	11	9	13	9	4	7

Source: K. R. Srinivasa Murthy and Malcolm S. Salter, "Should CEO Pay Be Linked to Results?" *Harvard Business Review,* May–June 1975, p. 70.

TABLE 11-19
Percentage of companies in which top executive compensation is closely related to financial performance

	Dominant-business performance		Related-business performance		Unrelated-business performance		All classes performance	
Measure of performance:	High	Low	High	Low	High	Low	High	Low
Profitability	9%	22%	31%	33%	75%	43%	29%	32%
Return on equity	18	33	31	44	50	43	29	40
Earnings per share	27	44	92	67	100	43	68	52
Any one of above measures	36	36	92	78	100	43	71	56
Number of companies	11	9	13	9	4	7	28	25

Source: K. R. Srinivasa Murthy and Malcolm S. Salter, "Should CEO Pay Be Linked to Results?" *Harvard Business Review,* May–June 1975, p. 70.

executive compensation is closely related to financial performance of the enterprise. Earnings per share had a greater impact on executive levels of compensation in high-performing related and unrelated business companies. Table 11-20 shows the use of stock options as a major form of executive compensation in unrelated businesses. Differences between the top two executives in compensation is shown in Table 11-21.

TABLE 11-20
Second-level executive's total compensation expressed as a percentage of top executive's compensation (excluding stock options)

	Dominant-business performance			Related-business performance			Unrelated-business performance		
Differential:	High	Low	All	High	Low	All	High	Low	All
High (less than 60%)	18%	11%	15%	0%	0%	0%	50%	29%	36%
Medium (60%–74%)	46	22	35	69	33	55	25	57	45
Low (75% or more)	36	67	50	31	67	45	25	14	18
Number of companies	11	9	20	13	9	22	4	7	11

Source: K. R. Srinivasa Murthy and Malcolm S. Salter, "Should CEO Pay Be Linked to Results?" *Harvard Business Review*, May–June 1975, p. 71.

TABLE 11-21
Companies emphasizing stock options for top executives

	Dominant-business performance			Related-business performance			Unrelated-business performance		
Degree of emphasis:	High	Low	All	High	Low	All	High	Low	All
Low (less than 20% of total compensation)	70%	78%	74%	25%	71%	42%	0%	43%	27%
Medium or high (more than 20%)	30	22	26	75	29	58	100	57	73
Number of companies	10	9	19	12	7	19	4	7	11

Note: This exhibit is based on data for 49 companies; 4 companies were excluded from the sample because of incomplete information. The degree of emphasis was determined by calculating the percentage of an executive's total compensation represented by his options when exercised. Both the gains from the options and total regular compensation were aggregated for as long a period as was possible.

Source: K. R. Srinivasa Murthy and Malcolm S. Salter, "Should CEO Pay Be Linked to Results?" *Harvard Business Review*, May–June 1975, p. 71.

In reviewing these data, it is evident that executive compensation is often unrelated to a company's financial performance. This trend tends to be inconsistent, with demands placed on middle- and front-line supervisors whose financial compensation is directly related to their operating effectiveness. For example, an outstanding manager may receive an annual increase in salary of 15 to 20 percent while a mediocre manager receives a token raise. To be consistent, compensation at all organizational levels should be measured in terms of a person's contribution to the success of the enterprise. Since corporate executives exercise the greatest influence in setting company goals, they should also accept the responsibility for financial success or failure. In this regard, it is interesting to note that General Motors executives in 1975 disregarded 60 percent of their annual rate of executive compensation.

Summary

The rising costs of wages and fringe benefits to a company require greater skills to motivate people through monetary incentives. Economic affluence has reduced the value of monetary incentives as a means of rewarding people for their performance. Further, a company must recognize that a given wage increase is not viewed in the same way by all personnel. A major concern to any firm is the relationship between psychological costs and wage increases. The high cost of raises forces most firms to use selectivity in granting substantial wage increases to corporate personnel. Thus, a wage incentive must overcome an employee's tendency to "play it safe," and it must provide motivation to implement creative ideas throughout the enterprise.

To meet new compensation needs enterprises must expand their methods of compensation beyond the scope of wages and fringe benefits. Major acts of legislation that altered compensation programs were the Social Security Act, minimum wage laws, and the Wagner Act. In 1971, fringe benefits represented 31 percent of an employer's payroll. An increasing trend is for management to pay the total costs of fringe benefits such as medical payments, retirement, and vacations. Services provided by an enterprise come in the form of work clothes, eating facilities, transportation, housing services, and savings on financial and legal services. To measure the impact of company benefits requires a survey of employee attitudes, a cost analysis of annual benefits, a willingness to alter existing programs to meet changing needs, and the recognition that financial solvency forces a firm to alter its benefit program in light of economic circumstances. The hidden costs of company benefits should be identified to avoid excessive expenditures, excessive demands, and increased governmental pressures to finance social services. Management must constantly strive to obtain the greatest return possible from its financial support of employee benefit programs.

One of the most difficult tasks for any manager is to determine a wage scale for a given job performed by an employee. Management should provide employees with objective data to justify payment or non-payment of existing wage rates in their industry. To structure a wage payment system in industry requires the establishment of performance standards, evaluation methods, and a means of altering a person's level of compensation. The point system, the factor comparison system, and the job-ranking system are the major methods used to structure a wage payment system. Regardless of the system used, management cannot view job evaluation as the total answer to determining wage rates.

The design of individual incentives in industry has become an area of contention between managers and their employees. A classic example is the limited use of merit raises by most corporations. Such programs in the past have reduced employee morale through mismanagement, favoritism, and employee distrust of merit payments. The piece rate system has been used to increase the income of employees in relation to increases in productivity. The drawback to the piece rate system is that excessive minimum standards of output can make it almost impossible for employees to earn supplemental income. Likewise, quotas and commissions have been used for years to increase the productivity of employees in sales-related tasks. One of the most successful group plans to reward employees for outstanding performance is the Scanlon Plan. The experiences of Atwood Vacuum Machine Company, Parker Pen Company, and Pfaudler Company illustrate the success of the Scanlon Plan in all types of corporate endeavors.

Changing methods of employee compensation are reflected in the trend of placing all employees on a salary. The experiences of Avon Products, Gillette, Black and Decker, Kinetic Dispersion, and Polaroid provide an excellent view of the methods used when placing all personnel on salaries. The experiences of these five companies suggest that a salary plan of compensation is economically feasible, personally rewarding, and a positive influence on management-employee relations.

The success of present pension programs is being eroded by economic, social, and legal influences on corporate pension programs. Increased vesting rights, increased participation by beneficiaries, increased employee mobility, and an increasing retirement population will continue to alter the traditional pension programs of most corporations. All these factors increase the cost, the scope, and the administrative task of keeping pensions abreast of changing environmental factors. Pension reform has been a major concern to labor and management since the establishment of pension programs after World War II. Responding to this concern, the United States Congress passed the Employee Retirement Income Security Act of 1974. This Act defined an employee's eligibility rights, vesting rights, funding requirements, termination insurance provisions, fiduciary responsibility, portability options, and reporting procedures. Prudent management requires adherence to policies that meet and exceed governmental guidelines to reduce the possibility of greater governmental controls over private pensions.

A study of 300 executives suggested that standardized packaged pay programs are a major source of dissatisfaction. Most executives sought noncash forms of compensation such as increased vacation time or expanded leisure time for personal business. Stock options and company-paid insurance policies were viewed as having limited value as a form of executive compensation. Further research determined that 75 percent of the executives studied preferred a "cafeteria" approach to executives' compensation. Most executives were willing to reduce the amount of direct cash compensation in return for larger supplemental pay items. A study by Malcolm S. Salter suggests that executive compensation is not related to a company's return on equity nor the company's earnings per share. To be consistent, compensation at all organizational levels should be measured in terms of a person's contribution to the success of the enterprise.

Discussion Questions

1. Explain the statement "Wage incentives do not have the same value for all personnel."
2. How do you account for the recent rise in fringe benefits for employees?
3. Have the increases in benefits for employees contributed to inflation in this country?
4. Would you rather work under a point system, a factor comparison system, or a job-ranking system if you had a choice?
5. Why has merit pay lost some of its effectiveness?
6. Why do you think that more companies have not developed plans similar to the Scanlon Plan?
7. What is your opinion of the idea of paying all employees a salary, including those holding jobs that have been traditionally paid on an hourly basis?
8. It was deemed necessary that all private pension plans be controlled. The result was The Employee Retirement Income Security Act of 1974 was passed. Why was this necessary?
9. What is meant when it is said that most executives prefer a "cafeteria" approach to executive compensation?

Notes

1. E. E. Lawler, Jr. *Pay and Organizational Effectiveness.* New York: McGraw-Hill, 1971.
2. Ibid.

3. Saul W. Gellerman. "Motivating Men with Money," *Management by Motivation, Fortune Magazine*, March 1968.
4. Fred K. Foulkes. "The Expanding Role of the Personal Function," *Harvard Business Review*, March–April 1975, pp. 82–83.
5. Reprinted with permission of Macmillan Publishing Co. from *Personnel and Industrial Relations*, 2nd ed., by John B. Miner and Mary Green Miner. Copyright © 1969 by Macmillan Publishing Co., Inc.
6. Charles Brennan. *Wage Administration,* rev. ed. Homewood, Ill.: Irwin, 1963.
7. Eugene Benge. *Job Evaluation and Merit Rating.* Deep River, Conn.: National Foreman's Institute, 1941.
8. William F. Glueck. *Personnel: A Diagnostic Approach.* Dallas: Business Publications, 1974, pp. 408–414.
9. Fred G. Lesieur and Elbridge S. Puckett. "The Scanlon Plan Has Proved Itself," *Harvard Business Review,* Vol. 47, No. 5 (September–October 1969), pp 109–118.
10. Ibid.
11. Ibid.
12. Robert D. Hulme and Richard V. Bevan. "The Blue-Collar Worker Goes On Salary." *Harvard Business Review*, March–April 1975, pp. 104–113.
13. Robert D. Paul. "Can Private Pension Plans Deliver?" *Harvard Business Review,* September–October 1974, pp. 22–34, 165.
14. Donald G. Carlson, "Responding to the Pension Reform Law." *Harvard Business Review,* November–December 1974, pp. 136–139. © 1974 by the President and Fellows of Harvard College; all rights reserved.
15. Wilber G. Lewellen and Howard P. Lanser. "Executive Pay Preferences," *Harvard Business Review,* September–October 1973, pp. 115–121.

CUSTOM FURNITURE CASE: AN EFFICIENT WORKER

Sally is one of the most efficient machine operators in the plant but lately John Taylor has noticed that she seems to spend an excessive amount of time in the rest room and in the employee's lounge. He sends for Sam Brown and the following conversation ensues:

John: "Come in, Sam. How's everything going in the plant?"

Sam: "Oh, everything is fine. Everyone is busy and I haven't heard too much griping lately. They all are doing what they are expected to do."

John: "How is Sally doing on her machine?"

Sam: "Same as always. You know she is one of our best operators. Why do you ask about her especially?"

John: "I've just noticed that in the afternoons she doesn't seem to be very busy."

Sam: "Well, she does meet standards before anyone else in the department."

Standards have been a touchy matter ever since the company set them and there is no incentive program for those who can exceed these standards. John does not want to get into this with Sam, because he knows that Sam feels that both the employees and the company would be more productive if there were some sort of incentive program. So he dismisses Sam:

John: "Well, thank you, Sam. If it's okay with you, I believe I'll call Sally in for a talk."

Sam: "That's fine with me. But I don't have any gripes with Sally. She is carrying her part of the load."

John has his secretary ask Sally to come in the first chance she has. He is not too surprised when she appears about 3:30 that afternoon.

John: "Come in, Sally, and have a seat. I've told Sam that I wanted to have a chat with you and he has agreed."

Sally: "Yes, sir. What is it that you want to talk to me about?"

John: "How much time do you have before you need to get back to your machine?"

Sally: "I've made my number of parts for today, so I don't suppose there is any hurry."

John: "Is that all you are interested in doing, Sally—just making exactly the number of parts that standards call for in eight hours?"

Sally: "Pardon me, sir, for asking. I don't mean to be impertinent, but why should I or any of us exceed standards when we don't get any extra pay if we do?"

John: "What's good for the company is good for the employees, Sally."

Sally: "Excuse me again, Mr. Taylor, but I can't buy groceries or pay rent with that. Besides Mr. Brown seems to be happy with my work and he doesn't complain when I get finished early. I suppose I could drag out the work over the whole day if this would be more satisfactory, but it sure gets tiresome, trying to look busy. I'd be glad to help some of the other operators if I could be paid something extra for doing it."

John: "No, Sally, we can't have that. Do you have any other suggestions?"

Sally: "Well, I've got a friend that works for a plant across town and they have some sort of plan where if they exceed standards, everybody gets some sort of bonus or something. I don't exactly understand the details, but this friend of mine is always talking about pitching in and helping somebody else so they can all share in the extra money."

John: "Well, thank you, Sally. I'll look into it."

1. What is your reaction to Sally's attitude?
2. What is wrong with having standards and no incentives for exceeding them?
3. What would you do in this situation if you were John?

DISCIPLINE

12

For the full story, turn to the case on page 358.

GENERAL PURPOSES
OF CHAPTER 12

1. To examine environmental influences on discipline and traditional methods of discipline
2. To contrast discipline by objectives to the traditional concept
3. To delve into the concept of discipline without punishment
4. To analyze the effects of discipline on morale

LEARNING OBJECTIVES

1. Name two changing values in society that **have** changed attitudes toward discipline
2. Cite at least six characteristics of traditional discipline
3. Contrast discipline by objectives with this traditional view
4. Name at least five requirements of an effective disciplinary program
5. Name the six steps outlined by John Huberman for discipline
6. Describe the relationship between morale and discipline

Discipline is essential in any organized human endeavor. Although it is assumed that all organizational members will cooperate with the objectives of an enterprise, it is unrealistic to expect total cooperation from everyone. Disciplinary policies should strive to educate employees so that they learn from their mistakes rather than take an approach that seeks to assess blame and inflict punishment. This short-term punitive approach does not alter the behavior of the employee involved, nor does it correct deviate behavior. For example, "crack-down" policies on absenteeism usually result in firing the offending employees because remedial precedures do not alter that behavior. Positive disciplinary action seeks to deal with causes, not symptoms.

Environmental Influences

Discipline to be effective should alter employees' behavior that does not comply with policies of the organization. Changing values in society have changed employees' attitudes toward disciplinary actions. In the past, management was free to take corrective action without undue pressure from unions and society. However, today employees influence the disciplinary action that a supervisor can take. Closely associated with changing values is the increased impact of legal rights on managerial decisions. For example, discharge procedures are outlined in union contracts, in company affirmative action programs, and in civil rights mandates. Thus, a manager must be aware of internal and external legal procedures that make disciplinary actions subject to scrutiny. A major new ingredient affecting managerial action is the right to appeal, to examine evidence, and to examine accusers. The presence of an arbitration system and grievance procedures further alters the environment in which a manager operates in carrying out disciplinary policies.[1]

Discipline by Tradition

Discipline by tradition seeks to list a person's crime, set a punishment for the crime, and apply the punishment to the person. Discipline under this procedure has the following characteristics:

1. Discipline is a one-way street in which a supervisor takes action against a subordinate for violation of company policies.
2. An employee's past behavior serves as the guide in determining punishment for present or future violations.
3. Punishment should fit the crime instead of correcting deviate behavior.

4. Punishment is used to deter other employees from violating corporate policies.
5. Continuous violations of a policy bring about greater severity of punishment for the more recent offenders of that policy.
6. When an individual offender in a group cannot be identified the procedure often followed is to take the disciplinary action against all group members.
7. Consistency of action is regarded as essential to avoid accusations of unfairness and injustice.
8. A second offense should receive a greater penalty even though the offense is identical to the first.
9. Punishment of offenses should be publicized to increase the deterrent effect on other employees.

Such a traditional philosophy of discipline brings impressive short-term results but fails to alter the behavior of people at work. Likewise, the negative impact of such a philosophy on employee morale remains long after the punishment ends.[2]

Discipline by Objectives

George S. Odiorne has outlined a positive disciplinary policy based on the following attitudes toward discipline:

1. Discipline at work is for the most part voluntarily accepted, and if not voluntarily accepted is not legitimate.
2. Discipline is not a punishment system, but a shaper of behavior.
3. The past provides useful experience in defining and changing behavior, but is not an infallible guide to right and wrong.
4. Contribution to objectives is a reasonable guide as to when to depart from rules and regulations.
5. Charts, lists, and compendiums of rules and regulations should be reviewed periodically against organization objectives to see if they are still productive.
6. The application of individual discipline by objectives makes each individual responsible for his output, and the individual differences are explainable in individual results.[3]

In reviewing the objective approach to discipline, it is apparent that the emphasis is on self-discipline. This approach places a supervisor in the position of shaping employee behavior toward the voluntary acceptance of company policies. In this way, supervisors can reduce the negative impact caused by traditional disciplinary methods. The objective approach to discipline still requires employee accountability for all actions. The purpose of accountability is not to fix blame but to enhance the learning process. Objective discipline can create a more favorable employee-supervisor relationship by reducing the "watch dog" reputation gained by many supervisors.

Requirements of Discipline

Progressive discipline seeks to warn, correct, and reform offenders rather than to "dish out" punishment. Rules should be definite as well as reasonable in order to enhance employee compliance. Enforcement of rules should be fair as well as uniform in order to prevent inconsistency of action by management. Penalties should relate to the offense as well as to mitigating circumstances. Disciplinary procedures should be outlined to protect the rights of all parties. Failure to follow prescribed procedures will usually negate any future enforcement of the rule that has been violated. To enhance the enforcement of company rules and procedures all supervisory personnel should receive additional training on how to deal with disciplinary issues.[4]

Positive discipline suggests that an offense be dealt with as it occurs. Failure to take action after warning an employee reduces a supervisor's authority, reduces the employee's respect for his or her superior, and creates a barrier to further disciplinary action. Closely related to timing is the supervisor's ability to discipline an employee in an impersonal manner. The nature of discipline itself arouses an emotional response between a supervisor and an employee that must be channeled in a constructive way to prevent future hostilities. A supervisor should speak in specific terms and should not apologize for the existence of a policy or rule. Once a supervisor has heard an employee's viewpoint, he or she should take appropriate corrective action. Having disciplined an employee, a supervisor must show through subsequent actions that personal relationships have not changed because of the necessary disciplinary action.[5]

To summarize the requirements of positive discipline consider the following guidelines:

1. Failure to notify employees of existing rules or changes in existing rules makes enforcement impossible.
2. Records of minor infractions should be removed after an employee has demonstrated compliance with company policy.
3. Supervisors should refrain from creating incidents that antagonize employees.
4. Inconsistent enforcement of policies should be documented as to why normal procedures were not carried out.
5. Supervisors should listen to employees' viewpoints and take action based on all the facts available.
6. Discharge of an employee should follow all stated guidelines for such disciplinary action.
7. Entrapment should be avoided because it breeds distrust and destroys justice of the entire disciplinary procedure.[6]

Review of Disciplinary Procedures

To burden an organization with excessive rules is to produce an enforcement policy of selectivity. Supervisors will enforce rules they agree with and ignore rules that they feel should not be enforced. This situation should encourage management to review all rules governing employee conduct in light of the contribution of such rules to corporate objectives. Rules that contribute to company objectives will reduce customer complaints concerning quality, protect the safety of all employees, reduce waste of physical resources, and prevent interruption of production activity. Odiorne has outlined some attitudes toward rules that normally contribute very little to the success of an organization:

1. We have always done it that way.
2. It is our policy.
3. The boss "now retired" installed that one.
4. It is generally a good thing.
5. Because I want it.
6. Don't make waves.
7. I don't have time to explain it to you, just do it.[7]

Periodic reviews of rules governing employee conduct can improve a supervisor's effectiveness.

Discipline Without Punishment

An excellent example of progressive discipline is the experiment conducted in a Douglas Fir plywood mill in 1963. This plan involved 300 hourly paid union employees. The company had been in operation twenty years. As is the case with many firms, growth may alter traditional employee-management relations from a benevolent, paternalistic philosophy to a more impersonal, authoritarian approach. Such shifts in policy created resentment among older employees and produced a tightly knit group of union employees who opposed managerial action. A major area of confrontation was the handling of disciplinary matters and the setting of satisfactory levels of work performance. Failure of front-line supervisors to enforce minor rules led individuals to take advantage of the situation. Ultimately, a supervisor demoted an employee after several annoying infractions. At this point the union filed a grievance because normal disciplinary procedures were ignored by management. The negative effect of the demotion was (1) a new person had to be trained to replace the demoted employee and (2) the demoted individual retaliated by lowering production and quality. Suspension of employees produced a ripple effect because the next most senior person replaced a suspended employee and job turnover became a constant nuisance to management.

The result of management and union dissatisfaction with work rules and disciplinary procedures produced a change in management philosophy. Three beliefs became the pivotal points around which company principles and policies were developed. First, the company set out to identify the variables and conditions that enhanced employee compliance with work rules and disciplinary procedures. Second, self-discipline and self-direction became a major factor in increasing an individual's feeling of worth. Third, repeated violations of company policies forced management to discharge noncooperative employees.[8] Figure 12-1 identifies the motivational factors that influenced employee performance.

John Huberman, in "Discipline Without Punishment," outlined six policies and procedures to implement this managerial philosophy. These are as follows:

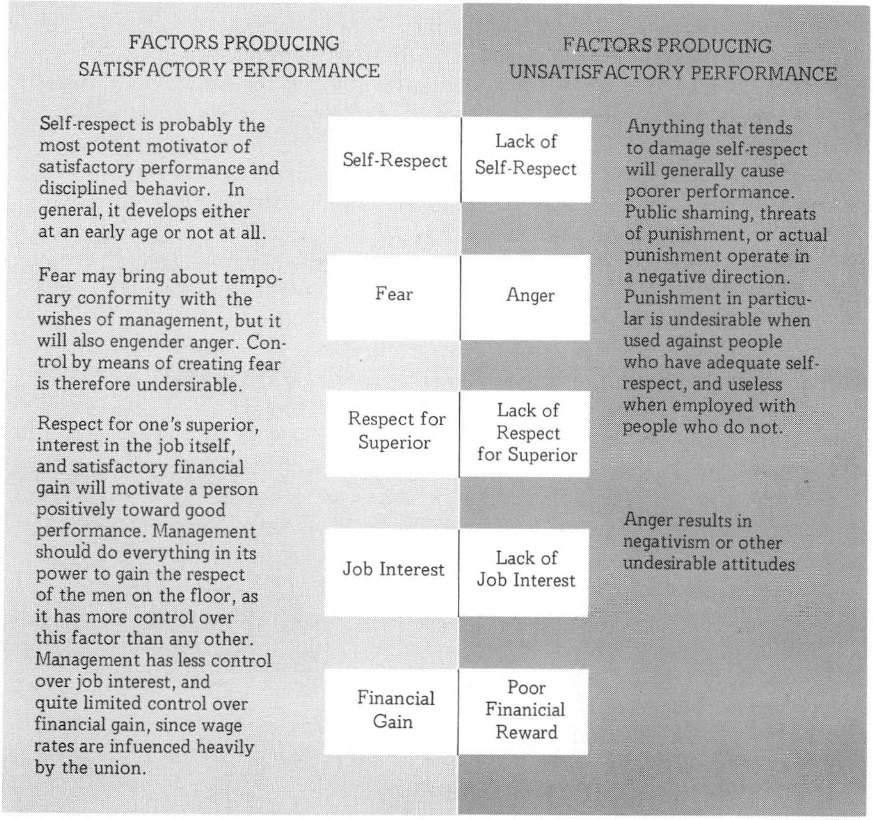

FACTORS PRODUCING SATISFACTORY PERFORMANCE			FACTORS PRODUCING UNSATISFACTORY PERFORMANCE
Self-respect is probably the most potent motivator of satisfactory performance and disciplined behavior. In general, it develops either at an early age or not at all.	Self-Respect	Lack of Self-Respect	Anything that tends to damage self-respect will generally cause poorer performance. Public shaming, threats of punishment, or actual punishment operate in a negative direction. Punishment in particular is undesirable when used against people who have adequate self-respect, and useless when employed with people who do not.
Fear may bring about temporary conformity with the wishes of management, but it will also engender anger. Control by means of creating fear is therefore undesirable.	Fear	Anger	
Respect for one's superior, interest in the job itself, and satisfactory financial gain will motivate a person positively toward good performance. Management should do everything in its power to gain the respect of the men on the floor, as it has more control over this factor than any other. Management has less control over job interest, and quite limited control over financial gain, since wage rates are infuenced heavily by the union.	Respect for Superior	Lack of Respect for Superior	
	Job Interest	Lack of Job Interest	Anger results in negativism or other undesirable attitudes
	Financial Gain	Poor Finanicial Reward	

Figure 12-1
Motivational factors in employee performance. Source: John Huberman, "Discipline Without Punishment," *Harvard Business Review*, July–August 1964, p. 66.

1. No disciplinary demotions, suspensions, or other forms of punishment will henceforth be applied.
2. In case of unsatisfactory work performance (e.g., carelessness in handling materials, inattention to duty) or breach of discipline (e.g., overstaying rest or lunch periods, unnecessary absenteeism, disregard of safety, failure to carry out the foreman's instructions), the following steps will be followed:

   Step One. The foreman will offer the worker a casual and friendly reminder on the job.

   Step Two. Should another incident arise within four to six weeks of Step One, the foreman will again correct it casually on the job but will later call the individual to his office for a serious but friendly chat. He will explain the need for and purpose of the rule(s); make sure the person understands the explanation; and express his confidence that the person will henceforth decide to abide by them. He will also listen to any reasonable excuse the employee may bring up. If he decides that the transgression was unintentional or based on a misunderstanding, he of course informs the employee that the matter is closed.

   Step Three. In case of further incidents within about six weeks, Step Two is repeated with some variation. First, the shift foreman is also present at the discussion; secondly, the employee's attention is directed to the possibility that he may dislike the work we have to offer, or he may find the relatively strict industrial discipline distasteful. In such case, would it be better to look for some other job or line of work? (Vocational counseling is available through the Personnel Office.) The foreman then expresses his hope that the employee will, in fact, decide that he likes the work and the company and will adapt himself to the requirements. This conversation is confirmed in a letter to the employee's home.

   Step Four. The employee who perpetrates another incident of poor workmanship or breach of discipline within six to eight weeks of Step Three is called off the floor into the foreman's office, again in the presence of the shift foreman. There he is directed to go home for the rest of the shift and consider seriously whether he does or does not wish to abide by company standards. He is informed that he will get full pay for the time, as a last expression of the company's hope that he will wish to stay and abide by the rules. He is also told that another occurrence of trouble within reasonable time will lead— regretfully—to termination.
3. If another incident should occur within reasonable time, the employee's services are terminated.
4. In case several incidents happen at unusually close intervals, Step Two or Step Three may be skipped.
5. If no further incident occurs within six to eight weeks of any one step (except Step Four), such step is cleared from the employee's record. Should another incident happen at a later time, the last step will be repeated. Considerable time—in the range of a year—would

have to elapse without incident before Step Four is cleared from the records.

6. In case of discovery of criminal behavior or in-plant fighting, termination results without preliminary steps. Such behavior is taken as conclusive evidence of lack of adequate self-respect and discipline even if it happens only once.[9]

The purpose of this system is to remove disruptive influences before they have a bad effect on people and materials. An individual is given the chance to demonstrate his or her desire to conform to the requirements of a given work situation. Every employee in any enterprise assumes certain responsibilities upon employment. This approach has increased supervisory effectiveness, has reduced employee grievances, has lowered managerial costs, and has reduced the financial drain of negative employee-management relationships. The morale of first-line supervisors, superintendents, and employees has shown dramatic improvement.

The experience of Douglas Fir plywood mill is not an isolated case of progressive discipline, as is shown in the following four cases of progressive discipline:

Let's consider several examples of discipline without punishment, with the only thing in common between them the fact that each one worked. Take Daredevil Dan, who operated his forklift truck as if the main aisle of the plant were the Indianapolis Speedway. One morning, what the manager had long been expecting happened: Dan dropped and ruined half a shift's work of finished material. The manager could have fired him or given him a stiff layoff. However, Dan, except for his speeding, was a first-class operator.

He could have embarrassed Dan by making a snide remark in front of the whole crew, such as "I think we're going to trade in your lift truck for a perambulator." Clever enough to get a yack from the boys and certain to wound a show-off like Dan. But the manager reasoned it would accomplish the opposite of his objective. Being a show-off, Dan would probably drive more wildly than ever to show everyone that the boss's cracks didn't bother him a bit.

What to do? The manager got Dan in private and cut him down with a couple of withering sentences: "Everyone's been telling me what a fool I am for letting you run that jeep. But I've been insisting that you were going to grow up one of these days." He left it at that. He gave Dan the opportunity to "grow up" without making him feel that he had to prove to the rest of the crew that he was unaffected by criticism. Furthermore, the manager assumed that Dan had a better side and appealed to it by putting on record his previous expressions of confidence. Dan, happily, rose to the occasion and was content to prove his mastery of the lift truck without endangering life and property.

Another case was a clerk-typist we'll call Lazy Leona, whose problem simply was that she was unambitious and bridled at the suggestion of hard work. However, her basic skills were excellent and her supervisor, although sorely tempted, decided against firing her. Motivating her was practically out of the question, the supervisor concluded. Counseling, an appeal to Leona's sense of fairness and responsibility, was bound to fail —she didn't have any, and such a session would probably result in tears, resentment, and mutual recrimination.

Discipline in Leona's case consisted of a four-pronged attack on the problem: (1) The supervisor gave Leona plenty to keep her busy and checked her progress regularly. (2) She gave her additional chores that forced her to work harder, although no harder than most of the girls, to get time for her additional tasks. (3) She spelled out standards and set a time limit each time she gave Leona a nonroutine job. (4) She moved Leona's work station to a spot among a hardworking group who, by example and/or pressure, would probably help Leona to turn in a fair day's work. In short, the supervisor gambled on having Leona either shape up or quit and, in this instance, her gamble paid off.

Then there's Superior Sam, an intelligent man and first-class operator whose problem was that the job was too easy for him. He frequently got bored and his favorite way of relieving boredom was to go visiting other workers in his own department and some of his buddies in other departments. Something had to be done. Yet when he was working, Sam was tops. Obviously, the management had to crack down on Sam, but it had to do it in a way that would spare his feelings and not give him the impression that he was being singled out and persecuted.

Sam was a reasonable man—that was the core of insight on which the manager based his strategy. The first step was to get the facts. He took notes on the time Sam actually spent doing the things he was supposed to do. Next, he made up a facsimile time card showing how much time Sam would have lost for the week if the time card were real and the time he spent away from the job were being deducted. Finally, he confronted Sam and let the evidence speak for itself. There were no histrionics, no verbal accusations, and everything was played in a low key. And Sam being Sam and basically rational and responsible, the approach worked.

We recall another case where a manager had a similar problem with Gregarious George, an amiable, not too bright subordinate who spent a good deal of time visiting other departments. The manager could have built up a case against this man (incidentally, a good worker when he worked) and eventually thrown the book at him. He preferred to handle the case differently. Whenever he suspected where the subordinate was visiting, he tracked him down, sneaked up on him, and told him in piercing tones, "Go back to work!" Undignified? Yes. Time-consuming? Yes. However, the boss maintained good relations with the man. And after having been startled out of his wits on several occasions, the subordinate quit visiting around.[10]

The Theory of Authority

Discipline in an organized work endeavor is based on acceptance of a manager's right to govern the activities of subordinates. Unless an employee accepts a supervisor's right to guide his or her actions, organized endeavors cease to function effectively. The right to govern the activities of people carries with it a managerial responsibility to guide their work in a prudent and pervasive manner.

Chester Irving Barnard, in *Functions of the Executive*, provides all progressive managers with a detailed outline of an effective technique for exercising authority in organized enterprises.

The necessity of the assent of the individual to establish authority for him is inescapable. A person can and will accept a communication as authoritative only when four conditions simultaneously obtain: (a) he can and does understand the communication; (b) at the time of his decision he believes that it is not inconsistent with the purpose of the organization; (c) at the time of his decision, he believes it to be compatible with his personal interest as a whole; and (d) he is able mentally and physically to comply with it.

(a) A communication that cannot be understood can have no authority. . . . Now, many orders are exceedingly difficult to understand. They are often necessarily stated in general terms, and the persons who issued them could not themselves apply them under many conditions. Until interpreted they have no meaning. The recipient either must disregard them or merely do anything in the hope that that is compliance.

Hence, a considerable part of administrative work consists in the interpretation and reinterpretation of orders in their application to concrete circumstances that were not or could not be taken into account initially.

(b) A communication believed by the recipient to be incompatible with the purpose of the organization, as he understands it, could not be accepted. Action would be frustrated by cross purposes. The most common practical example is that involved in conflicts of orders. They are not rare. An intelligent person will deny the authority of that one which contradicts the purpose of the effort as he understands it. In extreme cases many individuals would be virtually paralyzed by conflicting orders. They would be literally unable to comply—for example, an employee of a water system ordered to blow up an essential pump, or soldiers ordered to shoot their own comrades. I suppose all experienced executives know that when it is necessary to issue orders that will appear to the recipients to be contrary to the main purpose, especially as exemplified in prior habitual practice, it is usually necessary and always advisable, if practicable, to explain or demonstrate why the appearance of conflict is an illusion. Otherwise the orders are likely not to be executed, or to be executed inadequately.

(c) If a communication is believed to involve a burden that destroys the net advantage of connection with the organization, there no longer would remain a net inducement to the individual to contribute to it. The existence of a net inducement is the only reason for accepting any order as having authority. Hence, if such an order is received it must be disobeyed (evaded in the more usual cases) as utterly inconsistent with personal motives that are the basis of accepting any orders at all. Cases of voluntary resignation from all sorts of organizations are common for this sole reason. Malingering and intentional lack of dependability are the more usual methods.

(d) If a person is unable to comply with an order, obviously it must be disobeyed, or, better, disregarded. To order a man who cannot swim to swim a river is a sufficient case. Such extreme cases are not frequent; but they occur. The more usual case is to order a man to do things only a little beyond his capacity; but a little impossible is still impossible.

Naturally the reader will ask: How is it possible to secure such important and enduring cooperation as we observe if in principle and in fact the determination of authority lies with the subordinate individual? It is possible because the decisions of individuals occur under the following conditions: (a) orders that are deliberately issued in enduring organizations usually comply with the four conditions mentioned above; (b) there exists a "zone of indifference" in each individual within which orders are acceptable without conscious questioning of their authority; (c) the interests of the persons who contribute to an organization as a group result in the exercise of an influence on the subject, or on the attitude of the individual, that maintains a certain stability of this zone of indifference.

(a) There is no principle of executive conduct better established in good organizations than that orders will not be issued that cannot or will not be obeyed. Executives and most persons of experience who have thought about it know that to do so destroys authority, discipline, and morale. For reasons to be stated shortly, this principle cannot ordinarily be formally admitted, or at least cannot be professed. When it appears necessary to issue others which are initially or apparently unacceptable, either careful preliminary education, or persuasive efforts, or the prior offering of effective inducements will be made, so that the issue will not be raised, the denial of authority will not occur, and orders will be obeyed. It is generally recognized that those who least understand this fact—newly appointed minor or "first line" executives—are often guilty of "disorganizing" their groups for this reason, as do experienced executives who lose self-control or become unbalanced by a delusion of power or for some other reason. Inexperienced persons take literally the current notions of authority and are then said "not to know how to use authority" or "to abuse authority." Their superiors often profess the same beliefs about authority in the abstract, but their successful practice is easily observed to be inconsistent with their professions.

(b) The phrase "zone of indifference" may be explained as follows: If all the orders for actions reasonably practicable be arranged in the order of their acceptability to the person affected, it may be conceived that there are a number which are clearly unacceptable, that is, which certainly will not be obeyed; there is another group somewhat more or less on the neutral line, that is, either barely acceptable or barely unacceptable; and a third group unquestionably acceptable. This last group lies within the "zone of indifference." The person affected will accept orders lying within this zone and is relatively indifferent as to what the order is so far as the question of authority is concerned. Such an order lies within the range that in a general way was anticipated at time of undertaking the connection with the organization. For example, if a soldier enlists, whether voluntarily or not, in an army in which the men are ordinarily moved about within a certain broad region, it is a matter of indifference whether the order be to go to A or B, C or D, and so on; and goings to A, B, C, D, etc., are in the zone of indifference.

The zone of indifference will be wider or narrower depending upon the degree to which the inducements exceed the burdens and sacrifices which determine the individual's adhesion to the organization. It follows that the range of orders that will be accepted will be very limited among those who are barely induced to contribute to the system.

(c) Since the efficiency of organization is affected by the degree to which individuals assent to orders, denying the authority of an organization communication is a threat to the interests of all individuals who derive a net advantage from their connection with the organization, unless the orders are unacceptable to them also. Accordingly, at any given time there is among most of the contributors an active personal interest in the maintenance of the authority of all orders which to them are within the zone of indifference. The maintenance of this interest is largely a function of informal organization. Its expression goes under the names of "public opinion," "organization opinion," "feeling in the ranks," "group attitude," etc. Thus the common sense of the community informally arrived at affects the attitude of individuals, and makes them, as individuals, loath to question authority that is within or near the zone of indifference. The formal statement of this common sense is the fiction that authority comes down from above, from the general to the particular. This fiction merely establishes a presumption among individuals in favor of the acceptability of orders from superiors, enabling them to avoid making issues of such orders without incurring a sense of personal subserviency or a loss of personal or individual status with their fellows.

Thus the contributors are willing to maintain the authority of communications because, where care is taken to see that only acceptable communications in general are issued, most of them fall within the zone of personal indifference; and because communal sense influences the motives of most contributors most of the time. The practical instrument of this sense is the fiction of superior authority, which makes it possible normally to treat a personal question impersonally.[11]

Self-Evaluation on Discipline

Select the correct answer:

1. An effective supervisor views discipline as
   a. punishment for misconduct.
   b. a means to alter employee behavior to meet acceptable standards.
   c. both (a) and (b).

2. Punctuality is viewed as
   a. getting to work on time.
   b. completing job assignments on time.
   c. both (a) and (b).
3. An honest day's work consists of
   a. occasionally completing job assignments.
   b. regularly completing job assignments.
   c. both (a) and (b).
4. Acceptance of a supervisor's authority implies
   a. a willingness to follow a supervisor's directive.
   b. a willingness to carry out a supervisor's orders.
   c. both (a) and (b).
5. Cooperation with others implies
   a. a willingness to accept greater job responsibility.
   b. a willingness to do only assigned tasks.
   c. both (a) and (b).
6. A positive attitude toward discipline is viewed as
   a. preventive.
   b. corrective.
   c. both (a) and (b).
7. The aim of positive discipline is to
   a. instruct employees on accepted standards of behavior.
   b. punish an employee for infractions.
   c. both (a) and (b).
8. Positive discipline uses self-direction to
   a. improve employee motivation.
   b. improve an employee's self-image.
   c. both (a) and (b).
9. The purpose of corrective discipline is to
   a. penalize an employee for misconduct.
   b. recreate a positive work environment.
   c. both (a) and (b).
10. A supervisor who outlines expected behavior to new employees is using
    a. positive discipline.
    b. negative discipline.
    c. both (a) and (b).
11. One way to use positive discipline is
    a. to give orders properly.
    b. to hold weekly staff meetings.
    c. both (a) and (b).
12. An employee's response to a supervisor's directive is influenced by
    a. the employee's attitude.
    b. the supervisor's attitude.
    c. both (a) and (b).

13. Continuous employee violations of company policy are indicative of
    a. a lack of positive discipline.
    b. a supervisor not doing his or her job.
    c. both (a) and (b).
14. Effective self-direction is the result of training methods designed to
    a. create positive work attitudes.
    b. encourage constructive employee behavior.
    c. both (a) and (b).
15. Supervisors who manage the work of others using concepts of self-direction and self-development are practicing
    a. positive discipline.
    b. corrective discipline.
    c. both (a) and (b).
    The answers to the self-evaluation are as follows: 1 (b); 2 (c); 3 (b); 4 (c); 5 (a); 6 (a); 7 (a); 8 (c); 9 (b); 10 (a); 11 (a); 12 (c); 13 (c); 14 (c); 15 (a).

Morale Versus Discipline

Many people view discipline as a disregard for human rights because for them the term implies rigid rules and harsh punishment for infractions. Thus discipline is not often associated with such ideas as job enrichment and employee participation in decision making. But the word *discipline* can also describe a voluntary compliance with rules and commitment to the goals of an organization. It is hoped that this compliance is based on self-discipline that equates the interest of the firm with the employee's personal interest. A secondary motive for compliance is recognition that sustained membership in an organization carries with it responsibility for adherence to rules that govern organizational members. The disciplinary actions of management have a significant influence on the morale of employees. Positive discipline should produce a feeling of satisfaction and harmony in organizational relationships. Productivity is adversely affected when negative disciplinary procedures reduce morale and distort organizational relationships.[12]

The relationship between discipline and morale is outlined in Figure 12-2. The shaded areas show a situation in which morale is so low that the work unit's continued operation is doubtful. A second situation shows a work unit in which discipline is so lax that there is insufficient cooperation to carry out assigned tasks. The morale-discipline mix is a function of managerial leadership, employee attitudes, and job assignments. As noted in Figure 12-2 the presence of high morale carries with it an additional measure of discipline. Higher morale is a product of self-discipline that stresses employee accountability for his or her own actions. To maintain a balance between discipline and morale requires

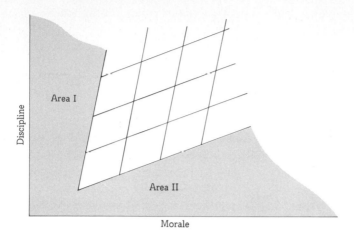

Figure 12-2
Source: Erwin Rausch, "The Effective Organization: Morale vs. Discipline," reprinted by permission of the publisher from *Management Review*, June 1971. Copyright © 1971 by American Management Association, Inc.

managerial flexibility to change a course of action if results are negative.

Figure 12-2 shows clearly that a firm with low morale and low discipline will not be very productive or competitive. Similarly, a firm with high morale but limited discipline is seriously endangering its stability because this situation seriously impairs management's ability to utilize the resources of the enterprise effectively. A complex decision-making process further frustrates an organization's ability to react to internal and external influences. An opposite corporate environment is based on authoritarian discipline that ignores the role of morale in designing organizational relationships. The success of this enterprise depends solely on the competence of its leadership. Under these conditions discipline is punitive and high turnover is reflected in the exodus of the more competent group members. As demands on the remaining personnel increase, morale drops to a point where opposition to leadership demands force a change in organizational relationships.[13]

Figure 12-3 provides four alternatives for a manager in implementing a morale-discipline continuum. Alternative C is the most desirable solution because it is the optimum trade-off between morale and discipline. However, individual and organizational influences may force a manager to take an alternative course of action. A change in leadership style that increases morale at the expense of discipline reduces a manager's ability to regain control. Thus, a manager should move toward alternative A in Figure 12-3 to enhance the ability to take corrective action. As with any managerial concept, the morale-discipline continuum seeks the optimum solution but corporate climate may require the implementation of a second alternative.

An effective manager realizes the need to alter managerial style to handle a variety of situations. To use the morale-discipline continuum, a manager should demonstrate an awareness of changing organizational relationships. An awareness of the impact of managerial decisions on morale and discipline provides a positive course of action to direct the future activities of the enterprise.[14]

Summary

Discipline is essential in any organized endeavor. Positive discipline seeks to educate employees so that they learn from their mistakes. Negative discipline seeks to assess blame and inflict punishment. Changing social and legal influences are altering the traditional techniques used to structure organizational relationships. Managerial action is further influenced by an employee's right to appeal disciplinary action, to examine evidence, and to examine accusers. Grievance procedures and the arbitration system have further influenced the environment in which a manager operates in carrying out disciplinary policies.

Traditional discipline lists a person's crime, sets punishment for the crime, and punishes the person. Such a traditional philosophy of discipline brings impressive short-term results but fails to alter the behavior

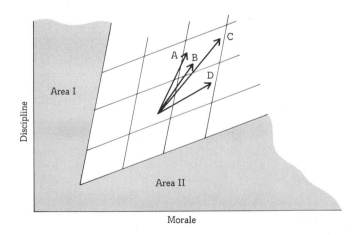

Figure 12-3
Source: Erwin Rausch, "The Effective Organization: Morale vs. Discipline," reprinted by permission of the publisher from *Management Review*, June 1971. Copyright © 1971 by American Management Association, Inc.

of people at work. Moreover, the negative impact of such a philosophy on employee morale remains with people long after the punishment phase. The objective approach to discipline places a supervisor in the position of shaping employee behavior through the voluntary acceptance of company policies. The objective approach to discipline still requires employee accountability for all actions.

Progressive discipline seeks to warn, correct, and reform offenders rather than "dish out" punishment. Rules and their enforcement should have uniformity in order to prevent charges of inconsistency and unfairness. Disciplinary procedures should be outlined to protect the rights of all parties involved in a disciplinary case. Having disciplined an employee, a supervisor must then demonstrate that personal relationships have not changed because of the disciplinary action. To burden an organization with excessive rules is to produce an enforcement policy of selectivity. Rules that contribute to company objectives reduce customer complaints concerning quality, protect the safety of all employees, reduce waste of physical resources, and prevent interruption of production activity. Periodic reviews of rules governing employee conduct can improve a supervisor's effectiveness.

The experience of Douglas Fir in 1963 suggests that discipline without punishment can become an organizational reality. Such a philosophy seeks to identify the variables and conditions that enhance employee compliance with work rules and disciplinary procedures. Self-discipline and self-direction become the motivational tools that influence employee actions. The purpose of this system is to remove disruptive influences before they have a negative effect on people and materials. The case histories of Dan, Leona, Sam, and George further illustrate successful use of progressive discipline without punishment in an organizational setting. Progressive discipline strives to replace extrinsic motivation with intrinsic motivation to bring about voluntary compliance with company operating procedures.

Discipline cannot exist in an organized work endeavor without employees' accepting the manager's right to direct their activities. The right to govern the activities of people carries with it a managerial responsibility to guide the work of employees prudently and persuasively. Chester Bernard provided progressive managers with an effective technique to guide their exercise of authority. A review of the self-evaluation instrument will give a manager a yardstick to measure his or her attitude toward discipline.

The balance between morale and discipline is a result of the use of positive discipline in structuring the environment. Morale and discipline imply compliance, acceptance of organizational objectives, and awareness of personal interests. The presence of low morale or reduced discipline produces chaos and confrontation, which can lead to the collapse of an organization. High morale is a product of self-discipline that stresses employees' accountability for their own actions. A proper balance between morale and discipline is necessary to produce a positive mix between organizational managerial, and employee needs. The presence of a laissez-faire or authoritarian leadership style tends to distort organizational relationships as well as to reduce productivity. An effective manager realizes the need to alter managerial style to handle different situations. To use the morale-discipline continuum a manager should demonstrate an awareness of changing organizational relationships. An awareness of the impact of managerial decisions on morale and discipline will provide a positive course of action to direct the future activities of the enterprise.

Discussion Questions

1. *What are some factors that have altered management's approaches toward discipline?*
2. *Discuss the dangers of using the terms* discipline *and* punishment *interchangeably.*
3. *Comment on the statement "If discipline at work is not accepted, it is not legitimate."*
4. *What should the main effort of progressive discipline be?*
5. *Why should records of minor infractions be removed after an employee has demonstrated present compliance with company rules.*

Chapter Case 12

It was the custom of most of the employees at the Ryan Company to arrive at the entrance door to the plant a few minutes before time to punch in. They would sit or stand around and talk, waiting for the clock to turn to 4:30 for the second shift. Joe and Jack were good friends and usually arrived at about the same time. However, on this particular day Joe got there first and in the process of waiting for Jack to come, he turned up last in line to punch the clock. Joe picked Jack's card out of the rack and punched in for him. About the time he replaced it in the opposite rack, Jack caught up with him and they started into the plant.

The supervisor stopped Joe and said to him "Joe, I saw you punch Jack's card. You know that you could be fired for that. The company is very strict about one employee punching in for another." Joe answered, "Well, if you saw me doing it, you had to see that Jack caught up with me before we entered the plant. Not more than a minute could have been missed on that clock."

"That's not the point," said the supervisor. "It is still against the rules to punch another guy's card. I'm going to recommend a three-day layoff without pay to personnel."

1. *Should the supervisor have disciplined Joe for an apparent infraction of a rule? Why or why not?*
2. *How about Jack? Should he have been disciplined?*
3. *How would you have handled this situation?*

Notes

1. George S. Odiorne. *Personnel Administration by Objectives.* Homewood, Ill.: Irwin, 1971, pp. 415–416.
2. Ibid., p. 417.
3. Ibid., pp. 418–421.
4. William M. Berliner and William J. McLarney. *Management Practice and Training,* 6th ed. Homewood, Ill.: Irwin, 1974, p. 643.
5. William F. Dowling, Jr., and Leonard R. Sayles. *How Managers Motivate: The Imperatives of Supervision.* New York: McGraw-Hill, 1971, pp. 129–131.
6. Odiorne, op. cit., p. 425.
7. Ibid., p. 423.
8. John Huberman. "Discipline Without Punishment," *Harvard Business Review,* July–August 1964.
9. Ibid., pp. 27–28.
10. Dowling and Sayles, op. cit., pp. 139–140.
11. Ibid., pp. 144–147.
12. Erwin Rausch. "The Effective Organization: Morale vs. Discipline," *Management Review,* June 1971.
13. Ibid.
14. Ibid.

CUSTOM FURNITURE CASE: CAR THEFT

On this particular morning John Taylor is having a conversation with Bill Jones and Sam Brown. It has just come to the attention of the company that one of the employees falsified his application when he was hired twelve years ago. On the form is a space for "Previous Arrests or Convictions" and Gil Stern answered "None," when actually, it has been learned, Gil was convicted for automobile theft when he was sixteen and was given a suspended sentence.

John: "Sam, did you know anything about this conviction of Gil's?"

Sam: "No sir! It's news to me. Gil has always been a model employee and I would never have guessed that he had ever been arrested, much less convicted."

John: "How about you, Bill? Did you know about this?"

Bill: "Nope. Gil has told me that he was a little reckless when he was younger, but he never mentioned any trouble with the law."

John: "Well, what do you think we should do about it?"

Sam: "Have you talked to Gil?"

358

John: "No, I wanted to talk to you first. Actually, I think it is your place, Sam, to get to the bottom of this. He works for you."

Sam: "Okay, I'll talk to him."

John: "Please do it privately. I don't want this to get around."

Sam asks Gil to stick around for a few minutes when his shift is over and most people are gone:

Sam: "Gil, I've got to bring up something that isn't going to be pleasant for either one of us."

Gil: "What's that, Sam? My work's all right, isn't it?"

Sam: "Sure, your work's fine. It's about something that's, well, sort of personal. Do you remember when you filled out the application for your first job here?"

Gil: "Sure, Sam. What about it?"

Sam: "Do you remember there was a question about whether you had ever been convicted of a crime?"

Gil: "Sort of. That was a long time ago."

Sam: "Well, you said that you had never been convicted, and now John Taylor says he has found out that you were convicted of car theft."

Gil: "Golly, Sam, that was when I was sixteen and the judge let me off. I just borrowed the car for a joy ride. I realize now how wrong it was, but you know, when you are young. . . ."

Sam: "Nevertheless, you lied on the application and that is grounds for dismissal."

Gil: "Do you mean I may lose my job over something that happened when I was a kid and that I didn't serve a day for?"

Sam: "I just don't know, Gil. John Taylor is pretty disappointed in you for doing this. Let me talk it over with him and give him the details as you have told them to me. Go on back to work and I'll talk to you later."

Sam reports his conversation with Gil to John and Bill Jones.

Bill: "Well, one thing's sure. We can't let him get away with this. I think that he should be fired!"

Sam: "Now hold on, Bill. He does work for me, you know. He's a good worker and I would really hate to lose him. Couldn't we give him some days off without pay as discipline? He wouldn't be easy to replace?"

John: "Well, it was a long time ago and he was very young. But still he *did* falsify his application."

1. What would you do if you were John Taylor?
2. Should Gil be disciplined in any way?
3. What about the money that the company has invested in Gil and the cost of replacing him?"

PERFORMANCE APPRAISAL

13

You will notice that I have given you an overall rating of Very Good.

In that case, I will want to look it over very carefully.

For the full story, turn to the case on page 373.

GENERAL PURPOSES
OF CHAPTER 13

1. To examine the traditional methods of appraisal
2. To look at some of the problems of these methods
3. To consider some guidelines for appraisal interviews
4. To take note of the system of management by objectives as an alternative method of appraisal

LEARNING OBJECTIVES

1. To name at least four purposes of performance appraisal
2. To list and give a brief description of at least six traditional methods of appraisal
3. To give five common problems that exist in appraisals
4. To name seven points to be considered during the appraisal interview
5. To define *management by objective*
6. To list the seven steps involved in a management-by-objectives appraisal system

Most managers no longer question whether there should be appraisal of employees. The question is how the evaluation or appraisal should be carried out. Some sort of system is necessary to such functions as salary administration, placement, transfer, and promotion. Decisions concerning these matters cannot be made without serious consideration. It is almost impossible to manage an organization without some form of appraisal. The very size of our organizations dictates that there must be a written record of evaluations since decisions concerning promotions and other matters may have to be made by a person who has no personal knowledge of the capabilities of the individual being considered.

History of Performance Appraisal

Merit-rating plans were probably the first of the appraisal plans now in general use in the private sector, although the U.S. Civil Service System developed an evaluation system in the 1850s. Robert Owen used a form of evaluation in his cotton mills in Scotland around 1800 when so-called character blocks were displayed at the work station of employees, indicating their rating from bad to good. During World War I, Walter Dill Scott saw his "man-to-man" system for evaluation adopted by the U.S. Army for the appraisal of military officers. During the 1920s and 1930s many industrial companies based in-grade increases on merit.

In the 1950s interest in management development programs increased and appraisal was considered to be an important part of any effective development plan. In recent years the term *merit rating* has come to be applied only to hourly employees. Even here it is not nearly as important as it used to be, because with the rise of unionism, promotion, pay, and other factors moved to a system of seniority rather than merit. The terms *performance appraisal* and *employee evaluation* have become more popular as applied to white-collar, managerial, and professional employees.

Purposes of Performance Appraisal

The principal purpose of performance appraisal, like most managerial tools, is to improve performance. Recognition can be given for past results and coaching can be used for future improvements. The employee needs feedback from his or her superior concerning performance and areas in which he or she needs improvement. A worker cannot be expected to perform well unless there is understanding about what is expected of him or her.

In addition to this purpose of improving performance are other objectives of performance appraisal:

1. Effective wage and salary administration. Proper salary action such as raises cannot be effectively administered without a review of the performance of the employees being considered.
2. Increase in managers' understanding of their employees. Evaluation should be on a daily basis but periodic appraisals will afford the opportunity on a regular basis for discussions between subordinate and supervisor that can truly be rewarding coaching and counseling experiences.
3. Examination of the hiring process. In the appraisal process ineffective performers should be weeded out and the number of those eliminated will provide an assessment of effectiveness of the firm's method of hiring and placement. This will aid allocation of resources, both capital and human.
4. Provide opportunities for self-development. During the process of appraisal, needs and opportunities for self-development of the employee may come to attention. Accomplishment of the self-development may be brought about through academic courses, self-study, or job-related considerations such as job rotation, job enlargement, or job enrichment.

One of the older and more traditional approaches to performance appraisal is by personal traits. Some of the traits to be measured are objective such as amount of work, but most of the traits considered are subjective: cooperativeness, attitude, initiative, enthusiasm, and dependability. It is very difficult to determine which traits will actually affect job performance. The main disadvantage of this type of appraisal is that the appraiser acts as both psychologist and judge. Not many supervisors are sufficiently trained to be either. As a result, the tendency is to give each person a higher rating than is probably deserved.

Appraisal Methods

Many types of appraisal are available to the manager. For our purposes, we have confined our discussion to the following:

1. Rating scale
2. Ranking
3. Paired comparison
4. Forced choice
5. Weighted checklist
6. Narrative
7. Management by objective

In the *rating scale* method, the traits to be measured are presented on a printed form and a rating scale is given for each trait. The rater indicates the degree to which the person being rated shows the trait as he or she performs the work assigned. Sometimes these degrees are placed along a continuum:

Attitude:

0	1	2	3	4
Shows little interest in job	Does not follow instructions	Shows interest in work; willing to accept help	Shows great enthusiasm in all efforts	Is looked to as a leader by fellow workers

The rater places a mark somewhere along the continuum indicating a personal perception of the extent to which the ratee possesses this trait. When the scores are added, the sum becomes that individual's rating for the period. The points may be shown on the form, but frequently they are omitted and the scores are tabulated by the personnel department. In this system, as was mentioned before, the supervisor is forced to assume the role of a judge.

Ranking consists of placing all employees as on the steps of a ladder from the highest down to the lowest in regard to their job performance and worth to the organization. Instructions may tell the rater to pick the top person first and next the poorest and to proceed to fill in the chart until all of the group has been placed somewhere on the ladder.

Paired comparison involves the comparison of each person being rated with all other persons in the work group, one at a time. A record is made of the number of times each person is ranked above another and from this listing the order for the group is derived. This system is difficult to manage if the group is very large.

Forced choice uses a rating form consisting of groups of four or five statements. The rater must select the statement that best describes the ratee and the one that is least applicable. Within these groups, there are usually a nearly equal number of favorable and unfavorable statements. The weighting of the statements is not revealed to the rater, so the rater does not really know which way the choice counts for the person being rated. Only one of the favorable and one of the unfavorable statements indicates high or low performance. Discussion of the results with the ratee is very difficult since the rater does not know the method of scoring.

The *weighted checklist* consists of various descriptions of levels and types of behavior for the job held by the ratee. Each statement is weighted. The supervisor checks those statements that seem to most accurately describe the individual being rated. The various weights are then averaged, and this average becomes the score of the ratee. This system does make the supervisor think more specifically about the behavior of the various work group members. However, it is very expensive to put into practice, especially in a firm with many diverse jobs.

Narrative is one of the most flexible systems for appraisal. The traits to be measured are the only notations given on the form and the supervisor makes relevant comments under each trait. This information is gained from a special notebook the supervisor is expected to keep in which he or she notes situations in which the ratee showed effective or ineffective action or behavior in relation to certain traits. Since the only practical way to use this notebook is on a daily basis, it takes a great deal of the supervisor's time. Employees may feel that every move they make is being recorded in the "little black book."

Management by objective is a system in which the employee sets goals at the beginning of the appraisal period; these goals are agreed on by both the rater and the ratee; and the appraisal is based on the degree to which these goals are met during the specified period. This is a very simplified explanation of MBO. A more detailed examination of the method appears later in the chapter.

Problems in Performance Appraisal

The Halo Effect

One of the most prevalent mistakes in appraisal is the tendency to allow an impression, either positive or negative, of one trait of an individual to color the rating on all the other factors. If an employee dresses poorly and presents an unkempt appearance, this negative impression may carry over to the rating on quality of work even though there may be no correlation between the two factors. This phenomenon is known as the *halo effect*. Isolated incidents may also enter into this error in appraisal. If the last incident the rater recalls involving the employee is a favorable one, then the appraisal may well be higher than is deserved. By the same token, a recent disagreeable experience with an employee may color the entire appraisal. It must be remembered that the appraisal is supposed to be of the whole person and to cover the entire period of evaluation.

Rating Everyone Average

Too many supervisors who have not taken the time to think about performance appraisal during the entire period for which it is developed do not have the facts to do an effective job of appraisal. They tend to give everyone an average rating. This also frequently happens when the supervisor does not want the rating to produce difficulties—if an employee is rated too highly, that employee may let production drop off; if the person is rated too low, there may be controversy in the appraisal interview—so he or she just rates everyone average. This type of evaluation shows a lack of integrity and is quickly seen through by members of the work group, including those who know that they are below average as well as those who realize that they deserve a better-than-average rating.

Last-Minute Appraisals

Employees know that appraisal is an important factor in their future with the company. It is unfair for a supervisor to wait until the day of or even the day before evaluations must be accomplished to give the matter attention. In the first place, appraisal is supposed to be an ongoing event, and in the second place, a good appraisal cannot be made in a few minutes, without all the facts at hand, and without individual attention to each person being rated. In most instances, pay raises and promotions hinge on this instrument. Each supervisor should face the task with concern and enough preparation to make the appraisal process meaningful and the appraisal interval a time in which to be a coach and a counselor to the workers, not a judge pointing attention to past mistakes.

Personal Bias

The proper job to be performed in appraisal is to rate the individual in relation to performance on the job. Too often performance is ignored and evaluation is based on the likes or dislikes of the rater as applied to the individual being rated. Even though the worker's job performance may be excellent, if that person's attitude and personality clash with the expectations of the rater, an overall rating of satisfactory may ensue. Unless job performance is suffering because of these attitudes and personality traits, they should not even be considered in the appraisal of overall performance.

Comparing One Person with Another

Each of us is as individual as our fingerprints. A system that makes comparisons of one employee with another is not fair. People should be compared with standards set for the jobs (of course, the standards should be fair ones) if comparisons must be made at all. In the section on management by objectives it is shown how evaluation can be accomplished with a system based on results, not traits or comparisons.

The Appraisal Interview

Unfortunately, some companies still believe that appraisal results should be shared only by the supervisor doing the rating and higher management. This creates an atmosphere of fear and distrust as well as frustration on the part of the workers resulting from the lack of feedback on the feelings of the supervisor and the company concerning their performance on the job. However, in most companies employees participate in an appraisal interview, even if the participation consists only of listening to the supervisor relate the results of the appraisal.

Ideally, this meeting should be conducted in private and without interruption. The supervisor should prepare for this meeting as carefully and painstakingly as he or she would prepare for an important meeting with his or her superior. If the rater has been evaluating several people, it is sometimes easy to get the evaluations confused, so it is a good idea to take a few minutes to review the form immediately before the interview. If the person has been given a low rating on a given point, the supervisor should be prepared to explain why. Have a few pointers in mind that can help the employee overcome this particular problem. Don't be afraid to ask the ratee for suggestions on how the difficulty can be overcome. At this same time it is helpful to make a list of some of the strong points of this particular individual. Depending on the situation and the people involved, it may be a good idea to talk about a weakness, then a strength, and then a weakness, and so on, thus not piling up criticism after criticism.

Some points the supervisor should consider during the interview itself are the following:

1. Conduct the interview in private with no interruptions.
2. Stick to facts as much as possible.
3. Make the person feel at ease.
4. Assure the ratee that the evaluation is for his or her benefit as well as that of the company.
5. Concentrate on the issue, not the individual.
6. Give praise if it is due.
7. Avoid lecturing and make the interview a dialogue, not a monologue.
8. Give the worker a copy of the appraisal and allow time for reading it.
9. Be prepared to suggest a program for maintaining or improving the rating.
10. Follow up on the progress being made with the program outlined.

Regardless of the system chosen for appraisal, the individual being rated should understand that its purpose is to assist in job performance. This meeting gives the supervisor an excellent opportunity to counsel and coach the subordinate and should not be taken as a chance to judge the employee and attempt to drive the worker toward goals that he or she has had no part in setting. The appraisal process is circular; the end of each appraisal period marks the beginning of a new one.

Management by Objectives

One of the most significant contributions made by the appraisal process to management of enterprises has been the development of the system of management by objectives as begun by Douglas McGregor and Peter Drucker and furthered by George S. Odiorne and others.

Douglas McGregor compares the traditional performance appraisal with Theory X when he states:

Performance appraisal is often perceived simply as a technique of personnel administration, but where it is used for administrative purposes, it becomes a part of a managerial strategy, the implicit logic of which is that in order to get people to direct their efforts toward organizational objectives, management must tell them what to do, judge how well they have done, and reward or punish them accordingly.[1]

He strengthens this position when he states:

Appraisal programs are designed not only to provide more systematic control of the behavior of subordinates, but also to control the behavior of superiors. For example, it is believed that an appraisal program will force the superior to face up to problems of poor performance and deal with them, that it will force him to communicate to his subordinates his judgements of their performances, etc.[2]

McGregor believed that Theory Y, which stipulates management by self-integration and self-control, is more appropriate and results in more growth and learning and in improved performance, which after all is supposed to be the main purpose of performance appraisal.

Ordiorne defined management by objective as follows:

In brief, the system of management by objectives can be described as a process whereby superior and subordinate managers of an organization jointly identify its common goals, define each individual's major area of responsibility in terms of results expected of him, and use these measures as guides for operating the unit and assessing the contribution of each of its members.[3]

The development of MBO can largely be attributed to the dissatisfaction of many with traditional approaches to appraisal and a search for a more fair and effective method. Under the systems of rating personality traits or comparing individuals, the subordinate, more often than not, failed to realize what was expected of him or her until *after* the performance review. Under MBO the subordinate participates in setting the criteria by which he or she is to be judged. These criteria are specified in terms of concrete results, rather than personality traits such as initiative, leadership, cooperation, and so on, and the emphasis is on output, rather than input.

There are several reasons why MBO has been gaining in importance both as an appraisal technique and as a system for total management:

1. With the growth in size and complexity of today's organizations, managers are forced to delegate more of their work.
2. Although the manager is still responsible for the results of subordinates' actions, it becomes increasingly difficult to be familiar with all these activities. More managers are coming to realize that achievements are largely the result of cumulative results accomplished by subordinates.
3. Today's employees, younger and better educated, will not stand for very close supervision. They want more self-determination and participation in setting the goals of the organization.
4. Job descriptions usually include duties and activities, not results. Little is mentioned about what the employee is supposed to accomplish. Thus, traditional appraisals tend to revolve around how a person's time is spent, rather than the more important matter of the results of the effort. This type of appraisal experience is unsatisfactory for everyone concerned. Because the manager is usually not qualified to assess personality traits, the assessment reflects personal likes and dislikes. There is little communication of ideas that might prove beneficial to both superior and subordinate under more favorable circumstances.

In an MBO system the focus is on participation and self-commitment, as well as on self-improvement and personal growth. This has many advantages, such as the following:

1. Genuine communication results between subordinate and superior because each knows what the criteria are for evaluation.
2. When the goals of the employee are his or her own, and these goals are known to be the criteria for evaluation, commitment to the goals is enhanced.
3. There is much more likelihood for agreement in the appraisals since the criteria focus on results, not personalities, and since the criteria were selected and agreed on prior to appraisal.
4. The MBO method provides a more realistic scheme for job improvement and personal growth.

Establishing the System for Appraisal

Several steps are involved in a successful MBO program for evaluation. Ideally, the employee should be allowed to write the job description.

However, this is usually not practical since job descriptions already exist and because a new employee cannot be expected to have enough knowledge of the job to complete this task or to know how the job fits into the picture of the total organization. We therefore consider the following to be the logical steps in an MBO system of appraisal.

1. Subordinate establishes own objectives for the performance period.
2. Objectives are discussed and mutually agreed on between superior and subordinate.
3. Methods of measurement are established for the performance period.
4. Objectives are written, indicating accomplishments planned during the coming performance period.
5. Progress checks are established for periodical review.
6. Accomplishments on each agreed on objective are reported on by the subordinate.
7. Results are jointly evaluated.

The employee states in specific terms what is planned for accomplishment during the performance period. Some of the requirements for completing this step follow.

1. All areas of job responsibility must be considered.
2. Objectives must be set in each area.
3. Goals must be specific.
4. Goals must be measurable.
5. Objectives must be consistent with company and department needs.
6. Self-development goals should be included.

The two parties must agree on what constitutes a reasonable list of individual goals for the person being rated. These goals must be in line with the goals of the organization and of the superior. At this point, the rater has a good opportunity to assume the role of counselor and coach, not judge. People are always more committed to goals they have set themselves than to goals that have been forced on them. The superior should assume an attitude of friendliness and trust, but the objectives of the organization must be kept in mind.

Methods of measurement should be established in advance by mutual agreement. They may include such items as dates of completion for specific projects, sales volume to be achieved (or production volume), and/or reduction of certain costs by a specified percentage within a specified length of time. Goals such as these lend themselves to precise measurement, and this is a basic requirement for an effective goal. However, other goals that may be just as important are not as easily measured, such as the preparation of a certain manual or other programs within a certain span of time. Here the effectiveness of the preparation may be more relevant than completion within a certain performance period. Still, if these goals cannot be measured, a proper evaluation cannot be accomplished. For instance, a goal such as to "develop a better attitude toward my work" may be very admirable, but it is practically impossible to measure objectively.

When the objectives are reduced to writing, the employee realizes that commitment is being made for the next performance period: six months or a year. A good list of objectives considers not only what is good for the organization, but also what is good for the individual. Goals must represent a sufficient task for the period, but not a task that is too ambitious for the person involved. In other words, they must be attainable. Both long- and short-term goals should be included and qualitative as well as quantitative objectives should be spelled out. It is important to state all goals clearly and simply.

Meetings should be arranged during which the supervisor and subordinate can discuss the effectiveness of plans and methods being used. This not only enables both parties to know where the employee stands in relation to target dates but also is an excellent time to reappraise goals and set new ones if necessary.

At the end of the performance period, the employee puts into writing the manner in which and the degree to which the goals set at the beginning of the period have been accomplished. The degree of accomplishment is important, as well as whether or not the goals have been accomplished. It should be determined whether the goal was too optimistic or conditions beyond the control of the individual prevented completion of the goal. Reasons for lack of accomplishment should be identified.

Joint evaluation of results takes place at the performance appraisal interview. It is very important that the subordinate be encouraged to participate in this interview and not just be informed of what he or she has or has not accomplished. In fact, the person being evaluated should be allowed to do a good deal of the evaluating. The interview should focus on results and not become a discussion of personality traits. The purpose of the evaluation is not to judge the subordinate for what he or she *is,* but to determine what has been accomplished based on the goals set.

If it seems appropriate, this meeting can also cover such concerns as relationships on the job, opportunities, or job-related problems. However, another date can be set for discussion of these matters if it is not comfortable for both parties to do it at this time. It is the opinion of many, including the writers, that the appraisal session or interview should be kept separate from salary reviews and promotion decisions.

Summary

Although it is agreed that there must be some system of performance appraisal for employees, there is no universally accepted method of accomplishing this appraisal. Some objectives of appraisal are (1) effective wage and salary administration, (2) increased understanding of employees, (3) examination of the hiring system, and (4) provision for opportunities for self-development.

Many of the traditional methods of appraisal, such as rating scales, rankings, paired comparison, forced choice, weighted checklist, and narrative, focus on personality traits deemed to be desirable. These methods measure the degree to which the ratee possesses the characteristics. Some of the problems resulting from traditional methods are (1) halo effect, (2) the tendency to rate everyone as average, (3) hurried appraisals, (4) personal biases, (5) comparisons of employees.

The appraisal interview is a very important event for the employee and it should be handled with care and preparation. Many believe that appraisal is most effective when it is based on a system of management by objectives, a system in which the subordinate sets goals for the performance period, which are reviewed by the supervisor and mutually agreed on. Evaluation is based on the degree to which these goals are accomplished rather than on personality traits or comparisons with other employees.

Discussion Questions

1. *Relate the benefits of MBO to such problems as communication, motivation, leadership styles, types of ogranzations.*
2. *Give some reasons why it might be difficult to install a system of MBO in an existing organization.*
3. *Why is it necessary that in the installation of an MBO system the impetus be from top management?*
4. *Do you believe that it is easy to establish objectives on which evaluation will be based?*
5. *Define* management by objectives *and briefly describe the various points expressed in Odiorne's definition.*
6. *What should be the main purpose of the evaluation of employees?*
7. *What are some advantages of allowing the person being evaluated to participate in the appraisal interview?*
8. *What type of system is used by your firm for appraisal? Do you believe this system is as effective as MBO might be?*

CUSTOM FURNITURE CASE:
THE EVALUATION

It was appraisal time again and John Taylor was dreading it. As usual he had put it off until the last minute and now the forms were due in the main office in a very few days. He took one of the forms from his desk and began to go over it:

Name _____ Position _____ Date _____
Length of time on job _____ Points assigned _____

	U	F	G	VG	E
Knowledge of work	1	2	3	4	5
Initiative	1	2	3	4	5
Quality of work	1	2	3	4	5
Dependability	1	2	3	4	5
Volume of work	1	2	3	4	5
Leadership	1	2	3	4	5
Attitude	1	2	3	4	5
Judgment	1	2	3	4	5
Dealing with people	1	2	3	4	5
Organizing ability	1	2	3	4	5
Application	1	2	3	4	5

Unsatisfactory:	10–15 points
Fair:	16–25 points
Good:	26–34 points
Very Good:	35–45 points
Excellent:	46–50 points

John decided to review Ron Davis, one of the salespeople, first since Ron had studied personnel administration in college and always expressed himself vocally at evaluation time:

John: "Well, Ron, it's evaluation time again. Seems as if we just went through this last week, but actually it has been six months."

Ron: "Yes, sir; time really flies when you are having fun."

John: "Very funny. Well, to get on with it. I have a lot more people to review. Actually you are the first."

Ron: "Yes, I know."

John: "Here is your form all filled out. Take a few minutes to look it over and if you have any questions, I'll try to answer them. You will notice that I have given you an overall rating of Very Good."

Ron: "In that case, I will want to look it over very carefully."

John: "Okay, but please remember that we don't have all day and your job is not on the line with this appraisal."

Ron: "The first thing that I don't understand is why you are giving me a rating of Good on initiative."

John: "Well, Ron, you know that we talked on the last review about your reluctance to call on the smaller accounts, and your figures do not indicate to me that you are doing any more of this than you were at this time last year."

374

Ron: "You can't live off those two-bit customers that you are always riding me about. I see that you have given me a 5 on volume of work."

John: "Oh, yes, you turn in plenty of volume. More than any other salesperson. Unfortunately, I had to rate you only 3 on quality of work—because you will not put enough effort into selling our higher-priced products."

Ron: "Ten percent of $100,000 is better than 25 percent of nothing."

John: "That is hardly the proper way to look at this situation, Ron. If all the salespeople just looked at volume and to hell with profit, the company could not keep its doors open."

Ron: "One more thing—what about this 'fair' rating on attitude?"

John: "That is mainly because of the way that you work or, in reality, refuse to work with the design department. You seem to think that we don't even need them and you very seldom use their services."

Ron: "I can't get along with those temperamental, or perhaps I should say artistic, people with their high-falooting ideas and their expensive specifications."

John: "They could help you raise your profit picture by specifying our higher-priced products."

Ron: "No thanks, I'll stick to being the top salesman in volume. That's the name of the game."

John: "I'm really sorry that you feel that way, but I've got to move on. Will you please sign your evaluation?"

When he looked at the form after Ron left, John noticed that Ron had written the words *with protest* above his signature. He hated to send this into the main office, but he did not know what else to do.

1. What is your opinion of the appraisal form?
2. How could John have handled this interview better?
3. What is the main problem in this situation?
4. What changes would you make in the appraisal system in use at present?

Appendix 1
JOB EVALUATION SYSTEM

I. General Information

A. Job Evaluation

One of the company's main objectives in relation to its employees is to insure that each employee is equitably compensated for the service he performs.

Since each employee is paid largely on the basis of how important his job is to the company, it is necessary to set a value on each job. This is done through a systematic method called job evaluation.

Job evaluation is the determination of the relative value of one job in relation to every other job in an organization. It is performed using the processes of description and classification. The purpose is to determine the relative worth of jobs by the use of some impersonal measuring stick.

Job description is used to collect the basic information about a job in an organized manner. It should include facts about tools and materials used, the primary purpose of the job, the degree of supervision required, and a concise description of the working procedure.

Job classification is the process of determining relative values for the different jobs using the description as a guide. Classification can be done by several methods. Our system is to use point values developed from ten factors.

Using this approach to job evaluation will

Assure a fair wage at all job levels.
Provide equal pay for equal work.
Clarify function, authority, and responsibilities of any given job.
Aid in selecting, placing, promotion, transferring, and training employees.

B. Job Descriptions

The job descriptions written in this report will serve as a basis for classifying jobs. It is necessary, therefore, to obtain full knowledge of the functions of each, in order to write a concise but complete description.

The descriptions are written to describe the requirements of the job and not necessarily what the present incumbent is doing. It is the job we want to describe not an individual.

The importance of adequate descriptions of the jobs cannot be overstressed. Job descriptions serve to record why a job was classified as it was and also to judge alleged changes in job content resulting from technological changes or from accumulations of minor changes.

Our method of writing descriptions will use the following six categories to summarize the job.

1. Primary function.
2. Tools and equipment.
3. Materials.
4. Source of supervision.
5. Direction exercised.
6. Working procedure.

1. *Primary function.* This should state in one sentence the main purpose for which this job has been established.

2. *Tools and equipment.* This should be a listing of those tools, machines, and equipment that are necessary for the satisfactory performance of the job being described.

3. *Materials.* This should consider both the materials and the materials produced. Materials used include those consumed, handled, transported, or transferred. Materials produced include only those materials where there is a physical or chemical change as a result of action taken by the incumbent on the job or by those for which he is responsible.

4. *Source of supervision.* This should include the title of the immediate superior on the job being described.

5. *Direction exercised.* This should include the titles of those jobs for which the incumbent of the job being described is responsible.

6. *Working procedure.* This should contain a concise but complete as possible listing of the functions which must be performed in order to satisfactorily complete the requirements of this job. In order that there be no misunderstanding as to what an individual incumbent of an occupation may be asked to do, the following statement should be included as the last line of all job descriptions: "It must be clearly understood that the above statements reflect the general details considered necessary to describe the principal functions of the job identified, and shall not be construed as a detailed description."

C. Job Classification

The method of classification used in this report is described as the Point Value Method. It is based upon an analysis of the relative worth of jobs in terms of basic factors of job content. The ten factors used herein are:

1. Experience.
2. Education and trade knowledge.
3. Initiative and judgment.
4. Physical effort.
5. Mental or visual effort.
6. Responsibility for equipment.
7. Responsibility for material or product.
8. Responsibility for operations.
9. Responsibility for safety of others.
10. Job conditions and unavoidable hazards.

In order to insure consistency in all evaluations, special consideration has been given to the following points:

378

1. In all job classification work, the factors are not intended to measure the man on the job. They are used only to describe characteristics or requirements necessary in any individual to perform the job successfully. To repeat, it is the *job* that is under consideration, *not the individual* who works on the job.
2. Classification will be made on the basis of performance of a "fair day's work," defined as follows: "A fair day's work is that amount of work that can be produced by a qualified employee when working at a normal pace and effectively utilizing his time where work is not restricted by process limitations."
3. Jobs will be placed in the appropriate degree in each factor by considering the specific requirements of each job and the descriptions of each degree.
4. Only the numerical values specifically set forth on the following pages may be assigned in the classification of a job and no interpolation may be made between degrees.
5. Jobs are to be classified without regard to existing wage rates.

D. Job Factors Used

The following table shows the point values for all the degree levels of the various factors.

Factors	1st	2nd	Degree 3rd	4th	5th
Skill					
1. Experience	16	32	48	64	80
2. Education and trade knowledge	14	28	42	56	70
3. Initiative and judgment	14	28	42	56	70
Effort					
4. Physical	8	16	24	32	40
5. Mental or visual	6	12	18	24	30
Responsibility					
6. Equipment	10	20	30	40	50
7. Material or product	8	16	24	32	40
8. Operations	8	16	24	32	40
9. Safety of others	6	12	18	24	30
Working Conditions					
10. Job conditions and unavoidable hazards	10	20	30	40	50

1. Factor No. 1—Experience. This factor appraises the length of time usually required by an individual, with the specified education and trade knowledge, to learn to perform the work effectively. The total time to become proficient at this job is based on the accumulation of periods when additional job knowledge is being acquired. Generally this will be less than the elapsed time on the job. Consideration was given for necessary time spent on directly related jobs required for progression to the job being studied. It does not include time required for apprenticeship or trades training which has been rated under Education. Included under Experience is only the time required to attain production standards.

16	*1st Degree.* Up to three months.
32	*2nd Degree.* Over three months up to one year.
48	*3rd Degree.* Over one year up to two years.
64	*4th Degree.* Over two years up to three years.
80	*5th Degree.* Over three years.

2. Factor No. 2—Education and Trade Knowledge. This factor appraises the job requirements in terms of the mental development needed to understand the work being performed. Such mental development or technical knowledge may have been acquired by formal schooling, company training programs, or through equivalent practical experience.

Points

14	*1st Degree.* Requires the ability to read and write, add and subtract whole numbers.
28	*2nd Degree.* Requires the use of simple arithmetic such as addition and subtraction of decimals and fractions; together with reading of simple drawings and some measuring instruments such as caliper or scale.
42	*3rd Degree.* Requires the use of fairly complicated drawings and/or shop arithmetic, variety of measuring instruments; some trade knowledge in a specialized field or process.
56	*4th Degree.* Requires the use of complicated drawings and specifications, advanced shop mathematics, handbook formulas, wide variety of precision measuring instruments, broad shop trade knowledge.
70	*5th Degree.* Requires a basic technical knowledge sufficient to deal with complicated and involved mechanical, electrical, or other engineering problems.

3. Factor No. 3—Initiative and Judgment. This factor appraises the independent action, exercise of judgment, the making of decisions, or the amount of planning which the job requires. This factor also appraises the degree of complexity of the work.

Points

14	*1st Degree.* Requires the ability to understand and follow simple instructions and the use of simple equipment involving very little independent thinking, since the employee is told exactly what to do.
28	*2nd Degree.* Requires the ability to work from detailed instructions and the making of minor decisions, involving the use of some judgment.
42	*3rd Degree.* Requires the ability to plan and perform a sequence of operations where standard or recognized operation methods are available, and the making of general decisions as to quality, tolerances, operation, and set-up sequences.
56	*4th Degree.* Requires the ability to plan and perform unusual and difficult work where only general methods are available, and the making of decisions involving the use of considerable ingenuity, initiative, and judgment.
70	*5th Degree.* Requires outstanding ability to work independently toward general results, devise new methods, meet new conditions necessitating a high degree of ingenuity, initiative, and judgment on very involved and complex jobs.

4. Factor No. 4—Physical Effort. Appraisal of the muscular exertion required by the job for the performance of a fair day's work. We selected the level which best describes the average degree of muscular exertion rquired throughout the shift.

Points	
8	*1st Degree.* Minimum physical exertion. Perform very light work such as sitting or standing for purposes of observations, and such work as very light assembly and adjustment. Plan and direct work. Weight and record.
16	*2nd Degree.* Light physical exertion. Use light hand tools and handle fairly light materials manually. Operate crane-type controls. Operate truck or tractor. Sweep, clean up.
24	*3rd Degree.* Moderate physical exertion. Handle medium-weight materials. Use a variety of medium-sized hand tools for performing tradesman's work. Climb and work from ladders. Operate heavy controls and valves.
32	*4th Degree.* Heavy physical exertion. Use heavy hand tools and handle heavy materials manually. Move heavy material. Operate heavy pneumatic tools.
40	*5th Degree.* Extreme physical effort. Extremely heavy lifting, pushing, or pulling.

5. Factor No. 5—Mental or Visual Effort. Consideration was given to the mental or visual concentration and attention required by the job for the performance of a fair day's work. We selected the level which best describes the average degree of concentration and attention required throughout the shift.

Points	
6	*1st Degree.* Minimum mental application required for performing highly routine, simple, rough, or closely directed work. Walk, clean up, use simple tools for rough work, handle crude materials, operate simple controls not requiring adjustment. Manually handle product off or on processing unit where little coordination with others or process is required.
12	*2nd Degree.* Light mental or visual application required for performing work where there is some variety, but actions to be taken and decisions made are limited to few possibilities. Work requiring some coordination with others or process. Set up, regulate, adjust simple machines and processes; weigh and count product, record data; ordinary crane hooking. Do simple trades work, such as concrete finishing, connecting pipe, simple torch cutting, or routine lubrication.
18	*3rd Degree.* Moderate mental or visual application required for performing manual work, machine operations, set ups, inspection and adjustments which require frequent decisions to detect and adjust for variance from proper operation. Operate cranes and tractors in congested areas or involving considerable variety of movement. Perform tradesman's duties not involving close tolerances.
24	*4th Degree.* Close mental or visual application required for performing tradesman's work involving close tolerances, or controlling machines and processes at rapid pace requiring close coordination or fine adjustment.

30   Plan or direct fairly complex work methods or operations, which control size, shape, or physical qualities of product. *5th Degree.* High mental application required for planning difficult work methods and sequences to obtain size, shape, or physical qualities of product. Extremely close visual attention to make fine adjustments required to control high speed operations, or to exercise very precise muscular control.

6. Factor No. 6—Responsibility for Equipment. This factor was used to appraise the obligation imposed on the workman for attention and care to prevent damage to the equipment used in the performance of the job. Consideration of the probable amount of damage resulting from carelessness in handling set-up operation, etc., for any one mishap. Losses which are possible but highly improbable, or losses inherent in the nature of the job and beyond the control of the employee, were not included. Equipment is defined as machines, tools, gages, test sets, etc., used in the performance of work. Equipment which is used on the job which is damaged due to collision or similar accident was considered.

Points

10	*1st Degree.* Probable damage to equipment is negligible.
20	*2nd Degree.* Probable damage to equipment is seldom over $100.
30	*3rd Degree.* Probable damage to equipment is seldom over $750.
40	*4th Degree.* Probable damage to equipment is seldom over $3000.
50	*5th Degree.* Probable damage exceedingly high, reaching several thousand dollars.

7. Factor No. 7—Responsibility for Material or Product. This factor appraises the responsibility for preventing waste or loss of raw material or partially finished product through carelessness. Consideration was given to the probable number of pieces which may be spoiled before detection and correction in any one lot or run, the value of the material and labor, the possibility of salvage. Do not use either maximum or minimum, but an average based on normal expectation.

Losses possible but highly improbable, or inherent in the job and beyond control of the employee, were not considered.

Material is that which was actually worked on. It was not always a product.

Points

8	*1st Degree.* Probable loss due to damage or scrapping of materials or product is seldom over $25.
16	*2nd Degree.* Probable loss due to damage or scrapping of materials or product is seldom over $250.
24	*3rd Degree.* Probable loss due to damage or scrapping of materials or product is seldom over $500.
32	*4th Degree.* Probable loss due to damage or scrapping of materials or product is seldom over $1000.
40	*5th Degree.* Probable loss of material which may be damaged or scrapped is very high, up to several thousand dollars.

382

8. Factor No. 8—Responsibility for Operations. This factor appraised the responsibility for utilizing capacity of equipment or process by maintenance of work pace and/or machine speeds. It also includes planning, instructing and directing the work of others. Consideration was given to the crew size and team work required, the importance and size of equipment and the degree of control exercised.

Points	
8	*1st Degree.* Primarily responsible for own work. Little or no responsibility beyond utilization of own time. May work as a gang member or closely directed simple work. Minimum amount of coordination with other personnel or operations.
16	*2nd Degree.* Responsible for coordinating with one or two own members 50 percent or more of the time performing simple routine work. Operation involved seldom controls production rates.
24	*3rd Degree.* Responsible for instructing, directing, setting up for, and maintaining the flow for a production center involving one or two helpers. Operation has relatively small effect on plant production.
32	*4th Degree.* Directing a major production center involving a maximum of five helpers. Operation has major effect on departmental production. May direct smaller group having major effect on plant production.
40	*5th Degree.* Directing a major production center involving six or more helpers. Operation has major effect on plant production.

9. Factor No. 9—Responsibility for Safety of Others. Consider, careless operation of machine or handling of materials or tools by the employees on the job being rated which may result in injury to others. Accordingly, this factor appraises (1) the care which must be exercised to prevent injury to others, and (2) the probable extent of such injury. (Injury to the employee on the job being rated is to be considered under job conditions and unavoidable hazards.)

Points	
6	*1st Degree.* Little responsibility for safety of others. Job performed in an isolated location, or where there is no machine involved and the material is very light.
12	*2nd Degree.* Only reasonable care with respect to own work necessary to prevent injury to others, and accidents, if they should occur, would be minor in nature.
18	*3rd Degree.* Considerable care and attention required to prevent lost-time accidents to others.
24	*4th Degree.* Constant care necessary to prevent serious injury to others, due to inherent hazards of the job, but where such other employees may act to prevent being injured.
30	*5th Degree.* Safety of others depends entirely on correct action of employee on job being rated and carelessness may result in fatal accidents to others.

10. Factor No. 10—Job Conditions and Unavoidable Hazards. This factor appraised the surroundings or physical conditions under which the

job was performed and the extent to which those conditions made the job disagreeable. It also appraised the hazards, to both accident and health, connected with or surrounding the job.

Points	
10	*1st Degree.* Ideal working conditions, complete absence of any disagreeable elements. Accident or health hazards negligible.
20	*2nd Degree.* Good working conditions, may be slightly dirty and have some exposure to accidents. May involve occasional exposure to dust, dirt, heat, fumes, cold, noise, etc. May involve exposure to accidents largely limited to cuts, bruises, or abrasions that can usually be treated adequately through first aid.
30	*3rd Degree.* Somewhat disagreeable working conditions due to exposure to one or more of the elements listed above, but where these elements are not continuous, if several are present. It may involve exposure to lost time accidents, such as crushed hands or feet, loss of fingers, eye injuries from flying particles. Some exposure to occupational disease, not incapacitating in nature.
40	*4th Degree.* Continuous exposure to several disagreeable elements or to one element which is particularly disagreeable and may involve exposure to an incapacitating accident or health hazards, such as loss of arm or leg, impairment of vision, etc.
50	*5th Degree.* Continuous and intensive exposure to several extremely disagreeable elements. Also may involve exposure to accidents or occupational disease which may result in total disability or death.

II. Data Collected

A. Job Descriptions
1. Job Number 1—Coil Line Operator
   Incumbent's duty is to operate the automatic coil tin-plate cutting machine, which entails the following specific tasks:
   a. Perform prestart checkup.
   b. Place coil on machine.
   c. Feed coil to cutting die.
   d. Transfer automated systems after manual check.
   e. Monitor machine functions.
   f. Prepare daily production report.
   g. Alter processes to meet various cutting die requirements.
2. Job Number 2—Oven Coater Operator
   Duty of this position is to operate the tin-plate coating machine which feeds the automatic oven. This is broken down into the following tasks:
   a. Perform prestart checkup.
   b. Check lacquer.
      (1) For thickness.
      (2) For temperature.
      (3) For molecular structure.
   c. Feed cut plate into coater.
   d. Begin manual process and change to automatic system.
   e. Make quality control inspection.

f. Change coater rolls as needed.

g. Perform minor maintenance on coater.

3. Job Number 3—Scroll Shear Operator

This job is to operate scroll shear machine used in cutting tin plate in the end manufacturing process and consists of the following:

a. To perform prestart checkup.

b. Begin initial process machine.

c. Switch to automated program.

d. Lift cut scroll plate off of machine and place on finished product cart.

e. Perform minor maintenance and adjustment on equipment.

f. Proper attention must be given to all safety procedures due to hazardous nature of job.

4. Job Number 4—Coiled Steel Lift Truck Operator

Duties are to provide the means of moving coiled steel in the various stages of production. The specific tasks of this position are outlined below:

a. Operate heavy-duty 40,000-lb.-capacity lift truck.

b. Unload rail shipments of coiled steel.

c. Mark each coil with its coil number and base boxes.

d. Move coil steel from unloading dock to an assigned inventory location.

e. Move coil from inventory to coil line.

f. Maintain operating log on lift truck.

5. Job Number 5—Five Compartment Press Operator

Duties of encumbent are to operate a five compartment aluminum T.V. press, as described by the following tasks:

a. Turn on power and air switches.

b. Perform prestart checklist.

c. Place coil of aluminum on input feeder.

d. Load the aluminum foil into press.

e. Start press and switch into automatic operation.

f. Pull dennison tag and put in accounting box.

g. Perform minor maintenance on press.

6. Job Number 6—Can Line Attendant

Incumbent of this position monitors the automatic can transfer line by performing the following functions:

a. Check can line to insure that feeder lines are clear.

b. Monitor feeder lines after can manufacturing starts.

c. React to automatic alarm system on feeder line.

(1) Remove defective cans responsible for line jam.

(2) Direct process to secondary line if necessary.

d. Make periodic adjustments on can feeder line.

7. Job Number 7—Aluminum Tray Inspector and Packer

To inspect and pack into shipping containers the output from the T.V. Tray Operation, the job consists of

a. Pull samples of finished trays from the production lines.

b. Check samples for correct die imprint.

c. Check sample for cracks.

d. Pack finished trays into shipping containers.

B. Job Evaluation Data

1. Job number 1—coil line operator

Factor	Degree	Points
1. Experience	4th	64
2. Education and trade knowledge	5th	70
3. Initiative and judgment	5th	70
4. Physical effort	2nd	16
5. Mental or visual effort	5th	70
6. Responsibility for equipment	5th	50
7. Responsibility for material or product	5th	40
8. Responsibility for operations	4th	32
9. Responsibility for safety of others	5th	30
10. Job conditions and unavoidable hazards	2nd	20
Total points		422

2. Job number 2—oven coater operator

Factor	Degree	Points
1. Experience	3rd	48
2. Education and trade knowledge	3rd	42
3. Initiative and judgment	3rd	42
4. Physical effort	3rd	24
5. Mental or visual effort	4th	24
6. Responsibility for equipment	5th	50
7. Responsibility for material or product	5th	40
8. Responsibility for operations	3rd	24
9. Responsibility for safety of others	4th	24
10. Job conditions and unavoidable hazards	3rd	30
Total points		324

3. Job number 3—scroll shear operator

Factor	Degree	Points
1. Experience	2nd	32
2. Education and trade knowledge	3rd	42
3. Initiative and judgment	3rd	42
4. Physical effort	3rd	24
5. Mental or visual effort	4th	24
6. Responsibility for equipment	4th	40
7. Responsibility for material or product	2nd	16
8. Responsibility for operations	3rd	24
9. Responsibility for safety of others	4th	24
10. Job conditions and unavoidable hazards	4th	40
Total points		308

4. Job number 4—coiled steel lift truck operator

Factor	Degree	Points
1. Experience	2nd	32
2. Education and trade knowledge	2nd	28
3. Initiative and judgment	3rd	42

4. Physical effort	2nd	16
5. Mental or visual effort	2nd	12
6. Responsibility for equipment	4th	40
7. Responsibility for material or product	4th	32
8. Responsibility for operations	2nd	16
9. Responsibility for safety of others	5th	30
10. Job conditions and unavoidable hazards	3rd	30
Total points		278

5. Job number 5—five compartment press operator

Factor	Degree	Points
1. Experience	2nd	32
2. Education and trade knowledge	2nd	28
3. Initiative and judgment	2nd	28
4. Physical effort	2nd	16
5. Mental or visual effort	3rd	18
6. Responsibility for equipment	5th	50
7. Responsibility for material or product	2nd	16
8. Responsibility for operations	1st	8
9. Responsibility for safety of others	5th	30
10. Job conditions and unavoidable hazards	5th	50
Total points		276

6. Job number 6—can line attendant

Factor	Degree	Points
1. Experience	1st	16
2. Education and trade knowledge	1st	14
3. Initiative and judgment	2nd	28
4. Physical effort	1st	8
5. Mental or visual effort	1st	6
6. Responsibility for equipment	5th	50
7. Responsibility for material or product	2nd	16
8. Responsibility for operations	1st	8
9. Responsibility for safety of others	2nd	12
10. Job conditions and unavoidable hazards	2nd	20
Total points		180

7. Job number 7—aluminum tray inspector and packer

Factor	Degree	Points
1. Experience	1st	16
2. Education and trade knowledge	2nd	28
3. Initiative and judgment	1st	14
4. Physical effort	1st	8
5. Mental or visual effort	1st	6
6. Responsibility for equipment	1st	10
7. Responsibility for material or product	1st	8
8. Responsibility for operations	1st	8
9. Responsibility for safety of others	2nd	12
10. Job conditions and unavoidable hazards	5th	50
Total points		160

C. Job Rating Sheet

Job rating sheet

Points	100–188	188–218	218–248	248–278	278–308	308–338	338–368	368–398	398–428	428–458	458–488	Wage Rate
Job Class	1	2	3	4	5	6	7	8	9	10	11	
	St											2.10
	1	St										2.18
	2	1										2.26
	3	2	St									2.36
	4	3	1									2.46
	5	4	2									2.50
	6	5	3	St								2.58
		6	4	1								2.66
		7	5	2								2.70
			6	3								2.82
			7	4	St							2.90
			8	5	1							2.96
				6	2							3.09
				7	3							3.14
				8	4	St						3.23
					5	1						3.30
					6	2						3.38
					7	3						3.46
					8	4	St					3.54
						5	1					3.62
						6	2					3.70
						7	3					3.78
						8	4	St				3.86
							5	1				3.94
							6	2				4.02
							7	3				4.10
							8	4	St			4.18

Appendix 2

Give Your Men a Faster Start
Make Job Goals Fit the Man
Ways to Handle Office Clashes
Find the Pivot Man

From: *Managing Your People,* 4th Edition, Nation's Business, Washington, D.C.

GIVE YOUR MEN A FASTER START
Nathaniel Stewart

Each time a man moves to a position of greater responsibility in business, the move represents a company's investment in his potential. It is a vote of confidence, an expression of belief that he can make the grade.

No matter what selection test scores show or what a man's personnel card reveals, a new manager—whether an outsider or an insider moving up—constitutes a risk.

You want him to make good.

The absolute necessity of seeing to it that new men do make good is reflected in the comments of many executives who have studied the problem at close range.

Typical of these is the following observation by Tom N. Sewell, personnel manager of the Texas Power & Light Company:

"We know of instances where lack of adequate orientation resulted in serious damage to the new man, his employes, and the company. We're determined to guard against any repeat of such instances."

An important first step to assure a new man's success is proper orientation. The conventional formalities of introducing the man to the organizational chart, his office location, his secretarial services, the executive dining room, parking facilities, some of his key associates and the whole gamut of personnel department requirements may be necessary—but they are not enough.

The company that wants to help a new man to quick adjustment and early productivity must understand three things:

• Why orientation is necessary.
• Who should conduct the orientation.
• What it should include.

The problem of orientation must be faced even in companies which advocate that every manager train his successor. There is a difference between sitting in the number one chair and in the number two chair in a division or a department.

There are changes in responsibilities, mental skills to be used, the use of executive time and effort, realignment of relationships, and the nature of teamwork at the new level.

Good coaching of subordinates by their superiors is a real asset in easing the transition to the new job, but the man still has to form his own perspective and call the shots as he sees them in getting on top of the new job. Moreover, in striving for achievement, new managers will try to make their own jobs as they see the need.

In an insurance company a recently promoted middle manager was regarded as a bust after the first month in his new post. The company expected him to produce new ideas, build more discipline into his unit, and project a plan to accommodate a new insurance program.

Unfortunately, the company did not alert him to the heavy backlog of work which he was to inherit.

The former department head had left much undone. There were unfilled commitments, an overflowing in-basket, a difficult grievance case scheduled for hearings.

The new man needed a month just to clear his predecessor's desk, handle pending matters and crash requests, and bring about some semblance of order before turning to other ventures.

In another case a manager in a real estate firm was severely criticized for missing the regular Friday morning staff meetings.

In his orientation, however, he had been informed that only the Tuesday meeting was essential and that attendance on Friday was optional. The fact was that all managers at his level were expected to attend both meetings. It was a long time before he recovered from the criticism he received.

Let's take a close look at the elements of effective orientation.

Why Orientation Is Important

Good orientation is particularly important for men in the middle management ranks, where even marginal performance can wreck careers.

Regardless of past performance or professional competence, the new man lacks a sense of belonging and is insecure to some degree. Dr. Alan McLean, a consultant in industrial psychiatry, has observed that the new man is in a position of isolation and emotional discomfort. He tends to seek a confidant in the company, someone secure in his own position and a person of integrity. But this is no substitute for effective induction. We must enable the man to get over any defensiveness or indecision. We must help him feel completely at home as boss of his unit.

It is also important to put the brakes on a new man tempted to charge ahead in order to make a good impression. Good orientation will tend to counteract this tendency.

Manager orientation is also important because a new man has an unusual psychological readiness to learn.

The director of training at Eastman Kodak Company notes these psychological conditions facing the new man: He is uneasy and sometimes downright scared; he is eager to learn; he wants to succeed. This kind of setting provides an excellent basis for effective learning through well planned orientation.

For the company, taking a new man on board provides a strategic occasion to take stock of the status of the unit he is to lead. Changing managers offers an opportunity to change departmental habits that result in wheel-spinning, dissipation of energy, unproductive time and effort, and even serious misunderstandings. It may also uncover envy or resentment among some of the man's new associates who may feel that they were passed over and thus may subtly sabotage his efforts.

It is also understandable that a company wants to get moving fast when the new man arrives, especially after the time lag incurred in recruiting or delay in transferring the man when he comes from within the organization. Investment of a little more time at the point of entry will save time and money later in correcting maladjustments in relationships and preventing boners on the job.

Who Should Handle Orientation

Orientation is primarily the job of the line official who had the final voice in selecting the new manager and the boss for whom he will work. These two should be expected to put aside sufficient time for face-to-face sessions with the man as well as to monitor his induction. This task cannot be palmed off on the management training director or the personnel department. The training director should later include the new man in the company's management training program, but this is another responsibility entirely.

To the extent that other parties get into the act—the former incumbent who may still be around or the assistant who held the fort during this transition—the new manager must be perceptive in determining how much of what they tell him is objective and how much personalized and opinionated.

The two men chiefly responsible should be willing to talk straight about past performance of the department, organizational planning under way, budgetary support, people and their relationships, pending policies and decisions which may affect the department. If a management consultant has looked over the company in recent years, pertinent information from this survey should be passed on.

Beneficial suggestions which have been put in cold storage should be brought to his attention. Appropriate reports, agenda and minutes of staff meetings, special documents of interest should be made available.

Within bounds of propriety, the company can expose certain confidential documents to the next man.

The briefing should be candid and deep enough to enable the new man to come away with a clear understanding of the set-up—almost as though he had researched in advance the company and department he was to join.

What to Cover

Dangers of overlooking important details will be lessened if those handling the orientation divide their presentation into three steps:

The big picture: This presents the company's objectives, plans, and expectations. It should portray the corporate sense of values, the public relations image as seen by outsiders, and the internal image of the organization.

It should provide a perceptive presentation of the company's present and potential product lines, the nature of the competition in the industry, the progress in research and development (if this is applicable), the company's profit position and what is needed to improve it.

It should also focus on shifting objectives, anticipated changes, and related matters. In summary, it should enable him to get the feel of the pulse of top management and how it views the company's future.

The operational picture: This concerns the setting in which the new manager will operate, have access to information, statistical data, and other resources, make decisions, sell ideas, consult with others, meet his own responsibilities, and contribute to the team effort.

The important questions of coordination and interoffice relations must be covered. His areas of responsibility should be spelled out, along with standards of performance, work plans and their completion, and how his progress is reviewed.

This is also the time to cover delegation—its extent and to whom.

In addition, it provides the framework of both the formal and the informal organization and their respective influence. Other information should relate to special problems of supervision, relationships with associates, and the status of morale and productivity of his unit.

The personal picture: Basically, this involves a frank and helpful presentation of how the man can grow on the job, avoid dead-ending, and measure up to the demands of his position in a way which will reflect well upon him.

Here attention is given to what the man can do himself to make an effective transition from his former job to the new one, ways to bolster his self-confidence, pointers on how to use his time effectively so that he can meet priorities and deadlines.

It provides the basis for discussion and counsel on how to deal with conflicts and pressures.

A good presentation or discussion should try to show how the new man can best measure up to the standards expected of him and also derive some enjoyment out of the new position. He should be cautioned that, while he may have overcome certain blind spots in his former job, he may develop new ones now. He should be advised how to counteract the new hazards. Moreover, some attention should be given to how he can find time to think—about the job, about improving relationships, about management improvement, and about innovations in his department or division. Particularly vital is letting him know where he can get more counsel and guidance if and when he needs it.

Throughout the orientation effort, there will obviously be some difference between the new man from the outside and the man promoted from within. However, this will be largely a matter of degree, allocation of time, and intensity. But the main essentials of the balanced presentation and the follow-up should apply more or less equally to both.

In essence, the orientation should indicate what the company can do for him and, more important, what he can do for the company.

How long should orientation take? It is not a matter of time so much as the extent to which it is well planned, intensive, unhurried and covers the important ingredients. After all, orientation has to be regarded as a kind of manager training, highly personalized and crucial to the interest of the company and the man.

A positive program, too, should have an element of follow-up. There should be some provision for keeping in close touch with the new man to determine how things are going, keeping posted on how his staff meetings are coming along, and where the boss or the company can help.

Review of the administrative manual may be necessary because of complex situations facing the new manager's department. Some mental index should be made of his mistakes and their consequences, as well as how speedily the mistakes are undone to the extent practicable. Controls on his performance should be relaxed at first but tightened up as he gains experience.

For all this, there is still much that the new manager will have to discover for himself. This is his task and has to be the product of his observations and judgment. Among the things he may have to smoke out for himself, once on the job, are such matters as crossing of lines of authority, the influence of one-boss rule and the legacy it leaves, the problem employes, backlogs of work not readily visible, deadwood, provincialism, hero worship of the former boss, inbreeding, line and staff rivalries, and communication breakdowns.

He will have to spot instances of mediocre men handling too many responsibilities, span of control which may be too wide and unmanageable, and supervisors too much absorbed in details which should be left to technicians and clerks.

He will be dominated by the question, "What's the set-up here?"

He may find few or none of these problems, the whole set-up may be favorable, and he may be blessed in inheriting a good situation from his predecessor. In a well managed company this will often occur. But the probing and stock-taking must nevertheless be done.

MAKE JOB GOALS FIT THE MAN
W. D. Schoenbeck

This happens to every man who manages others:

You assign a man to do a job. You think it will take him approximately four hours. Nearly four hours later you find that it is only half done. Further, you find that he has made several mistakes.

What are you going to do? And why?

In reality you cannot answer these questions until you know more about the situation. For example:

Was this the first time he had done this job?

Did he have the right tools?

Did he encounter unexpected obstacles and delays?

Were your instructions clear?

Is this a typical performance for him?

This simple illustration points up the fact that a manager must adjust his standard of performance as the facts in the situation vary.

In this case, if the man had been hired recently, you would make allowance for his newness. If he had run into unavoidable problems, you would accept this performance. If this were the only case in which he failed to measure up, you would take his record into account.

One cannot supervise long—indeed, it is not necessary to supervise at all—before realizing that you cannot expect an inherently less capable employe to match the results of your best worker; nor can you apply the same yardstick of performance.

Experience is another variable that calls for a standard that varies from person to person. Health, age, sex, physical condition and other factors must be taken into account.

Situations also vary. Some work must be done in unfavorable conditions; other work is done under ideal conditions. Some work is done with exactly the right tools and equipment; other work requires improvisation. Some actions can be planned in advance; others are taken on an emergency basis.

Some assignments are new; others are routine. Some are unusual and involve a strong element of safety; others can be done automatically, almost without thought. Some assignments take weeks to complete; others are done in a matter of minutes.

Obviously you cannot apply the same fixed standard to people and assignments that vary so greatly.

To set a firm standard geared to your best worker means that only one person measures up. To set a standard at the level of your poorest worker means that everyone else is above standard. To set an arbitrary standard somewhere in between may mean that some of your men can achieve standard without half trying, while others struggle mightily to make it. These applications of a rigid standard frequently have adverse effects on the employes. Men who exceed the standard with little effort often reduce the effort; and the men who strain to do what is expected often buckle under the strain.

What is needed then is a standard that is flexible and fair.

Some may ask: Is it fair to expect more from one person than another? Actually, it is unfair not to do so. The range of abilities is great, in unskilled and skilled jobs alike. And there are so many other variables that a flexible standard is the only thing that can be fair to all.

The most realistic, practical standard of an employe's performance is the ratio: Does Do/Could Do.

How the Ratio Works

On an individual basis, this relates the employe's actual performance, the Does Do, to his potential performance, the Could Do. On a group basis, it relates the actual performance of the group to the potential capability of its members. This provides a dynamic standard that responds to the many variables that bear on specific work performance. It enables each employe to be appraised in terms of his own attitude, abilities, and effort and the conditions which affect his work.

To use this standard you must: 1, know what each of your men is capable of doing; 2, observe how well each is performing up to his ability.

A logical question concerning a variable standard is: Are there no minimums? If everyone's performance is measured in personal and variable terms does this mean that any performance can be considered acceptable?

The answer is: No.

There are reasonable expectations for each employe in specific circumstances, and if he does not measure up, something must be done.

Two instances in which an employe's performance is not satisfactory are:

1. When his Could Do—his demonstrated or potential ability—is not enough.
2. When his Does Do—his actual performance—falls unduly below his otherwise acceptable Could Do.

Let's apply this standard to the illustration. If, for example, the employe could not do more than half the work expected of him with the proper training, tools, and instruction, he is unacceptaable on the particular job.

On the other hand, if he could have done the whole job as expected, but did not do so, another course of action is suggested.

The gap that exists between what an employe Does Do and what he Coud Do is one you must analyze specifically for each employe. You need to know:

1. Why does the gap exist for this particular employe?
2. When did it start to develop?
3. Has it existed long?
4. How big is it now?
5. Is it getting larger or smaller?
6. What effect is it having on group productivity and morale?
7. Is the employe aware of it?

Answers to these questions will guide your measurement of the individual's performance and indicate what corrective action is needed.

Why does the gap exist? It is impossible for an employe to work up to 100 per cent of his capacity 100 per cent of his working hours. Individuals have an optimum pace which is best for them. This varies widely, and you need to know what you can expect of each man. A small gap between an employe's optimum rate, Does Do, and his top rate, Could Do, is not a major concern. The gap that needs close scrutiny is the one that exceeds reasonable expectations for that individual. When such a gap exists, you need to learn why.

When did it start? If you can determine when the gap became unreasonable, you will be in a better position to analyze it. It is natural, of course, for a new man's Does Do to fall well below his Could Do. In some cases, advancing age may become a factor. In between these extremes, however, are innumerable starting points for let down of performance. The specific starting time, in many cases, may hold the key to the solution of the problem.

Has it existed long? Correcting bad habits is not easy, particularly if the habits are of long standing. So, from a remedial viewpoint, it is better if the gap in an employe's performance has not been allowed to exist very long. Early observation is a big help. Furthermore, if an employe realizes himself that he is performing his behavior, he will not be so responsive to your suggestions for improvement. If a standard is lowered, knowingly or unknowingly, and is allowed to operate at that level for some time, it may become the accepted standard.

How big is it? A gap that has been permitted to grow and grow has gotten out of control. It may be difficult, now, for the employe to regain the level he once Could Do, even if you point out that what he Does Do must improve. It is important to know just what you can expect of each man, and not to allow a gap to overdevelop.

Is it getting larger or smaller? It is important to know if the gap is expanding or contracting. Is this a steady process in the right direction or wrong direction? What is the likelihood of complete recovery or ultimate failure?

Effect on group? Frequently, a group will carry a substandard performer. This is true, particularly, if the employe is well liked or if other factors are going for him. However, when the man's inadequate performance hurts them, or if he is unpopular, the group may resent him. If a group gives up on an incompetent associate, it is clear that you have been overly tolerant—that you have permitted your standard to slip from your grasp.

It may indicate that you have adjusted your standard downward for a marginal employe without taking all the effects fully into account.

Is employe aware? Have you called it to his attention? Could he, otherwise, assume that he was doing his share?

Using the Formula

The Does Do/Could Do ratio is realistic in that it permits adjustment of standards to varying circumstances. It is idealistic in that it appraises a man in terms of his own capability, experience, qualifications, and attitude. It is practical, because it makes sense that a supervisor should have flexibility built into his standard.

Using the Does Do/Could Do ratio means using personal supervision. It means giving individual consideration to individual employes; and this is the way to bring out the best in people.

The more the numerator, Does Do, approaches the denominator, Could Do, the closer a person's performance approaches his potential;

and as one potential level is attained, the horizon of a new one often appears. This is significant in all walks of life, because our society is in need of people who give their best, and who are not willing to settle for less.

WAYS TO HANDLE OFFICE CLASHES
George S. Odiorne

Effective managers recognize that personal conflict is unavoidable in even the best run business. So they learn how to deal with conflicts.

Some conflicts can be spotted before they erupt—and headed off with judicious application of a few principles of good human relations. In other cases, the storm breaks without warning and the executive's responsibility is to keep its destructive effects to a minimum.

It's not surprising that conflicts exist in business. Our economic system is competitive. This means competition between firms, between small groups, between ambitious individuals who have a desire for promotion, preferred position, or recognition.

In a special and circumscribed way, knowing how to fight in the right way is part of the personal skill the successful manager must—without talking about it—develop if he's going to rise in the organization and keep his company competitive.

There are three basic things you should know about conflicts:

- Why people fight.
- How to be a good referee.
- The rules for business conflict.

Each of these merits close examination.

Why People Fight

Hope of winning rewards or fear of losing something are the most common reasons for personal competition in business.

Take the case of the manager of quality control who found that every time a customer rejected a shipment he caught the blame, even though the manufacturing boss had approved shipment of the defective work.

One day, after a shipment had been returned and the production head had blithely shifted the responsibility, the quality control man was furious. He knew that if the situation continued he would not only suffer personally but the company would lose as well. So he mapped out his plan and dropped his bombs at the right moment. Waiting until he was in the presence of the general manager, he made some pointed accusations, backed by facts. The general manager, who abhorred fighting, got the point and spelled out procedures to prevent a recurrence. Until the fight took place he had let the situation drift.

Another common cause of conflict is the desire to establish one's position. A personnel manager found that many decisions affecting labor relations were being made without his knowledge. Many were contradictory and self-cancelling. He could see that, unless he moved vigorously, the situation would soon be chaotic. The next time the staff was assembled he stood up and reprimanded the whole crowd. Some heated arguments followed. Later, one of his subordinates present summed up: "I guess we were all going off half-cocked until Harry straightened us out—but hard."

Sometimes people fight just to let off steam. This can be either good or bad. Consider a case which backfired in a midwestern company. A number of feuds suddenly developed that took up so much time of important people that they couldn't keep on top of production.

The manager called a dinner meeting to thrash the whole thing out. Several hours of discussion revealed that there really wasn't much basis for the bickering except that they were wearing on one another's nerves and "letting off the pressure on each other," as one of them put it. They agreed to save their complaints for a monthly dinner meeting where they'd air most of them at once, clear the air and get on with the job. In some companies staff meetings are regularly scheduled solely for this purpose.

Still another reason why people squabble is to escape something they can't bear patiently. This may be nothing more than boredom, but more often it's some kind of unpleasantness. In some instances it's continuing evidence of their own inadequacy. The latter causes the most mischief since it's rarely constructive.

How to Referee Business Conflicts

Since experience teaches people how to get things done without a battle, most managers will see fighting from the viewpoint of the third party. This role is somewhat similar to that of a referee. How should a referee act? When and how should he move to settle squabbles? Here are some guides:

Try to foresee a battle. Big conflicts usually follow a series of warning signals. Knowing your people, talking and working with them constantly, and eliminating causes of conflict will prevent most of the blows from falling.

In a large New Jersey factory, the foremen of two departments were constantly quarreling over a lack of mutual cooperation and conflicting actions which made life hard for both. The foreman of assembly complained that the packing foreman wasn't keeping the packing station clear and it was backing up and stopping the assembly line. The packing foreman complained that the assembly people changed labels and models without notifying him in advance, requiring delays in getting proper packing equipment and materials set up.

Charges and countercharges grew louder at staff meetings. Finally, the manager moved in. He switched the men's positions—the assembly foreman was assigned to packing and the packing foreman to assembly. Neither had experience in the other's activity, and soon each was yelling for help. Each man went back to his own department chastened and more appreciative of the other fellow's problems.

Don't take sides before getting the facts. People under emotional stress will always present every angle favorable to them. Realizing this, you, as a referee, must be scrupulous in getting all the facts without bias. You may ultimately have to serve as judge and make a decision, but this should come only after you dig into the root causes of the conflict, deciding what is best for the company. When you've done that, state your judgment in unequivocal terms.

Take the case of the superintendent who was approached by supervisor Bill with a tale about the refusal of supervisor George to release a skilled machinist from his department for a special assignment with Bill.

"All he would say is that he can't do it," Bill reported.

The superintendent immediately called George, dressed him down over the phone and told him to get the desired machinist on his way to the other department pronto.

"I can't do it," the supervisor replied, "as I told Bill, that man has been out with the flu and won't be in for another week."

The abashed superintendent made a hasty retreat.

Sell your decision and stick to it. Having gotten the facts, announce your decision and explain it to both sides. The rightness of the decision and its value to the company should be made clear. Once these steps have been taken, the decision should be firmly held to. The referee who lets players talk him out of a decision is in for plenty of trouble.

Rules for Business Conflict

Just as it is inevitable that hostilities will crop up in the relationships of people under you, it is equally certain that you will find yourself embroiled in conflicts from time to time. How should you act when this happens?

Interviews with old campaigners in business, and observation of some soundly—and some poorly—executed business battles point up a number of useful rules:

Rule 1. Always be reluctant to fight. Since it's part of the folklore of business, especially of the human relations school of management, that conflict of wills is engaged in only by ruffians, an executive should always appear extremely unwilling to fight. If he is forced to defend himself, he should preface it by a remark such as "I didn't want to get into this, but since it was forced on me. . . ."

400

It's wise strategy to master the outward façade which one presents to avoid any display of emotion. Petulance and sullenness are especially bad.

The manager who sulks over getting beaten out of a promotion or an order, or being transferred to the Managua sales office, is sure to arouse clucking disappointment among other managers. People like mature individuals around them, and maturity is most tangibly demonstrated by self-control and a lack of destructiveness.

In business a man must take his licks without complaining, and act as though the outcome were exactly what he wished. He may later tell his wife that he got a rotten deal but around the shop it's unacceptable to sulk.

Losing one's temper is taboo. This means more than abstaining from the mean remark. Anger is easily detected, since it entails a whole series of physiological changes in a man. His breathing increases, blood circulation rises, the face gets flushed, veins distend.

All these signs are apparent to the casual observer and indicate that a man is not in control of himself. In even the most contained individual, such anger may make itself known through reddening of the ears, or fidgeting. This, of course, arms the other person. He can keep a cool head, which never loses when confronted with a hot one. The sophisticated businessman keeps cool.

Rule 2. Keep your values in line. Well intentioned people sometimes slip from their code of ethics under the pressures of combat. The boss who is generally fair in his judgment may be tempted to discriminate or use psychological brass knuckles under stress. This always produces bad results in the long run. In building a business, or a career, the principal values to remember are:

Protect yourself. Don't let the heat of battle cause you to do things which will damage your reputation or make permanent enemies. They may come back to haunt you after you've won the fight at hand.

Protect the company. The only acceptable conflict is one for the good of the firm. Every squabble must be made to take that turn. If it results in damaging the company it will react against the people involved, whether they started it or just fought back.

Protect others. Innocent bystanders may be hit when you throw your javelins. These fallen sparrows of business warfare may be watched over by members of a sort of business bird-lovers association who are quick to rally to their support.

Rule 3. Hard work is the most effective weapon. Better than any other strategy is the open secret of working the other fellow into the ground.

Take the case of two men who were bucking for a vacant vice presidency. The first spent more than he could afford in joining a club where the executives gathered. He met them casually at the bar, and by faint praise and other subtle means sought to undermine his adversary. The other studied, worked, sweated, and produced more. He was a hands-down winner.

Rule 4. Build strong alliances. Despite the competition which exists between executives, some forms of cooperation are required. Attending certain trade association meetings or perhaps joining in a common activity, such as a toastmaster's club, is sound strategy.

Without being pressed to do so, a young sales manager who was ambitious and competitive developed harmonious relations with the plant people. He built a reputation as "one sales guy you can work with." He ultimately moved into the top sales position, and into the assistant general managership. The reason? He could get things done when others couldn't. Furthermore, when he had a real gripe and had to battle the plant, he knew the ropes and could get action more effectively.

Some men feel it's a mistake to look too good in competition. The younger man who looks and acts too much like the top executives may attract the strongest efforts of his associates to sabotage his climb to the top.

In one large firm such a superior-appearing man was moving rapidly through the industrial relations department. He attracted the type of attention which invited his colleagues to feel that "nobody can be that good, let's look for some flaws." When they were found and exposed, he was thrown a few impossible jobs which he flubbed. Then he was routed into a job on the company's charitable foundation from which there was no return.

Rule 5. Work to win, not to kill. Being congenial and helpful toward losers is sound strategy to follow up a victory. The trick is to convince the losers that they lost to a better man, and to convert them into allies. The winner should avoid destroying capable men simply because they fought and lost.

In one company a division manager had been crossed by the corporate training director on several occasions.

Hardly 24 hours after he was elected executive vice president, he stalked into Industrial Relations and ordered the training director fired.

Word of this childish action spread throughout the firm. Several others in staff positions immediately began to look for jobs. When the company attempted to replace the fired man, no reputable professional would accept the job with the firm "which pulled such a dirty trick on Bill X."

Competition in business must end with an amicable settlement, even when one man wins and another clearly loses. Fights and competition are usually disruptive while they are going on, and may result in uneasiness and dissatisfaction among those who have lost or have been close to the encounter. It becomes imperative for the winner to sort out such problems and solve them promptly.

A case in point involved a controller who had acquired a name for being ferocious on costs and rather cold-hearted about people. Eventually he was picked for general manager. He altered his tactics immediately. He asked others' opinions, became tolerant of folly, indulgent of errors that previously would have put him in a rage.

After a few months of this, the others became convinced that "Harry is a new man since he got promoted."

Actually, he still burned to tell people to quit wasting money, but he realized that his first job was to build the team around him before he began calling hard plays for them to execute.

Rule 6. Attack groups with caution. Think carefully before you engage in a clash of wills with many people. When everybody but yourself seems wrong-headed and stubborn, perhaps the logical first step is to ask yourself, "Is it them, or is it me?"

One of the real tests of business squabbling at the higher and middle levels of management is its ultimate effect upon the team. Attacks made simply for effect or to stir up excitement usually don't solve much and disrupt the possible gains from teamwork.

Studies show that people are more productive as a group when they like one another. Simple exercise of restraint and good manners among members of a management team can avert the disruptive effects of divided purpose and prevent factions from springing up.

The kinds of battles in which people line up votes for or against their proposals in management committees may have a serious effect in lost unity. This loss of team effort and willingness to see the other fellow's problems can be much more serious than giving in, even on a point which one holds strongly.

FIND THE PIVOT MAN
Joseph G. Mason

Every company has a few people who wield influence far out of proportion to their vested authority or their actual position on the table of organization. These are the action men—the people who provide leverage points to make the organizational gears mesh and turn. No organization can function without them.

Unless the manager wants to provide all the push himself, he would do well to learn to spot such pivotal types among his subordinates. He can then use them deliberately when he needs such help.

You can usually spot pivot men by their need for action.

They are men or women with the ability to grasp a good idea—either their own or someone else's—and push, pull, coax or coerce it through the company.

If such a person is in a formally recognized supervisory position, chances are he will display the grasp of leadership described by W. E. Zisch, president of Aerojet-General Corp.

"The manager's greatest skill," Mr. Zisch says, "is dealing with persons who are stellar performers in their specialized fields. As such, they are beyond the manager's competence in their individual specialties.

But they are also dependent in large measure for their own success on his ability to weld them into a team whose over-all performance will reflect more credit and satisfaction on each than each could get by himself."

A pivot man, however, often is a person far removed from any claims to authority or leadership. It could, for example, be the girl with the soldering iron, described by William J. Coughlin, who has it in her power to make or break the quality image of even a General Electric or a Westinghouse. If she is the kind of person with an instinctive pride in a job well done, who combines this with the infectious ability to pass on her desire for excellence to the other girls in her section, she may be worth more to the company than a dozen quality control men farther down the production cycle. She is the person who provides the production leverage for that section.

Identifying such people is not always easy. They do not wear big labels saying, "I am a pivot man." Chances are they seldom think of themselves as such. And, unless you are actively searching for signs and symptoms, they can easily be overlooked.

What do you look for? Finding any single characteristic is no guarantee that the person is indeed a real or potential pivot man. But it can be a signal for you to seek out additional characteristics in the individual. Once you locate your own pivotal people, you may be able to open up fresh, if unofficial, channels for action on your ideas or for getting fresh ideas on your current problems.

Two qualities that run through pivot men are curiosity and awareness in their many forms.

The Ready Suggester

Often the most difficult part of solving a problem is simply to get started on it. This is where the type of pivot man you need may be what, for lack of a better term, can be called "the ready suggester." This is the person who, no matter what kind of problem is presented to him, will usually have several suggestions for solving it. These ideas are not always good, or even potentially good, but they can serve to get some action going in an otherwise static situation. Just the necessity to check out the practicality of some of the ideas will often get other people thinking constructively toward what will be the real solution.

The ability to come up with suggestions on various problems, particularly if they have some merit, can also be the tip-off to someone who should be watched for possible promotion to supervisory ranks. The characteristic indicates a certain degree of mental flexibility which is one of the better traits for any supervisor to have. This flexibility gives a person the ability to shift easily from one task to another without becoming upset or irritated. It is also, to some degree, a function of self-confidence—another trait advantageous for a supervisor.

But remember that the search for pivot men is not necessarily a search for the potentially promotable. It is, rather, a search for those people who can help you get action when you need it. And often what you need is a supply of ready ideas—no matter what the rank of the suggester.

The Broadly Knowledgeable

One of the handiest persons to have around in a tight situation is one with a broad range of interests and knowledge—especially when what is called for is a new idea to solve an immediate problem. Because new ideas are usually combinations of old ideas or old ideas in new forms, the person with a breadth of knowledge will usually have a greater potential for producing ideas.

People with a broad degree of knowledge are apt to be especially valuable for supervising others who are also highly competent in their jobs. Professional workers, such as scientists or technicians, are apt to bridle at the so-called professional approach to supervision. They don't respond to anyone who gives the impression of being a supercharged salesman. They will respond to a man whose authority is based on demonstrated knowledge and ability—even to the point of forgiving him some otherwise disagreeable personality characteristics.

Lee A. Iacocca, vice president of Ford Motor Co., emphasizes the importance of both spotting people who have a broad range of knowledge, and taking positive steps to help them broaden that knowledge. "We shift our management people from job to job at planned intervals to give them the broadest possible experience and to maximize the number of areas in which to test their capabilities," he reports. "You'd be surprised how good a salesman you can make of an engineer, or how good a product-planner you can make of a finance man."

A Man with a Memory

A good memory is, of course, important to the acquisition of general knowledge. But frequently, when you need a quick solution to a short-term problem, the type of person who can remember an odd-shaped piece of metal he has in the storage room at just the time such a piece is needed may also be able to remember how a similar problem was handled the last time it occurred. In fact, an "odds and ends" type of memory frequently typifies a mind with a potential for creative solutions to problems.

Gen. Lucius Clay, a director of Continental Can Co., is one who is noted for his memory. According to his associates, he has a photographic memory that enables him to keep track of minute details, and he often confounds them with the things he knows.

Memory alone will not assure that you have spotted a pivot man. But it is one of the key indicators that the person could, under certain circumstances, be the first one to come up with information or help when you need it in a hurry.

The Driver

The quality of drive is a relatively easy one to observe. It shows itself usually by a man's dogged determination to see a job through.

But watch out. Drive, to be constructive, must be coupled with one or more of the other intellectual assets. Persistence may easily be confused with stubbornness or obstinacy—neither of which may be what an executive with a tough job is looking for. The person with well motivated drive can be an excellent pivot man to swing a long-term project or one with multitudinous details to be resolved.

Drive is, moreover, a relative factor. One organization, in a fit of psychological soul-searching, had all supervisory personnel evaluated for various personality characteristics. One man was found to rate very low on the scale of "dominance"—a more formal word for drive. But investigation showed that his was an excellently run department. Further investigation provided the reason: His employees ranked even lower on the dominance scale, and he was, therefore, able to function as an effective leader.

The Deep Thinker

In a world geared to cost-cutting programs, production norms and output minimums, deep thinkers or contemplative types of workers occasionally find the going rather rough. The old humorist's admonition, "Don't think—work," is often applied with serious intent when some worker's attention seems to be off the job in front of him. Yet the naked ability to think and to reason is an important skill for pivot men.

What's important is the quality of thought, and one measurement of the quality of the thinking lies in the nature of subjects being thought about. The late Charles Kettering, of General Motors research fame, once chided a group of industrial editors about their concern for the current events in their industries, rather than for future trends and possibilities.

"You are mostly worried about the seething of current effects," he said. "Now you can't do anything to fix anything today. You had to fix it 10 or 15 years ago. So all of this is just turbulence."

The avoidance of turbulence in favor of constructive endeavor is a measure of the quality of the thinking available to you in a potential pivot man. Even on the production line there are some workers who, without benefit of a college diploma or not even having completed high school, have the intellectual abilities to think and reason constructively. You should know who they are, and learn to motivate them toward thinking about your problems.

The Pace-changer

Many organizational problems stem from the inability of the people charged with solving them to be able to get a fresh, uninhibited look at the over-all situation. This is where the person with the ability to change the pace can be the pivot man either to get the organization moving again, or to accelerate a movement.

An example of such a pace-changer is George Lesch, president and chief executive officer of Colgate Palmolive Co. His background was in accounting, but he made his mark as a man with a distinct flair for the unorthodox. Most of his Colgate record was compiled as an executive of the company's Mexican subsidiary. There, instead of simply copying marketing methods used in the U.S., Mr. Lesch struck out in new directions with such ideas as using sound trucks carrying fetching señoritas called "Miss Colgata" and "Miss Fabuloso Fab" to demonstrate the virtues of the Colgate products in the primitive villages. When Mr. Lesch required an executive vice president, he went outside Colgate and selected a man without any previous experience in the soap and toiletry field, in an effort to get new and pace-changing thinking in the management for the benefit of Colgate.

The Fighter of Routine

Really creative minds resist efforts to restrict and channel their thinking. If the creative urge is strong enough, it will show up in continuing efforts to get in on other jobs, or other problems, or, at the least, to acquire some knowledge of other people's work. This is the first clue you may have of a pivot man.

Sometimes, of course, a refusal to settle down to one type of work or one phase of a job may indicate simply an objection to authority of any kind. This again calls for a judgment to be made both on the motivation behind the routine-bucking and also on the quality of results obtained.

The Creative Skeptic

Often the pivot man turns up with qualities in places you'd least expect.

The mere thought that they should encourage skepticism in any form, for instance, is enough to send many managers into a royal purple funk. Skeptics, they feel, are disloyal, destructive and wasteful in an organization.

But a certain degree of skepticism is the best weapon an organization has against complacency and even irresponsibility.

The key factor, again, is the quality and motivation of the characteristic itself.

The creative, or constructive, skeptic doubts many things—particularly the obvious things that everyone else accepts perhaps too readily. The destructive skeptic has destruction or belittlement as his motivation. The difference can often be distinguished by an adroit question or two. The noncreative skeptic will usually assume that things are going from bad to worse and nothing can be done about it, so why try.

The creative skeptic normally feels that no matter how bad or how wrong something is, it can always be made better. He may even have some ready suggestions for betterment.

Chances are any creative skeptics you identify will have their principal benefits to you in serving as problem bloodhounds or as people who point out new opportunities.

Often opportunities exist to expose such people deliberately to problems they don't normally meet, and to solicit their thinking on these.

Such a chance occurred when Ford Motor Co. bought Philco. Ford's automotive designers were asked for their ideas on how to improve the styling of Philco products. Amid some only half-kidding remarks about "TV sets that look like Thunderbirds," William Balderston, Jr., product planning manager for consumer goods at Philco, asserted that the interchange had "tremendous advantages in terms of fresh ideas."

The Unusually Observant Person

Workers who are alive to what is going on around them can be a source of major irritation to management. They can feed the rumor mill and few secrets escape them. At the same time, if an executive can cultivate such people, they can also be his first warning of something about to go wrong or something that could stand improvement. These people are apt to have what psychologists refer to as problem sensitivity—the ability to crystallize and formalize problems long before anyone else realizes they exist. Lee Atwood, president of North American Aviation Co., points out the value of this trait to his company. "Most of our business," he says, "consists of finding imaginative answers to unheard-of-problems."

It may be that the person in your organization who always knows what's going on can help you spot your unheard-of problems in time to keep them from becoming major.

In applying the pivot man theory within any company, objections can be thought of quite easily. Yet they are usually objections in theory rather than practice. In practice, all the pivotal men are in operation; they act. They often act as the informal and not always recognized fulcrum to get the work out. Learning to recognize these pivot men enables a manager to achieve better results.

Appendix 3

From: *Managing Yourself*, 4th Edition, Nation's Business, Washington, D.C.

HOW TO SELL YOUR IDEAS
Eugene Raudsepp

Millions of dollars arc lost to business every year because many valuable ideas stay locked up in the minds of executives and their subordinates.

Many men can't sell their ideas to the boss. The basis of this may be simply the fear of rebuff, sometimes based on past rejections. It also can be a reluctance to face up to the enormous task of preparing an effective, salable presentation for an idea. Or some men may feel that the extra effort it takes to convince others of the value of an idea is unimportant compared with having conceived it in the first place. They don't seem to realize that ideas must be sold.

Putting an idea into salable shape requires persistent effort. It may demand more work than origination of the idea. In addition, a lot of courage, imagination, foresight, initiative, resourcefulness, and staying power are needed.

A leading management consultant in training and personnel relations, points out: "In many cases, the person you are submitting your idea to will not even realize that there is a need for it. You may have to begin at the beginning and go through the whole reasoning process that you yourself followed."

Presenting a new idea is in many ways one of the most crucial aspects of the creative process. Many a brilliant idea dies stillborn at this stage because the manager fails to communicate his brain child to others persuasively. Here are some guideposts that will increase your chances of success:

In most companies the person who must be sold the new idea first is your immediate superior. Selling it to top management then becomes much easier. Eugene Von Fange suggests that the best way to secure your superior's backing is to "imagine what he believes is important, and then approach him from this vantage point."

If you have to present the idea to a committee, you should try to sell it before the time of the meeting to one or two members. These individuals often appreciate advance confidence and will rally to your side if the going gets rough during the presentation.

Before actually presenting the idea, you should give a short history of the problem, what led you to investigate the area and how you proceeded to solve the problem and create the new idea.

A research associate with a top manufacturer, who has been training industry groups in selling ideas for over a decade, advises:

"Show by your conversation that this idea isn't the first one that's popped into your head. You've thought about the problem and you've made various approaches or made refinements until you're satisfied you've got something worthwhile. The purpose of this advice is to build up status so that when you open your mouth, something worth while happens. The person who goes off half-cocked continuously may be fine to stimulate others around him in an idea session, but when you're ready to 'sell' an idea, demonstrate that you've thought it through."

He emphasizes the need for utmost clarity in the presentation. "Remember, if you have an idea, it is a thing you have worked with for some time. It's clear in your mind but may not be clear to anyone else. It embarrasses a 'buyer' to be told of an idea that he just can't make heads or tails out of; he is resentful."

Don't get overly anxious in anticipating rejection. This can spoil your presentation. On the other hand, you should be prepared to explain the reasoning you used to arrive at it.

The presentation should be made as concise as possible. People get impatient with long-winded preliminaries.

You should be sure, however, that you cover all the pertinent facts.

Mr. Von Fange cautions: "When speaking to a manager, remember that if there is one bother in his life, it is the man who rambles for half an hour on something that could be said in 20 words." He further notes that there is "a curious and widespread tendency to surround proposals or requests with so many commentaries that the request itself can hardly be discerned."

In situations where the audience includes one or several professional people, you'll need to include counterarguments to your idea and discuss these also. This two-sided approach will help you convince the more sophisticated persons of your thoroughness.

The two-sided approach has additional advantages, especially in taking the wind out of objections and arguments that might arise later.

"This approach is superior with those who initially disagree with you because it disarms the objections which they are mentally rehearsing while receiving your message. It is dangerous to assume that arguments favoring the other side will do no harm if left unvoiced. If your audience has these arguments in mind, it is better to bring them out where they can be dealt with," says Prof. James N. Mosel of The George Washington University.

Don't Go Too Fast

The presentation of the new material should be delivered no faster than it can be understood and absorbed. Clear and lucid language is absolutely necessary. Take special care to eliminate trade jargon unless the people who are listening are equally at home with such language.

E. J. DeWitt, president of Wallace Supplies Manufacturing Company, feels that most failures are attributable to the tendency to use specialized language.

"We have had tape recordings of engineers trying to tell management what would be management's gain if engineers' recommendations were to be followed. Reruns of these tapes have been most instructive. Time after time verbal impasses developed. Time after time restudy showed a bogging down over a technical phrase in a layman's discussion. . . .

Most people—engineers included—tend to talk with their everyday vocabularies. Unfortunately, the vocabulary of the specializing engineer is not one with which most laymen will be comfortable."

Arguments answering objections or criticisms should be well prepared, but it's a good idea not to offer them before they are actually needed. An argumentative approach creates the impression of unnecessary defensiveness. It may change the entire feeling or attitudes of the people who are listening.

Says a Harvard University professor, "A man who goes into his job with the conviction that people are going to resist any idea he presents with blind stubbornness is likely to find them responding just the way he thinks they will. The process is clear: Whenever he treats the people who are supposed to buy his ideas as if they were bullheaded, he changes the way they are used to being treated and they will be bullheaded."

Special attention has to be paid to the practical details of the idea, how it can be carried out. Mr. Von Fange advises, "We should avoid any rash tendency to attempt to sell our ideas before we have a definite plan and program to support it. For management very generally, and very properly, will refuse to approve any proposed undertaking that is not well planned with regard to its execution." The advantages, as well as the costs and difficulties involved, should also be pointed out. Nothing kills the survival chances of a new idea faster than a purely technical or abstract way of presenting it.

When selling an idea to top management, remember that a strong dollars and cents case must be made. The possible savings potentials or profit potentials and primary selling features should be demonstrated and the presentation should include plenty of "business benefits to us" and not solely "how it works."

People are notoriously poor visualizers, especially when it concerns something unfamiliar. Therefore, whenever possible, it's a good idea to augment your verbal presentation with sketches and charts. Verbal descriptions sometimes are boring and, especially with new ideas, often aren't clear.

When you present an idea your reputation and good judgment are tested. If the idea or presentation is inadequate, it will affect your future in the company and make any future selling of ideas even more difficult. The image your boss has of you is highly important in getting your idea accepted. If you have a reputation for trustworthiness and expertness, it will be easier to sell your idea.

Use the Soft Sell

Overselling should be avoided. While enthusiasm can be contagious, a superabundance, especially at the beginning of the presentation, will put people on the defensive.

"It is easy to get too enthusiastic about an idea, especially if it is your

412

own," another consultant points out, "and when you begin to overesti-mate rewards and overstate your opinion of them, it may create doubts among people who would otherwise want to give your idea serious con-sideration. Actually, the idea itself may be perfectly good in a more modest sort of way, but obvious overselling can frighten people out of wanting to take a chance on it."

Be particularly cautious when the new idea involves radical change. Your bosses may resent or resist the new idea merely because they were so intimately involved in the past. Talk about the good times ahead, rather than the bad times past.

If the idea is too radical or too big, it should be presented piecemeal, in logical sequence. This prepares the group to accept it gradually.

In the opinion of still another expert, ideas which entail major changes or expenditures are best broken up into three or four parts, each of which can then be installed or introduced separately.

"This progressive step-by-step method," he notes, "is often acceptable to management when the overall 'big idea' involves sweeping changes."

Be careful to avoid an air of superiority or pride when presenting an idea. This may make your listener feel small or inferior and build resis-tance.

It will help a great deal if you know as much as possible about the people to whom you must present your idea—their temperaments, apti-tudes, idiosyncrasies and preferences.

By putting yourself in the boss's shoes all the way through, by trying to imagine how you would react, were the positions reversed, you will be able to do a much better job of interpreting and selling your ideas.

Important to Test

One way to help make a sale is to offer to test the idea, if this can be done.

"Any idea that can be subjected to a road test should certainly get one. When ideas are debated instead of tested, a poor idea, supported by a good debater, makes a better showing than a good idea, supported by a poor debater. When ideas are tested, good ideas stand out."

The director of research for a major manufacturer suggests: "Think through every problem likely to arise in carrying out your proposal. Then provide an acceptable answer to show you've anticipated and planned for every such circumstance. A busy executive has all sorts of worries of his own. If, in order to approve your proposal, he has to stop and solve a problem relating to your baby, the easiest and quickest thing for him to do is to say no."

At the end of the presentation, you should sum up the more salient points, the anticipated advantages of the idea, the need that exists or can be created for the idea, and why you think the idea should be adopted.

Leaving copies of a clear, well written report with your listeners will give them a chance to study it later, and perhaps to arrive at your con-clusions.

HOW TO MAKE A BUSINESS DECISION
Peter Drucker

Over the next 20 years the emphasis in management will be on the understanding of decision-making.

Coupled with the advances of the past 20 years in organization theory, human relations, economic analysis, and market research, this understanding should bring a tremendous improvement in our managerial skill and performance.

Right now we are developing a whole tool-box for decision-making. But any manager can obtain the most important thing with few if any new tools: That is, he can understand that decision-making is a rational and systematic process and that its organization is a definite sequence of steps, each of them in turn rational and systematic.

This may not be adequate to give the best possible decision for every situation but it will be adequate for many business decisions—and in every case it can improve decision-making and lessen the weight of the decision burden.

Business decisions will always have to be based on judgment. They will always remain decisions for a future which will continue to be unpredictable. They will always entail risks. But studies made over the past ten years now have reached a point where every businessman, by following fairly simple steps, can greatly improve his performance as a decision-maker. These steps are basically four:

1. *Defining the problem:* What kind of problem is it? What is its critical factor? When do we have to solve it? Why do we want to solve it? What will solving it cost?
2. *Defining expectations:* What do we want to gain by solving it?
3. *Developing alternative solutions:* Which of several plans offers the surest way to avoid things that are unexpected?
4. *Knowing what to do with the decision after it is reached.*

Attention to these rules will help the businessman avoid the three most common pitfalls in the making of business decisions. These are:

- Finding the right answer for the wrong problem—few things are as useless.
- Making the decision at the wrong time. Far too many decisions are postponed when they should be made, without realization that postponing a decision might also be a decision—often an irrevocable one. Contrariwise many decisions are being made long before the decision is necessary. One tendency is as dangerous as the other.
- Making decisions that do not result in action. A decision without a definite action-plan and without adequate control of its execution is not an effective or even a finished decision.

We have also learned why people make these mistakes. The first and perhaps the main reason is that they do not organize their decision-making. They tend to do by intuition those parts of the process that can best be done rationally, and tend to be rational and fact-based in those parts that should be matters of judgment.

The second main reason for poor decision-making is wrong distribution of the time spent. Too many people spend time finding the answer —far too few spend time finding out what the problem is. Yet the right definition of the problem is both the most important and the most difficult job in decision-making. In the great majority of decisions once the problem is defined, the answers are easy.

Finally businessmen tend to look upon a decision as a problem rather than as an opportunity. As a result they tend to settle for the solution which has the lowest cost even though it promises the lowest gains and entails the greatest risk. Yet every decision is an attempt to balance gains, costs and risks.

Only by looking upon a decision as an opportunity as well as a problem can we discipline ourselves to the point where we objectively look at the alternatives and pick the one that offers the best balance between gains, costs and risks.

Such an objective look will consider these questions:

What Is the Problem?

All we can see at the beginning are symptoms. Symptoms in a business can be as deceptive as symptoms in human illness. To doctor symptoms while leaving untouched the basic problem will, however, provide only the most temporary relief.

A simple yet fairly common example is the scheduling problem in a manufacturing plant where, despite all efforts to plan and to schedule, production always gets into trouble, where overtime to meet delivery promises always runs up extra costs without ever quite giving satisfaction. In one such case management had practically decided to spend a substantial amount of money to increase the capacity of the plant. Then somebody pointed out that they did not know where the delay actually occurred.

When this was examined it soon became clear that the trouble was not in manufacturing at all and that no reasonable increase in plant capacity would end it. The trouble was in marketing. Salesmen promised immediate delivery for all items in the catalog including specialties that were not regularly stocked. They also gave the company's most marginal customer the same delivery promise as the company's best customer. As a result rush orders for specials or orders for small runs continuously disrupted whatever schedules manufacturing had made. These had to be pushed through separately and disrupted the entire shop. As soon as this was brought to the attention of the sales manager he could solve the problem by deciding that promises of rapid delivery were not needed except for the major current items and for actual or potential major customers. This of course involved a risk; it might lose some marginal customers or some of the business on specials. But the risk seemed so slight (subsequent experience showed it to be nonexistent) and the gains so great that the decision was fully justified. It at once cleared up what had been plaguing the company for years and had seriously eaten into its profits.

One tool, in the majority of cases, will enable a businessman to decide what the problem really is. Its technical name is "critical-factor analysis." The critical factor is the one element in the situation which has to be changed, moved, or removed before anything else can be done. By isolating this strategic element we usually manage to break through the surface of the symptoms and come to grips with the real problem.

For ten years a large company had been having trouble filling its number two spot, executive vice president. Eight men had been appointed to the position in ten years; every one of them had either left after a short time or had been asked to leave. Among them were men of forceful personality and men who were meek; men from inside the company and men hired from the outside, young men and older men. When the president recommended a ninth candidate to the board of directors, one of the board members said: "Isn't it time we found out why eight good men did not work out?"

He set out to interview the eight former holders of the position and found out rapidly that the critical factor in the situation was the president himself. While he had delegated all responsibility to the executive vice president and refused to make any decisions he still tried to hold the full authority of the chief executive office, expected the vice presidents to report to him and only to him, issued orders without informing the executive vice president and altogether behaved as if he were still the actual operating head of the business.

The critical factor was that authority and responsibility of the job were not compatible. The solution was to move the president to the position of chairman of the board and give him clearly defined authority for major policy matters but ask him to stay out of operating decisions. Instead of hiring an executive vice president, the company went looking for a new president and, incidentally, found the right man among the eight who, in the executive vice presidency, had not worked out earlier.

Timing is part of this job of defining the problem. The rule is simple: Don't make a decision before it can be effective. But don't postpone it after it has reached a point where it has become timely.

This concept is one most of us learned during World War II, that of lead-time. We all know today that if we want a new strategic bomber by 1963 we have to start working on it in 1956. Similarly if we want to have a steel plant by 1972 we have to commit ourselves this year to having one built.

And we know that a company that needs top management people ten years hence better start now to put some men into responsible positions where they can be trained and tested. It takes at least ten years to prepare a man for a top management position, even in a fairly small company.

The lead-time should always determine the timing of a decision. To make a decision several years before we actually have to make it to get

416

results when we need them is tempting fate; it is wise not to strain one's capacity to predict the future any further than it has to be strained. But once the lead-time has been reached, postponing a decision is in itself a decision—a decision not to do anything. If this should turn out to be wrong we will be in trouble. Occasionally procrastination can be made good through a crash program; but under the best of circumstances this is expensive. In most cases a decision that has been postponed beyond its proper timing has gone for good, and with it goes opportunity.

Finally, as part of the job of defining the decision, we set out the specifications for the acceptable solution. One element in this is the objectives. What must we accomplish? Is it enough for the decision to overcome a present difficulty? Or must it also prevent recurrence of the crisis? Is the decision to be purely defensive, to protect a company against expected moves of competitors? Or is it to move the company ahead and give it an advantage over competition or a new opportunity to grow and to expand?

The other element in these specifications, and the one most commonly slighted, is a careful examination of the risks a business can afford.

There are no riskless decisions nor can there ever be. Yet no business can possibly accept unlimited risks.

The question, "what risks can we afford to take?" is therefore basic. In deciding to build a new plant there is, for instance, the question: Which risk are we more willing to shoulder, the risk of being saddled with idle plant capacity on which we have to pay interest and amortization; or the risk of losing customers and markets through failure to supply an increased demand?

Any pricing decision similarly weighs the risk of an inadequate profit margin. In introducing a new product, the risk of becoming obsolete has to be balanced against the risk of introducing a new product with its tooling or development expenses, the costs of getting it to the market and its risk of failure.

Not all the risks involved in a decision can always be spelled out, let alone reduced to figures. Yet it is almost always possible to define clearly the outside limits of the risks the business is able to take. That is the point beyond which risk-taking should not be carried. This in turn will give the businessman a better understanding of the nature of the decision he faces and a much clearer idea what decision is likely to be the right decision under the circumstances.

Defining Our Expectations

Most of the earlier books on problem-solving or decision-making went into details about finding the facts. Many businessmen pride themselves that they always base their decisions on facts.

Our modern study of decision-making leads us to take a dim view of this assertion.

Actually we must always base our decisions on assumptions regarding the future; and the only facts we can ever have are in respect to the past.

This is a good deal more than academic quibbling. It spotlights one of the basic difficulties of the businessman who has been brought up to have great respect for facts and to hunt for them when he faces a major decision. Yet his decision will, in the final analysis, be of necessity an appraisal of what he expects to happen in the future.

What we need is to define the expectations for the future that govern our decision. This, incidentally, is the only way by which we can build into the decision some mechanism toward later review and improvement. For only if we clearly spell out what we assume will happen can we be sure of knowing when a decision needs to be reviewed and revised because actual events differ from our expectations.

Defining our expectations also enables us to find out what historical records—what facts—we ought to consult. I have yet to sit in on a major decision in a business where we are not flooded by facts and figures—and where we do not complain bitterly that we cannot get any of the relevant facts. The fault, I hasten to add, is ours. We have not thought through what our expectations were and therefore do not know what facts we need. As a result we have millions of figures—but no real knowledge whether they are relevant and what they have to tell us. Once we have thought through what we expect to happen we can then define clearly what figures we need, what among them we can get, and where we have to do without facts and have therefore to guess—and to pray.

Developing Alternative Solutions

Once the problem and the expectations have been defined and analyzed we are ready to talk about solutions. The important letter in this word is the final "s." The temptation is extremely great to come up with the "right" solution at once. This is one of the major weaknesses of decision-making. The "right" solution, that is, the obvious one, rarely is really the one that will give us the best answer to the needs and opportunities of the situation. In fact the "right" solution often represents only the prejudices we started out with—so much so that we usually don't have to analyze the problem or study the available facts to arrive at this solution.

The way to avoid this common pitfall is to make sure that we always consider the full range of solutions that are possible within the objectives we have set and within the risk we have decided we can afford. To make sure that we really consider the alternatives, it often helps to start out with the most absurd of all conceivable solutions. We should also insist, both for ourselves and for our associates, that the pros as well as the cons for every alternative solution are spelled out in considerable detail. Any statement that begins with the word "obviously" should be challenged. You will be surprised how many times the attempt to prove what at first seemed a perfectly obvious statement leads to the conclusion that the opposite is actually more likely to be true.

One large company that has spent a great deal of time and thought on decision-making has concluded that we ought to drop our emphasis on action-recommendations in all staff reports. The argument is that the emphasis on a recommendation forces the writer to settle on one alternative and thereby to argue against all others when his job really is to study all of them and to give management the fullest information to choose between them.

Making sure that all the alternatives are considered is necessary because we normally see only what we expect to see and therefore tend to overlook the unexpected. It is lack of imagination rather than lack of intelligence that is the problem we have to overcome in decision-making. Considering all the alternatives is also the only way we have to make sure that we do not overlook opportunities.

An example here is that of a small manufacturer of plumbing equipment who found his sales going up sharply while his profit remained stable or actually shrunk. He diagnosed the trouble as resulting from his factory, which was old, crowded and in a congested area so that it could not be expanded. He decided to build a new factory with greater capacity —and as a result found himself out of business within a year.

He had diagnosed the problem correctly; he could indeed not produce efficiently in the old location nor could he expand production. But he considered no alternative except that of building a new plant which he was financially incapable of doing.

Any number of alternatives were available. He could have subcontracted part of his production and kept in his plant only that part for which the plant was best equipped. He could have rented or bought a plant instead of building one. He could even have stopped manufacturing altogether and, capitalizing on his standing in his market, had his goods made for him by outside suppliers. He could have become a distributor for somebody else's goods. Or he might have merged, marrying his marketing skill and market standing with the production skills and low cost of some other company which needed a market outlet. Actually, the company never even considered any of these alternatives—it was so obvious that it had no choice except to continue in the old plant or build a new one.

It is particularly important to consider the alternatives when the decision that seems to be most logical and most nearly right is to do what everybody else has been doing. When the problem is to copy a new product of a competitor or to meet a new competitive price, the temptation to play follow-the-leader is always great. Yet in such situations a different solution often produces the greatest results and offers the greatest opportunities.

How to Use a Decision

Now we are ready to make the decision. We know what we can do, that is, the range of alternatives. We know what each of them requires in the way of efforts and costs, what each of them is likely to produce in the way of gains, and what the risks of each are. We now can compare the range of actions available to us against the specifications in respect to objectives and risks.

This does not normally give us automatically the right decision.

In the first place we rarely find a situation in which any of the available actions is perfect—and we find none at all which are riskless. Usually two or three courses of action are equally desirable and equally undesirable. We have always to exercise judgment. But at least we will have narrowed the range of judgment considerably. We will also have made sure that everybody connected with the decision talks about the same thing and considers the same factors. We will know what we actually decide when we pick one course of action over another. This decision, while still judgment and risk-taking, will be a rational decision with definite expectations and definite reason behind it.

Still we have to make sure that it is converted into action. By and large, the people who make the decision are not the ones who take the actions needed to make a decision effective. We must therefore make sure that the decision is understood by the people who must carry it out. The first thing to note is who these people are. Every decision requires an action-plan which spells out who has to do what, when, where and why before the decision can be effective. Then we have to make sure that the people who have to take action really are willing and able to take it. This is the time for meetings, for presentations, for discussions and for participation. Here is the place to apply all we have been learning during the past 20 years about working with people.

Finally we have to build into the decision the measurement of its effectiveness. The foundation for this is laid when we spell out the expectations on which we base our action—the things which we expect will happen and in anticipation of which we have made the decision. This enables us to say concretely what the decision should achieve; and also what, outside of the decision itself—for instance in the national economy or in the technology of our business—has to happen for the decision to remain effective.

When we decide to build a paper plant a certain way, we assume certain price relations between various kinds of cardboard, wrapping paper and writing paper. When these price relations change we will have to decide whether the plant has to be changed or whether the product-mix for which it was built is still the most advantageous one. To be able to do this we have to put into the decision to build the plant a clear, unmistakable and policed instruction to let us know immediately as soon as the price relations, which we assumed and expected, change in any significant way.

This is, of course, simply saying that no decision we make, and especially no long-range decision, can be assumed to be the right decision. The odds against human beings being able to predict the future are overwhelming; and no system can possibly beat them. Hence we must make sure at least that the decision will be reviewed as soon as events indicate that we had the wrong expectations and what the right expectations should have been.

The steps outlined here may seem laborious. Actually they are time savers. Today most executives spend a tremendous amount of time on fact-finding, on picking the right decision and especially on making the decision effective. Even more time is spent bailing out decisions that have gotten into trouble as the future unfolded. Time spent on these things is cut sharply in a rational organization of decision-making. Time is spent instead on the first phase, the definition of the decision, and on the third phase, the thinking through of the alternatives. But the time spent on these steps is a fraction of the time we now spend agonizingly finding the answers and "selling" the decision.

A rational approach to decision-making not only results in better decisions—and above all in clearer decisions—it also results in easier and faster decisions. It does not—and this point cannot be emphasized often enough—result in riskless decisions. It does not replace the mature manager's responsible judgment by a computer or an infallible system. It enables the manager, however, to make the commitments and take the risks with greater clarity, more simply and with greater chance of success.

MAKE YOURSELF A BETTER MANAGER
Joseph G. Mason

Only the individual can make himself a better manager.

The company and the boss can help, of course, with formal training programs and personal coaching. But in the long run all personal development is just that—personal.

The manager should use his capabilities to make a success of training he has been given and to develop the attitudes and experience that must be truly self-developed because they cannot be taught.

It is useful, then, to look at some of the things the individual executive can do if he wants to become a better manager. These steps involve him, his attitudes, his actions. He won't need anyone else's approval or cooperation to put them into practice, and the only person he needs to share them with is always available.

One of the most common misconceptions about being an executive is that there is some mystical pattern or mold into which the aspiring manager should cast himself.

This is certainly the first attitude you should discard.

You cannot make the most of your own inborn talents if you try to develop along the lines of any ideal pattern of personality characteristics. There are no set patterns for success.

Consider the most common example of regimented personalities: the military. Certainly if any group has an image of inflexible sameness, it is a military organization.

Yet in "The Professional Soldier," Morris Janowitz points out that most distinguished commanders were men who deviated from the image.

General Douglas MacArthur, for example, is cited as having had a "career based on a flouting of authority." And the description by Marquis Childs of Dwight Eisenhower may come as a shock. As a West Point cadet, according to Mr. Childs, "Eisenhower was a roughneck. He broke the rules just as often as he dared. Law-abiding classmates were shocked at his daring. . . . His conduct was that of the tough boy from the wrong side of the tracks defying the code, and yet managing by his resourcefulness to live with it."

Certainly if such individualists can succeed in a military organization, individualists should also do well in even the most image-conscious business enterprise.

One industrialist who expressed himself on this point is Alfred C. Fuller, founder of the Fuller Brush Company. "Of the first 200 men who achieved executive position in the Fuller Brush Company," he relates, "only three had previously earned as much as $50 a week in other employment. They were, without exception, little men of no previous attainment, or inadequate background, and almost no training for their jobs. Neither they nor I could 'think big'; we just knew how to work hard."

The late Moorhead Wright, of the General Electric Company, not only supported the feeling that the best service a company can give its managers is to allow them to be their own men, but also raised some interesting questions regarding theoretical images for managers:

"If you are going to work toward any sort of ideal personality pattern," he asked, "what, in the face of such a pattern, are you going to say to the managers now in place? Shall we say that they must conform to this ideal pattern or be fired?

"How," he continued, "do we account for the fact that we now have some managers—good managers—who are tough and rugged personalities, others who are quiet and thoughtful men, others who are aggressive-salesman types, and others just as widely assorted?

"The truth is," he concluded, "there just isn't any standard pattern of personality traits that makes a good manager."

Get Experience Where You Are

General Electric interviewed 300 men with managerial responsibilities. An outside research group was used and individuals were guaranteed anonymity.

Asked, "What do you consider the thing that was most important in your development?" 90 per cent of the managers replied that it was their day-to-day work. Only 10 per cent ascribed major importance to educational background, special courses, job rotation.

The outstanding factors were the manner in which the man himself was managed in his daily work, the climate in which he worked, and his relationships with others—particularly his immediate superiors.

One executive, commenting on his experience as preparation for the work he is now doing in the aerospace industry, states the case this way:

"Experience is not always a good teacher, nor is past experience necessarily and universally relevant to the future. On the other hand, it would indeed be strange if, after two decades of studies, experiments, and participation with the military in design, test, evaluation, and use of equipment in the air as well as on the ground, in observations on the use of this equipment in the field, under a full spectrum of conditions from primitive to plush—if at the end of all this I didn't have some firmly held views on what kind of developments are likely to succeed, what kind of developments are likely to fail, and why."

One thing to watch for in going after new experience in your present job is to make sure your assigned work is being done first. Many eager junior executives realize that even limited management authority brings opportunities to develop themselves through different experiences, but they then make the mistake of working so hard to broaden their horizons that they forget to cover the daily bases they are paid to cover. While your present job offers a base for future growth, you probably won't prosper if the work that is assigned to you isn't being done.

But opportunities to take on new responsibilities and gain the experience that comes from solving problems are all around any manager. They exist in the improved utilization of people; better control of dollars; more efficient and effective use of time; maximum utilization of company facilities. Few companies, or even divisions, departments, or sections of companies, can claim that they are doing the best that can be expected in all of these areas, and anyone looking for opportunities will find plenty of them.

Help Your People Grow

Henry Kaiser says, "I make progress by having people around me who are smarter than I am—and listening to them. And I assume that everyone is smarter about something than I am."

You can become a better manager if you develop others to help you.

Determine the best qualities of each of your people, and then give them the opportunities to maximize those qualities for the benefit of the company. This requires an awareness by the executive of the potential that lies within every man to develop new capabilities when the climate is right.

No executive should limit anyone's opportunities for growth by arbitrarily deciding that this man or that man has the capacity to grow, while someone else does not. All men have the capacity to grow to some degree if encouraged to develop those qualities in which they are initially strong. The development policy should be one of individual attention and encouragement, rather than crystal-ball selection and limitation.

One company that makes a deliberate policy of allowing its people to maximize whatever potentials they may have as individuals is Aerojet-General Corporation. Although called highly unorthodox for its organization and operating methods, the company has achieved startling successes in the highly competitive aerospace industry by following such far-out procedures as allowing the scientists who develop new devices to trot them out and attempt to sell them to prospective customers. So far the policy has paid off with more successes than failures, and has come to be the way things are done throughout the company.

Aim for Professionalism

"I like pros," one manager emphasizes. "I like to listen to them; watch them in action; work with them; know I have one on the job when there is a major commitment to be met. I don't care how snobbish it sounds, I always prefer to deal with a pro."

Being a professional in a job is more than just doing what you are paid to do. Professionalism is more a matter of the attitudes that manifest themselves in a man's general approach to his work.

One such characteristic is often a man's willingness to stick his neck out either before or to a greater degree than his colleagues when a new proposition is presented.

Another characteristic of the pro is his complete mastery of the job, no matter how complex the problems.

Still another easily observed quality in the real professional is his personal sense of responsibility. He seldom waits for problems to come to him. He goes looking for them, and when he finds one he can get his teeth into, he makes it his own personal problem and doesn't quit until that problem has been licked.

Frank Fischer, of Cresap, McCormick and Paget, cites the opposite of this attitude as the symptom of a stale climate in a company. In the stale climate, he says, executives tend to be acquiescent—they don't develop strong feelings about anything and never bother to disagree over issues.

Such men, he points out, tend to play follow-the-leader; they lack a feeling of urgency and therefore tend to postpone decisions. This, Mr. Fischer indicates, is when a business begins to run down.

Guard Your Moral Values

Few men in any field ever reach the top without a strong sense of morality.

The occasional man who does gain a position of prestige or power without an honest character will eventually be uncovered.

Power or authority demands integrity of the highest type, for without it a man will sooner or later give in to the temptation to abuse his authority. Even in lesser positions, a strong and sincere sense of morality is a requisite for winning and holding the respect and confidence of others in the face of the everyday temptations to deal and contrive rather than to think and plan.

A man cannot be a little bit dishonest in business. He is either honest or he is not; he either has integrity or he does not. He doesn't need to be a psalm-singer to be a moralist. As a matter of fact, unless he does have true and deep religious convictions, to adopt a superreligious pose merely for the sake of appearances would indicate a lack of integrity.

The practice of honesty has, in most industries, become a way of life.

Corporate reputations for honesty often pay off in dramatic ways. Donald Douglas built such a reputation for his aircraft company and worked to preserve it. At the time Douglas was competing against Boeing to sell Eastern Airlines its first big jets, Eddie Rickenbacker, who headed Eastern, is said to have told Mr. Douglas that his specifications and offers for the DC-8 were close to Boeing on everything but the noise suppression.

He then gave Mr. Douglas one last chance to outpromise Boeing on this feature.

After consulting his engineers, Mr. Douglas reported back that he did not feel he could make the promise.

Mr. Rickenbacker is said to have replied: "I know you can't. I wanted to see if you were still honest. You just got yourself an order for one hundred and sixty-five million dollars. Now go home and silence those damn jets!"

It is apparent that individual improvement must be largely an individual matter. While education can do much to advance an executive's personal development, only the executive himself can supply or develop the inner qualities that transcend methods, techniques, procedures and systems.

You start where you are with what you have and build on it. Only you can make yourself a better manager.

PUT NEW LIFE IN YOUR CAREER
Auren Uris

Three major causes of executive failure can trip up an otherwise experienced and capable businessman.

Thousands and thousands of executives represent living puzzles—to themselves and others. They seem to have a great deal on the ball. They may be likable, imaginative and skilled in both technical and managerial areas. Yet they perform at merely get-by levels; or in some cases their performance sags to a level that may mean demotion or separation from their jobs. Why?

The three main causes for ineffectiveness boil down to:

- Career confusion and indecision.
- Distortion of job objectives.
- Misjudgment—that produces the right action at the wrong time.

To say the capable man who operates below his capacity is just under-motivated is far too glib an answer.

Conversations with personnel experts, particularly those concerned with the employment of executives, reveal a more specific diagnosis.

Paul H. Kiernan, managing director of Kiernan & Co., personnel consultants, says, "I've seen a lot of capable people who failed to get ahead because of an ailment that may be called career indecision. In my experience the symptoms are unmistakable. The individual, although impressively qualified, fails in his job. When you talk to him you eventually get to the real reason. The man feels he's in the wrong job or with the wrong company or may even think he belongs in an entirely different profession."

It's not unusual for a manager to have doubts about himself and his professional future, but such hesitations may arise from different causes. Temporary career dissatisfaction is not career indecision.

It's perfectly reasonable to become dissatisfied with one or another aspect of a job. One's salary is seldom high enough. There's always one colleague—or it may be one's boss—who makes life less pleasant than it might be. And in the world of work not all assignments are plums. The man who feels he's been stuck with an unpleasant task may be permitted a feeling of discontent.

Such surges of negative feeling, however, usually are relatively short-lived.

As a matter of fact, John Handy, also well known in the executive search field, speaks of "cyclical restlessness." This he describes as "growing out of boredom, an edgy home situation or some chafing in a job relationship." The result is the individual has an impulse to "get out of there."

Career indicision, however, is a decidedly different phenomenon. For one thing, it exists at a deeper level of feeling. For another, rather than being temporary, it is an ever present obstacle to constructive thought and action on the job.

Career indecision may be difficult to diagnose. After all, it is only one of the possible causes for performance failure. Accordingly, the first thing to be done in attempting to diagnose is to rule out other such obvious possibilities as incompetency, improper training, family worries, poor health.

Once these are ruled out, one may make a more positive identification. In the last analysis, it is only the individual victim who can sufficiently clarify his own feelings and firm up the diagnosis.

The person who is disabled by career indecision is typified by the employee with considerable experience both as a salesman and as a sales manager. "In your next job," he was asked, "would you like to continue as a sales manager or get back into selling?" He thought for a moment and said, "Neither."

"But suppose you could have any job you wanted?"

"I don't know what I want to do," was the reply.

Managers in their forties and over frequently fail to have a satisfactory answer to a basic career question: "What do I really want to do?" Here are some of the possible backgrounds that lead to indecisiveness about career goals:

The fed-up feeling. The victim sees a job as a rat-race. Regardless of what virtues it has, he is aware only of its pressures or its continuing frustrations.

The childhood dream. In their teens, most people develop inordinate ambitions. They see themselves and their futures suffused by a rosy glow of accomplishment. They see no particular problem in out-Henry-ing Ford or out-Thomas-ing Watson.

As we mature, most of us outgrow these fancies. The world takes on a more realistic light. But in the case of the individual suffering from career indecision, maturing has not taken place. Still living in the dream world of childhood aspiration, he views any accomplishment as inadequate. In such a situation, the individual is bound to suffer from disappointments—no matter what he may accomplish.

The campus hero. "I was top man on the campus at old State U.," reminisces one unsuccessful manager. "Those were the great days. It's been downhill ever since."

Outstanding accomplishment in school that is not continued in the working world can damage a man's self-esteem. He suffers from career indecision because he cannot adjust to his disappointing status in a world with different standards for accomplishment.

The South Sea Island fantasy. Some individuals daydream about a languorous land where the living is easy and they are lords of all they survey. If they could only kick over the apple cart—this usually includes wife, financial problems, the job—and make it to the gem-like isle, all life's problems would be solved. If the daydream is strong enough, everyday realities are bound to be unprepossessing.

The best way of dealing with career indecision is to keep it from getting started. A series of questions asked early enough and repeated from time to time can go a long way towards prevention:

Is there any job or profession I would rather be in than my present one? Don't kid yourself on this answer and rule out responses such as, "I'd like to have my boss's job" or "Any job that will pay me twice as much."

Do I have a clear-cut idea of where I'd like to be in the next two or three years?

Is this career goal realistic in view of education, experience, skills, achievement and so on?

What steps have I taken to make my next career move not only possible but likely?

What more can I do?

Am I doing the one thing that is usually the strongest guarantee of advancement—scoring a positive success in my present job?

The importance of facing reality is shown by studies made by the Foundation for Re-Employment, a nonprofit organization that some companies call in when they are forced to separate people due to mergers, automation, or other cost-cutting programs. Seventy to 90 per cent of the people trained by the Foundation find their own new jobs within 60 to 90 days, but as much as one third of them shift to new careers—the self-analysis the Foundation puts them through convinces them that they have been in the wrong job all along.

It's fine to be attracted to functions where the money is or action is. Yet, not everyone has what it takes to be a good marketing man or finance officer or director of research and development.

And too many promising executives fall by the wayside because they assess wrong values to their career targets, suggests Paul H. Henson, president of United Utilities and the U.S. Independent Telephone Association. "The future belongs to those who can contribute something of value to their companies."

Distortion of Objectives

Industrial psychologists have pointed out that the ability to define an objective is a major element in the pattern of successful executives. The converse is also true: "In many cases, inability to zero in on career objectives explains below-par achievement," points out Sidney Friedman, chairman of the board of Meadow Brook National Bank, which operates 66 branches in the greater New York area. Here are some of the situations that indicate the existence of distortion of your career objectives:

The wrong promotion. A particular promotion may be sought too early or too late in a man's career. He may aim too high or too low. In short, he has set his sights on an inappropriate "next rung."

One example is the eager beaver who sets out to leapfrog straight to the top. He probably lacks the experience and the ability to hold the job, even should he get it. He's probably underestimating the capabilities of competitors closer to the throne, who are more logical choices. And perhaps without the backing of certain key individuals—members of the board, veteran members of the policy-setting top echelon group—he lacks the power platform necessary to win the prime spot.

Or a manager may set his sights too low. He may be satisfied with routine raises and methodical advances which are more the result of inertia than initiative.

"A successful promotion usually must be thoughtfully planned and prepared for on both sides," says James M. Jenks, president of Alexander Hamilton Institute. "The company should preplan the promotion, but equally important, the man himself should plan his promotion strategy in advance. It is his responsibility to be gassed up and ready to go when each of his promotion opportunities presents itself."

Shortsighted triumph. Sometimes a manager exaggerates the importance of a target simply because he can accomplish it easily. This type of distorted perception can pop up in many guises.

Some men try to look good in a hurry. One businessman attends a meeting at which a serious problem of sagging production has been discussed. He decides that over the week-end he'll prepare a detailed analysis that he'll submit not to his boss, but to the general manager. He knows bypassing is risky. But he feels his victory is worth taking a chance. Comes Monday morning and he slips his carefully bound 25-page analysis of the problem on the manager's desk. Later on, the general manager thanks him for his "thoughtful report." But his boss never forgives him, and even the general manager keeps him at arm's length thereafter.

The missed challenge. "They're not going to send me to Siberia," you tell your wife. "They picture it as a promotion, but the last man to have the job quit after a year. My challenge will be nil in the sticks."

Your analysis may be correct. On the other hand, if the job in the sticks is a bona fide opportunity to show what you've got on the ball, you may commit a major error in career strategy not to take it.

There are two fast tests to assess the situation.

If there is an actual opportunity for an energetic and ingenious manager to show what he's got, then an assignment in "Siberia" may be the best possible assignment.

A heart-to-heart talk with the superior making the assignment should quickly establish motivation.

Comments management consultant Robert Sibson: "Many of the so-called people problems of business are caused by the fact there is too little direct, honest communication between people—or too much of the other kind."

Status versus accomplishment. This particular kind of target distortion is common among the inexperienced. The young executive often values status higher than he should. Accordingly, he will devote inordinate amounts of energy in winning evidences of status—anything from a larger office to a prestige assignment. But today more than ever before, executive performance is given weight over other qualifications such as school tie, appearance, personality and so on.

Rex Vivian, of Ward Howell Associates, Inc., a spokesman for the Association of Executive Recruiting Consultants, points out that increasing precision with which corporations and their executive recruiters select and evaluate management people leave the executive only one solid rock on which he can build his career, and that is his ability to get results.

The executive who gets to know the right people might be ill-advised to abandon such efforts. But these days it makes good sense to at least match status-seeking efforts with equal energy expended in doing the best job possible.

Dead-end unawareness. "It's shocking," observes one career counselor, "to see how many men are in dead-end jobs without knowing it." Many executives turning in a good performance have the fond expectation that one day their efforts automatically and inevitably will be recognized by a deserved promotion. Trouble is, there is often no place for them to go in their present companies.

This does not necessarily mean that there are no positions above theirs. What is meant is that the hard facts of the situation wall in the man: A promotion he vaguely expects is already sewed up by another. Or, while a promotion or better assignment is theoretically possible, he lacks specific qualifications—anything from personality make-up to education—to make the step.

In general, maintaining clear and effective aim on your career targets requires three elements:

1. Appraisal of capabilities. If you want to be president, make sure you've got what it takes. If you want to be head of R & D, check on your qualifications.
2. Appraisal of greatest satisfactions. Don't kid yourself. If you'd make a much happier V. P. than you would a president, you'd be making a serious error to try for the top spot.
3. Appraisal of required action. What must you do or do without in order to achieve your selected career goal? If you want to go into the financial field, and there are gaps in your education, training or experience, you must be willing to take the steps that will fill in the gaps—regardless of time, energy or cash. If you're not willing to take these necessary steps, target distortion has set in—with inevitable likelihood of failure.

Charles A. Berns, chairman of "21" Brands, Inc., sums it up this way: "Analyze your job, don't just do it. Then analyze what it takes to be successful at the next job above your present one that you want to shoot for."

Right Action—Wrong Time

One of the most dangerous approaches to managerial success is adoption of the character stereotype—the hard-nosed manager, for example, or the great persuader. The fact is, each company has its own set of needs and standards for executive excellence. Further, each job tends to call for specific qualities for which a Johnny-one-note approach is not appropriate.

Aggressiveness and persuasiveness should be tools to accomplish a result rather than elements of personality. The well rounded executive can move aggressively in certain situations, be completely relaxed in others. Or he can be persuasive when there's something to be gained by persuasion.

Consequently, misdirected or fumbling applications of any of the tools of an executive's trade indicate an ineptness that is likely to show up in under-par performance.

The regional sales manager of a chemical products company was well aware that the successful sales executive is supposed to be aggressive.

He showed his drive by close supervision of his men. Reading their call reports, analyzing their weaknesses, trying to strengthen them.

But at meetings with fellow-sales managers, he dramatically presented plans to solve current sales problems; or, indulged in fervid, even hostile arguments with his colleagues on one or another point of sales policy.

Unknowingly, he killed his chances for advancement in his company. As his boss remarked: "He hasn't got enough sense to know when not to fight. What we need out of him is less competitiveness and more 'companiness.' He doesn't realize that he's a constant disruptive force."

Many managers have erected their own roadblocks by using inappropriate executive tools.

Another business executive is faced with the need to arrive at a decision regarding merchandising of a new product line. He calls a meeting of his staff, starts a discussion of possible approaches. Then, when a decision is required to decide on a specific action, he sits back and puts various proposals to a vote. In some cases, participation and "majority rules" may be called for. However, not now. The considered judgment of a single man—his decision—is required.

The selection and use of the right approach at the right time is a function of:

Executive methods. By now, the art-science of professional management has been developed to the point where guesswork is largely outdated. The executive who has a top-heavy workload now knows that there are a number of proven techniques for handling this problem. He can, for example, increase the areas of responsibility of some of his subordinates. Or delegate some of the work to new people to lighten his load.

Leadership. Some of the correct actions are functions of leadership, rather than procedure. Yet, here, too, the manager must understand his leadership role well enough to know when he must command, when he must persuade, when he should seek participation from his subordinates, and when he alone must respond to the exigencies of the situation.

In the final analysis, career progress depends not only on the avoidance of the three basic pitfalls: career indecision, target distortion, and inappropriate action. Equally important is the positive planning for forward motion based on improving capabilities, experience and training.

The noteworthy aspect of the three roadblocks is their insidiousness. They often exist without the victim being aware of them. In most cases, once the spotlight of self-analysis has exposed them to view, they will respond to remedial treatment in a most satisfying manner.

HOW TO ENJOY YOUR JOB

Employees of a small eastern manufacturing corporation swear to the truth of this story about their president.

On a sunny Saturday afternoon a few years ago, the president, then a vice president, was bent over his desk in deep concentration. Suddenly he was shaken from his meditation by the excited voice of a colleague who had burst into his office.

"What in heaven's name are you doing here, Frank!" his colleague exclaimed.

Not that it was unusual to find this vice president on the job on Saturdays. But this Saturday was different. There was cause for alarm. The vice president had an appointment that very hour in church. It was his wedding day.

This absent-mindedness—which made the bridegroom late for his own wedding—is hardly a typical trait of corporate executives. However, his all-absorbing love of job is characteristic. It is a quality that has helped propel many a man to the top of his organization. For many successful managers, work is synonymous with life itself; and job satisfaction feeds on the challenge of an unfinished problem.

Nation's Business interviewed psychologists, psychiatrists, consultants and executives on the subject of executive job satisfaction to seek a better understanding of its elements and the part it plays in effective management.

The key findings are:

1. Executives need special kinds of job satisfaction.
2. Today's industrial organization can be the scene of great frustration and great enjoyment.
3. Executives can achieve richer job satisfaction and more productivity at the same time.

Kinds of Satisfaction

For every executive, some phases of the job are more enjoyable than others. Usually these are functions he does well or with ease because of his experience and skill. Since on the highest managerial levels there is frequently considerable leeway in what an executive does and when and how he does it, there is danger that he may spend too much time doing what he likes best to do.

Take the case of the company president who got to the top via the sales route. Now, as president, he spends six months of the year on the road seeing customers and loves it. But the company's organization structure is outdated, plans for a cost control system are in mid-air and a building program has bogged down.

The president is too busy enjoying the one part of his job which he knows best.

"There's a big difference between making play out of work and playing at work," notes Dr. Robert H. Felix, former director of the National Institute of Mental Health. "Enthusiasm and enjoyment in one's work are important for both physical and mental health," he says.

However, the man who seeks job pleasure at the expense of other requirements lacks maturity and a recognition of the scope and responsibility of the job.

Surveys of executive job satisfactions have pointed up some specifics.

432

Executives' stated satisfactions range from liking to work with figures to liking to be an integral part of the organization. Executives also say they derive their greatest satisfactions from the increased importance of their firms in the economy, working with their people toward a common goal, solving tough problems, feeling vital in the operation of company programs, and having the freedom and opportunity for creative planning.

Another satisfaction, notes Dr. Felix, comes from "being in a position where policies and programs are influenced by you at the raw level." It's the satisfaction of power combined with the need to create.

The executive in truth "creates a course of action," as Bernard J. Muller-Thym, management consultant, puts it. Moreover, in creating this course of action, the executive "initiates changes that make a contribution which can be recognized as useful," says Dr. Edwin M. Glasscock, consultant with Farr and Glasscock Associates.

At the root of executive satisfaction, however, is what Dr. Felix calls a certain "divine discontent," an "itch that must be scratched." This is the dissatisfaction with things as they are that spurs the imagination and creativity.

"A lot of executives I know get a tremendous kick out of their jobs, the prestige and the money, but they are ulcerous worry warts," says John Sargent, of Cresap, McCormick and Paget, management consultants. "They are frustrated and dissatisfied, but they love it," he notes.

"In my experience," comments Dr. James Farr, of Farr and Glasscock, "the best executives are the most dissatisfied, in that they must have challenge and are always under pressure to measure themselves against some task."

So, the deepest and truest satisfaction for executives seems to arise from a discontent that stimulates creative powers which bring accomplishments that the executive himself sees or senses.

Frustrations and Enjoyment

In such times as these when the chill of recession has pervaded business generally, the economic atmosphere provides little cause for cheer among executives. As many firms have retrenched and reshuffled their programs and organizations, it has left some misfits and much dissatisfaction.

Even in more buoyant times, the nature of some large business organizations is a source of frustration and dissatisfaction for executives. Multiple divisions, dispersed plants, frequent changes in products, production and distribution make timely information and communications difficult. A tendency toward specialization, close control, rigid policies and many levels of authority may conflict with the drive for independence, variety, individualism and breadth of duties and authority.

For many executives in both large and small organizations, government restrictions, high taxes, labor union power and resulting worker attitudes, not to mention touchy world conditions, are environmental causes of worries.

As managers move up to the highest ranks of their companies, new sources of tension and anxiety arise. Competition among managers becomes stiffer and rivalries for promotion are more intense. At the summit there is a loneliness and isolation that makes it easy to understand what William Howard Taft meant by a comment he made after his first few months in the White House. "Nobody drops in for the evening," he bemoaned.

Ranking executives must cope with what Dr. Felix terms "one of the saddest things in administration—the yes-man." Dr. Felix, a psychiatrist who administers a $40 million a year program himself, says some administrators become tense if there is disagreement around them, so they surround themselves with yes-men. This makes for more anxiety because the executive never can trust the candidness of his subordinates' answers. Even when he cracks a joke, he finds that often the response is hollow loyalty laughter.

Troubles and dissatisfactions can grow in situations of overlapping responsibilities where job limits are not defined, asserts executive recruiter J. Francis Canny. Improper placement of executives in jobs that are either far too big for them, or not big enough can lead to dissatisfactions.

Perfectionist tendencies can be causes of dissatisfaction, too, says Dr. Glasscock. Many executives are so conscientious they try to devote too much attention to too many things. This leaves most activities in a half-done state that breeds worry.

For middle managers sometimes a special problem can cause great disappointment. They come to realize that they are against a blank wall as far as advancement is concerned, with many years ahead of them before retirement.

For some middle and upper managers, many of life's goals have been attained: The children are educated and married, the home is paid for, the insurance is paid up, the executive heights have been reached. The challenge is gone.

Industrial executives, however, can find enjoyment to surpass any of the frustration in their jobs. Although some large organizations can become bureaucracies with layers of authority that stifle creativity, most businesses certainly aren't functioning that way today, comments Mr. Muller-Thym. They are dynamic and growing. The large organizations for instance, provide large opportunities, responsibilities and great varieties of challenges to the creative talents of their executives. They offer a source of pride in the company's reputation and its impact on the economy.

Natural tensions arising from competition and demands on abilities and energies now and then are beneficial. "Being keyed up by the excitement of an important action that must be taken helps you deliver with maximum punch," explains Dr. Felix. "Your reaction time is faster, you are keener and usually you don't tire until the job is done." So for those irregular times when peak performance is required, your tensions can help you.

Executives can reach a higher level of job enjoyment and satisfaction and at the same time increase their effectiveness and the productivity of their subordinates. This fortunate fact can be realized in several ways.

Dr. Farr, who is a psychological consultant to top management in the field of managerial effectiveness, suggests these steps:

• Deliberately begin to see your job, not as managing a business so much as managing people, and set this as a number one challenge.

The responsibility of getting other people to do the job that is to be done will undoubtedly increase the scope of your position. The more effective you become, the more successful your department or organization or company can become and the more satisfaction you can attain from this accomplishment.

A common problem in the business world is that the man who built up a company is aggressive, confident, even egotistical. He frequently doesn't delegate authority to his subordinates. So, although he is a business builder, he's not a people builder. "Building people is far more challenging and satisfying work," insists Dr. Farr.

• Start thinking about what you will do in guiding your company's destiny and let your subordinates decide how it will be done.

Dr. Farr says too many executives have a narrow concept about authority; they don't let their people have the responsibility for planning and organizing the way in which some project or policy will be carried out.

• Develop the habit of asking yourself what you are worrying about. Don't let anxiety build up.

Anxiety exaggerates the harmful elements of a situation. You can seek the answers from subordinates, associates or superiors, depending on what the worry is. It is particularly common for anxiety to build up in a manager who hesitates to ask for a full explanation of an order or policy because he believes he might give his boss the impression he is confused or not sharp enough to interpret the meaning of an instruction.

• Give your subordinates every opportunity to measure and judge themselves.

They are effective because their superior says they are, or because they have some other means by which they may measure and realize their accomplishments.

All of these suggestions are aimed at enabling you to manage more effectively, more productively and with greater satisfaction.

Careful selection of your subordinates helps assure more job enjoyment, says Dr. Felix. You should have confidence in their professional or technical abilities and confidence in them as people with integrity, loyalty and discretion, he adds. The executive who knows he makes mistakes and has people who will frankly tell him about them has more security in administering, Dr. Felix maintains. "To keep this kind of staff, give them a chance to come up with ideas and never take credit for their ideas," he adds. "Creative people are what make organizations great."

The conditions under which greatest productivity can be achieved are without question the same conditions which provide maximum job satisfaction, according to Mr. Muller-Thym.

Those companies that are diverse and growing provide opportunities for maximum energies, intelligence and decision-making. Managerial satisfaction comes from these growth conditions.

Mr. Canny emphasizes the importance of proper placement. This exists when executives are in jobs where there is just enough room for them to grow.

This makes for top performance and satisfaction. Full communication through an organization, so that managers know about the important decisions that are being made, also aids managerial effectiveness and job satisfaction.

Even a manager who sees the promotion path clogged can set goals and challenges for himself that can yield productivity and satisfaction of accomplishment simultaneously. He can set his sights on new sales or profits or other targets that he can achieve in his present job with his present authority.

Great creative satisfactions can be derived from helping to run a producing organization, properly conceived and planned, which serves the public need and becomes a source of financial gain to many, according to Dr. Felix.

These satisfactions can be rich and full if the administrator has a philosophy he believes in and a clear sense of values to guide him.

INDEX

442

Process, departmentation by, 50
Product, departmentation by, 49
Production committees, 118
Production restrictions
    and training, 76–78
    work groups, 69–76
Productivity
    and decision making, 71
    and job satisfaction, 435–436
    and morale, 150–157
Product organization, 50–51
"The Professional Soldier"
    (Janowitz), 421
Profit-sharing program, American
    Motors, 310
Projection, as defense mechanism,
    178
Projective surveys, 134–135
Prudential Insurance Co., human
    relations studies, 12–13
Psychological influence, 129
Puckett, Elbridge S., 311
Punishment, discipline without,
    344–348
Purcell, Theodore V., 260

Ranking, appraisal method, 365
Rating, average, in performance
    appraisal, 366–367
Rating scale, appraisal method, 365
Rationalization, as defense
    mechanism, 178
Rausch, Erwin, 354, 355
Read, W. A., 155
Regression, as defense mechanism,
    178
Research, human relations, 9–12
Responsibilities, as job classification
    factors, 382–383
Restlessness, cyclical, 426
Rickenbacker, Eddie, 425
Risk, in decision making, 417
Rohan, Thomas M., 133
Rosen, Benson, 264–269 passim
Rosen, H., 283
Routine-bucker, as pivot man, 407
Rubber Workers Union, 252
Rumors
    in communication, 95–96
    as defense mechanism, 178

Safety needs, 224
Salter, Malcolm S., 327, 328, 330, 331
Sargent, John, 433

Satisfaction. See Job satisfaction
Scanlan, Burt K., wage payment
    system guidelines, 172
Scanlon Plan applications, 310–314,
    333
Schmidt, Warren H., 116
Scott, Walter Dill, 363
Sears, Roebuck and Co., flat
    organization, 45
Seashore, Edith W., 69n
Self-evaluation, in discipline, 351–353
Self-realization needs, 225
Sewell, Tom N., 390
Sex Stereotyping, HBR survey on,
    263–270
Sheet Metal Trades Union, 313
Sherman, Arthur W. Jr., 44
Sibson, Robert, 429
Skeptic, as pivot man, 407–408
Social interaction needs, 224
Social Security Act, 297
Social Security provisions, 298
Soliman, Hanafi M., operative theory
    of organization, 151–152, 153
Spanish-Speaking Americans in
    business, 271–272
Specialization, 255, 257
Staff and line, 47
Stagner, R., 283
Standards
    group, 69
    and incentives, 305–309
Stock options, in executive compen-
    sation, 331
Structure and climate, organization,
    254–255
Subordination, dynamics of, 180–184
Suggester, as pivot man, 404–405
Suggestion systems, 118
Supervision
    consultative, 117
    democratic, 117–118
    and morale, 154–156
    and motivation, 186
Supervisor
    as change agent, 114–115
    as communication barrier, 94–95
    production centered vs. employee
        centered, 12–13
Sutermeister, Robert A., 74
Sybron Corp., 313

Tagiuri, Renato, 279
Tannenbaum, Robert, 116

444

77 78 79 80 9 8 7 6 5 4 3 2 1